European Media Policy for the Twenty-First Century

Media policy issues sit at the heart of the structure and functioning of media systems in Europe and beyond. This book brings together the work of a range of leading media policy scholars to provide inroads to a better understanding of how effective media policies can be developed to ensure a healthy communication sector that contributes to the well-being of individual citizens, as well as to a more democratic society. Faced with a general atmosphere of disillusionment with the European project, one of the core questions tackled by the volume's contributors is: what scope is there for European media policy that can exist beyond the national level? Uniquely, the volume's chapters are structured around four key policy themes: media convergence; the continued role and position of public regulatory intervention in media policy; policy issues arising from the development of new electronic communication network environments; and lessons for European media policy from cases beyond the EU. In its chapters, the volume provides enriched understandings of the role and significance of policy actors, institutions, structures, instruments and processes in communication and media policy.

Seamus Simpson is Professor of Media Policy at the University of Salford, Manchester, UK. His research interests are in European and global communications policy, areas in which he has published widely. His research has been funded by the Economic and Social Research Council (ESRC) and the European Commission. He was part of the PricewaterhouseCoopers team which undertook the first EU-funded evaluation of the pan-European communications regulator, BEREC, in 2012. He is Chair of the Communication Law and Policy Division of the International Communication Association and an ICA Board of Directors member. In 2015, he joined the 'Oxford Research Encyclopedia: Communication' as a Senior Editor (Oxford University Press).

Manuel Puppis is Associate Professor in Media Systems and Media Structures in the Department of Communication and Media Research (DCM), University of Fribourg, Switzerland. He currently serves as chair of Communication Law and Policy Section of the European Communication Research and Education Association (ECREA) and board member of the Swiss Association of Communication and Media Research (SACM). His research interests include media policy, media regulation and media governance, media systems in a comparative perspective, political communication and organization theory.

Hilde Van den Bulck (PhD) is full Professor of Communication Studies and head of the *Media, Policy and Culture* research group at the University of Antwerp, Belgium. She combines expertise in media culture and identity with expertise in media policies and structures, looking at the impact of technological, economic, political and cultural developments on media structures and policies, with a focus on public service broadcasting. In both areas she has researched and published in books and ISI journals.

Routledge Advances in Internationalizing Media Studies

Edited by Daya Thussu, University of Westminster

1 Media Consumption and Everyday Life in Asia
   Edited by Youna Kim

2 Internationalizing Internet Studies
   Beyond Anglophone Paradigms
   Edited by Gerard Goggin and Mark McLelland

3 Iranian Media
   The Paradox of Modernity
   Gholam Khiabany

4 Media Globalization and the Discovery Channel Networks
   Ole J. Mjøs

5 Audience Studies
   A Japanese Perspective
   Toshie Takahashi

6 Global Media Ecologies
   Networked Production in Film and Television
   Doris Baltruschat

7 Music, Social Media and Global Mobility
   MySpace, Facebook, YouTube
   Ole J. Mjøs

8 Media Power and Democratization in Brazil
   TV Globo and the Dilemmas of Political Accountability
   Mauro P. Porto

9 Popular Television in Eastern Europe During and Since Socialism
   Edited by Timothy Havens, Anikó Imre and Katalin Lustyik

10 The Global News Challenge
   Marketing Strategies of International Broadcasting Organizations in Developing Countries
   Anne Geniets

11 Al Jazeera and the Global Media Landscape
   The South Is Talking Back
   Tine Ustad Figenschou

12 Online Journalism in Africa
   Trends, Practices and Emerging Cultures
   Edited by Hayes Mawindi Mabweazara, Okoth Fred Mudhai and Jason Whittaker

13 Modernization, Nation-Building, and Television History
   Edited by Stewart Anderson and Melissa Chakars

14 Media Across Borders
   Localizing TV, Film and Video Games
   Edited by Andrea Esser, Miguel Á. Bernal-Merino and Iain Robert Smith

15 Asian Perspectives on Digital Culture
   Emerging Phenomena, Enduring Concepts
   Edited by Sun Sun Lim and Cheryll Ruth R. Soriano

16 Digital Politics and Culture in Contemporary India
   The Making of an Info-Nation
   Biswarup Sen

17 European Media Policy for the Twenty-First Century
   Assessing the Past, Setting Agendas for the Future
   Edited by Seamus Simpson, Manuel Puppis and Hilde Van den Bulck

European Media Policy for the Twenty-First Century

Assessing the Past, Setting Agendas for the Future

Edited by
Seamus Simpson, Manuel Puppis
and Hilde Van den Bulck

NEW YORK AND LONDON

First published 2016
by Routledge
711 Third Avenue, New York, NY 10017

and by Routledge
2 Park Square, Milton Park, Abingdon, Oxon OX14 4RN

First issued in paperback 2018

Routledge is an imprint of the Taylor & Francis Group, an informa business

© 2016 Taylor & Francis

The right of the editors to be identified as the authors of the editorial material, and of the authors for their individual chapters, has been asserted in accordance with sections 77 and 78 of the Copyright, Designs and Patents Act 1988.

All rights reserved. No part of this book may be reprinted or reproduced or utilised in any form or by any electronic, mechanical, or other means, now known or hereafter invented, including photocopying and recording, or in any information storage or retrieval system, without permission in writing from the publishers.

Trademark notice: Product or corporate names may be trademarks or registered trademarks, and are used only for identification and explanation without intent to infringe.

Library of Congress Cataloging-in-Publication Data

Names: Simpson, Seamus, editor. | Puppis, Manuel, 1977– editor. | Bulck, Hilde Van den, editor.
Title: European media policy for the twenty-first century: assessing the past, setting agendas for the future / edited by Seamus Simpson, Manuel Puppis, and Hilde Van den Bulck.
Description: New York: Routledge, 2016. | Series: Routledge advances in internationalizing media studies; 17 | Includes bibliographical references and index.
Identifiers: LCCN 2015038256
Subjects: LCSH: Mass media policy—Europe—History—21st century.
Classification: LCC P95.82.E85 E943 2016 | DDC 302.23/094—dc23
LC record available at http://lccn.loc.gov/2015038256

ISBN 13: 978-1-138-59806-5 (pbk)
ISBN 13: 978-1-138-85650-9 (hbk)

Typeset in Sabon
by codeMantra

Contents

Tables and Figures ix
Acknowledgements xi

1 Contextualising European Media Policy in the
  Twenty-First Century 1
  MANUEL PUPPIS, SEAMUS SIMPSON AND HILDE VAN DEN BULCK

SECTION I
Understanding Media Policy in an Environment of Media Convergence

2 Beyond the Buzz: Why Media Policy Researchers
  Should Study Teletext 23
  HILDE VAN DEN BULCK AND HALLVARD MOE

3 Electronic Press: Turning a New Leaf for Convergent
  Media Content Regulation? 40
  IRINI KATSIREA

4 #Tweetgate: When Public Service Broadcasters and
  Twitter Go to War – An Irish Perspective 59
  JENNIFER KAVANAGH

SECTION II
The Relevance of Public Regulatory Intervention in Media Policy

5 Is Self-Regulation Failing Children and Young People?
  Assessing the Use of Alternative Regulatory Instruments
  in the Area of Social Networks 77
  EVA LIEVENS

Contents

6 Media Policy and Regulation in Times of Crisis 95
CORINNA WENZEL, STEFAN GADRINGER
AND JOSEF TRAPPEL

7 Digital Switchover: EU State Aid, Public Subsidies
and Enlargement 118
MARK WHEELER

SECTION III
Regulatory Policy Issues in Advanced Communication Network Environments

8 New Networks, Old Market Structures? The Race
to Next Generation Networks in the EU and
Calls for a New Regulatory Paradigm 139
MARIA MICHALIS

9 The Net Neutrality Debate from a Public Sphere Perspective 161
FRANCESCA MUSIANI AND MARIA LÖBLICH

10 Access to the Network as a Universal Service Concept
for the European Information Society 175
OLGA BATURA

SECTION IV
Lessons for European Media Policy from Cases beyond the EU

11 Between Norms and Accomplishment: Lessons
for EU Media Policy from EU Enlargements 195
BEATA KLIMKIEWICZ

12 Convergent Media Policy: Reflections Based
upon the Australian Case 219
TERRY FLEW

13 Communications and Social Inclusion: Universal Service
Policies in Europe and Latin America 238
MARIA STELLA RIGHETTINI AND MICHELE TONELLOTTO

List of Contributors 263
Index 269

List of Tables and Figures

Tables

6.1	Media Policy Documents	100
11.1	Freedom of the Press Rankings by Freedom House (2005–2013) for the Czech Republic, Hungary, Poland and Slovakia	202
11.2	'Press Freedom Index' by Reporters Without Borders (2005–2014) for Czech Republic, Hungary, Poland and Slovakia	203
11.3	The average share of transmission time devoted to European works in the CEE Member States between 2005 and 2010	209
13.1	Empirical dimensions of Universal Service Obligations regulatory regimes: orientation and organization	243
13.2	Variation in growth of Internet users *between 2008 and 2012*	244
13.3	The Evolution of the legal framework on USO in Telecommunication (UE–UK–FR–ES–IT)	246
13.4	The Evolution of the legal framework of US in Argentina, Brazil, Chile and Venezuela	249
13.5	Orientation in USO programs	251
13.6	Core USO actors in EU and Latin American regulatory regimes	252
13.7	The organization and orientation of the USO regimes in EU and Latin American States	253
13.8	Procedures for selecting of USO providers	255

Figures

11.1	Freedom of the Press ranking by Freedom House (2005–2013) for the Czech Republic, Hungary, Poland and Slovakia	202
11.2	Press Freedom Index by Reporters Without Borders (2005–2013) for the Czech Republic, Hungary, Poland and Slovakia	204
11.3	The average share of transmission time devoted to European works in the CEE Member States between 2005 and 2010	209

Acknowledgements

The idea for this volume emerged from deliberations which took place at the 2013 European Communication Research and Education Association (ECREA) Communication Law and Policy section workshop held at Mediacity UK in October 2013. The editors would like to thank ECREA and participants at the workshop for their valuable contributions.

1 Contextualising European Media Policy in the Twenty-First Century

Manuel Puppis, Seamus Simpson and Hilde Van den Bulck

The Current State of the Media Landscape: Convergence and Its Problematics

The European media environment is complex. It derives much of its character from a set of heterogeneous political and economic structures, languages and cultures, and social and education systems. This is evident both within and between the 28 Member States of the European Union (EU) and numerous non-member states elsewhere on the continent. Added to the mix is a set of structures and processes constituted at the EU level which sit both in complement – and often in tension – with the national level. It is within this context that the seismic changes which have affected and continue to shape the media sector have taken place and find specific expression. Much of that change can be accounted for by ongoing processes of convergence taking place at a number of levels. Notwithstanding the commercial hyperbole that inevitably accompanies developments in media that exemplify convergence, it is still the case that the contemporary media sector is radically different in appearance even from that recognised less than 20 years ago when the agenda of convergence focused on the coming together of broadcasting, IT (Information Technology), publishing, and telecommunications and was given particularly controversial airing at EU level through the European Commission's Green Paper on Convergence (European Commission, 1997). The defining development in the interim has been the rise to prominence of the Internet as an increasingly sophisticated, international communication platform through which an online world of media production and consumption has developed, epitomizing much of the benefits and potential – but also the problems – of media convergence.

These changes have presented media policy makers and policy scholars alike across Europe with a burgeoning roster of policy challenges. Such has been the growth of the online world, with its – by nature – high profile in the commercial sphere and public eye, that it is understandably tempting to conclude that to make sense of and prescribe policies for the online media environment requires a brand new set of lenses and tools. However, two important points are worth making. First, despite the degree of change witnessed thus far, it is still the case that a very significant part of media production and consumption takes place in what might be termed the traditional manner. This is particularly relevant where currently linear television and radio broadcasting continue to thrive, despite significant utilisation of the Internet's capacity. Thus, in policy terms, many of the traditional conundrums and vexations of media systems – such as media ownership and concentration, universal service, and the role of public service content and providers – continue to confront key policy actors nationally and at the EU. Second, it is the case that whilst the infrastructural, service and content based contexts of media are increasingly those of the Internet, many of the tools and perspectives of media policy developed historically provide an important basis from which to develop better understandings of the policy challenges of convergence. This is not to argue for a wholesale transposition of offline media policies and practices – as well as analyses of them – to the online environment. Rather, it acknowledges that policy knowledge about the fundamentals of human communication structures and processes, developed through many decades and across successive waves of infrastructural, content and service-based changes in media technologies, are relevant experience repositories and knowledge tool kits for European media policy in the twenty-first century. What is more, understanding evolutions in policies regarding relatively un-researched media such as teletext, provide often strong resonances of current debates (see Chapter 2 [Moe & Van den Bulck], this volume).

One of the most daunting current and future media policy challenges in Europe, and indeed beyond, concerns the roll out, deployment and use of upgraded and new infrastructure. As was the case from the earliest days of electronic communication, the network provides the physical conditions for human communication agency to play out, with all its potentials and problematics. The refurbishment of the fixed link electronic communications network and further development of wireless infrastructure are arguably the largest infrastructural communication policy challenges of at least the last 50 years and have the pursuit and realisation of sophisticated media convergence at their core. The EU's Digital Agenda, for example, has set ambitious targets for accessibility to high speed broadband services to be realised by 2020 (European Commission, 2010). The policy goal of creating widespread next generation networks based on optical fibre technology is, in particular, both large and complex. It presents a major time consumptive and costly civil engineering challenge, before even the cost of the electronic components of the network itself is considered. The pattern, extent and timing of roll out of this new enabling infrastructure is of the utmost significance. It raises network access issues which relate to, and take forward, traditional analyses of universal service in Europe in both broadcast and telecommunication-based media, both intra- and cross-EU Member State.

The enabling nature of such new networks and their future course has inevitably called into question the usage of existing electronic communications infrastructure. A number of policy issues appear particularly pertinent. The demands of the mobile communications network operators for spectrum, allied to the capacity promises of fixed-link next generation networks (NGNs), have raised questions over the use of spectrum for digital terrestrial TV (see Chapter 8 [Michalis], this volume). Second, the affordances of NGN technologies to take media convergence to a new level of breadth and intensity have also called forth a series of policy issues in respect of the applications which sit on such networks, as well as the content and services delivered through them. Whilst rich capacity and high speed communication are the promised endpoint of the journey to NGN, en route considerations of how to manage communication traffic for network efficiency, security and economic equity have become high profile. Equally significant has been the debate on whether to offer better quality – that is, higher speed – Internet access services based on the ability to pay. All currently key parts of the debate on net neutrality (see Chapter 9 [Musiani & Löblich], this volume), the idea of neutrality is open for – and arguably in pressing need of – re-interpretation. Ideas of equity, balance and parity of esteem and treatment are staples of the traditional communication system expressed in universal and public service practices of broadcasting and telecommunication. However, in contrast to the traditional public interest Internet philosophy of non-intervention to achieve 'neutrality', securing these new public interest staples of the online world requires direct intervention (Simpson, 2015). In other words, drawing on the traditional and re-working it in the context of the new, has the potential to create a set of viable media policies for the still converging media environment. Acceptance of this as a policy principle and modus operandi is merely the start of a complicated process of designing and implementing effective European media policies for the twenty-first century. Such a project has entailed within it a number of daunting tasks explored by various contributors to this volume: a fundamental re-working of the governance of media convergence (Chapter 12 [Flew]) is needed that addresses a range of issues to do with the regulation of traditional media content now delivered predominantly online, such as journalism (Chapter 3 [Katsirea]) or universal service (Chapter 10 [Batura]; Chapter 13 [Righettini & Tonellotto]); the development of effective regulation online to protect children (Chapter 5 [Lievens]) and understanding social media and its place in hybrid and new public service media environments (Chapter 4 [Kavanagh]), to name but a few. As these contributions suggest, this policy project goes beyond the technological and industrial-economic questions that are receiving the lion's share of attention in the age of convergence and encompasses the search and need for a media system that can guarantee, for example, the production of quality journalism and original radio and televisual programming in an environment dominated by international Internet service companies that show no interest in providing these types of content. A key question, then, is by whom – and how – can this vital policy project be delivered?

The Relevance or Otherwise of Public Sector Intervention in a Market-Dominated Media Environment

The nature of the changes described above point strongly towards a consideration of the magnitude of policy action required to deal with them and leads to the question of the respective roles of public and private interests in their realisation. It is important to underline that, in Europe, media law and policy developments pre-convergence mainly took place at the national level and different media fell under different legal and policy regimes, reflective of the Zeitgeist in which they originated and dominated the media scene. The press, after a heavily controlled origin in the authoritarian era, was considered part and parcel of the democratisation of western societies. Not surprisingly, freedom of expression in many constitutions was written down as freedom of the press, which has remained a strong starting point for any press regulation up to this day (Czepek, Hellwig & Novak, 2009). Press freedom was formulated first and foremost in relationship to the state, either in a negative interpretation as freedom from interference from the state, restricting the press mainly to commercial and some social-profit initiatives and, in a positive sense, as the obligation of the state to create a media system necessary for a working democracy (Baker, 2001). Guidelines and restrictions mainly were and have been limited to self-regulation.

After a brief experimental period in the early 1920s, radio was quickly nurtured by the state, following the belief in the visible hand of government and the social responsibility of the state towards the media. The most well-known exponent hereof, of course, is public service broadcasting (PSB). This view extended to television as it started to spread post–World War II and lasted well into the 1980s (Price, 1995; Van den Bulck, 2001). Whereas the 'liberalisation' and marketisation of broadcasting – an extension of a neo-liberal approach to society and the belief in the invisible hand of the market from the 1980s onwards – ended the public service broadcasting monopolies, in most European countries television remained subject to much regulation with regards to content and commercial communication. Even at the EU level (e.g., through the Television Without Frontiers Directive) this type of control was maintained (Wheeler, 2004).

Telecommunication, for a long time, was not considered as part of media law and policy and its regulation, based in international agreements (on frequencies, for example), was technology- (rather than content-) based. Telephony was not regulated with regards to what could be said on the telephone as it was not considered as part of mass (one-to-many) communication, to which media regulation and policies applied, but to interpersonal (one-to-one) communication of which regulation was limited with regards to the right to privacy, the latter mainly defined in relationship to the state (Bannister, 2005).

Convergence has shaken up these old regimes considerably. Clear distinctions between media – and in particular between mass and interpersonal communication – have become less relevant. Convergence has blurred distinctions between media content and markets and has opened up traditional markets to services and service providers, most notably those from the once distinct sector of telecommunications, now widened definitionally as information and communication technologies (ICT) (d'Haenens & Brink, 2001; Hendriks 1995). Similarly, convergence, and especially the introduction of Web 2.0 social media, overturned the distinction between 'senders' and 'receivers' of mass media messages as audiences became not just consumers but active producers, so-called prosumers. This has led to a blurring of the boundaries between the public and the private.

As a result, convergence is not just a technological and economic reality. A discourse of convergence has permeated media and Information and Communication Technologies (ICT) policy-making (Sampson & Lugo, 2003). In these policy debates, two main positions can be identified. Optimists, from a technological determinist position, promote convergence and its innovative possibilities, usually with economic growth as the ultimate goal. This is often accompanied by a technological nationalism, policy stakeholders promoting convergence to improve economic investments and political prestige (Van den Bulck, 2008). Convergence also features positively in a discourse of technological democracy as an engine for increased autonomy of, and new possibilities for, the citizen-user (Iosifidis, 2006). This argument is embraced both by stakeholders attempting to obtain a dominant position in new and potentially lucrative markets, and by the cultural and minority sector that believes new media can fulfil 'old' ambitions regarding alternative media for voices not heard elsewhere (Cammaerts & Carpentier, 2007). Optimists by and large argue that, due to the explosion of services, devices, and platforms, regulation has become obsolete or at least impossible to impose effectively and that, more than ever, the market will take care of itself. This view is reflected in so many policy debates and outcomes that Freedman (2005, p. 6) refers, with concern, to 'the hegemony of market-led approaches to the provision of goods and services'.

However, there are other voices. Pessimists, from an equally determinist position, see convergence as a threat to existing relationships and to the carefully established equilibrium in specific media markets, undermining once stable value chains and thus the viability of existing actors and positions. Convergence, together with globalisation, are seen by pessimists as further enhancing the power of transnational multimedia groups, undermining existing positions and future developments of local players that provide content and opportunities for local producers. Convergence thus hampers the social role of media, made explicit in public service broadcasting (Sampson & Lugo, 2003), but also secured historically through healthy local media markets. Convergence is therefore considered ultimately to push the homogenisation and commercialisation of culture (De Bens, 2004). For the most ardent pessimists, this constitutes the potential end of much that is considered good and important in human communication. Hence, these authors advocate the need for more regulatory intervention or re-regulation in spite of issues of enforceability (Van den Bulck, 2008).

Pessimists suggest that convergence makes national or regional media policy more relevant than ever. Yet, it is argued, convergence and globalisation make media policy-making increasingly complex. First, as already noted, they have opened up traditional media markets to new players, most notably those from the once distinct telecommunications sector and its spin-offs. Convergence also results in new configurations between old and established players. Second, media policy-making is no longer reserved to national governments, as power has been eroded by the growth of multi-level governance. Policy-making responsibilities are increasingly shared by various policy actors at the regional, national and inter- or supranational levels (Collins, 2008). European governments have been faced with the growing involvement of the EU, and the impact of the European Commission and European Courts in media and ICT policy-making (Donders, Loysen & Pauwels, 2014). Adhering to a neo-liberal 'markets can cater for diversity' discourse, putting economic goals first and cultural and public interests second, the EU has been instrumental in pushing convergence ever since it liberalised the use of cable networks and then point-to-point distribution systems (Østergaard, 1998). This has also been highly evident in recent EU policy on the so-called digital switchover (see Chapter 7 (Wheeler), this volume). Some have consequently espoused a certain defeatism regarding the (im)possibility of regulating convergence: whilst regulation may still be valuable to ensure socially agreed values, it has become obsolete due to a lack of enforceability. At the same time, there are indications that national and regional governments remain powerful actors in the media policy arena, particularly in sectors such as broadcasting (see Chapter 11 [Klimkiewicz], this volume; Sinclair, 2004). The enormous diversity of media markets in Europe further indicates a level of path dependency: choices made in the past impact the present and will continue to do so in the future (Brevini, 2013). Small EU Member States, for example, have adopted various models of 'controlled liberalisation', opening up their media markets, but with due protection for domestic players in the interests of preserving national identities, culture and language (Lowe, Berg & Nissen, 2011).

Enduring and New Forms of Media Regulation and Policy-Making

In policy processes, optimists and pessimists can be seen to fight it out while trying to find solutions to various policy problems. The result is that certain new forms of media regulation and policy-making have emerged with traditional regulatory regimes being called into question, as a corollary. To start with the latter, longstanding, taken-for-granted norms and regulations such as freedom of expression and privacy have become subject to debate. Whereas not all examples of renewed discussions about freedom of expression are the straightforward result of media convergence, as the French case of *Charlie* exemplifies, many others are. Old media such as broadcasting incorporating 'new' media such as Twitter can create controversy (see Chapter 4 [Kavanagh], this volume), questioning the extent of the right to freedom of political expression. The trend of Internet trolling, whereby someone posts or tweets negative, hateful or just off-topic messages to provoke or harm others (see Phillips, 2015), the result of audiences becoming producers of media texts on Facebook and Twitter, tests the limits of an individual's freedom of speech in a mass-mediated interpersonal communication environment. Social media and other new media developments, particularly online, further break the barriers between the public and the private, thus pushing renewed attention to the notion of privacy and its protection against surveillance. Interestingly, whereas in the past the right to privacy was mainly defined in relationship to the state, today concerns regarding surveillance and breaches of privacy are more focused at the corporate level, as giants like Facebook and Google accumulate data and thus knowledge about individuals to an extent unrivalled even by the state (Cohen, 2008).

Converging and new media also create entirely new challenges for policy makers and regulators. Next to the rethinking of net neutrality discussed above, several examples of new media regulation and policy-making result from boundary negotiations. Convergence puts under pressure business models, as in the case of newspapers, and existing value chains, as in the case of audio-visual media content. This leads commercial media players, traditionally favouring free market solutions, to seek protection from governments to help maintain 'old' boundaries. An example in the press field is recent efforts by publishers to curb (public service) broadcasters' online news provision (see Chapter 3 [Katsirea], this volume). The Flemish so-called 'signal integrity case' (Van den Bulck & Donders, 2014) is an example of a successful alliance between commercial and public service television broadcasters to protect the use of their signal against distributors' commercial valorisation without prior consent. Shifts in the value chain and the creation of new 'windows' to create profits with audio-visual content has reignited debates about copyrights. While production companies and content commissioners (traditionally broadcasters, today also Over The Top (OTT) services such as Netflix) renegotiate the exploitation rights of new windows, the EU fosters the simplification of copyright processes to promote the cross-national distribution of European audio-visual works. As a result, copyright promises to remain on the agenda in the immediate future. Given these challenges, nation-states across Europe are not only required to rethink their existing regulation but also their policy-making processes and institutional arrangements for achieving policy objectives. Thus, the so-called governance concept, which refers to the 'entirety of forms of rules that aim to organise media systems' (Puppis, 2010, p. 138), has in considerable measure called forth the attention of researchers and practitioners alike (d'Haenens, 2007; d'Haenens, Mansell & Sarikakis, 2010; Ginosar, 2013; Karppinen & Moe, 2013; Meier, 2011). Governance now covers a range of self- and co-regulatory forms in addition to the traditional role played by the state (see Chapter 5 [Lievens], this volume).

The Role of Different Media Policy Actors in Setting Media Policy Agendas

Policies and regulation are the result of a political process. Contrary to views of policy-making as a mechanical, technocratic and objective process, media policy 'is a deeply political phenomenon' (Freedman, 2008, p. 1). Media policy-making can thus be conceived of as a struggle for influence in which different actors try to push through their interests and ideological positions. Aside from government bodies, parliament and political parties, various interest groups (such as trade associations and unions), civil society organisations and – last but not least – the regulated companies themselves are important actors in this process.

Media corporations, the advertising industry and distributors, among others, are directly affected by these very policies and regulatory interventions. The interests of owners thus have implications for policy-making. Whereas scholars taking a pluralist perspective on politics argue that there is no clear centre of dominant influence on the policy-making process and that no single interest group possesses enough power to impose a certain solution (Dahl, 1961), scholars in the critical tradition emphasise that the media themselves take an increasingly active role in policy-making. On the one hand, media organisations rely on lobbying efforts to prevent regulation that would interfere with their economic interests (Freedman 2008, pp. 93–97). On the other hand, coverage of media policy in the public interest may be at risk. In modern democracies the mass media are the primary source of political information. They 'provide an arena of debate and a set of channels for making policies, candidates, relevant facts and ideas more widely known as well as providing politicians, interest groups and agents of government with a means of publicity and influence' (McQuail, 2005, p. 4). The mass media offer citizens access to information and a full range of different views so that they are able to make informed judgements about political issues. Obviously, the media distribute chances for attention (and influence) with their decisions to cover or not to cover a certain political issue (Habermas, 2006). However, the media can deviate rather strongly from the ideal of acting as a neutral intermediary between citizens and the political system that channels input into the political arena and communicates output to the public when it comes to media policy (Mancini & Swanson, 1996, p. 9; Mazzoleni & Schulz, 1999, p. 250; Puppis, 2015). Scholars argue that commercial media are in an ideal position to control public perception of any possible debate concerning the regulation and structure of media. Treating media policy as a non-issue and providing it only minimal coverage or distorting the issue to suit their own purposes helps in controlling the decision-making agenda and promoting policy inaction (Freedman, 2010; McChesney, 2008; Page, 1996).

Existing studies show that news organisations rarely scrutinise themselves, their company's business development and relations to advertisers, media mergers, or proposed regulatory reform. This bias in media coverage of the media industry and media policy has been recognised as the second face of power. It limits 'the scope of the political process to public considerations of only those issues that are comparatively innocuous' (Bachrach & Baratz, 1962, p. 948). The powerful role of the media in media policy-making by way of lobbying and biased reporting may have serious repercussions for the media's contribution to the functioning of modern democracies. If the media successfully assert their own interests, this adds to the 'neo-liberalisation of media policy' (Freedman, 2008, p. 224), favouring light-touch regulation at the expense of the public interest. It is at least debatable whether a purely commercial media system would still provide an arena of debate, make ideas widely known and cater for the political needs of citizens.

Whereas the actors at the beginning of the communication process have plentiful opportunities to influence media policy-making and future regulation, the same cannot be claimed for media users. Whereas each one of them can decide to get involved in media policy-making as an individual, the audience itself is not an actor. It is not organised, lacks resources and a joint strategy (Jarren & Donges, 2006). Thus, in absence of dedicated associations of media users (Baldi & Hasebrink, 2007) or of audience councils within regulatory agencies or public service broadcasters, media policy is dominated by actors of the political system, media organisations, parties and industry associations.

Recent media convergence not only challenges existing policies and regulation but also the politics of media policy. First and foremost, the regulated industry and the industry actors involved in policy-making are changing. As noted above, technological convergence is mirrored by commercial convergence, leading to activities that are 'crossing the traditional national and sectoral boundaries' (Levy, 1999, p. 8) of previously separated media and communication industries. At first, cable operators and telecommunication companies started to court customers by offering one stop shops for telephone, internet and broadcasting (triple play), breaking up long-standing monopolies. Later, with internet companies like Apple, Amazon, Google, Microsoft or Netflix developing into content producers, boundary-crossing suddenly expanded beyond infrastructure. 'There are big shifts occurring in how we identify the key media industry actors, as the relationship between devices, platforms, services and content are becoming increasingly blurred' (see Chapter 12 [Flew], this volume). With the promise of delivery of all kinds of services and content via IP technology, companies in the newly converged media industry need to find ways to offer users exclusive content. Alliances and competition between telecommunications, film, broadcasting and computing companies brought about new constellations and conflicts in media policy-making. Given their vastly different business models and market positions, these companies advocate different policy solutions that help them in securing the attention of the audience. The above-mentioned signal integrity case, the discomfort of television stations with OTT services, distributors refusing to offer HbbTV or German publishers demanding a *Leistungsschutzrecht* against Google News illustrate the case. It can be expected that these powerful companies will use all their leverage to influence the political process, including effecting media policy silence and, rather differently, through noisy social media campaigns. This diversity of industry actors raises the question of regulatory parity.

Yet convergence might also spark another change within the actor-constellations of media policy. Members of the audience, in the past seen as relatively powerless, now have opportunities to articulate themselves that exceed the option to decide for or against using certain content. It is easier than ever before to organise and act as a collective due to the Internet. Media and technology companies are often confronted with the digital outrage of their customers, for example. On a transnational level, the Internet Governance Forum gives civil society a better chance to bring non-commercial interests to the table (Raboy & Padovani, 2010). Yet it remains to be seen whether online protest and multi-stakeholder governance actually lead to a permanent change of practice in the industry or whether it constitutes only the proverbial storm in a tea cup. After all, the high hopes for democratisation and more democratic policy-making associated with the internet have mainly remained unfulfilled (Hesmondhalgh, 2013, pp. 313–339). There is little reason to believe that the result will be different in media policy, a policy area that does not attract as much citizen interest as others.

The Consequences of Media Policy

The different actors in the field of media policy that try to influence political decisions and decision makers themselves – irrespective of whether they all act in the public or their private interest – expect regulation to further specific policy objectives. Yet often media policy does not deliver the intended outcomes. Rather, as Merton (1936) demonstrates, there are unanticipated consequences of purposive action. This is not to say that unforeseen consequences are necessarily undesirable from the standpoint of single actors. The lack of adequate knowledge tends to be the main reason for an incorrect anticipation of the consequences of policy action. Merton lists five causes of unanticipated consequences: ignorance, error, imperious immediacy of interest, basic values and self-defeating prophecy. Ignorance refers to a lack of knowledge, specifically knowledge that could easily be obtained. Practical constraints like time pressure further ignorance. Instead of clarifying objectives and performing a comprehensive analysis to identify the most appropriate means to desired ends, policy makers might simply choose to rely on muddling through (Lindblom, 1959). Error may occur 'in our appraisal of the present situation, in our inference from this to the future objective situation, in our selection of a course of action or, finally, in the execution of the action chosen' (Merton, 1936, p. 901). Imperious immediacy of interest, in Merton's terms, refers to instances where actors want the intended consequences of an action so much that they choose to ignore unintended consequences. Related to this are basic values, instances where unintended consequences are ignored because of normatively underpinned necessity of certain action. Finally, predictions of future developments are precarious, particularly as they become a new element in a well-established and, until recently, stable system.

Although it is difficult to remedy how interests and values influence the evaluation of policy consequences, attempts at solving the problem of ignorance and error can be addressed pragmatically. One way to provide knowledge to decision makers is through so-called regulatory impact analysis. Such impact assessments try to enhance the empirical basis of political decisions, but have also attracted criticism. For instance, scholars question attempts to measure priceless goods or point to the limitations of de-contextualised approaches (Radaelli, 2004). Both aspects are of the highest significance for media policy, as non-economic objectives of regulation are difficult or arguably impossible to measure accurately. Media policy decisions can directly affect political and social beliefs and values that are central to the democratic process and often involve both economic and social value objectives (Napoli, 1999). Moreover, national characteristics of political systems and media systems cannot be ignored.

Another important source of knowledge for policy makers is media and communication policy academic research. Given the importance of media and communication for modern democracies and the manifold consequences of regulatory (non-)intervention, scholars have to deal with 'an analytical burden more complex than analysis in other policy areas' (Napoli, 1999, p. 568). This can be a daunting task. Yet there are good reasons to try to inform policy makers (Just & Puppis, 2012). Research can help in interpreting situations, selecting a course of action and designing policy measures: without research, policy decisions are not as informed as they should and could be (Braman, 2003).Additionally, academic research enjoys greater independence from vested interests and can focus on issues and policy alternatives that go beyond the normal short-term horizon of policy makers (Frieden, 2008; Melody, 1990). Media and communication policy scholars can contribute to expanding the range of possibilities contemplated by policy makers and help them in understanding the available choices (Braman, 2003). There are also potential pitfalls of informing policy-making (Just & Puppis, 2012). For instance, scholars may be inclined to limit themselves to a more pragmatic selection of subjects and approaches in order to meet the perceived needs of policy makers. And policy makers may use research to legitimise decisions that have already been taken (Buckingham, 2009). Nevertheless, media policy scholars should not avoid dialogue with political actors.

Arguably, politicians' need for fresh insights on how to reform media regulation is greater than ever due to convergence, commercialisation and social change. The 'search for a new communications policy paradigm' (van Cuilenburg & McQuail, 2003, p. 181) occupies policy makers on both the European and national levels. Indeed, technological change can be seen as the key driver for communication policy research. As Rowland (1984: 426) stated 30 years ago, 'most of the discussions of public policy for the mass media [...] have been driven by questions about the role and promises of the "new technologies"'. Research produced in this spirit should be the subject of scrutiny. For Levy (1999, p. 143), 'much of the discussion about the regulatory implications of convergence are characterised by differing forms of determinism which assume that consumer behaviour will be led by technological change and that regulation should follow suit'. Yet, as Hesmondhalgh (2013, p. 113) reminds us, the evolution of technologies is influenced by many decisions and unintended consequences. Thus, there is need for research that avoids reductionist explanations and that offers analyses that go beyond the economic. Media policy research needs to focus not only on the consequences of decisions but also on the consequences of the decision not to decide: non-decision-making in the interest of powerful incumbent and new commercial interests, for example, might prevent progressive change (Freedman, 2008, p. 224).

European Media Policy: The National Level and the EU

One of the most striking aspects of the development of media in Europe over recent decades has been the emergence of the EU as both an actor and site for the growth of media policy. Traditionally, broadcast media were considered part of culture and did not fall under the European Union Treaty but, instead, were mainly the concern of the Council of Europe (CoE), an intergovernmental organisation that promotes human rights, democracy and rule of law. As the EU started to recognise the economic potential of the media and wider ICT sector, its interest grew, resulting in the extension of its remit. As a result, whereas the CoE remains relevant in traditional fields such as public service broadcasting, the general tendency to consider media as economic goods and the stronger powers of enforceability of EU directives compared to the recommendations of the CoE, have resulted in a growing presence for the EU in media and ICT matters. Indeed, the electronic communications sector has developed in the last 30 years or so into one of the most important policy domains for the EU. It has now in its portfolio a range of policy initiatives of various kinds – and from these a set of policy responsibilities and competences – across the core aspects of media: broadcasting, telecommunication, and the Internet. The least strongly developed of these areas is broadcasting policy due to the persistently strong gravitational pull of the national level. Nevertheless, EU media policy is manifest in sets of legislation, policy recommendations, direct funding initiatives, implementation monitoring activity and sectorial research and analyses. The EU institutions which concern themselves with media – principally the

European Commission, the European Parliament and the European Council of Ministers – often articulate their perspectives in terms of the ongoing convergence between these historically separate quarters of communication. The influence of the EU is not restricted to Member States but affects non-EU-member states as well. Acceding countries, EEA members and Switzerland are either required to – or voluntarily – align to EU policies, including EU competition regulation, audio-visual policy, cultural policy and telecommunications policy (Puppis, 2012; Schneider & Werle, 2007; Sciarini, Fischer & Nicolet, 2004).

A number of the key features of the EU's engagement with the media sector are worth rehearsing. First, it is important to distinguish between the EU's desire to intervene in particular policy matters and its actual legal competence to do so (Knill & Lehmkuhl, 2002). Much of the EU's formal *acquis* is derived from competences assigned as a result of the Treaties establishing the European Union. Thus, its most well developed powers relate to decisions of an economic nature. Prominent here have been the regulatory framework established for telecommunication (Thatcher & Coen, 2008); policy action regarding state aid to broadcasting (Donders et al., 2008) and, latterly, (would be) providers of NGNs (Simpson, 2012); and rulings on market structure and proposed changes to it (Harcourt, 2006), such as mergers and acquisitions. By contrast, the EU's powers in terms of regulating communication content, particularly that associated with traditional terrestrial broadcast systems, are relatively weakly founded (Humphreys, 2008). A second major issue is a consideration of precisely which institutional actor or actors characterise the EU (Christou & Simpson, 2014). Both intra- and inter-institutional variety within the EU means that differences of approach are historically evident in the treatment of media policy matters. The European Commission has, through its remit, often taken the lead in legislative or other policy initiatives which would develop the EU's presence in the media field, if enacted. However, within the European Commission there is often evidence of differences of opinion, between, for example, those whose remit is competition policy and those interests advocating a more direct industrial policy perspective. Differences on media policy have also been evident between the European Commission, the European Parliament and the European Council of Ministers (Levy, 1999). The politically sensitive matters of the nature and activity of public service broadcasters, the creation of a pan-European regulatory authority for electronic communications and the debate on Net Neutrality provide three contrasting examples where differing institutional positions have been seen vying for position as the media policy process unfolds at EU level. This well established trait, whilst a source of intellectual fascination for scholars, can be one of vexation for policy makers at the EU institutional level.

A third related media policy issue concerns the ongoing struggle between advocates of more intensive supranational policy apparatus and processes and those asserting the need to maintain the primacy of the national level in media policy decision taking. The products of the ensuing debate tend naturally to manifest themselves at the EU institutional level, though the issue goes beyond this context and is particularly complex and often potentially contradictory in electronic media. In broadcasting, the well-documented pull of the national level has been particularly strong historically, based on the specifics of culture and language, but also undoubtedly with an economic underpinning. The telecommunication sector is in something of a middle-ground position in this kind of analysis. Strong arguments were propounded historically about the need to ensure national markets in Europe reflected the increasingly international character of the sector. The liberalisation package agreed by Member States certainly held the promise of this, but the reality, as often lamented by the European Commission, has been a set of liberalised national EU telecommunications markets dominated by national incumbents with little evidence of a Europeanised character in development. European media policy approaches to the Internet have been tentative, to say the least. Historically dominated by the minimalist governance origins of its global policy-making environment, EU Internet policy has developed in a largely uncoordinated – even haphazard – fashion, underpinned by the fear of untimely or inappropriate intervention. The promotion of commercial and social self-regulation in a generally market-liberal mindset has witnessed a mix of occasional hybridised public-private governance models, the attempted extension of current legislation in place elsewhere in media to Internet matters or evidence of dis-coordination and disjuncture as national initiatives emerge ahead of, and possibly at odds with, the direction of travel being pursued at EU level. There has been only a limited positive response by the EU to the idea of extending public service media into the online realm (see Trappel, 2008).

The politico-legal nature of the EU and its potential influences on policy-making aside, a fourth major influence on media policy through the decades has been the uneasy relationship between the EU's penchant for taking measures with an industrial policy character and, by contrast, those bearing a neo-liberal market character. The tension between the two is still is clearly manifest in the media field. This has been particularly evident since the global financial crisis and subsequent economic slump. There are clear signs that the neo-liberal market overdrive of the EU pursued through the 1990s and into the subsequent decade in telecommunication has been tempered by calls to create structured investment in new networks and services that might assist with economic recovery (see Chapter 8 [Michalis], this volume). There is little doubt that the financial crisis has had a negative effect on the attractiveness of the EU project in the eyes of European citizens. All this leads to the conclusion that the EU in general is a political project in a state of flux. A particularly important issue concerns the evolutionary nature of the EU's size and composition (see Chapter 11 [Klimkievicz], this volume, ragarding media policy). The degree and effect of enlargements are significant as well as, by contrast, threats to the EU's core from calls for Treaty

Conclusion

All of the issues discussed in this context-setting chapter are exemplified and given more detailed treatment in the remaining chapters of this volume. Together, they aim to provide inroads to a better understanding of how effective media policies can be developed to ensure a healthy communication sector that contributes to the well-being of individual citizens, as well as a more democratic society. The issues of media convergence, the continued role and position of public regulatory intervention in media policy, policy issues arising from the development of new electronic communication network environments and lessons for European media policy from cases beyond the EU form the core themes around which the volume's chapters shape their analysis. Faced at the time of writing with a general atmosphere of disillusionment in the European project, a key issue for media policy scholars and policy makers alike is, What scope is there for European media policy that can exist beyond the national level? At this juncture, it is important to reiterate the well-established point that the development of communication can improve the quality of human existence through the act of reaching out, exchange of thought and practice and the development of learning and, ultimately, understanding. Whilst the national and local context is clearly important for the EU and other European states, in a media sector increasingly dominated by online activity, engagement with the international policy context is not only beneficial but could be deemed imperative. Retrenchment to the national level completely could prove not only stagnatory but, ultimately, retrograde. This applies in media to contexts of technological research, content creation, production, consumption and market regulation and governance. All this activity points to the continued strong relevance of the EU, in particular, in the burgeoning and increasingly diverse media sector. A key issue may be not whether it will become less relevant in European media policy, but rather, to what extent – and how – it can become more relevant.

References

Bachrach, P., & Baratz, M.S. (1962). Two faces of power. *American Political Science Review*, 56(4), 947–952.

Baldi, P., & Hasebrink, U. (Eds.). (2007). *Broadcasters and citizens in Europe: Trends in media accountability and viewer participation*. Bristol, UK, and Chicago, IL: Intellect Books.

Baker, C.E. (2001). *Media, markets and democracy*. Cambridge, UK: Cambridge University Press.

Bannister, F. (2005). The panoptic state: Privacy, surveillance and the balance of risk. *Information Polity*, 10, 65–78.

Braman, S. (2003). Introduction. In S. Braman (Ed.), *Communication researchers and policy-making* (pp. 1–9). Cambridge, MA/London: MIT Press.

Brevini, B. (2013). *Public service broadcasting online: A comparative European policy study of PSB 2.0.* Basingstoke, UK: Palgrave Macmillan.

Buckingham, D. (2009). The appliance of science: The role of evidence in the making of regulatory policy on children and food advertising in the UK. *International Journal of Cultural Policy*, 15(2), 201–215.

Cammaerts, B., & Carpentier, N. (2007). *Reclaiming the media. Communication rights and democratic media roles.* Bristol, UK: Intellect Books.

Citi, M., & Rhodes, M. (2007). New modes of regulatory governance in the European Union: A critical survey and analysis. In K.-E. Jorgensen, M. Pollack & B. Rosamond (Eds.), *Handbook of European politic* (pp. 463–482). London: Sage.

Cohen, N.S. (2008). The valorisation of surveillance: Towards a political economy of Facebook. *Democratic Communiqué*, 22(1), 5–22.

Collins, R. (2008). Hierarchy to homeostasis? Hierarchy, markets and networks in UK media and communications governance. *Media, Culture & Society*, 30(3), 295–317.

Czepek, A., Hellwig, M. & Novak, E. (2009). *Press freedom and pluralism in Europe: Concepts and conditions.* Bristol, UK: Intellect Books.

Dahl, R.A. (1961). *Who governs? Democracy and power in an American city.* New Haven, CT/London: Yale University Press.

De Bens, E. (2004). Media between culture and commerce: An introduction. In E. De Bens (Ed.), *Media between culture and commerce* (pp. 9–24). Bristol, UK: Intellect Books.

d'Haenens, L. (Ed.). (2007). Media governance: New ways to regulate the media [Special Section]. *Communications*, 32(3), 323–362. doi: 10.1515/COMMUN.2007.020.

d'Haenens, L., & Brink, S. (2001). Digital convergence: The development of a new media market in Europe. In L. d'Haenens & F. Saeys (Eds.), *Western broadcasting at the dawn of the 21st century* (pp. 125–145). Berlin/New York: Mouton de Gruyter.

d'Haenens, L., Mansell, R. & Sarikakis, K. (Eds.). (2010). Media governance: New policies for changing media landscape [Special Issue]. *Communication, Culture & Critique*, 3(2).

Donders, K., Loysen, J. & Pauwels, C. (2014). Introduction: European media policy as a complex maze of actors, regulatory instruments and interests. In K. Donders, C. Pauwels & J. Loysen (Eds.), *The Palgrave handbook of European media policy* (pp. 1–16). London: Palgrave Macmillan.

European Commission. (2010, 19 May). *A digital agenda for Europe*. COM(2010) 245. Retrieved from http://eur-lex.europa.eu/legal-content/EN/TXT/PDF/?uri=CELEX:52010DC0245&from=EN.

European Commission. (1997). *Building the European Information Society for us all.* Final Policy Report of the High-level Expert Group, Directorate General for Employment, Industrial Relations and Social Affairs, Unit V/B/4. Brussels.

Fernández Alonso, I., and de Moragas i Spà, M. (Eds.). (2008). *Communication and cultural policies in Europe*, 4 (pp. 151–182). Barcelona: Generalitat de Catalunya: Department de al Presidencia, Col. leccioLexikon.

Freedman, D. (2005). *How level is the playing field? An analysis of the UK media policy-making process.* London: Goldsmiths Media/Economic & Social Research Council.

Freedman, D. (2008). *The politics of media policy.* Cambridge, MA/Malden, MA: Polity Press.
Freedman, D. (2010). Media policy silences: The hidden face of communications decision making. *The International Journal of Press/Politics, 15*(3), 344–361. doi: 10.1177/1940161210368292.
Frieden, R. (2008). Academic research and its limited impact on telecommunications policymaking. *International Journal of Communication, 2,* 421–428.
Ginosar, A. (2013). Media governance: A conceptual framework or merely a buzz word? *Communication Theory, 23*(4), 356–374. doi: 10.1111/comt.12026.
Habermas, J. (2006). Political communication in media society: Does democracy still enjoy an epistemic dimension? The impact of normative theory on empirical research. *Communication Theory, 16*(4), 411–426.
Hendriks, P. (1995). Communications policy and industrial dynamics in media markets: Toward a theoretical framework for analysing media industry organization. *Journal of Media Economics, 8,* 61–76.
Hesmondhalgh, D. (2013). *The cultural industries* (3rd ed.). Los Angeles/London/New Delhi/Singapore/Washington, DC: Sage.
Héritier, A. (2002). New modes of governance in Europe: Policy making without legislating? Political Science Series.Vienna: Institute for Advanced Studies.
Humphreys, P. (2008). The principal axes of the European Union's audiovisual policy. In I. Fernández Alonso & M. de Moragas i Spà (Eds.), *Communication and cultural policies in Europe.* Collecció Lexikon 4 (pp. 151–182). Barcelona, Spain: Universitat Autònoma de Barcelona.
Iosifidis, P. (2006). DTT and the role of PSBs in driving digital switchover. Paper presented at the *RIPE conference* in Amsterdam, November, 2006.
Jarren, O., & Donges, P. (2006). *Politische Kommunikation in der Mediengesellschaft. Eine Einführung* (2nd ed.). Wiesbaden, Germany: VS-Verlag.
Just, N., & Puppis, M. (2012). Communication policy research: Looking back, moving forward. In N. Just & M. Puppis (Eds.), *Trends in communication policy research. New theories, methods and subjects* (pp. 9–29). Bristol, UK/Chicago, IL: Intellect Books.
Karppinen, K., & Moe, H. (2013). A critique of 'media governance'. In M. Löblich & S. Pfaff-Rüdiger (Eds.), *Communication and media policy in the era of the Internet. Theories and processes* (pp. 69–80). Baden-Baden, Germany: Nomos.
Knill, C., and Lehmkuhl, D. (2002). The national impact of European Union regulatory policy: Three Europeanization mechanisms. *European Journal of Political Research, 41,* 255–280.
Kohler-Koch, B., and Rittberger, B. (2006). Review article: The governance turn in EU studies. *Journal of Common Market Studies, 44,* 27–49.
Levy, D. (1999). *Europe's digital revolution – Broadcasting regulation, the EU and the Nation State.* London: Routledge.
Lindblom, C.E. (1959). The science of 'muddling through'. *Public Administration Review, 19*(2), 79–88. doi: 10.2307/973677.
Lowe, G.F., Berg, C.E. & Nissen, C.S. (2011) Size matters for TV broadcasting policy. In G.F. Lowe & C.S. (Eds.), *Small among giants: Television broadcasting in smaller countries* (pp. 21–41). Göteborg, Sweden: Nordicom.
Mancini, P., & Swanson, D.L. (1996). Politics, media, and modern democracy: Introduction. In D.L. Swanson & P. Mancini (Eds.), *Politics, media, and modern democracy. An international study of innovations in electoral campaigning and their consequences* (pp. 1–26). Westport, CT: Praeger.

Mazzoleni, G., & Schulz, W. (1999). 'Mediatization' of politics: A challenge for democracy? *Political Communication, 16*(3), 247–261. doi: 10.1080/105846099198613.

McChesney, R.W. (2008). *The political economy of the media: Enduring issues, emerging dilemmas.* New York: Monthly Review Press.

McQuail, D. (2005). *McQuail's mass communication theory* (5th ed.). London/Thousand Oaks, CA/New Delhi, India: Sage.

Meier, W.A. (2011). From media regulation to democratic media governance. In J. Trappel, W.A. Meier, L. d'Haenens, J. Steemers & B. Thomass (Eds.), *Media in Europe today* (pp. 153–166). Bristol, UK/Chicago, IL: Intellect Books.

Melody, W.H. (1990). Communication policy in the global information economy: Whither the public interest? In M. Ferguson (Ed.), *Public communication – The new imperatives: Future directions for media research* (pp. 16–39). London//New Delhi, India: Sage.

Merton, R.K. (1936). The unanticipated consequences of purposive social action. *American Sociological Review, 1*(6), 894–904. doi: 10.2307/2084615.

Napoli, P.M. (1999). The unique nature of communications regulation: Evidence and implications for communications policy analysis. *Journal of Broadcasting & Electronic Media, 43*(4), 565–581.

Østergaard, B.S. (1998). Convergence: Legislative dilemmas. In D. McQuail & K. Siune (Eds.), Media policy: Convergence, concentration and commerce (pp. 95–107). London: Sage.

Page, B.I. (1996). The mass media as political actors. *PS: Political Science & Politics, 29*(1), 20–24. doi: 10.2307/420185.

Phillips, W. (2015). *This is why we can't have nice things: Mapping the relationship between online trolling and mainstream culture.* Cambridge, MA: MIT Press.

Price, M.E. (1995). *Television, the public sphere and national identity.* Oxford: Clarendon Press.

Puppis, M. (2010). Media governance: A new concept for the analysis of media policy and regulation. *Communication, Culture & Critique, 3*(2), 134–149. doi: 10.1111/j.1753-9137.2010.01063.x.

Puppis, M. (2012). Between independence and autonomous adaptation: The Europeanization of television regulation in non-EU Member States. *Communications, 37*(4), 393–416. doi: 10.1515/commun-2012-0022.

Puppis, M. (2015). Political media regulation. In G. Mazzoleni (Ed.), *The international encyclopedia of political communication.* Oxford, UK/Malden, MA: Wiley-Blackwell (forthcoming).

Raboy, M., & Padovani, C. (2010). Mapping global media policy: concepts, frameworks, methods. *Communication, Culture & Critique, 3*(2), 150–169. doi: 10.1111/j.1753-9137.2010.01064.x.

Radaelli, C.M. (2004). The diffusion of regulatory impact analysis – Best practice or lesson-drawing? *European Journal of Political Research, 43*(5), 723–747. doi: 10.1111/j.0304-4130.2004.00172.x.

Rowland W.D., Jr. (1984). Deconstructing American communications policy literature. *Critical Studies in Mass Communication, 1*(4), 423–435. doi: 10.1080/15295038409360051.

Sampson, T., & Lugo, J. (2003). The discourse of convergence: A neo-liberal Trojan horse. In. T. Hujanen & G.F. Lowe (Eds.), *Broadcasting and convergence: New articulations of the public service remit* (pp. 83–92). Göteborg, Sweden: Nordicom.

Schneider, V., & Werle, R. (2007). Telecommunications policy. In P. Graziano & M. Vink (Eds.), *Europeanization: New research agendas* (pp. 266–280). Basingstoke, UK: Palgrave Macmillan.

Sciarini, P., Fischer, A., & Nicolet, S. (2004). How Europe hits home: Evidence from the Swiss case. *Journal of European Public Policy, 11*(3), 353–378. doi: 10.1080/13501760410001694228.

Simpson, S. (2012). New Approaches to the Development of Telecommunications Infrastructures in Europe? The evolution of European Union policy for next generation networks. In N. Just & M. Puppis (Eds.), Trends in communication policy research (pp. 335–351). Bristol, UK: Intellect Books.

Simpson, Seamus (2015). 'Convergence, Net Neutrality and European Media Policy'. Paper presented to the FACE conference, 'European Media Policy 2015: New Contexts, New Approaches', 9–10 April, Helsinki.

Sinclair, J. (2004). Globalisation, supranational institutions and media. In J. Downing (Ed.), *The Sage handbook of media studies* (pp. 65–82). London: Sage.

Thatcher, M., and D. Coen (2008). Reshaping European regulatory space. *West European Politics, 31*(4), 806–836.

Trappel, J. (2008). Online media within the public service realm? Reasons to include online into the public service mission. *Convergence: The International Journal of Research into New Media Technologies, 14*(3), 313–322.

Van den Bulck, H. (2001). Public service television and national identity as a project of modernity: The example of Flemish television. *Media, Culture & Society, 23*(1), 53–69.

Van den Bulck, H. (2008). Can PSB stake its claim in a media world of digital convergence? The case of the Flemish PSB management contract renewal. *Convergence: The International Journal of Research into New Media Technologies, 14*(3), 335–350.

Van den Bulck, H., & Donders, K. (2014). Pitfalls and obstacles of media policy making in an age of digital convergence: The Flemish signal integrity case. *Journal of Information Policy, 4*, 444–462.

Van Cuilenburg, J., & McQuail, D. (2003). Media policy paradigm shifts. Towards a new communications policy paradigm. *European Journal of Communication, 18*(2), 181–207. doi: 10.1177/0267323103018002002.

Wheeler, M. (2004). Supranational regulation. Television and the European Union. *European Journal of Communication, 19*(3), 349–369.

Section I
Understanding Media Policy in an Environment of Media Convergence

2 Beyond the Buzz
Why Media Policy Researchers Should Study Teletext

Hilde Van den Bulck and Hallvard Moe

Introduction

When the British Broadcasting Corporation's (BBC) Ceefax, the first teletext service developed in 1974, went off-air in London on April 18, 2012, following television's analogue switch-off, it caused a wave of tributes both on new media platforms like Twitter and Facebook and in the traditional medium of newspapers. Dismissed as a 'bout of nostalgia' by some, this massive response echoes the longstanding and wide-reaching success of teletext in countries all over Europe. Teletext's popularity for a long time survived and was even helped by the arrival of the Internet, digitisation and mobile and social media. In several countries teletext for many years was popular on the Web, and in 2012 the teletext mobile media app was the most popular (and most downloaded) app of Flemish public service broadcasting (PSB).

Teletext's success with European audiences contrasts sharply with its neglect by academics and especially media policy researchers. Studying the academic and public interest in teletext, McKinnon (2012) found that the focus was mainly on innovation and on users, hardly on policy. The limited attention granted to policy issues, focused on the failure to introduce teletext in the U.S. (Graziplene, 2000; Sterling, 2006). This academic neglect obliterates the fact that teletext services in many countries at times were controversial. In some countries, teletext was seen as an expansion of public service broadcasters into an area many saw as the territory of newspaper publishers and, later on, as an inroad into debates between public service broadcasters and commercial competitors that marked especially the first decade of the 2000s. Elsewhere, in the 1990s, teletext became a probe into the digital future, as broadcasters envisioned a convergence between broadcasting and the Internet, and moved to exploit the commercial potential of teletext. In short, several developments and discussions regarding teletext appear to pre-echo more contemporary contested policy debates. This suggests that more policy research attention to teletext and, more generally, a better historical awareness of policy debates would provide valuable lessons for policy discussions of today and tomorrow.

Therefore, taking the 'forgotten' case of teletext in two European countries as an empirical reference, this chapter offers a critique of media policy researchers' preoccupation with the latest buzz or hype (whether it is 'public value tests' or 'Double Irish Arrangements') and argues for a need to focus on and understand the overlooked but central developments of media technologies and services that exist under the radar. This allows us to critically assess the long-term and wide-reaching viability of 'hot' terms and issues in policy debates.

The aim of this chapter, then, is twofold. On the conceptual level, setting the programme for the future, we argue for a historical awareness and the need to look beyond the current issues put on the agenda by dominant policy actors. To this end, the theoretical framework discusses conceptual issues in policy research including buzzwords and policy indifference and subsequently highlights some of the current, much-discussed issues we believe can benefit from more historical contextualisation. This is subsequently illustrated empirically with examples from the development of teletext services in Norway and Flanders (the northern, Dutch-speaking part of Belgium), their growth and success, the role of teletext for media policy and its place in media convergence, focusing specifically on the relationship between public service broadcasters' Norsk rikskringkasting's (NRK) and Vlaamse Radio and Television's (VRT) teletext and commercial competitors and on the relationship between teletext and web services. The text concludes by evaluating how an understanding of developments in teletext confirms that the field of media policy research does not need novel approaches as much as it needs sound inquiry of central, but under-researched, developments of regulations or lack thereof.

Policy (Research) Fallacy: Buzzwords and Policy Silences

Media and communication law and policy research is, like the rest of our culture, preoccupied with the newest, with novelty, with innovation. Much of our energy goes into understanding, mapping and grasping new events, new media technologies – as they develop, while the issues are fresh and current. There are good reasons for this: policy-making is well served by research-based knowledge, funding bodies tell us so, and the media too. There are problems with this preoccupation, though. Twenty-five years ago, Richard Collins commented that 'the policy researcher's task is to be an historian of the present without the assistance time affords "real" historians by winnowing away the chaff of irrelevant data and contingent associations and revealing fundamental structures' (1990, p. viii). In the face of escalating globalisation, thorough marketisation and through-and-through digitalisation, the task is hardly easier today. Media industry buzzwords – those catch-all terms that flow from a specific field to reach the wider public, and lose precise meaning – certainly existed pre-WWW [World Wide Web] (Mjøs, Moe & Sundet, 2014), but appear stronger, more ubiquitous and more persuasive today. But to do sound media policy research on emerging phenomena on the fly, so to speak, is risky.

Indeed, this overly intense focus on the here and now with a tendency towards hype creates certain problems for a better understanding of policy-making. Des Freedman called for policy researchers not to be blinded by 'the current rush of legislative and regulatory initiatives' and to be attentive to non–decision-making and policy silences (2010, p. 4). As the analysis below shows, the (lack of) policy-making regarding teletext may not be a case of policy silence, that is, a conscious attempt by certain elite stakeholders to prevent policy from being made; still, it is worth trying to understand why 'nobody cared' about teletext resulting in policy neglect, as such an analysis brings to the fore less-visible processes affecting policy-making – or the lack thereof. McKinnon (2012, p. 3–6), for instance, connects policy neglect to technological determinism. He argues that policy (research) seems led by technological developments rather than societal needs and developments, as it 'excludes the possibility of democratic interventions into the engineering of technology [...] while covertly imprinting old social meanings onto new forms' (2012, pp. 5–6). Others relate (the absence of) policy-making to the level of industrial development that a new medium envisages (Carey & Elton, 2010), to contemporary and generative metaphors (Lakoff, 1983; McKinnon, 2012) that a new medium fits into or breaks away from and to issues of diffusion of technological innovations (Rogers, 1983, p. 7). This is the location of agency over the adoption of a media innovation.

Teletext appears to be an instance of policy neglect, and this will be explored in this chapter. The chapter further wants to make a recommendation for and demonstrate the usefulness of incorporating a historical perspective in this search for and understanding of issues neglected by policy makers and academics alike. Analysing why teletext was not prominent in media policy debates and regulation (or in the research thereof) and what issues were in fact key to the development of teletext can provide fertile ground to better understand later media (policy) developments.

Convergence, the Media Ecology Equilibrium and Historical 'Blindness'

The importance of a historical analysis in media policy research in general, and a better understanding of teletext policies (or lack thereof) in particular, lies in the way in which teletext provides interesting pre-echoes of contemporary debates, in particular with regards to the impact of digitisation and the ensuing convergence on contemporary media ecosystems.

In media policy research, the relationships between various old and new media have long been seen as a battle between competing media outlets and companies (see, e.g., Doyle, 2002). More recently, however, a media market is conceptualised as an ecosystem. 'Media ecosystem' refers to the careful balance between the different players in certain (inter)national, regional or local media (Fransman, 2010; Lopez, 2012). The term is highly ideological as it claims the authority and normality of natural cycles for man-made, industrial-economic activities (cf. Gitlin, 1982, p. 216). Yet, it provides an interesting view on the relationships between various (old and new) players in the media market.

Changes to media ecosystems have been pushed by media innovation and convergence, the latter here considered as an increasing connectivity and interaction between media activities and an erosion of once-distinct boundaries between media at the level of production, organisation, content, distribution and consumption. As such, convergence changes relationships, not just between different technologies but also between markets and industries (Jenkins, 2004). Neither the term nor the trend is new. As early as 1983, coinciding with the early years of teletext in many countries, Ithiel de Sola Pool pointed to a 'convergence of modes' (1983, p. 23). However, convergence only became a buzzword in technological, economic and policy circles in the 1990s, when digitisation started to make real waves in the media sector (Humphreys, 1996; McQuail & Siune, 1998). It has remained a dominant issue in discussions about media structures and policies up to the present moment, to the extent that Sampson and Lugo (2003) identify a 'discourse of convergence' that has permeated media and ICT policy-making, confirming Jenkins' suggestion (2004) that it is a continuing process for which the end is not in sight.

Many policy battles have been fought around the notion and implications of convergence. The long, ongoing battle between publicly funded broadcasters and commercial media companies over the formers' expansion into new media services is one example. On a European level, commercial television companies found support with representatives of the printed press in the discussion over where the limits for media services funded by the public should go (see, e.g., Donders & Moe [2011] for different perspectives across Europe). On a national level, the signal integrity case in Flanders is another example (Van den Bulck & Donders, 2014). The latter refers to policy debates regarding the impact, first of delayed viewing on the commercial revenues of broadcasters undermining their traditional business model and thus viability, and second, of distributors' programme overlays (for instance, content/services added to the broadcasters' programme signals) on the integrity of programme content and thus consumers' rights (for instance., to an advertising-free environment for children on public service broadcasting).

Academically, the concept of convergence is contested because of its over-emphasis on a strict media divide pre-convergence (Herkman, 2012; Ytreberg, 2011), a tendency to ignore pre-digital reshuffling of relationships and an oversimplification of the complexity of media and technological change (Storsul & Stuedhal, 2007). For instance, there was a strong conviction that the 'old', analogue media ecosystem had a value chain in which there were quite clearly delineated positions for the press, broadcasters and providers, mirrored in medium-specific media regulations. However, as the analysis below will demonstrate, even in the analogue era, technological innovations such as the introduction of teletext altered the balance in the media industry's ecosystem with potential effects for other players, including businesses and consumers.

The study analyses the evolution of teletext (policies) in Norway and Flanders. The research is based on the analysis of relevant government documents (legislation, parliamentary debates) and internal documents and publications about teletext from broadcasters. For the Flemish case, the study has been much enhanced by in-depth interviews with privileged witnesses, including Stijn Lehaen (then Head of Digital Media, interviewed May 2012), Jo Martens (VRT study department, April 2012), Emmanuel Rottey (then Chief Editor of News Gathering, Online and Social Media, 9 October, 2014), Linda Van Crombruggen (Teletext 1981–2007, interviewed 22 October 2014). Interviews were transcribed and, like the documents, analysed by means of a coding tool that was inspired by the conceptual literature. Information from written primary and secondary sources and from oral sources was triangulated.

Teletext in Norway and Flanders: A Brief History

On 8 May 1980, 'Teletekst', the Flemish public service version of teletext, officially started on an experimental basis as a free add-on service of the broadcast institution (Dewulf, 1990). Originally, few funds were allocated to the project and Teletekst was operated by volunteers who did this in addition to their regular jobs (Van Crombruggen, 2014). As a result, the original offer was limited to 40 pages, of which only a few could be 'refreshed' and for which there was not enough time for regular updates. However, Teletekst (decoders) turned out to be a success with audiences and, as a result, in May 1981 teletext obtained its own newsroom and additional staff. This allowed teletext to meet the growing demand for new subjects and faster news coverage (Dewulf, 1990, pp. 13–14). By 1983, all 100 pages were in use, with an improved layout and divided into seven chapters, each with its own table of contents.

1983 also saw the introduction of teletext (Norwegian: 'Tekst-TV') in Norway. With parliamentary approval, the public service broadcaster NRK launched the service for a three-year trial period starting in February (Nilssen, 1985, pp. 62–63; Vestbø, 2002). Parliament approved an increase in the 1983 budgets of €250,000 for the new media platform (Parliament 1981). Much like in Flanders and elsewhere in Europe, the first years were characterised by small scale, both in the volume and resources spent. Norway is a small country and was among the last in Western Europe to introduce television (in 1960) and colour television (in 1970) (Enli, Moe, Sundet & Styvertsen, 2013), and by 1983 the user base for teletext was miniscule, with an estimated 10,000 receivers (Nilssen, 1985). For the NRK, informational services were put front and centre, in addition to the prospects of catering to the hearing impaired through subtitling.

In 1985, Teletekst's success in Flanders pushed further expansion. Based on information obtained from an academic audience study conducted in 1984 (De Meyer, Fauconnier & Hendriks, 1984), adjustments were made. In February of that year, new equipment allowed the expansion to 800 pages, the use of a third television line allowed for faster manoeuvring through the pages and each of the (now eight) chapters – news, sports, weather/traffic, radio/tv/tt, financial, leisure time, consumer, daily/weekly papers – were given their own number and table of contents (Dewulf, 1985, pp. 42–43; see also Dewulf, 1990, p. 18). Subtitling was split into two separate services, one for each public service television channel. Following the BBC example and encouraged by audiences, the continuous news flash was introduced (Dewulf, 1985, p. 45). Throughout the late 1980s, Teletekst further developed in providing news and service information. To this end, it established a network both outside the institution (information from the Brussels stock exchange about futures and currency market data; from the Belgian national airport, Zaventem, for flight information; and the national royal weather service KMI for weather updates, amongst others) and within the institution to help establish specific pages (Dewulf, 1990, p. 24).

A similar expansion took place in Norway, though at a slower pace. By 1985 (2 years into the trial period), the number of pages was 125, with news being the major category, and sports, programme guides, and information about teletext being other categories. The NRK knew well that the service constituted a new form of media content distribution – what we later came to know as 'on demand'. 'News is available as long as the broadcasting signal is turned on. [...] the news is updated continuously. It takes mere seconds from the time a news story is ready at the editorial desk to when it is distributed across the country. The viewer can read the story in peace, just when it suits him or her' (Head of NRK teletext Nilssen, 1985, p. 62). With this quite radical potential in mind, the development continued into the 1990s.

In Flanders, the legal break-up of the public service television monopoly in 1987 and the arrival on February 2 of the first Flemish commercial television channel, VTM (Saeys, 2007), resulted in the introduction of a new teletext service. VTM text differed notably from its public service counterpart. While news and information were important, VTM had a distinct commercial side, with advertising banners, regular raffles and interaction through 0900 paid telephone lines. The news content was provided by the press group Concentra, then publisher of regional newspaper *Het Belang van Limburg* and shareholder in VTM (Van den Bulck, 2014). The further introduction onto the Flemish television market of commercial channels (VT4 and 2BE (1995), Vitaya (2000), VijfTV (2005), etc.) was often accompanied by complementary teletext services along the more commercial lines set out by VTM text. Similar trends towards extending teletext to commercial broadcasters could be observed in Norway.

Meanwhile the public teletext services in Flanders and Norway continued to flourish and expand. Teletekst was the first service in the public service institution to digitise the news input via an Electronic News System (Dewulf, 1990, p. 28). What is more, its content and services diversified to include carpooling information and hitchhiking services Taxistop and Eurostop, to commodity tests organized by from consumer service Testaankoop to information on the quality of sea water (Dewulf, 1990, 27–28), and detailed information for pigeon fanciers and other lesser known sports (Van Crombruggen, 2014). Special attention was given to youngsters through the development of TT-junior, a service which included games, birthday wishes, theatre reviews and the like (Dewulf, 1990, p. 28; Van Crombruggen, 2014). Meanwhile the commercial broadcasters' teletext services in both countries explored their commercial opportunities, including the introduction of erotic pages and interactive options. The expansions were mirrored by their success with audiences. In Flanders, for instance, a 1997 survey with a representative sample of Flemish television households (VRT Studiedienst, 1998) showed that no less than 93% used one of the existing Flemish teletext services.

In the early 2000s, teletext became caught up in the digitisation of broadcasting and the introduction of online services, sometimes leading the way, sometimes falling 'victim' to these developments. In Flanders, the public service institution's convergence of its various newsrooms was preceded by the merger, on January, 1, 2003, of the teletext newsroom on the one hand, the online newsroom, vrtnieuws.net (now deredactie.be), and sporza.be on the other hand (De Redactie, 8-5-2010). This meant a split of the old teletext newsroom, as subtitling remained under the wings of television, but those providing news, sports and services were moved to new, separate homes (Van Crombruggen, 2014). In Norway in the late 1990s, teletext was positioned against the budding online experiments as the latter grew out of individual editorial staff initiatives, while teletext was embraced by the commercial arm of the NRK. In essence, what some saw as commercial potential in teletext stood in stark contrast to the explicit public service motivations presented by the first online attempts (Moe, 2012).

The next innovation for teletext in Flanders was the move from analogue to digital. Starting November 2009 onwards, the teletext pages of VRT's general interest channel, één, could be consulted not just via television and the Internet, but also using a mobile app for smartphones. In 2012, it was VRT's most downloaded app (Lehaen, 2012). However, by 2014 Teletekst's future seemed less secure. While subtitling remains important, with 25 people working in this department, the information role of Teletekst is being reduced at the advantage of the website. The services of Teletekst will continue until a critical bottom threshold of users has been reached (Rottey, 2014). In Norway, teletext made a similar journey into the new media platforms, but here too, after 2010 user numbers began to drop and editorial staff was cut. In March 2014, the last editorial staff members left NRK teletext as the institution switched to a new mode of news production where stories for teletext were transferred from other editorial groups (e.g., Bach & Ashraf, 2013).

Teletext as Academic/Policy Silence

A study of the regulatory and policy documents relating to media in Flanders show a considerable lack of interest in or concern for teletext. Teletext was not mentioned in the media decree until the late 1990s, when teletext was introduced in the section on (the prohibition of) advertising on public service teletext (see below), and today references to teletext are limited to where issues with regards to other media 'also apply to teletext' (Vlaamse Regering, 2014). Similarly, in the successive management contracts between PSB institution VRT, one of the key teletext providers in Flanders, and the Flemish government, mention of teletext is sparing and limited to a few lines (e.g., Vlaamse Regering, 2011). A similar lack of legislative and policy attention can be observed in the Norwegian situation. Its introduction was uncontroversial, and in the years since its introduction, more high profile issues such as those concerning the provision of satellite television, and the end of the monopoly era, have been taken up on the agenda. Below, we elaborate on how teletext in the late 1990s provided a back door for ad funding on NRK online, a case that illustrates the little attention given to the medium by policy makers and legislators alike. Since the NRK remit by and large has been formally less well-defined than elsewhere in Europa (see, e.g., Moe, 2008), the fact that teletext has not featured in legislative documents should come as no surprise.

In Flanders, academics too stayed silent on the topic; with the exception of one special issue of an academic journal in the early years of teletext, the medium received little or no attention, especially not from policy researchers. In the limited literature on the topic, some reference is made to possible reasons for the lack of academic and policy attention to teletext that also occurred elsewhere. For one, teletext was typically a new technology lurking in the shadows, while at the time of its introduction (during the mid-1970s through the 1980s) videotex (online information) stood in the spotlight. As is now clear, videotex eventually did not work out, while teletext had a considerable success, at least in Europe. The first reason is of a technological nature. As Carey and Elton explain:

> this situation suggests that those championing the former [videotex] were probably right about the market being ready to accept services of the kind they envisaged (the services met a real need). But these champions may have underestimated the technological hurdles standing in the way of getting an easy-to-use version of their service into the market fairly soon (2010, p. 70).

Second, Carey and Elton suggest (p. 220) that a lack of policy and policy research attention could result from the fact that the start of teletext did not really involve the building of a new industry, a new economy, but instead appeared as little more than an add-on for broadcasting. This was indeed the case in Flanders and Norway. In both cases, as elsewhere in Europe, teletext originated and developed in the context of PSB, which held a broadcast monopoly and, at the time of the start of teletext, was not allowed any commercial revenue (Van den Bulck, 2001). In Flanders, a possible alternative platform for a teletext initiative was the cable, as an Ostend cable company's relaying of Ceefax in the late 1970s suggests (Dewulf, 1990, p. 10). Flanders was an early and widespread adopter of cable broadcasting (Saeys, 2007). However, the cable industry at the time was decentralised in several, relatively small scale, 'intercommunals', that is, collaborations between two or more municipalities (Stevens, 2009). As such, they did not have the size or financial means for new media initiatives, although later on, they would adopt teletext to provide their cable subscribers with practical information.

As a result, Flemish and Norwegian teletext services were originally, and for a long time, considered as part of existing metaphors, a re-interpretation of, but no real shift in, the paradigms of print and broadcasting. Teletext was initiated as an 'add-on' service to public service television and thus considered part and parcel of this medium, to the extent that in the PSB's organisational charts, teletext was never recognised as a medium in its own right. For instance, in the Flemish case, throughout its history, Teletekst fell under the responsibility of the head of television news – 'like a stowaway' (Boussé, 1985; Van Crombruggen, 2014). Some Teletekst workers saw this additional news source as the fusion of the print and broadcasting paradigm: as the 'printing press from a distance', 'Guttenberg on the TV screen' and 'the final step in the realisation of McLuhan's Guttenberg Galaxy' (Verpoorten, 1985, pp. 30–31). Later on, others saw the future of teletext more from a computer perspective in its potential as a permanently updateable and consultable database (Dewulf, 1985, p. 45). Therefore, the notion of teletext as an extension of mass communication was soon well established in the minds of policy makers and industry.

Unlike Norway, where there was no real interest by the industry, in Flanders there was considerable cooperation and consultation with the industry. The start of Flemish teletext was pushed by Fabrimetal, the umbrella organisation of household electronics manufacturers (Dewulf, 1990, p. 11). The development of affordable television sets with teletext decoders greatly added to the spread and popularity of early teletext (Piens, 1990, p. 89). In the 1990s, Dutch home electronics maker Philips in Eindhoven (NL) developed a television set that could store teletext pages so that viewers did not have to wait for the entire carousel to go past. The industry also developed suitable remotes and fast texts systems (Van Crombruggen, 2014). As such, in the vocabulary of Carey and Elton (2010, p. 32), teletext was a case of 'piggybacking on replacement cycles'. Television was well-established in households, and as people regularly replaced their old sets, new sets provided options for teletext without extra cost or effort. 'This provided a highly favourable context for the rapid diffusion of teletext' (p. 33), but did encourage a whole new and potentially profitable industry to develop.

While these elements may explain the policy neglect and, to a certain extent, the lack of policy research, it does not fully account for the overall academic neglect of teletext as, for instance, a news medium. News analysis has been the staple of communications research, and as the example of Twitter illustrates, new news media can attract enthusiasm from media scholars. So why did this not happen for teletext as a news medium? One reason may be the fact that teletext journalism and teletext news is succinct and matter-of-fact and thus does not allow for multidimensional analyses of aspects typical of print and audiovisual news. Crudely put: for researchers, teletext news is 'boring'. Journalism research shows a preference for feature articles, op-eds or scoops – journalism that makes an impact. The day-to-day routine life of the profession, unsurprisingly, gets less attention. If one disregards the technological innovation in the first years, teletext journalism has been all about routine, about the steady, 'dry' – but trusted – provision of vital information.

What is more, there are several methodological difficulties involved in studying teletext. This is not only because, in the age of the Internet, media researchers have found challenges with accessing archived material (see, e.g., Brügger, 2008, for a helpful discussion). Earlier media forms bring challenges too: old films have a tendency to burn, and separating first and later editions of print newspapers is not necessarily easy. Teletext has its own challenges. While broadcast television, and to some degree radio, in recent decades has been more consistently archived, often by public libraries, the task of recording and archiving teletext is different. Technically, teletext is a simultaneous broadcast at any point in time of a range of informational pages that together make up the teletext system at that point in time. For a recipient to archive this flow, recordings would have to be made of an equal number of parallel page streams. Suffice to say, this may not have been the first task on the agenda of media researchers interested in teletext.

Back to the Future I: Public Service Broadcasters Versus the Commercial Press

One of the media policy debates that has received a lot of attention throughout Europe over the last few decades has concerned the expansion of public service broadcasters, and especially their news provision, to new platforms, including the Internet. Across Europe, publicly funded broadcasting institutions have built an online presence of varying scopes. Most, however, aim at providing online news, also in text-based form – much like the online news provided by the commercial press. Amidst the 'crisis' of journalism – the problem with replacing losses in subscription and paper copy sales and attempts at raising 'pay walls' around online content – the free, publicly funded offers of public service broadcasters have met with criticism from the commercial press. How should we understand the stakeholders in this battle? What are the claims made, and on what grounds? Is the situation a result of public service broadcasters exploiting tax money to impinge on the territory of the press, or is it just a natural extension of the public service mission onto a new media platform? These are difficult questions, without generally applicable answers, and to answer them requires contextual understanding – of policy and of media systems. One additional dimension that might help is the historical development of additional services for public service broadcasters. Here, teletext is relevant.

Flanders provides a case in point. The start of teletext on PSB in 1980 was preceded by extensive consultation and negotiations with the printed press, represented by the *Belgische Vereniging van Dagbladuitgevers* [Belgian Association of Newspaper Publishers] (Dewulf, 1990, p. 11; Van Crombruggen, 2014). The press recognised that, in principle, use of teletext was a broadcasting issue, but at the same time it considered the medium as a potential competitor. A compromise was reached that every evening between 9 and 10pm, the headlines would be put onto Teletekst, where each newspaper had its own page. Audience research in 1984 (De Meyer, Fauconnier & Hendriks, 1984) further confirmed to both broadcasters and press that teletext was no competition for newspapers, as people indicated their newspaper reading had not diminished due to teletext use. Both were seen as different media with their own specific characteristics, including the brevity of teletext information. In subsequent years, according to Van Crombruggen (2014), teletext often served as an accelerator or as a system through which new technological possibilities and digitisation. For instance, the financial newspaper *Financieel Economische Tijd* (FET, now *De Tijd*) studied the teletext technology and then went on to rent BRT lines to send financial data to its subscribers. In 1995, the FET would be the first to have an online 'newspaper', rather resembling a digital brochure (Beyers, 2004, p. 12). Thus, teletext is considered by some as the forerunner of online newspapers (Beyers, 2004). The relationship with the press remained stable until the introduction of the VRT news website, which was contested by the press as unfair competition for their own online initiatives (Van den Bulck, 2008). The arrival of the first commercial teletext service of television station VTM, VTM text, did not really provoke any debate with the printed press for the simple reason that, by law, the channel was owned by the Flemish press companies so they could control this 'competitor', and VTM text had more commercially oriented than news oriented.

The Flemish case suggests that a look back at teletext tells us that there are direct historical parallels to the current discussion between policy stakeholders regarding the presence of PSBs on other digital platforms. The arguments used in discussions about teletext between PSBs and the press in Flanders are a pre-echo of the debates surrounding the start and success of the PSB's news website (Van den Bulck, 2008). Digging deeper and comparing cases in more countries can help to better understand this and other cases where there are historical parallels to contemporary debates regarding boundary maintenance between media sectors, which digitisation has increased. This can also help to further clarify what has changed since the early discussions regarding teletext. For instance, what is the actual role of the EU as a promoter and arbiter of convergence, if we consider that debates about media boundary transgression precede the EU's involvement in media matters?

Back to the Future II: Teletext and the Internet

One key historical development that has been considered to be at the basis of many policy debates is the development of the Internet and the subsequent convergence and conflicts between old and new media and platforms. Carey and Elton (2010) argue that there is a need to study the role of teletext in the development of the Internet. They claim that, beyond the well-known and much repeated history of the Internet that 'focuses narrowly on the technological development of the Internet as a U.S. Defense Department project that began with the Arpanet in the late 1960s' (Carey & Elton, 2010, p. 10), there is another story of the Internet to be told:

> From the late 1970s through the mid 1990s, videotex[t] and teletext were the experimental field laboratories for content development. […] Between them, however, they developed advertising, news services, games, shopping, and even [an] auction. […] All these services led the way to models of content on the Web today'.
> (Carey & Elton, 2010, p. 10)

It can be argued, then, that our understanding of policies and regulation regarding the Internet and other telecom-based initiatives can be improved by an analysis of developments in teletext in this regard.

A good example to illustrate this point is to be found in Norway. The NRK is one of the 'purest' public service broadcasters in Europe in terms of funding: no ads and little other commercial income streams. However, for 10 years, from 2000 to 2010, it had banner ads on its website. How did this happen? The answer does not lie in discussions about the Internet or web strategies for the NRK. Nor does it lie in political documents concerning online media or even digital television: it lies in strategy documents about teletext and in political discussions and regulations concerning teletext. In short, in 1997, the NRK established the commercial subsidiary NRK Aktivum to take care of all business activities. Already in June 1997, Aktivum presented an ambitious plan for commercial exploitation of teletext service. Ads and shopping services on teletext could generate €2.5 million in the coming two years, argued Aktivum. Crucially, Internet activities had to be developed in parallel: 'Within a short period of time, these two functions will have melded together' (Wam in Larsen, 1997). On this basis, a lengthy policy process started that was about teletext and its relation to the PSB remit, its commercial potential, etc. But for the NRK, it was also about the Web. When in 2000, after lengthy debates in Parliament, the 'yes' to ads was finally given, the NRK first launched ads on its teletext service and then extended that same approach to its website. As a result, teletext became a test bed for commercial income streams at the NRK and effectively paved the way, or to use a more appropriate metaphor, it opened a backdoor, for advertising on the website – which continued for 10 years.

In the Flemish case, too, there were a number of interesting discussions surrounding teletext that pre-echo debates that pop up in Internet discussions. Looking back after 10 years of teletext in Flanders, Dewulf (1990, pp. 9–10) explored some potential reasons for its success and referred to the active role of the audience that the medium allows for: the viewer can autonomously decide what he or she wants to read, when and for how long. As its main attraction, he saw the combination of quick and up-to-date information for wide audiences (news, sports, weather, traffic, radio and television programming) with very specific, focused services for a diverse group of target audiences (financial information, subtitling for the deaf and hearing impaired). In short, he referred to the 'consultation' function of teletext, which later on proved an important factor in the success of the Internet. It showed that, unlike policy makers, audiences experienced teletext through the prism of paradigms established outside of broadcasting and print (Elton & Carey, 1983). This had potential impact on later television developments. Indeed, in their discussion of the development of Interactive Television (ITV), Carey & Elton (2010) explain that while in the U.S. a negative attitude towards ITV dominated, in Europe and particularly the UK, there were far fewer trials and attitudes were less negative. 'In the United Kingdom, people had experience with a limited form of enhanced television through Teletext, which taught them simple skills about how to interact with television and may have created an appetite for more advanced services' (Carey & Elton, 2010, p. 270). Again, knowledge of developments in older technology adaptations such as the uptake (or not) of teletext and, equally important, of the paradigmatic history can further our understanding of varying responses to contemporary developments.

Second, while instrumental in developing new forms of journalistic language (later used by Twitter), Flemish teletext also raised social concerns that resemble those about media content on other (new) media such as the Internet. To accommodate younger generations, in the 1990s the youngster pages of one of the Flemish teletext services were extended with games and additional pages during school holidays. At some point, a pen pal service was included in which young people could be brought into contact and exchange letters (Van Crombruggen, 2014). However, this was terminated when the pen pal service resulted in a child falling victim to a grown-up disguised as a child, a pre-echo of debates about sexual predators on Internet and social media (cf. Wolak, Finkelhor, Mitchell, & Ybarra, 2008).

The point illustrates that in order to understand policy issues regarding the Internet today, we need to look at a history that goes beyond the Internet. Sometimes we need to look to broadcasting policy, sometimes to privacy policy and sometimes to teletext.

Conclusion: Looking Back to Look Forward

The above analysis of the development and characteristics of teletext as a case of policy (research), bring us, finally, to three main claims. First, the analysis of many of the debates and arguments relating to teletext have been shown to be pre-echos of contemporary debates in media policy. Therefore, to improve the quality of contemporary policy analysis, media policy researchers need to connect with media historians and media histories to overcome much of the historical blindness that typifies media policy research. Historical awareness of how technologies and policy issues have developed make us better equipped to answer current questions in a more authoritative way. Our study thus seems to confirm Collins' (1990) concern for historical contextualisation and his invitation to media policy researchers to acknowledge that it is really hard to be media policy researchers without the time to look back at the topic we are studying; in other words, without the benefit of hindsight.

Our second, and seemingly contradictory, claim is that media (policy) history is too important to be left to media historians. This study of teletext from a policy perspective indicates that there are still a lot of interesting and important media policy analyses to do of media issues and developments that happened a while ago. Against the trend amongst policy researchers of following the latest buzz or hype, doing policy research on issues that are not going on right now, is a perfectly legitimate and rewarding endeavour. However, and this is our third claim, it would be a shame to stick to media (policy) history as a goal in its own right, as media (policy) history can provide better answers to urgent issues. It is precisely this combination of historical insights with an analysis of contemporary issues that can provide useful answers to the pressing policy issues of the day.

References

Bach, David and Ashraf, Ahmed Fawad (2013). NRK legger ned Morgennytt. [NRK shuts down morning news broadcast program Morgennytt] In *Aftenposten*, http://www.aftenposten.no/kultur/NRK-legger-ned-Morgennytt-7405013.html [accessed 25.11.15]

Beyers, H. (2004). Online-kranten in Vlaanderen: Een historisch overzicht van midden jaren '90 tot vandaag, *e-view*, 2. Retrieved from http://comcom.uvt.nl/e-view/04-2/inhoud.htm.

Boussé, L. (1985). De blinde passagier [The Stowaway]. In BRT-teletekstredactie (Eds.), *Teleteks* (pp. 5–28). Brussels, Belgium: BRT uitgave.

Brügger, N. (2008). The archived website and website philology – A new type of historical document? *Nordicom Review, 29*(2), 155–175.

Carey, J., & Elton, M.C.J. (2010) *When media are new: Understanding the dynamics of new media adoption and use*. Ann Arbor, MI: University of Michigan Press.

Collins, R. (1990). *Television: Policy and culture*. London: Unwin Hyman.

De Meyer, G., Fauconnier, G., & Hendriks, A. (1984). Het gebruik van teletekst in Vlaanderen [The use of teletext in Flanders], *Communicatie, 14*(2), 9–13.

De Redactie (2010). VRT-Teletekst blaast 30 kaarsjes uit. [VRT-Teletekst blows out 30 candles], http://deredactie.be/cm/vrtnieuws/cultuur%2Ben%2Bmedia/media/1.763452, (accessed 10 November 2014).
Dewulf, B. (1985). De toekomst van teletekst [The future of teletext]. In BRT-teletekstredactie (Eds.), *Teletekst* (pp. 43–51). Brussels, Belgium: BRT uitgave.
Dewulf, B. (1990). Tien jaar BRT-teletekst: een terugblik. [Ten years of BRT teletext: A look back]. In B. Verpoorten (Ed.), *Teletekst: Televisie om in te bladeren*, (p. 932). Brussels, Belgium: BRT uitgave.
Donders, K., & Moe, H. (Eds.). (2011). *Exporting the public value test: The regulation of public broadcasters' new media services across Europe*. Gothenburg, Sweden: Nordicom.
Doyle, G. (2002). *Media ownership: the economics and politics of convergence and concentration in the UK and European media*. London, UK: Sage.
Elton, M., & Carey, J. (1983/2006). Computerizing information: Consumer reactions to teletext. *Journal of Communication*, 33(1), 162–173. doi: 10.1111/j.1460-2466.1983.tb02382.x.
Enli, G.S., Moe, H., Sundet, V.S., & Syvertsen, T. (2013). From fear of television to fear for television. Five political debates about new technologies. *Media History*, 19(2), 213–227.
Fransman, M. (2010). *The new ICT ecosystem: Implications for policy and regulation*. Cambridge, UK: Cambridge University Press.
Freedman, D. (2010). Media policy silences: The hidden face of communications decision making. *The International Journal of Press/Politics*, 15(3), 344–362. doi: 10.1177/1940161210368292.
Gitlin, T. (1982). Television's screens: Hegemony in transition. In M.W. Apple (Ed.), *Cultural and economic reproduction in education: Essays on class, ideology and the state* (pp. 202–246). London: Routledge & Kegan Paul.
Graziplene, L.R. (2000). *Teletext: Its promise and demise*. Cranbury, NJ: Associated University Presses.
Herkman, J. (2012). Introduction: Intermediality as a theory and methodology. In J. Herkman, T. Hujanen & P. Oinonen (Eds.) *Intermediality and Media Change* (pp. 10–27). Tampere, Finland: Tampere University Press.
Humphreys, P. (1996). *Mass media and media policy in Western Europe*. Manchester, UK: Manchester University Press.
Jenkins, H. (2004). The cultural logic of media convergence. *International Journal of Cultural Studies* 7, 33–43. doi: 10.1177/1367877904040603.
Lakoff, G. (1983). The contemporary theory of metaphor. In A. Ortony (Ed.), *Metaphor and thought*. Cambridge, UK: Cambridge University Press.
Larsen, S. (1997, July 23). NRK med 20 mill. på 'ny' tekst–tv. [NRK puts 20 mill NOK in 'new' teletext] *DagensNæringsliv*, p. 27.
Lehaen, S. (2012). *Personal Communication Stijn Lehaen, then Head Digital Media*. Brussels: VRT, May 2012.
Lopez, A. (2012). *The media ecosystem: What ecology can teach us about responsible media practice*. Berkeley, CA: Evolver Editions.
Martens, J. (2012). *Personal Communication Jo Martens, VRT study department*. Brussels: VRT, April 2012.
McKinnon, J.K. (2012). *Postmodernism: The role of user adoption of teletext, videotex and bulletin board systems in the history of the Internet*. MA thesis, Simon Fraser University.

McQuail, D., & Siune, K. (Eds.). (1998). *Media policy: Convergence, concentration and commerce*. London: Sage.

Mjøs, O. J., Moe, H., & Sundet, V.S. (2014). The functions of buzzwords: A comparison of 'Web 2.0' and 'Telematics'. *First Monday*, 19(12).

Moe, H. (2008). Public service media online? Regulating public broadcasters' Internet services – A comparative analysis. *Television & New Media*, 9(3), 220–238.

Moe, H. (2012). Between public service and commercial venture: The Norwegian Broadcasting Corporation on the Web 1994–2000. In M. Burns & N. Brügger (Eds.), *Histories of public service broadcasters on the Web* (pp. 75–90). New York: Peter Lang.

Nilssen, Olav. (1985). Tekst-TV i dag og i morgen [Teletext today and tomorrow], in *NRK/TV 25 år:1960–1985 [NRK/TV 25 years: 1960–1985]*. Oslo, Norway: NRK.

Norwegian Parliament. (1981–1982). Innst S. nr 192 Forsøk med tekstfjernsyn [*Proposition to Parliament No. 192. Tests with teletext*]. *www.stortinget.no/no/*.

Piens, P. (1990). Teletekst infrastructuur bij de BRT. [Teletext infrastructure at BRT] In B. Verpoorten (Ed.), *Teletekst: Televisie om in te bladeren*, (pp. 89–114). Brussels: BRT uitgave.

Pool, de Sola, I. (1983). *Technologies of freedom. On free speech in an electronic age*. Cambridge, MA: Harvard University Press.

Rogers, E.M. (1983). *Diffusion of innovations*. London: Colliers MacMillan.

Stevens, D. (2009). *Toezicht in de electronische communicatiesector: Constitutionele en institutionele aspecten van de wijzigende rol van de overheid. Proefschrift*. [Supervision in the electronic communication sector: Constitutional and institutional aspects of the changing role of the government. PhD] Leuven: Faculteit Rechten.

Rottey, E. (2014). *Personal Communication Emmanuel Rottey*, then Chief editor News Gathering, Online and Social Media. Brussels: VRT, 9 October.

Saeys, F. (2007). 'Statuut, organisatie en financiering van de openbare televisieomroep in Vlaanderen'. [Statute, organisation and financing of public service television] In A. Dhoest & H. Van den Bulck (eds.) *Publieke televisie in Vlaanderen: Een geschiedenis*, (pp. 23–52). Ghent: Academia Press.

Sampson, T., & Lugo, J. (2003). The discourse of convergence: A neo-liberal Trojan horse. In. T. Hujanen & G.F. Lowe (Eds.), *Broadcasting and convergence: New articulations of the public service remit* (pp. 83–92). Göteborg, Sweden: Nordicom.

Schlesinger, P. (1985). From public service to commodity: The political economy of teletext in the UK. *Media, Culture & Society*, 7, 471–485. doi:10.1177/016344385007004005.

Schön, D.A. (1993). Generative metaphor: A perspective on problem-setting in social policy. In A. Ortony (Ed.), *Metaphor and Thought*. Cambridge, UK: Cambridge University Press.

Sterling, C.H. (2006). Pioneering risk: Lessons from the US teletext/videotex failure. *IEEE Annals of the History of Computing*, 28(3), 41–47.

Storsul, T., & Stuedahl, D. (Eds.). (2007). *Ambivalence towards convergence: Digitalization and media change*. Götenburg, Sweden: Nordicom.

Van Crombruggen, L. (2014). *Personal Communication with Linda Van Crombruggen*, Teletekst editor 1981–2010. Brussels: VRT, October 22nd.

Van den Bulck, H., & Donders, K. (2014). Pitfalls and obstacles of media policy making in an age of digital convergence: The Flemish signal integrity case, *Journal of Information Policy, 4*, 444–462.

Van den Bulck, H. (2014). *Media: Structuur en werking*. [Media: Structure and processes] Antwerp: Acco.

Van den Bulck, H. (2001). Public service television and national identity as a project of Modernity: The example of Flemish television, *Media, Culture and Society, 23* (1): 53–70.

Van den Bulck, H. (2008). Can PSB Stake its Claim in a Media World of Digital Convergence? The Case of the Flemish PSB Management Contract Renewal. *Convergence: The International Journal of Research into New Media Technologies, 14*(3), 335–350.

Verpoorten, B. (1985). Teletekst: het lezend-luister-oog. [Teletext: the reading-listen-eye]. In BRT-teletekstredactie (Eds.), *Teletekst* (pp. 29–39). Brussels, Belgium: BRT uitgave.

Vestbø, A. (2002). Leve tekst-TV – Den stivbente grafikkens retorikk [Long live teletext – the rhethoric of rigid graphical design]. *Mediert, 1*, 8–17.

Vlaamse regering (2014). Decreet van 27 maart 2009 betreffende radio-omroep en televisie.[Decree of March 27 2009 regarding radio broadcasting and television] Brussels: Vlaamseregering.

Vlaamse Regering (2011). Beheersovereenkomst VRT 2012–2016. [Management Agreement VRT 2012–2016] Brussels: Vlaamse Regering.

VRT (1998). Het grote teletext onderzoek. [The big teletext study] Brussels: VRT Studiedienst.

Wolak, J., Finkelhor, D., Mitchell, K.J., & Ybarra, M.L. (2008). Online 'predators' and their victims: Myths, realities and implications for prevention and treatment, *American Psychologist, 63*(2), 111–128. doi: 10.1037/0003-066X.63.2.111.

Ytreberg, E. (2011). Convergence: Essentially confused?, *New Media & Society, 13*(3), 502–508. doi: 10.1177/1461444810397651.

3 Electronic Press
Turning a New Leaf for Convergent Media Content Regulation?

Irini Katsirea

Introduction

Media convergence, the 'phenomenon involving the interconnection of information and communications technologies, computer networks and media content' (Flew, 2014) has posed challenges for policy makers from its inception. The prevalent model for most of the twentieth century was that media content delivered through specific platforms was subject to different regulatory requirements. The breakdown of silos separating these platforms and the concomitant change of familiar patterns of consumption raises the question whether traditional regulatory structures are still appropriate.

An aspect of convergence that has so far received scant attention is that between the newspapers' online presence and that of broadcasters. Whereas public service broadcasters have been the target of state aid complaints by the press and have even been restricted in their online activities at the national level beyond the requirements of EU Law, the newspapers' web presence has rarely been questioned (European Commission, 2010).[1] Newspapers are not just 'news' printed on 'paper', but are also understood as news content available on websites carrying videos that are reminiscent of television. A notable development of recent times has been the exponential increase of video content available on newspaper websites, often produced by major newspapers as well as news agencies such as Reuters and the AP, which were once specialised in print only (Pavlik, 2008)

The need for broadcasting regulation has historically been justified on grounds of spectrum scarcity, of the natural tendency of broadcasting markets towards concentrations of power and of the unique pervasiveness of broadcasting (Barendt, 2007). These factors were not deemed to exist in the case of the press, which was therefore only subjected to general laws such as libel, contempt of court and obscenity. The diametrically opposed treatment of broadcasting vis-à-vis the press has deeper roots in the ideology of Social Liberalism, which was prevalent when broadcasting was born as a mass medium in the 1920s, as opposed to that of Market Liberalism, which held sway when the 'free press' was born in the mid nineteenth century (Vick, 2006). The thinly masked attempts to conceal this ideological battle behind objective explanations eventually failed. The technological justification for the disparate treatment of press and broadcasting collapsed with the advent of digitalisation, while the economic and cultural arguments are also highly contestable.

The growing convergence between the two sectors in the online domain begs the question whether their divergent regulation is still appropriate or whether convergence of media content regulation in the form of broadcasting deregulation or, conversely, of a tightening of press standards is desirable. In the UK, the phone-hacking scandal prompted demands for a more stringent press regulation regime. Whereas Leveson mostly evaded the issue of convergence (Leveson, 2012), the House of Lords Select Committee on Communications (2013), as well as the Australian Convergence Review, recently recommended a relaxation of standards for all convergent, non-public service news media (Australian Government, 2012). The Convergence Review proposals foundered on political opposition, and those of the Select Committee have not materialised so far either.

As long as no political consensus on regulatory convergence can be reached, the question of how to satisfactorily distinguish between text-based and video-based media in the online domain will remain relevant. In recent times, this question has surfaced in the context of the classification of newspaper publishers' video sites as on-demand Audiovisual media services (AVMS). This issue has generated great controversy, the press sector being loath to face regulatory burdens, and is considered as a particularly challenging area by national regulatory authorities (de Bueger, 2013; Machet, 2011).

This chapter will examine, first, the regulatory framework of the Audiovisual Media Services Directive (AVMSD) and the extent to which it can apply to the electronic press (European Parliament and Council, 2010). Subsequently, the chapter will discuss the contrasting positions of the British and Austrian regulatory authorities concerning the regulation of video material on the websites of print publications. It will focus, in particular, on the criteria employed by these authorities for drawing the regulatory boundary between newspaper websites that deserve to be regulated as AVMS and those that do not. In doing so, this chapter will analyse the determinations reached by the British and Austrian regulatory authorities. It will take guidelines issued and audience research commissioned by the former as well as insights from the discipline of media studies into account. At the time of completion of this chapter there is no judicial determination on the many open questions thrown up by the AVMSD's imperfect framework. A highly anticipated ruling by the Court of Justice of the European Union on the Austrian authorities' approach in Case C-347/14, *New Media Online* is still pending.

The EU Legal Framework for Online Newspapers: The Audiovisual Media Services Directive

The AVMSD, the successor to the Television without Frontiers Directive (TwFD), is the most important regulatory instrument for the audiovisual sector in Europe (Council of the European Communities, 1989; Gibbons & Katsirea,

2012; Katsirea, 2008). It was adopted in 2007 after a lengthy legislative process with the aim of extending the scope of the TwFD beyond traditional television to the so-called 'on-demand' or 'non-linear' AVMS. The main rationale behind the adoption of the AVMSD was the creation of a level playing field for linear and non-linear services (European Parliament and the Council, 2010). Nonetheless, the AVMSD only pays lip service to the principle of technological neutrality, while effectively divorcing itself from it by endorsing a system of graduated regulation. As Recital 58 of the AVMSD explains, on-demand services are subjected to a lighter regulatory regime compared to linear services on the grounds that they 'are different from television broadcasting with regard to the choice and control the user can exercise and with regard to the impact they have on society'.

The principle of graduated regulation is not the only aspect of the AVMSD that signifies a departure from the principle of technological neutrality. The exclusion of radio and of the press from the Directive's scope also signals a break with this principle. It is the second of these exclusions that is of interest for our purposes. Recital 28 of the AVMSD states that 'The scope of this Directive should not cover electronic versions of newspapers and magazines'. It is doubtful whether this statement suffices to completely exclude audiovisual material made available on the website of a print publication from the AVMSD remit. The exclusion has only made its way in a recital, not in the Directive's main text. Recitals set out the reasons for the enactment of a Directive. They are legally non-binding but can guide the Directive's interpretation by the courts (European Parliament, the Council and the Commission, 2014, Guideline 10).

The 'principal purpose' criterion is one of the seven cumulative criteria that an on-demand AVMS needs to meet in accordance with Article 1 of the AVMSD. It seeks to exclude all services where any audiovisual content is merely incidental to the service. The Directive mentions websites that contain audiovisual elements only in an ancillary manner, such as animated graphical elements, short advertising spots or information related to a product or non-audiovisual service, as well as gambling services, on-line games and search engines as examples of services that should be excluded from its scope.

The requirement under Article 1 of the AVMSD that an AVMS must consist in the provision of programmes also has a bearing on the classification of online newspapers. A 'programme' is defined in Article 1(1)(b) of the AVMSD as 'a set of moving images with or without sound constituting an individual item within a schedule or a catalogue established by a media service provider and the form and content of which are comparable to the form and content of television broadcasting'.

The Directive refers in the same article to feature-length films, sports events, situation comedies, documentaries, children's programmes and original dramas as examples of programmes. The attribute of comparability to television broadcasting is further elaborated upon in Recital 24. This recital explains that AVMS are television-like when 'they compete for the same audience as television broadcasts, and the nature and the means of access to the service would lead the user reasonably to expect regulatory protection within the scope of this Directive'. The recital goes on to clarify, however, that the notion of a 'programme' should not be understood in a static but in a dynamic way, taking into account developments in television broadcasting, so as to 'prevent disparities as regards free movement and competition'.

This raises the question whether the principal purpose and the programme criteria in conjunction with Recitals 24 and 28 mean that the electronic press falls in its totality out of the Directive's ambit. The following section will try to clarify the position of the electronic press within the Directive's regulatory framework. By examining the implementation of the AVMSD in the UK and Austria, the section will seek to answer the question of whether the audiovisual material on the websites of print publications can be regulated as an AVMS.

The Implementation of the ATVOD in the United Kingdom

In the UK, the regulation of on-demand AVMS has been delegated to the Authority for Television on Demand. (ATVOD). In March 2010, The Office of Communications (Ofcom), the UK communications regulator, designated ATVOD, a previously self-regulatory body, as the co-regulator for on-demand programme services (ODPS). The first characteristic of an on-demand programme service, and the one most relevant for our purposes, is that it is, in accordance with s. 368 A(1)(a) of the Communications Act of 2013, a service whose 'principal purpose is the provision of programmes, the form and content of which are comparable to the form and content of programmes normally included in television programme services'. ATVOD has the power to establish whether a service falls within the ODPS definition, to require the notification of an on-demand service and to ensure that it complies with statutory obligations, including editorial content rules on material likely to incite hatred, material harmful for minors and on commercial references (Authority for Television on Demand [ATVOD], 2012). Determinations made by ATVOD may be the subject of appeal to Ofcom (Office of Communications [Ofcom], 2012a). Service providers are obliged to pay an annual fee to ATVOD in relation to each notified service. The tariff for regulatory fees is the subject of a yearly public consultation and needs to be approved by Ofcom.

The regulation of audiovisual material made available on the website of a print publication was the subject of some of the first appeals made to Ofcom against ATVOD scope determinations. In the following, we will concentrate on the *Sun Video* case, but also draw insights from other ATVOD determinations and Ofcom appeal decisions. *Sun Video* was one of eight determinations made by ATVOD in cases involving audiovisual material on newspaper/magazine websites.[2] ATVOD argued that the video section of the *Sun's* website constituted an ODPS, given that the video content was aggregated on a discreet section of the website, which was presented as a consumer destination in its own right. Also, the programmes could be made sense of without reference to the newspaper offering and were comparable to the form and content of TV programmes. Newsgroup Newspapers appealed ATVOD's determination in *Sun Video* to Ofcom. In December 2011, Ofcom overturned the determination and upheld the appeal (Ofcom, 2011). After Ofcom's appeal, ATVOD withdrew the other seven determinations.

Ofcom's decision in *Sun Video* provides a thorough examination of s. 368A (1) of the Act in light of the fact that the case raised 'important and difficult questions under complex new legislation and for which no precedents exist' (Ofcom, 2011). Ofcom set aside ATVOD's determination on the grounds that it placed too much emphasis on the video section of the *Sun's* website without taking sufficient account of the totality of what was provided on the website. Moreover, Ofcom criticised ATVOD for not sufficiently considering the written content of the *Sun's* website and its relationship to the audiovisual material. On the basis of its own review of the evidence available both at the time of ATVOD's determination and at the time of the appeal, Ofcom reached the conclusion that the video section of the *Sun's* website did not have the principal purpose of providing audiovisual material.

Ofcom considered that an on-demand programme service would be more likely to have its own homepage or to be catalogued and accessed via a separate section of the relevant website, to be presented or styled as a television channel, to have substantial duration/complete programmes that can be watched independently rather than 'bite-sized' clips, to have no or a limited number of access/content links between the audiovisual material and other content, to have more prominent audiovisual than written material. These characteristics are non-determinative. Therefore, a service having the required principal purpose would not need to display all of them; the presence of some of them could possibly suffice. In Ofcom's view, the video section of the Sun website did not meet these criteria given that it did not have its own homepage, it was not presented as a consumer destination in its own right, its audiovisual material lacked independence and was of short duration, there were access and content links between the audiovisual material and other content of the website, and finally, the accompanying written material was more prominent (Ofcom, 2011). Given its negative finding on the principal purpose, Ofcom did not need to consider the comparability of the video section to the form and content of television programmes.

Ofcom's decision in *Sun Video* leaves no doubt that there is some room for the video sections of online newspapers and magazines to be considered on-demand AVMS if they are sufficiently substantial and self-standing (Mac Síthigh, 2011). This ambivalence in Ofcom's legal treatment of newspapers' and magazines' video sections is also reflected in ATVOD's 'Guidance on who needs to notify'. This Guidance, also known as 'Scope Guidance', advises on the criteria that are applied by ATVOD when deciding whether a service falls under the definition of an ODPS (ATVOD, 2014a).

The Scope Guidance contains a non-exhaustive list giving some introductory examples of services that are likely to be considered as ODPS such as catch-up services for broadcast television channels and television programme archive services. It further includes two lists of factors to be taken into account when deciding, first, whether a service is TV-like, and, second, whether it has the principal purpose of providing TV-like content. The factors in these lists are derived from Ofcom appeal decisions as Ofcom recommended also in *Sun Video*. It is the second of these lists that is particularly interesting for our purposes. It emphasises: the existence of a point of entry to a service with its own independent identity; the degree and nature of any linkage between the video on demand, and in particular the TV-like content and other content; the question as to which of these types of content is the primary means of conveying the information sought to be conveyed; the prominence, quantity and proportion and relevance to the consumer of the TV-like programmes.

ATVOD does not consider that the AVMSD aimed to totally exclude from regulation all online services which also contained the electronic version of a newspaper or magazine (ATVOD, 2014b). Nor did it consider that the discussion concerning the classification of the electronic press was closed by the Ofcom decision in the *Sun Video* case. Ofcom only held that at the relevant time the video section did not have the required principal purpose. It did not, however, rule out the service developing in the future in a way that brings it within the scope of regulation.

The Implementation of the AVMSD in Austria

In Austria, AVMS are regulated by the Austrian Communications Authority (*Kommunikationsbehörde Austria* [KommAustria]). KommAustria was established in 2001 as the regulatory authority for broadcasting in Austria. In 2010, KommAustria was transformed into an independent panel authority with the powers of a court. KommAustria comprises five members, which are independent and not bound by any instructions, and receives administrative support from the Austrian Regulatory Authority for Broadcasting and Telecommunications (*Rundfunk und Telekom Regulierungs-GmbH*, RTR). Until 31 December 2013, KommAustria's decisions in matters of broadcasting regulation were reviewed by the Federal Communications Senate (*Bundeskommunikationssenat*, BKS). Since 1 January 2014, the BKS has been dissolved, and the Federal Administrative Court (*Bundesverwaltungsgericht*, BVerwG) assumed its function as the appellate authority against KommAustria's decisions.

The focus in this section will be on KommAustria's decisions in relation to the regulation of the electronic press. The first of these decisions concerned a regional daily newspaper published in Austria, the *Tiroler Tageszeitung*.

On 9 October 2012, KommAustria held that the newspaper's video section constituted an AVMS that would have to be notified to the regulatory authority (KommAustria, 2012). The *Tiroler Tageszeitung* operated a website which contained the newspaper's online edition. The videos in the website's 'Video' section contained edited reports between 30 seconds and a few minutes in length which could be searched by category, chronologically or by way of a full-text search. Some of the videos could also be accessed via links within articles in other parts of the website, whereas others had no direct connection to the website's text material. The video section had the same design and general navigation system as the remainder of the website.

The respondent argued that the videos only constituted a subordinate element of the overall website, complementing its text-based offering. Therefore, the provision of programmes was not the principal purpose of the website. Moreover, the videos in question did not constitute 'programmes' and were not 'television-like' in view of their short duration. KommAustria disagreed. It came to the conclusion that the videos were TV-like, because they aimed to inform, entertain or educate, and they were comparable in form and content to programmes broadcast on television. A minimum duration was not required.

As regards the principal purpose of the service, KommAustria argued that it would be misguided to examine the entire range of services offered by a service provider. Instead, it was necessary to determine on the basis of quantitative criteria whether the provision of audiovisual content was the principal purpose of a service. For KommAustria, the crucial question in this context was whether the audiovisual offering in question – leaving other services offered by the same provider aside – performed an independent function. A provider could not escape regulation by arguing that only an extremely small part of its entire service was devoted to audiovisual material when this material was indeed independent. The presentation of this material in a subdomain or in a separate homepage was not decisive, but could at best be taken into account when assessing the domain's independence. These considerations led KommAustria to conclude that the video section constituted an AVMS, given that it could be used independently of the other website content.

The owner of the *Tiroler Tageszeitung* appealed to the BKS to contest this outcome. In its ruling of 13 December 2012, the BKS upheld KommAustria's decision (*Bundeskommunikationssenat,* 2012a). It held that there was no difference between the videos that were available on the appellant's website and similar programmes shown on linear TV. The law did not prescribe a minimum duration of programmes. Besides, many of the videos lasted more than a couple of minutes so that there was no material difference from traditional television. The BKS also agreed with KommAustria's 'independent function' test and with its findings concerning the principal purpose of the website. It observed that the videos in question were stored in a subdomain that was exclusively devoted to audiovisual material and that could be consumed without recourse to any textual content. The audiovisual material did not merely serve to complement the text-based elements of the website but could be consumed independently.

Having outlined the Austrian regulators' approach to the regulation of the electronic press under the AVMSD, the final section will compare this approach to Ofcom's position.

The UK and Austrian Positions Compared

The first two criteria identified by Ofcom in *Sun Video* are formal. First, the service would need to be accessed via its own homepage or via a separate section of the relevant website. The Austrian regulators, by contrast, attach little importance to the existence of a separate homepage or even subdomain or to the existence of audiovisual material also in other parts of the website.

Indeed, it is not entirely clear why the availability of the audiovisual material also in other parts of the website should undermine the principal purpose of the video section. Nor is it clear why the video section would need to be endowed with its own homepage so as to more readily qualify as an independent service having the required principal purpose. This criterion can readily be circumvented by integrating such material within the overall website.

To be sure, Ofcom qualifies the requirement of a separate homepage by saying that it is not determinative, and that a website could 'provide a number of distinct services under cover of a single homepage' (Ofcom, 2011, no. 57; Ofcom, 2013a, paras 48, 49). However, in the *Everton TV* case, which concerned the TV section of the Everton Football Club's website, the fact that the homepage was the main initial destination for users suggested, in Ofcom's view (2013), that the TV section was not an independent service.

Second, the audiovisual material would need to be styled as a television channel. Ofcom agreed with News Group's submissions that the overall site was designed as a primarily text-based experience and that most users would have been unlikely to consider it as anything other than the online version of the *Sun* newspaper, especially in view of the presentation of the homepage and of the existence of the masthead on every page.

Ofcom's grounds for disputing the video section's TV-like presentation and style are overly formalistic. First, by shifting the focus from the video section to the entirety of the website, Ofcom easily arrived at the conclusion that the feel and look of the site was that of an online newspaper. Second, Ofcom's findings concerning the existence of the masthead on every page sit uneasily with its suggestion that names, labels and logos are not determinative, as well as with its abovementioned assumption that a single website could embrace a number of distinct services (Ofcom, 2011, para. 90 point c). If this is the case, why should it matter that these services bear the same masthead? It would be illogical to deny the classification of a pocket of TV-like territory as a distinct service on the grounds that it bears the same insignia as the remainder of the website.

These findings set clear pointers as to how to avoid the classification of a sub-service as an ODPS by ensuring its integration in the overall website. However, they risk stifling a more principled discussion about what kind of hybrid services should fall within the scope of the definition. The Austrian authorities, by contrast, accepted that the *Tiroler Tageszeitung* video section fulfilled the 'TV-likeness' and 'principal purpose' tests without focusing on its styling and presentation, but only on its content and on the fact that it targeted the same audience as traditional television.

We will now turn to the three substantive criteria introduced by Ofcom: the duration of the audiovisual material, its independence and its prominence compared to the written material. Interestingly, neither the duration of the videos nor their extent compared to the written text matter according to the Austrian regulators unless they are completely peripheral (*Bundeskommunikationssenat*, 2012b). The only decisive criterion in their view is the videos' functional independence from the written text.

As regards the duration of the audiovisual material, Ofcom explained that this was not a determinative criterion in itself. In other words, a service displaying material of short duration can still be considered to have the required principal purpose if its overall characteristics justify this conclusion. Indeed, in the *BBC Top Gear YouTube* and *BBC Food YouTube* cases (Ofcom, 2013b; 2013c), the short duration of the clips on these services did not alter the fact that their principal purpose was the provision of audiovisual material. However, in the present case, Ofcom considered the generally limited duration of the audiovisual material to be one of the factors indicating that the video section did not have the required principal purpose.

However, the benchmark against which Ofcom measured the duration of clips on the video section is not clear. Ofcom has repeatedly stressed that the typical duration of content depends on the genre in question, and that 'short form content may be more likely to be typical in some genres, such as children's programming and adult content programming' (Ofcom, 2012b, para. 59).

No attempt was made to attribute the clips on the video section to specific genres. Presumably, they could in their vast majority be characterised as 'news' in a broad sense, spanning the entire spectrum from 'serious' news to 'infotainment'. News clips on the *Sun* video section would hence have to be compared to news programmes on linear television. However, what would be the right comparator: individual news items or entire news bulletins? The average duration of news items on BBC1 and BBC2 is under three minutes, and hence comparable to that of news items in the video section. The fact that news items on linear TV are commonly bundled within longer news bulletins might militate against such a comparison. However, the prevailing logic of news is that of 'fragments of information with little apparent overall coherence apart from that imposed by the bulletin format' (Eldridge, 1995). Also, the 'BBC 60 second news' is an established news format, which might become more commonplace in future.

Ofcom's next substantive criterion is the independence of the audiovisual material from the other content in the newspaper's electronic version. Ofcom held that most of the audiovisual material on the video section lacked independence. It was linked to a written text and related directly to it in that it was either the source of this text, or provided the same content in audiovisual form or was an enhancement of it. This observation allows Ofcom to draw the conclusion that the video clips were subservient to the written content and an ancillary part of the electronic newspaper. The focal question asked by the Austrian authorities, by contrast, is about the comprehensibility of the video content without the aid of accompanying articles. No emphasis is put by them on the existence of links between the former and the latter.

It is submitted that Ofcom's analysis risks underestimating the interconnectedness between the two modes of communication – text and video – in the online domain as well as the powerful impact of the latter. If, as Ofcom claims, the audiovisual material itself was the source of the text, could not the opposite conclusion be drawn, namely that the latter was subservient to the former? Interestingly, Ofcom, in attempting to explain the relationship between the two media, notes initially that the audiovisual material 'amplified or enhanced what was written' only to say the exact opposite a few paragraphs later, namely that 'the written text generally provides context and gives meaning to, and enhances the information provided by, the audiovisual material …' (2011, paras 142, 151). This apparent contradiction suggests that neither the audiovisual material is subservient to the text nor is the text subservient to the audiovisual material, but that the two are intertwined.

This conclusion is consistent with insights from media studies which suggest that different media, when combined online, do not simply lead parallel lives, nor are they subordinated the one to the other. Instead they form a parent-child relationship so that one medium comes to contain the other. When video clips are inserted in a web newspaper, they take on a different role as they become 'subsumed into a larger, newspaper-like rhetorical whole' (Fagerjord, 2003). Ofcom's attempt to delve into the content of the audiovisual material and of the text-based article to which it was linked so as to establish their exact functionality seems misguided in view of their close interdependence.

Ofcom, by arguing that video content in an electronic newspaper website only satisfies the 'principal purpose' criterion if it is wholly independent of the written text, in effect removes big parts of this sector from regulatory scrutiny. Only in the event where an online newspaper dedicates a distinct section of its website to the publication of TV-like programmes that are wholly unrelated to the rest of its offering, could it be classified as an ODPS. One historic example of such a case is the transmission of Channel 5 programmes on the *Express* and *Daily Star* websites in the past. This is a rather exceptional occurrence so far, but such cross-media cooperation is likely to become more frequent in the future (Rahvar, 2011).

The last substantive criterion that Ofcom, but not the Austrian regulators, considered is the prominence of the audiovisual compared to the written material. Ofcom diligently noted the length of the written articles as well as the duration of the audiovisual material that was embedded within it. Leaving the numbers to speak for themselves, Ofcom (2011, paras 143) implied that, to name but one example, the 16-paragraph article on Amy Winehouse's last recording was more prominent than the two pieces of audiovisual material that were embedded within it, the one three minute and 21 seconds long, the other two minutes and 13 seconds long. Ofcom thus arrived at the conclusion that the written content accounted for most of the prominent content on the website. This unsubstantiated conclusion leaves the question unanswered as to how to compare written with audiovisual content. Taking the sheer volume of the latter into account, one could argue that audiovisual content takes up more space and hence is more prominent. Moreover, regulation could easily be evaded by embedding audiovisual material within a great deal of text. These are the reasons why the quantitative approach has been rejected by other regulators such as the Dutch CvdM and the Belgian CSA (Betzel, 2011, 58; Valcke & Ausloos, 2014, 319).

The 'Step Back'

Finally, Ofcom has taken what it calls a 'step back' to have more general look at relevant provisions of the AVMSD. First, Ofcom paid particular attention to Recital 11, which clarifies that it is the Directive's aim to avoid distortions of competition between linear and on-demand services by creating 'at least a basic tier of coordinated rules', as well as recitals 21 and 24, which emphasise that regulation should only cover services which compete with television broadcasting. Ofcom held that the pertinent question to ask so as to do justice to these recitals is whether viewers would consider the audiovisual material on The Sun's website as among their competing options to linear television programmes. Ofcom held this unlikely to be the case. This conclusion is supported by a research report commissioned by Ofcom in 2012 so as to better understand which services are competing alternatives to linear television. The report features the Guardian video section among the services definitely not considered TV-like (Essential Research, 2012, 68).

The clearly negative verdict on the possibility of classifying video content on a newspaper website as a reasonable substitute for linear television can interestingly be contrasted to the more nuanced position taken in an earlier 2009 Essential Research study (Essential Research, 2009). The 2009 study found that the users considered the video content on the Telegraph website to be *less* TV-like, because it was an enhancement of a website primarily concerned with written content (Essential Research, 2009, 39). Nonetheless, this conclusion was qualified by saying that the video content 'did to some extent remind participants of TV news video watched on mainstream news programmes' because it was felt to be professionally made and to be destined for TV (Essential Research, 2009, 40). Participants' familiarity with the *Telegraph* brand meant that they were conscious of being in a newspaper environment. At the same time, this familiarity reassured them and made the experience more TV-like. Tellingly, the Telegraph website was positioned in the grey area of the spectrum of on-demand services included in the 2009 study.

What is the most likely explanation for this disparity in assessment of the TV-likeness of online newspapers' video content between 2009 and 2012? Viewers' expectations of what is a reasonable substitute for linear TV can undoubtedly change over time. Interestingly, the factors that were identified by participants when assessing on-demand services shifted between the first and the second study. In 2009, familiarity, mainstream viewing and the professional production and packaging of content were together with the platform on which content was accessed the most significant drivers of 'TV-like'.

On the contrary, the 2012 study identified a more differentiated range of factors, which had to be taken into consideration, but did not rank them in order of importance. Familiarity and the platform as part of the overall viewing experience were still considered to be important. However, a number of new factors were identified as equally if not more important such as the viewer's control over the viewing experience and the length and volume of content. The length of content, in particular, has evolved from being considered less important in 2009 to being 'a telling characteristic' in 2012.

Is this finding of the 2012 Essential Research report sufficient to justify Ofcom's conclusion? Certainly not, given that the report only gives an indication of viewers' perceptions. The report (2012, 4) itself draws attention to the fact that its findings do not determine whether any particular service falls within the ODPS definition and are hence no substitute for applying the statutory criteria. Also, the 2012 research is meant to 'complement', not to replace the 2009 research. Consequently, the findings of the 2009 study cannot be ignored.

Ofcom's negative verdict stands out in sharp relief against the Austrian regulators' resounding yes to the TV-likeness of the videos offered in the Tiroler Tageszeitung website. This appealingly straightforward observation is, however, somewhat impressionistic, wholly unsupported by audience research.

The second and final step of Ofcom's 'step back' focuses on the reference in recital 24 AVMSD to users' reasonable expectation of regulatory protection as a key characteristic of services that fall within the scope of regulation. This led Ofcom to ask whether users of the Sun video section would have expected its content to be regulated under the Directive. Ofcom answered this question in the negative. The only reason it gave for its verdict is that the user would likely have considered himself as viewing the electronic version of the Sun newspaper.

However, this finding does not yet answer the question whether the user would have expected regulatory protection. The Directive links the expectation of regulatory protection to 'the nature and the means of access to the service' (European Parliament and the Council, 2010, rec 24). On the contrary, the 2012 Essential Research report (2012, 22) suggests that the devices participants used to access a service did not have great bearing on whether they thought a service to be TV-like and hence to expect regulatory protection. It was rather the nature of the service that weighed more on their judgement. Rather inconsistently, the report lists later the viewing experience, i.e. the means of access to audiovisual content on a small screen or on a TV screen among the ten factors that inform users' impression of a service. If we consider the means of access to the Sun newspaper online, it would more likely be on a PC screen or 'on a smartphone on the bus' than 'on a big screen on the sofa' (Essential Research, 2012, 36). Depending on the weight that is attached to the access factor, this could be an argument against the users' expectation of regulatory protection. On the other hand, the probable expansion of connected TV in the near future means that the boundaries between PC and TV screen will be blurred and the device used to access a service will become even less relevant as a yardstick for regulatory protection.

If the Directive solely relies on the method of access to a service to establish whether the user would reasonably expect protection, this is problematic because of technological convergence. Moreover, defining the scope of the Directive with regard to users' expectations gives rise to legal uncertainty. Ascertaining these expectations is difficult given that they are not set in stone but are also informed by the existence of the Directive. Besides, this way of proceeding takes for granted that users not only reflect on the type of service that might be subject to regulation but that they also have some insight into the actual scope of the Directive. Both assumptions seem unwarranted, the second one particularly so in view of the complexity of the Directive's regulatory regime and of the ambiguities as regards its scope.

The question that the Directive should have asked instead is whether the user would *merit* regulatory protection. This question would have been a useful starting point for a more fruitful discussion about VOD content in general, and about newspaper websites in particular, and possible risks they might pose to under-age users or to the general public, *inter alia* due to the use of shocking or violent imagery. By focusing on the hypothetical users' perspective instead, the Directive introduces another element of uncertainty into the equation, and skews dialogue away from the crucial question whether its scope is circumscribed in a manner that adequately caters for users' interests.

Conclusion

The approaches of the UK converged regulator, Ofcom, and of its co-regulator, ATVOD, as well as those of the Austrian authorities on the question of the regulation of newspaper websites display contrasting views, and bring the interpretative difficulties with the definition of an AVMS, in particular the criterion of 'principal purpose', to the fore.

Ofcom, in the *Sun Video* case, overturned on appeal ATVOD's determination, thus prompting it to reconsider its view. Whereas ATVOD attempted to expand its remit by focusing on the video section of the website, Ofcom clipped ATVOD's wings and made clear that the object of assessment should be the website as a whole. However, ATVOD's desire to expand its regulatory remit does not sufficiently explain its approach in *Sun Video*. Its decision was not simply a mistake made by a co-regulator still in its infancy, as has occasionally been intimated. It was a perfectly defensible position, reflecting a belief in the need for more regulation of the online press. The conflict between ATVOD's strict regulatory approach and Ofcom's more liberal, market-oriented one was fought on novel grounds, and Ofcom used *Sun Video* as a 'model case' on the basis of which to clarify the statutory criteria and to enhance legal certainty (Metzdorf, 2012).

But has the desired outcome been achieved? A careful examination of Ofcom's remarkably systematic analysis which, however, teems with ill-founded presuppositions, shows that a number of questions remain unanswered. Would the video section need to have its own homepage? If names do not matter, why should it make a difference whether the video section bears the newspaper masthead? These formal criteria seek to ascertain that the video section has a separate identity from the rest of the newspaper, but they are readily open to circumvention. More crucially, they fail to provide convincing pointers so as to distinguish between services that deserve to be subjected to regulation and others that can safely fall through the net. The uncertainty is even greater as regards the substantive criteria: the duration of the audiovisual material, its independence and its prominence compared to the written material. The ambiguity is compounded by the non-determinative nature of these factors. Ofcom's holistic approach makes it hard to predict the mixture that would bring a hybrid service within the scope of regulation.

Admittedly, the uncertainty in Ofcom's test is to a great extent conditioned by the AVMSD's principal purpose criterion. The Directive's emphasis on the principal purpose of a service is a source of considerable uncertainty that could lead to over- or under-regulation of elements of a service. Two alternative approaches are conceivable: first, the regulation only of the video content of an electronic newspaper, but not of its text components, irrespective of its predominance within the overall service or second, the submission of the entire service under the AVMSD requirements on child protection, hate speech, audiovisual commercial communication, consumer information and possibly the right of reply (Craufurd Smith, 2007, p. 263).

This second approach, if paired with an extension of the AVMSD reach to all commercial on-demand services, including text and audio, would enable the creation of a common floor of basic standards online. The European Parliament recently also stressed the need 'to align the rights and obligations of broadcasters with those of other market players by means of a horizontal, cross-media legal framework' (European Parliament, 2014). The Austrian regulatory authorities chose, however, the first, more modest approach. This approach has the advantage of staying loyal to the AVMSD scheme while avoiding a head-on confrontation with the press sector.

Even though the basic tier of AVMSD requirements is largely met or even exceeded by statutory and self-regulatory measures applicable to the printed press, newspaper and magazine publishers vehemently object to an AVMSD-type regulation. They take issue with specific aspects of the AVMSD such as the prohibition of audiovisual commercial communications that promote discrimination, claiming that they are incompatible with press freedom (VDZ and BDZV, 2013, 17). However, their main objection is to statutory regulation as such as well as to any notification requirement. They doubt that technical convergence has led to content convergence or to a convergence in the usage of linear and non-linear media. Should such convergence have taken place though, they demand a deregulation of on-demand AVMS after the model of the externally pluralistic press.

The expectation of the press to act as role model for the regulation of on-demand services seems complacent in a converged world. It is widely recognised that the distinction between linear and non-linear services drawn in the AVMSD is progressively becoming irrelevant, and that a more consistent minimum standard, which will offer viewers greater protection, is needed (Ofcom, 2013d, 3). This harmonised standard is likely to be pitched at a higher level than the current framework for on-demand services, possibly extending to matters relating to taste and offense, but at a lower level than current broadcast regulation.

At the same time, the asymmetry between print and broadcast media is also likely to become increasingly problematic in view of the heightened opportunity and demand for high quality video content accessed online as a result of the superfast broadband roll-out (New Zealand Law Commission, 2013, para. 12). The convergence between press, broadcasting and other video-on-demand services online is expected to lead to a certain rapprochement between the longstanding models for press and broadcasting regulation. The authorities in charge of video on demand, while claiming objectivity when resisting or assisting this rapprochement, are in fact indebted to an ideological system, veering towards the ideals of Market or Social Liberalism. Against this background, the Austrian approach offers a clear-cut and pragmatic, though by no means ideologically, neutral solution to a problem that is only beginning to emerge.

Notes

1. See § 11d (2) Nr. 3 of the German Interstate Treaty on Broadcasting and Telemedia of 31. August 1991 as amended by the 15. Interstate Treaty of 1 January 2013, which excludes non-programme-related press-like services from the public service mandate.

2. Elle TV; Sunday Times Video Library; News of the World Video; Sun Video; Telegraph TV; Guardian Video; The Guardian YouTube Channel; FT Video; The Independent Video at http://atvod.co.uk/complaints/determinations.

References

Australian Government. (2012). *Convergence review. Final report*. Retrieved from http://www.abc.net.au/mediawatch/transcripts/1339_convergence.pdf.

Authority for Television On Demand [ATVOD]. (2012, 3 May). *Statutory rules and non-binding guidance for providers of on-demand programme services (ODPS)*. Retrieved from http://atvod.co.uk/uploads/files/ATVOD_Rules_and_Guidance_Ed_2.0_May_2012.pdf.

ATVOD. (2014a, 5 February). *Statement on the adoption of new guidance on the scope of the regulations relating to video on demand services*. Retrieved from http://atvod.co.uk/uploads/files/Statement_on_New_Scope_Guidance_FINAL.pdf.

ATVOD. (2014b, 5 February). *Guidance on who needs to notify. Application and scope of the regulations for video on demand (VOD) services, Edition 4.0*. Retrieved from http://atvod.co.uk/uploads/files/Guidance_on_who_needs_to_notify_Ed_4.0_Feb_2014.pdf.

Barendt, E. (2007). *Freedom of speech*. Oxford: Oxford University Press.

Betzel, M. (2011). Finetuning classification criteria for on-demand audiovisual media services: The Dutch approach. In *IRIS special, the regulation of on-demand audiovisual services: Chaos or coherence?* Strasbourg: European Audiovisual Observatory, 53–62.

Bundeskommunikationssenat (Austria). (2012b, 24 September). *Cultvisual*. KOA 1.950/12-042. https://www.rtr.at/en/m/KOA195012042/KOA_1.950-12-042.pdf.

Bundeskommunikationssenat (Austria). (2012a, 13 December). *Tiroler Tageszeitung*. GZ 611.191/0005-BKS/2012. Retrieved from http://www.bundeskanzleramt.at/DocView.axd?CobId=49930.

Council of the European Communities. (1989, 3 October). *Directive 89/552/EEC of 3 October 1989 on the coordination of certain provisions laid down by law, regulation or administrative action in Member States concerning the pursuit of television broadcasting activities*. OJ L298/23. Retrieved from http://eur-lex.europa.eu/legal-content/EN/TXT/PDF/?uri=CELEX:31989L0552&from=EN.

Craufurd Smith, R. (2007). Media convergence and the regulation of audiovisual content: Is the European Community's Audiovisual Media Services Directive fit for purpose? *Current Legal Problems*, 60(1), 238–277. doi: 10.1093/clp/60.1.238.

De Bueger, T. (2013, October). *Supervising on-demand audiovisual media services: Best practices and methodology*. Background document to the 38th European Platform of Regulatory Authorities (EPRA) meeting, Vilnius, Lithuania. Retrieved from http://www.epra.org/meetings/vilnius-38th-epra-meeting.

Eldridge, J. (Ed.). (1995). *The Glasgow media group reader, volume 1. News content, language and visuals*. London: Routledge.

Essential Research. (2009, December). *The regulation of video-on-demand: Consumer views on what makes audiovisual services 'TV-like'*. Retrieved from http://www.stakeholders.ofcom.org.uk/binaries/research/tv-research/vod.pdf.

Essential Research. (2012, October). *On-demand services: Understanding consumer choices*. Retrieved from http://stakeholders.ofcom.org.uk/binaries/broadcast/tv-ops/vod/Research_Report.pdf.

European Commission. (2009, 28 October). *E 2/2008. Financing of ORF.* K(2009)8113. Retrieved from http://ec.europa.eu/competition/state_aid/cases/22 3847/223847_1014816_27_1.pdf.
European Commission. (2010, 26 January). *State aid E 5/2005. Annual financing of the Dutch public service broadcasters – The Netherlands.* C(2010)132. Retrieved from http://ec.europa.eu/competition/state_aid/cases/198591/198591_1079191_160_1.pdf
European Commission. (2013, 24 April). *Preparing for a fully converged audiovisual world: Growth, creation and values.* COM(2013) 231. Retrieved from http://eur-lex.europa.eu/LexUriServ/LexUriServ.do?uri=COM:2013:0231:FIN:en:PDF.
European Parliament. (2014, 12 March). *Preparing for a fully converged audiovisual world.* P7_TA-PROV(2014)0232. Retrieved from http://www.europarl.europa.eu/sides/getDoc.do?pubRef=-//EP//TEXT+TA+P7-TA-2014-0232+0+DOC+XML+V0//EN.
European Parliament, & the Council (2010, 10 March). *Directive 2010/13/EC of 10 March 2010 on the coordination of certain provisions laid down by law, regulation and administrative action in Member States concerning the provision of audiovisual media services.* OJ L95/1. Retrieved from http://eur-lex.europa.eu/LexUriServ/LexUriServ.do?uri=OJ:L:2010:095:0001:0024:en:PDF.
European Parliament, the Council, & the Commission. (2014). Joint practical guide for persons involved in the drafting of legislation within the community institutions. Retrieved from www.eur-lex.europa.eu/techleg/10.html.
Fagerjord, A. (2003). *Rhetorical convergence: Earlier media influence on web media form.* (PhD, thesis), University of Oslo, Oslo. Retrieved from http://fagerjord.no/rhetoricalconvergence/.
Flew, T. (2014). Media convergence. *Encyclopædia Britannica.* Retrieved from http://www.britannica.com/topic/media-convergence.
Gibbons, T., & Katsirea, I. (2012). Commercial influences on programme content: The German and UK approaches to transposing the EU rules on product placement. *Journal of Media Law, 4*(2), 159–188. doi: 10.5235/Jml.4.2.159.
Katsirea, I. (2008). *Public broadcasting and European law. A comparative examination of public service obligations in six member states.* Boston, MA: Kluwer.
Kogler, M.R. (2011). Fernsehähniches TV-On Demand – Was ist (k)ein 'Audiovisueller Mediendienst auf Abruf'? *Medien und Recht, 4,* 228–232.
Lord Justice Leveson (2012). *An Inquiry into the culture, practices and ethics of the press: Report.* London: TSO.
Machet, E. (2011, May). *Content regulation and new media: Exploring regulatory boundaries between traditional and new media.* Background document to the 33rd European Platform of Regulatory Authorities (EPRA) meeting. Retrieved from http://www.epra.org/attachments/ohrid-plenary-1-exploring-regulatory-boundaries-background-document.
Mac Síthigh, D. (2011). Co-regulation, video-on-demand and the legal status of audio-visual media. *International Journal of Digital Television, 2*(1), 49–66. doi: 10.1386/jdtv.2.1.49_1.
Metzdorf, J. (2012). Regulierung der elektronischen Presse in Grossbritannien? – Ein Anwendungsbeispiel zum Erwägungsgrund 28 der AVMD-RL. In J. Taeger (Ed.), *IT und Internet – Mit Recht gestalten* (pp. 497, 513). Edewecht: Olmir. Ofcom.
New Zealand. Law Commission. (2013). *The news media meets 'new media'. Rights, responsibilities and regulation in the digital age.* Law Commission report 128. Retrieved from http://r128.publications.lawcom.govt.nz.

Office of Communications [Ofcom]. (2011, 21 December). *Appeal by news group newspapers limited against a notice of determination by ATVOD that the provider of the service 'Sun Video' has contravened section 368BA of the Communications Act 2003*. Retrieved from http://atvod.co.uk/uploads/files/Ofcom_Decision_-_SUN_VIDEO_211211.pdf.

Ofcom. (2012a, 15 August). *Procedures for the handling of appeals of ATVOD decisions in relation to what constitutes an on-demand programme services*. Retrieved from http://stakeholders.ofcom.org.uk/binaries/broadcast/tv-ops/vod/appeals-procedures.pdf.

Ofcom. (2012b, 14 December). *Appeal by Channelflip Media Limited against a notice of determination by ATVOD that the service 'Channel Flip' (www.channelflip.com) has contravened section 368BA of the Communications Act 2003*. Retrieved from http://www.atvod.co.uk/uploads/files/Channel_Flip_appeal_decision.pdf.

Ofcom. (2013b, 13 January). *Appeal by BBC Worldwide Limited against a notice of determination by ATVOD that the provided of the service 'Top Gear YouTube' (www.youtube.com/topgear) has contravened sections 368BA and 368D(3)(ZA) of the Communications Act 2003*. Retrieved from http://stakeholders.ofcom.org.uk/binaries/enforcement/vod-services/top-gear-youtube-decision.pdf.

Ofcom. (2013c, 13 January). *Appeal by BBC Worldwide Limited against a notice of determination by ATVOD that the provided of the service 'BBC Food YouTube' (www.youtube.com/bbcfood) has contravened sections 368BA and 368D(3)(ZA) of the Communications Act 2003*. Retrieved from http://stakeholders.ofcom.org.uk/binaries/enforcement/vod-services/bbc-food-youtube-decision.pdf.

Ofcom. (2013d, 30 September). Ofcom response to the European Commission. Green paper: Preparing for a fully converged audiovisual world: Growth, creation and values. Retrieved from http://stakeholders.ofcom.org.uk/binaries/international/international-responses/green-paper-sep13.pdf.

Ofcom. (2013a, 26 June). *Appeal by Everton Football Club against a notice of determination by ATVOD that the provider of a service has contravened section 368D(3)(ZA) (requirement to pay a fee) of the Communications Act 2003 whilst operating an ODPS*. Retrieved from http://www.atvod.co.uk/uploads/files/Everton_TV_Ofcom_Appeal_Decision.pdf.

Pavlik, J. V. (2008). *Media in the digital age*. New York: Columbia University Press.

Peer, L., & Ksiazek, T. B. (2011). YouTube and the challenge to journalism: New standards for news videos online. *Journalism Studies, 12*(1), 45–63. doi: 10.1080/1461670X.2010.511951.

Rahvar, Z. (2011). *Die Zukunft des deutschen Presserechts im Lichte konvergierender Medien*. Nomos: Baden-Baden.

Select Committee on Communications. House of Lords. (2013, 27 March). *Media convergence*. HL154 2012–13. Retrieved from http://www.publications.parliament.uk/pa/ld201213/ldselect/ldcomuni/154/154.pdf.

Tambini, D., Leonardi, D., & Marsden, C. (2008). *Codifying cyberspace: Communications self-regulation in the age of Internet convergence*. London: Routledge.

Valcke, P., & Ausloos, J. (2014). Audiovisual media services 3.0: (Re)defining the scope of European broadcasting law in a converging and connected media environment. In K. Donders, K. Pauwels, & J. Loisen (Eds.), *The Palgrave handbook of European media policy*. Basingstoke, UK: Palgrave Macmillan.

VDZ & BDZV (2013). Common submission to the Green Paper: Preparing for a Fully Converged Audiovisual World: Growth, Creation and Values, 24 April

2013, COM (2013) 231 final, 30 September 2013 from http://HYPERLINK "http://www.ec.europa.eu/digital-agenda/en/news/consultation-green-paper-preparing-fully-converged-audiovisual-world-growth-creation-and-values" www.ec.europa.eu/digital-agenda/en/news/consultation-green-paper-preparing-fully-converged-audiovisual-world-growth-creation-and-values.

Vick, D.W. (2006). Regulatory convergence? *Legal Studies*, 26(1), 26–54. doi: 10.1111/j.1748-121X.2006.00005.x.

4 #Tweetgate

When Public Service Broadcasters and Twitter Go to War – An Irish Perspective

Jennifer Kavanagh

Introduction

On the night of 24 October 2011 the national Irish public service broadcaster, Raidió Teilifís Éireann (RTÉ), transmitted a debate between all seven candidates seeking the office of President of Ireland. This debate, one of a series across the terrestrial Irish channels, was instrumental in deciding the eventual winner of the election as polls showed a massive swing of support from Séan Gallagher to the eventual winner, Michael D. Higgins, as a result of this debate (RedC Research and Marketing, 2011).

The broadcast was transmitted on the main station, RTÉ 1, during one of the flagship current affairs programmes, *The Frontline*, and during primetime. However, the debate also underpinned a moment when the clash between broadcast regulation and social media regulation occurred.

> By common agreement, the following moment was to prove decisive in what had often been a controversial campaign. At 10.39pm, a tweet was posted to a Twitter feed '#aras11'. The Twitter account responsible was '@mcguinness4Pres'. It read: 'The man that Gallagher took the cheque from will be at a press conference tomorrow. #aras11'. (Irish Independent, 2011)

What transpired came to be known as #tweetgate and will be used in this paper as a case study in the interface between the calls for more inclusive media and a balanced approach to broadcasting on news and current affairs, especially in a delicate situation such as national elections. It demonstrated the difficulty for broadcasters to self-regulate instantaneous communications for inclusion in current affairs programming and the realistic ability of broadcasters to maintain and exercise editorial control over such communications. It also highlights an actual instance of media convergence between new and traditional and the challenges that can be faced when they combine.

This chapter will use this debate as a means to study the public service broadcasting regulation in Ireland with regard to the clash between traditional and new media, the legal obligation to balance voices in election settings and the regulatory challenges posed by the incorporation of new media in current affairs programming from the Irish context, with lessons that may

60 *Jennifer Kavanagh*

be used internationally. The chapter will first assess the legal and policy framework in which Irish public service broadcasting operates. It will assess the constitutional, legislative and case law interpretations in the area. It will then look in detail at the regulations concerning broadcasting and legally required duties of balance, especially in times of elections and referendums in Ireland. The chapter will then move on to the details of the debate, the implications of the debate and the reports carried out into the conduct and editorial decisions taken during the debate. The chapter will also use the recall Poll carried out by the polling company RedC as commissioned by RTÉ to highlight the implications of the debate on the actual poll. The chapter will then assess the implications of reviews into the programme and their impact on the regulation of broadcasting in Ireland and how social media has been brought into this regulation framework.

Legal and Policy Framework Shaping Broadcasting in Ireland

Ireland is a common law country with a written constitution. This means that the basic and foundation laws and rights of the State are contained in the written constitution and further developed in legislation, which must follow the basic principles enshrined in the constitution and may then be interpreted by the Courts. In order to set out the legal framework, the principles surrounding balance and plurality in election debates will be discussed, then the analysis will assess the specific legal sources from which the regulatory environment in which Irish public service broadcasting operates.

The regulation of the broadcasts during and concerning elections and referendums in Ireland is based on the principle of equality and fair access to broadcast time in order to communicate policies and debate issues of national importance. In Ireland paid political advertising is not allowed on broadcast media, except public election broadcasts or party political broadcasts (Rafter, 2011). The link between freedom of expression and the free and equitable circulation of ideas was set out in the following terms in *Bowman v. The United Kingdom* (1998).

> Free elections and freedom of expression, particularly freedom of political debate, together form the bedrock of any democratic system. The two rights are interrelated and operate to reinforce each other: for example, as the Court has observed in the past, freedom of expression is one of the 'conditions' necessary to ensure the free expression of the opinion of the people in the choice of the legislature'. For this reason, it is particularly important in the period preceding an election that opinions and information of all kinds are permitted to circulate freely.

In Ireland the main cases dealing with the equal division of time are *Coughlan v. Broadcasting Complaints Commission* (2000), where Hamilton CJ found that there was no balance between the viewpoints put forward. It was held that the transmission of ten broadcasts supporting the 'yes' proposition was unconstitutional and that the balance of time should be held equally between those for and against the proposition. However, Barrington J was of the belief that political party broadcasts, besides ensuring that they do not place the authority of the state in jeopardy, should be free of any form of regulation, including whether they should be in favour or oppose policy measure for the sake of balance. Barrington J stated that:

> Political party broadcasts are in a totally different position. Of course they must not break the law or advocate the overthrow of the State. But apart from this, the second respondent (RTÉ) is not entitled to concern itself with their content. The politicians are entitled to use all the arts of advocacy to persuade the citizens of the correctness of their proposals ... it [broadcasting regulation] cannot interfere to negative the collective advice of the politicians to the electorate. The fact that all the political parties are agreed on a particular aspect of national policy may be a political fact of the utmost importance.
> (*Coughlan*, 2000)

The import of the political party plays a role in the debate and conduct of such policy discussions. Considering the wider democratic implications of regulating and balancing speech, in this case regarding a referendum, Barrington J made the following observations:

> A distinguishing feature of a democratic society is that political leadership rests, not on power, but on persuasion. Likewise political authority rests on the consent of the electorate. It is right and appropriate that political leaders should use their authority and the arts of persuasion to lead the people towards the decision which their judgement tells them will best promote the common good.
> (*Coughlan*, 2000, p. 44)

In *Madigan v. RTÉ* (1994), judicial review was sought on the decision of RTÉ not to give the petitioner time to represent his views as an independent candidate for the Dublin area in the European elections. The petitioner's main complaint was that, as an independent candidate amongst a wide field of other independents and party candidates, the time allowed in proportion to others was not a fair and equal attempt to achieve the objects of the relevant legislation. The policy of referring to results of previous elections as a means of achieving proportionality was, first, not applied (pp. 472, 476) and, second, misrepresented a fluid situation (pp. 472, 477). Kinlen J did question this approach by emphasizing that fairness did not equal equality (pp. 472, 481). Kinlen J deferred to the RTÉ authority and its interpretation of the situation, stating that:

> It is the duty of the RTÉ authority to give a fair and balance[d] directive, to be impartial without in any way intruding on the view of the

authority itself ... It is clear ... that the approach of the authority is fluid and may change hourly in regard to all sorts of factors the authority sees [as] relevant. (pp. 472, 481)

On considering the approach of both the High Court and the Supreme Court in these issues, the balance is based on a fair and proportionate assessment of support for the candidates involved. It is clear that the notion of mathematical equality is unobtainable in a situation such as election coverage. Support may change, policy emphasis may change and there does need to be a recognition that the broadcaster needs to be able to react to such changes in the 'education of public opinion' without being stifled in reporting by legal calculations to reduce risk of litigation and thereby chill the very coverage which was intended to be carried out by the media under the Constitutional framework of Article 40.6.1 (i).

The issue of equality and plurality of voices on the media is especially important in the time of elections and referendums. The role of television, which is subject to the majority of the rules, was stated by Keane J in *Coughlan* ([2000] 3 IR 1) as follows:

It is obviously important that so powerful a broadcasting medium should fairly reflect, so far as is practicable, the wide diversity or interest and views which one would expect to find competing for attention in a truly pluralist and democratic society. ([2000] 3 IR 1)

Furthermore the legal framework accepts the currency of news to matters of public importance. For example, in *Observer and Guardian v. The United Kingdom* the judge specifically referenced the fact that news is a perishable commodity and there is a currency to news relating to matters of public importance (*Observer and Guardian v. The United Kingdom*, 26). This point also resonated with the Irish judiciary in the case of *Leech v. Independent Newspapers* (2007). Chartlon J had no issue with accepting that news was a perishable commodity. The means of balancing such speech to ensure equality of access is demonstrated in the next section.

Constitutional Protection

In the Irish Constitutional framework, the right to freedom of expression on matters of politics is to be found in both Articles 40.6.1 (i)[1] and 40.3.1[2] to establish the boundaries and use of the constitutionally stated and interpreted rights to both freedom of expression for its political use and its general use. Article 40.6.1(i) incorporates the 'criticism of government policy' as part of the rightful liberty of expression that is bestowed on the organs of public opinion in their mandate of educating public opinion. The interpretation of these rights has focused on the political nature of speech rights. There are a number of complexities though with the framing of the article as it is split in terms of its treatment of the citizen and the media. The first part of the right considers the right of the citizen to express their convictions and opinions. The second half of the article contemplates the media. In its construction of the right, it covers all forms of media in use in 1937. This has been interpreted to include all forms of media. Then the article, in a rather patriarchal fashion, looks on the media as the organs of public opinion and the educators of public opinion and holds that the criticism of government policy is part of their objectives. Therefore, if legislation was to be passed with the aim of restricting such activities, then this legislation would be struck down as unconstitutional. However, this right is tempered with the responsibility to maintain public order and morality.

A number of court cases have analysed and tested the limit of the right to freedom of expression in the Irish Constitution. Article 40.6.1(i) has been interpreted as a political right to expression as the wording of the article specifically references the 'convictions and opinions' of the citizen, references the role of the media as the 'organs of public opinion' and also includes the criticism of government policy as part of the 'rightful liberty of expression'. In the case of *Murphy v. Independent Television and Radio Commission* (1999), Barrington J, judge of the High Court, stated that 'the framers of the Constitution had deliberately included them in the one sub-section for a reason. He drew the conclusion that the reason was that they were concerned with the influencing of public opinions' (1999). Also in *Irish Times v. Ireland* (1998), where Barrington J also acted as judge, this right to freedom of expression was classed as positive right which the State had a role to play in defending and added that as Ireland is a common law jurisdiction, that the citizen was entitled to say whatever they wished once it was not illegal to say it. However, Article 40.6.1 (i) of the Irish Constitution is not the sole source for a right to freedom of expression within the constitutional framework. From the case of *Attorney General v. Paperlink* (1984) a general right to communicate was interpreted from the text of the Constitution as part of the personal rights of the citizen. Therefore, the Irish right to freedom of expression has both liberal communication aspect and political expression aspects that can both be deployed to both protect and regulate speech in the political context. The interpretation of the Irish right from the Constitution is also influence by the domestic application of the European Convention. Here the right is constructed in terms of opinions and information unlike the Irish right that terms speech in relation to convictions and opinions only. The right does not make specific reference to its place within the democratic relationship of governance but it could be argued that the inclusions of 'without interference by public authorities', is a parallel protection on the use of disproportionate legal responses to political speech issues. The restrictions listed in Article 10.2[3] focus on the duties and responsibilities of freedom of expression and allow for restrictions necessary in democratic society. These restrictions include grounds that may be used in the censoring or restriction of political expression. The phrase 'may be subject to such formalities, conditions, restrictions or penalties as are prescribed by law and are necessary in a democratic society' allows for flexibility and scope for discretion with the judges of the European Court of Human Rights.

Legislative Protection

The aim of the high regulation of broadcast media in Ireland during such periods is to give equal time to those contesting elections. This division of time has been the subject of constitutional litigation, legislation as per the Broadcasting Act 2009, and Broadcasting policy per the Public Service Broadcasting Charter and individual codes set out by the Broadcasting Authority of Ireland. Emerging bodies of case law and guidelines have come to ensure that balance is present in the debate of policy from all those contesting elections at the time of elections. The current guidance in Ireland regarding Election is found in the Broadcasting Code on Referenda and Election Coverage made pursuant to s. 42(1) of the Broadcasting Act.[4] These codes are created to ensure that balance, impartiality and objectivity is employed in the production and editing of news and current affairs programmes during election or referendum time. However, during all other times there is a general duty placed on broadcasters to be impartial when discussing matters of current affairs. Issues such as the moratorium on broadcasts for certain durations prior to the ballot and party political broadcasts are also covered.

To promote this aim of plurality of voices, at every election and referendum the broadcasting regulator lays down a series of guidelines for the conduct of fair coverage. The Broadcasting Act 2009 amended previous legislation which governed the broadcasting regulatory environment in Ireland and with it stated the duties of Broadcasters. Under s. 39, every broadcaster is to ensure the following:

> All news broadcast by the broadcaster is reported and presented in an objective and impartial manner and without any expression of the broadcaster's own views (and) the broadcast treatment of current affairs, including matters which are either of public controversy or the subject of current public debate, is fair to all interests concerned and that the broadcast matter is presented in an objective and impartial manner and without any expression of his or her own views, except that should it prove impracticable in relation to a single broadcast to apply this paragraph, two or more related broadcasts may be considered as a whole, if the broadcasts are transmitted within a reasonable period of each other.

The Public Service Statement of RTÉ sets out its role within the Irish State, in particular regarding its role in a democratic society and in matters of public importance (Raidió Teilifís Éireann [RTÉ], 2010).

> RTÉ sees its mandate as the provision of national media services essential to the democratic public interest. ... They provide a space where public conversation, debate, performance and entertainment can be sustained. (RTÉ, 2010, p. 1)

This is further emphasised in the specific objects of RTÉ in relation to News and Current Affairs where it commits to 'comprehensive, independent and impartial news and current affairs programming' across its radio, television and online services (p. 2). RTÉ also sets out the principles it seeks to fulfil regarding the public interest amongst others: creating opportunity for fair debate and discussion on the issues of the day across RTÉ services, encouraging and enabling audience contributions to RTÉ programmes and respecting human dignity and upholding rightful freedom of expression (p. 4).

Impact of European Human Rights Law in Ireland

The development of the political speech rights in Article 10 of the Convention has seen the European Court of Human Rights act as a form of watchdog on the activities of States when seeking to regulate media. In *Lingnes v. Austria* (1986), the Court emphasised the role of the press in imparting information and ideas on political issues as well as other areas of public interest.

> Freedom of the press furthermore affords the public one of the best means of discovering and forming an opinion of the ideas and attitudes of political leaders. More generally, freedom of political debate is at the very core of the concept of a democratic society, which prevails throughout the Convention. (p. 13)

This position was again emphasised in *Observer and Guardian v. UK* (1991), where the court restated the role of the press and added:

> Not only does the press have the task of imparting such information and ideas: the public also has a right to receive them. Were it otherwise, the press would be unable to play its vital role of 'public watchdog'. (p. 26)

The discussion of matters of public importance and policy issues is dependent on strong media protections as outlined by the court above. This is probably the motivation behind the structure of Article 40.6.1(i), which especially mentions the role of the media, in particular the press and the radio but encompasses all forms of media as part of the protection for freedom of expression in the protection for political speech.

Comparing the Legal and Policy Regulation Objectives

On considering the examination of the specific laws governing political speech and then moving on to underpin the legislative and policy basis upon which public service broadcasting in Ireland operates, it is clear that the primary concern of this right rests with the promotion of unfettered and free speech, especially in relation to political speech. The protection of political speech is regarded as the bedrock of democracy; this is of utmost importance during the period of election communication, and this aspect has been recognized in Irish jurisprudence when the determination of broadcasting restrictions during election periods.

The concepts of balance and plurality in election and referendum periods are held as central tenants in the regulation of the media, especially during times of elections such as the presidential election, and in particular during debates such as the *Frontline* debate. As can be seen, taking both the high protection for political speech and the need for clear and equal balance for all participants in debate, this causes specific problems when the plurality of voices in election debate contexts is taken into account. Also, the law accepts the perishable quality of news and this impacts on the inclusion of social media sources but the regulatory issues surrounding the inclusions of such information have not been set out. Not only must the voices in election settings be taken into consideration but also the views and questions of citizens in electoral situations, especially when there are serious questions that need clarification regarding the background and suitability of individuals for high political office. This was the situation which was to unfold in the Irish Presidential Debate on the National Broadcaster.

The *Frontline* Debate

The Presidential Election of 2011 in Ireland was to mark a watershed moment in the ability of social media and television debates to influence the outcome of elections. In this particular instance, *The Frontline,* which was a topical debate programme on the national broadcaster RTÉ, held a debate between all the candidates in front of a studio audience and broadcast it to the entire Nation[5]. In this debate the presenter read out a tweet in studio. This tweet made allegations of unethical conduct by the then–front-runner candidate, Séan Gallagher. The gravity of the tweet was to change the perceptions of the general public and in essence was the reason why Séan Gallagher lost his status as front runner as shown in the polling data.

In this debate, the candidates were asked a series of questions from both the presenter and the audience on various issues which were current and important to the selection of the President of Ireland. A number of tweets were read out to candidates to probe issues raised in the debate and clarify any points which they had made earlier in the broadcast. Some of the key questions posed by the presenter to Séan Gallagher are listed in reverse order and excerpted from the live tracker that was released by RTÉ during the programme. The tracker, as published, reads in reverse order. However, the full tracker shows all the questions to all the candidates over the time period of the broadcast from 21.40 to 23.30.

> 2224 Gallagher is asked, does he still feel he should run for President, given the possibility of scandal in the future. Pat asks him how did he mislay a cheque for €89,000 in a bank account? Gallagher says the cheque was made out to the wrong account. He says the matter was resolved and there was no breach of law. He says he is '100% tax compliant'.
> 2159 Gallagher says he has met Pat Kenny as many times as he has met Brian Cowen. He says he was at about two Cairde Fáil dinners. McGuinness cautions Gallagher about what he is saying and that a man told him that Gallagher took a cheque for €5,000 for Fianna Fáil. He says Gallagher is in 'deep, deep trouble'.
> 2154 McGuinness says there was something 'very rotten at the heart of the last administration' and Gallagher was 'up to his neck in it'.
> 2154 Davis says she is the only 'truly Independent candidate'.
> 2152 Norris says Gallagher paid himself over €800,000 from one of his companies. Norris says the election of Gallagher would prove that the Irish people 'have not learned very much'.
> 2151 Gallagher says he has stood back from all his business obligations in order to devote himself to the campaign.
> Higgins says the Celtic Tiger was 'mismanaged' and 'misdirected'. He adds that he does not believe that Gallagher will be President and that voters are rallying behind him.
> 2149 The panel is asked what they think of the possibility that the electorate will put a former Fianna Fáil member, Gallagher, into office, eight months after FF was ejected from government. (RTÉ, 2011)

During the programme, a tweet was read out to the front runner, Seán Gallagher, which sought to further question him about his dealings with certain individuals. The question from the tweet was as follows, and asked directly to Seán Gallagher by the host.

> Now a development which I want to put to Seán Gallagher, on the Martin McGuinness for President Twitter account, Sinn Féin are saying that they are going to produce the man who gave you a cheque for five grand. Now do you want to change what you said? Or are you simply saying that it simply didn't happen? Or are they up to dirty tricks or what? (Broadcasting Authority of Ireland [BAI], 2012, p. 6)

Seán Gallagher was very unhappy with the conduct of the debate and complained to the broadcast regulator in Ireland, the Broadcasting Authority of Ireland [BAI]. Following complaints from both Seán Gallagher and members of the public, the national broadcaster, RTÉ, and the broadcasting regulator reviewed the conduct of the debate in line with best practice. The editorial review in RTÉ and the review by the BAI assessed the general conduct of current affairs programming in Ireland and the use of social media to add greater context to current affairs programming.

Impact of the Debate

Polls on the day of the election showed that the debate dramatically changed people's voting intentions as was shown in polling undertaken by the broadcaster. People did not vote for Séan Gallagher because of the contents of the tweet, as can be seen in the dramatic change of support in the wake of the debate (Red C Research and Marketing, 2011). The lead candidate claimed that the use of this tweet was the reason why he lost the election (Irish Independent, 2011). In the fallout from this tweet, a presidential election was lost by the frontrunner candidate. The RedC poll demonstrated a massive swing of support from Gallagher to the eventual winner of the Presidential election (RedC, 2011). Reviews of the editorial decisions of the night were commissioned and court actions were threatened. The programme which carried the debate was later replaced. The highly regulated area of current affairs broadcasting in the time of Elections combined with an unverified tweet to create the perfect regulation storm. However, most of the vitriol which was directed at the national broadcaster was misplaced on consideration of the debate. Two issues were raised by Séan Gallagher's representatives: the nature of the questions raised by members of the public and the tweets which were read out on air[6]. From the airing of the debate to the time of the election result, the impact of the debate was exceptionally harmful to Séan Gallagher. A Recall Poll conducted by Red C demonstrates the effect of the debate on the popularity of Séan Gallagher. The polling company asked voters if the debate and the surrounding controversy had affected their final decision to vote. For those who answered, 45% stated that the debate did not impact their decision. 35% responded that the debate impacted it a lot and for 20% the controversy impacted their decision a little (Red C Research and Marketing, 201, p. 35).

Reaction to the Debate

The reaction from the Séan Gallagher camp was understandably strong.[7] Even the polls from the national broadcaster showed that the debate had changed his front-runner status. In the RedC Report (Red C Research and Marketing, 2011), the swing in support from Séan Gallagher to his nearest rival, Michael D. Higgins (who eventually was elected President), was astounding. The polling data shows on the night of the debate a massive swing of support from Séan Gallagher to Michael D. Higgins, as demonstrated in the Red C poll where there is a direct swing of support between both candidates in the wake of the debate.

Unsurprisingly, there were a number of complaints by individuals about the conduct of the debate (BAI, 2012). In all, six complaints were received by the BAI and all were upheld. All of the complaints related to the use of the unverified tweet in the debate. However, most complainants did not acknowledge the line of questioning by Martin McGuinness that lead to the inclusion of the tweet. For all six complaints, RTÉ defended their actions in the same manner. In the defence to the complaints to the BAI, RTÉ tried to use the 'retweeting' of the message by various well-known journalists in Ireland as a means of adding context to the use of the tweet. It was also felt that, as Martin McGuinness was present in the studio, the claim of producing the individual involved could be verified. Also, they defended their actions by stating that the matter was already in the public domain, by means of Twitter, and therefore they were only relaying what was stated there. In defamation proceedings, such a point regarding the primary source of circulation would have been sufficient, but such a defence is not provided for under the regulations contained in the Broadcasting Act of 2009. In all six complaints, the decision was upheld on the grounds that the use of an unverified tweet was unfair to Seán Gallagher, that steps could have been taken to discover the provenance of the account and that the failure to provide such clarification was unfair to the candidate. In the response and consideration of the complaint from Mr. Gallagher's solicitors, the BAI and RTÉ elaborated more on the issues involved but arrived at the same conclusions.

In terms of the internal response from RTÉ, a report was published as a result of an editorial review (RTÉ, 2011). This editorial review was carried out by Steve Carson and Rob Morrison. Steve Carson was the Director of Programmes for RTÉ and Rob Morrison was the former Head of News and Current Affairs for UTV. This review was carried out after the BAI upheld the complaints from individuals described above. Even though this report was supposed to cover the same ground as the BAI complaints, the focus of the report was on the manner of editorial control of questions to the candidates, time allocations to candidates and the selection of the audience members. The report also assessed any training needs for those working in the news and current affairs section. The report did not analyse the production and editorial decisions which lead to the selection, verification and use of the tweet at the heart of the debate. The report, which was eight pages in length, did comprise some useful guidance for those with editorial control in current affairs; it was conducted with the assistance of peer review from the likes of the BBC and UTV, but the issue of the tweet was only mentioned in terms of training needs for staff working the area of current affairs. The most robust provisions related to social media were incorporated in revised journalism guidelines, which emphasized the personal nature of tweets and the need to seek advice from senior editors for the inclusion of such material in a news broadcast (RTÉ, 2012). However, the issue of verification has not been given the weight that would be expected when compared to the assessment of the BAI.

BAI Compliance Committee stated that it felt the reports and findings demonstrated and highlighted 'serious and significant editorial failings that took place during a television debate of utmost public importance and interest' (BAI, 2011). It stated that the Committee took the view that such failings could have been avoided if good practices had been followed and the broadcast had been conducted to the standard required for a presidential election. It noted the public apology from the broadcaster and its admission that significant failures had occurred. On the basis of the report, the BAI declined to commence a statutory investigation under the provisions of sec. 53 of the Broadcasting Act.

In its response to the individual complaints, the BAI stated that verification of information is important especially in news and current affairs (BAI, 2012). The broadcast of unverified information was unfair and there were no apparent efforts made to verify the source and accuracy of the tweet and its context. The tweet could have been verified with Martin McGuiness or his team, who were present in studio. Also information was available to clarify the tweet and the failure to provide this tweet was unfair to Séan Gallagher.

Since the resolution of the #tweetgate issue, the BAI has now released a new code of fairness, objectivity and impartiality in news and current affairs. In the guidance notes and statement of outcomes, the issue of the use of social media in news and current affairs situations has been set out by the regulator. The guidance notes set out in Rule 15 states that broadcasters will have in place 'appropriate policies and procedures for handling contributions via social media' (BAI, 2013). The BAI advises that the code relates primarily to the on-air use of social media. However, it extends the regulation of social media to the output of broadcasters online if it is relevant to an investigation.

Media consumption has changed significantly over the past number of years, and as a consequence there has been a proliferation of sources of information, not least social media platforms such as Twitter. This use of social media is now reflected in the revised RTÉ journalism guidelines, in place since 2011. Two of the principles underpinning the rules contained in this guidelines are accuracy and responsiveness. Accuracy in respect of news and current affairs is of paramount importance in sustaining the high levels of trust that Irish audiences currently have in Irish broadcast media. This drive for accuracy is also reflected in the journalistic codes which operate in both the general regulatory forums for Irish broadcasting and also internal codes within RTÉ. Accuracy is often not just about getting the facts right. Where there are matters of public controversy or matters of current public debate, a variety of views and opinions often need to be considered in addition to the stated facts. This is reflected in the Broadcasting Act 2009, which is the principle act regulating broadcasting in Ireland, Often, in the case of social media, it is important to be aware that online sources of information are not subject to the same degree of regulation, and from a news and current affairs perspective, there is no statutory requirement for fairness, impartiality and objectivity. This aspect of social media and media regulation has now been reflected in the updated journalistic guidelines in RTÉ, in place since the completion of the investigation into the RTÉ programme.

This demonstrates the changing environment and the pressure on broadcast media to be the first, but it also important to be right. The remainder of the guidance note reiterates that the onus is on the broadcaster to assess the provenance and surrounding issues behind a tweet which is considered for inclusion in a broadcast. It is here that the conclusions of the BAI complaints process were included into the guidance notes of the regulation of broadcasting. The guidance notes reiterate that production and editorial staff must consider the reliability of the source, the veracity of the information, the potential for bias and respect for privacy for the individual involved. In the consultations on the code, the Authority stated that even though the code does not make any direct rules for the treatment of social media, it stressed that all the rules relating to appropriate practices, procedures and requirements for fairness, objectivity and impartiality also apply to social media as a news source (BAI, 2013). They agreed that additional procedures should be followed for social media. RTÉ did incorporate this point into the revised journalism guidelines; it is scant on detail but emphasizes the need to clear the use of such material with producers.

The reports highlighted a number of issues with the conduct of the debate, from the editing of questions to the use of unverified Twitter feeds to pose questions. Notwithstanding the fact that there is no automatic right to access the airwaves, is it right that access is based on the identity of the speaker rather than the content of their message. The reports of the regulatory body and the national broadcaster considers the inclusion of diverse voices in a debate less important than including a diversity of opinion. Because the tweet was the primary issue of complaint for all six complainants to the BAI, the report by RTÉ is questionable due to the avoidance of the tweet issue. The report here focused on the questions which were posed by the audience and the editorial controls and procedures adopted. By using social media as a means of enabling and encouraging audience contributions, it is possible to pick up incorrect information, especially in the fast-moving environment of Twitter. However, it needs to be determined where is the liability for harm caused in such instances, if any, and whether the information can be verified. Broadcasters are depended upon to communicate information in a balanced, impartial and accurate manner. Therefore, the recommendation for training about such media is a positive move.

New Media – New Challenges

When the right to political speech is isolated for consideration in such situations, there should be a growth of voices, but balanced voices, in the debate. Social media can facilitate this pluralistic conversation. Political speech is given the widest possible degree of freedom by the courts, yet unregulated speech is also harmful to the debate. In the particular instance of the #tweetgate incident, there was a good reason to place such allegations before the candidate. However, the majority of reports and investigations have failed to point out that as the candidate was there in the studio, and there was ample time for a right of reply to the allegations being put before him. Such debate is common in an election campaign; it is part of the testing period for those who seek higher office in a country. The fact that Seán Gallagher did not answer a question in a manner which satisfied those watching and tweeting about the debate is not the responsibility of the national broadcaster but a concern for the candidate himself. When comparing and contrasting the response of both bodies to the role of freedom of political expression and the balancing of communication time between participants, the overwhelming conclusion is that the right to political expression was upheld by the conduct of the debate. When issues are raised which refer to the public activities of an individual, then the issues must be pursued. There may have been verification issues regarding the provenance of the tweet which is perceived to be a at the heart of the issue. Yet when the conduct of the debate is reviewed, it is the inability of Seán Gallagher to give a clear answer to allegations put to him by another prospective candidate which undermined his performance that night.

On the issue of media regulation and social media, such an event should not equate to a rationale to curtail debate. It is important that questions are put to a candidate when they consent to participate in a national debate with other candidates seeking the same office. Speech and its validity cannot be measure in terms of the identity of the speaker but rather in terms of its content and what it can add to the quality of a debate. The level of regulation which has been placed into the Irish news and current affairs broadcasting environment could have gone further, but both the regulator and national broadcaster should be commended for not going further. The current state of the regulation emphasizes the need for good journalistic practice when all sources of information are considered, including social media; but the circumstances described in this situation do sound a cautionary note for those seeking to base information from the output of social media. The content of the legislation and regulation documents emphasise the need for balance in the discussion of current affairs and in particular at the time of elections.

Conclusion

In the section of this chapter titled 'Legal and Policy Framework Shaping Broadcasting in Ireland', it is explained that Irish law and media regulation place a high value on the balancing of voice in the media in election settings.

This includes election debates, where public interest is required for citizens to assess those who are seeking their vote for political office. The format of the debate described in this chapter adhered to previous court decisions in the area in giving equal time to participants. However, the BAI Compliance Committee stated that the debate fell short of acceptable standards. The development of adding in contemporaneous commentary from Twitter was, in fact, adhering to the principles of RTÉ in their public service statement encouraging and enabling audience contributions. In the *Frontline* debate this encouraging and enabling of contributions included not only the studio audience but the entire viewing public. The reaction from the debate in the form of the internal RTÉ report and BAI report both focused on editorial failings within the programme. However, regarding the issue of the tweet, which is the main focus of this chapter, the regulatory response did not forbid the use of social media as a contemporaneous means of adding, encouraging and enabling audience contributions. The reports focused on the need for verification of the sources of the information contained in social media contributions. Therefore, the impact of #tweetgate in the Irish media regulatory framework upholds all aspects of constitutional and legislative protection for freedom of expression, but in a responsible manner which emphasizes freedom of expression but also balance for all involved.

Notes

1. Article 40.6.1 makes specific reference to the liberty for the exercise of a number of rights. These rights are expression of convictions and opinions in Article 40.6.1(i), the right to assemble peacefully and without arms in Article 40.6.1(ii), and the formation of association and unions in Article 40.6.1(iii). The collection of these rights are generally referred to as the civil and political rights. They directly affect political protest, speech and the formation of parties and unions that have an influence on the direction of governance and political protest in a democracy.
2. Article 40.3.1 encompasses all the general rights of the citizen, and the right to communicate has been interpreted into this right. See the discussion of *Paperlink v. Attorney General*, below, in this chapter.
3. Article 10.2: The exercise of these freedoms, since it carries with it duties and responsibilities, may be subject to such formalities, conditions, restrictions or penalties as are prescribed by law and are necessary in a democratic society and in the interests of national security, territorial integrity or public safety, or for the prevention of disorder or crime, protection of health or morals, protection of the reputation or rights of others, prevention of the disclosure of information received in confidence or maintenance of the authority and impartiality of the judiciary.
4. The Codes are updated for each election and referendum (BAI, n.d.).
5. Various YouTube clips show the nature and character of the debate and its most controversial aspects See, e.g., Martin4President2011 (2011).
6. Tracker from RTE on the debate shows the development of the issues and the general responses from all the participant's and the host (RTÉ News, 2011).
7. Séan Gallagher's strong reaction to the conduct of the debate can be seen on the YouTube channel of the Irish Times (Irish Times, 2012).

74 Jennifer Kavanagh

References

Attorney General v. Paperlink (1984) 1 ILRM 1.
Bowman v. The United Kingdom (1998) 26 EHRR 1.
Broadcasting Authority of Ireland [BAI]. (2011). Statement by the BAI Compliance Committee: The Frontline presidential debate. Retrieved from http://www.bai.ie/?p=2905.
BAI. (2012). Broadcasting complaint decisions. Retrieved from http://www.bai.ie/wordpress/wp-content/uploads/CC_Decisions_August2012_v2_vFinal.pdf.
BAI. (2013). BAI code of fairness, objectivity and impartiality in news and current affairs – Guidance notes. Retrieved from http://www.bai.ie/wordpress/wp-content/uploads/201300701_FairnessGuidance_vFinal.pdf.
BAI (n.d.) *Codes & Standards*. Retrieved from http://www.bai.ie/index.php/codes-standards-2.
Castells v. Spain (1992) ECtHR 11798/85.
Corcoran, J. (2011). RTE accused over fake tweet that scuppered Gallagher's Aras bid. *Irish Independent*. Retrieved from http://www.independent.ie/irish-news/rte-accused-over-fake-tweet-that-scuppered-gallaghers-aras-bid-26796139.html.
Coughlan v. Broadcasting Complaints Commission (2000) 3 IR 1.
Doherty v. Referendum Commission (2012) IEHC 211.
Ireland. Law Reform Commission. (1993). *The report on the civil law of defamation*. Retrieved from http://www.lawreform.ie/_fileupload/Reports/rDefamation.htm.
Irish Times. (2012, May 15). *Sean Gallagher speaks about debate controversy*. Retrieved from http://www.youtube.com/watch?v=zGcNMIRlKq8.
Irish Times v. Ireland (1998) 1 IR 359.
Leech v. Independent Newspapers [2007] IEHC 223
Lingnes v. Austria (1986) ECtHR 9815/82.
Madigan v. RTÉ (1994) 2 ILRM 472.
Martin4President2011. (2011, October 25). *Séan Gallagher's lies exposed on RTE's Frontline* [Video file]. Retrieved from https://www.youtube.com/watch?v=uUhFdi7iRL0.
Murphy v. Independent Television and Radio Commission (1999) 1 IR 12, 17.
Murphy v. Ireland (2004) 38 EHRR 13.
Oberschlick v. Austria (1991) ECtHR 11662/85.
Oblique v. The Promise Productions (1994) 1 ILRM 74.
Observer and Guardian v. The United Kingdom (1991) ECHR 13585/88.
Rafter, K. (2011). Hear no evil – See no evil: Political advertising in Ireland. *Journal of Public Affairs, 11*(2), 93–99. doi: 10.1002/pa.393.
Raidió Teilifís Éireann [RTÉ]. (2010). Public service statement. Retrieved from http://www.rte.ie/documents/about/rte-pss-2010v1.pdf.
RTÉ. (2011). As it happened: Frontline presidential debate. Retrieved from http://www.rte.ie/news/2011/1024/307841-president_tracker/.
RTÉ. (2012). *Editorial review of the frontline*. Retrieved from http://www.rte.ie/documents/about/report-of-the-editorial-review-of-the-frontline.pdf.
RTÉ. (2013). Journalism guidelines. Retrieved from http://www.rte.ie/documents/about/rte-journalism-guidelines-oct-2012-final.pdf.
RTÉ News. (2011). As it happened: Frontline presidential debate. *rte.ie/news*. Retrieved from http://www.rte.ie/news/2011/1024/307841-president_tracker/.
Red C Research and Marketing. (2011). RedC Presidential Election Recall Poll – Full. Retrieved from http://redcresearch.ie/wp-content/uploads/2011/11/RTE-Recall-Poll-Presidential-Election-28th-Oct-2011.pdf.
Thorgerison v. Iceland (1992) ECtHR 13778/88.

Section II
The Relevance of Public Regulatory Intervention in Media Policy

5 Is Self-Regulation Failing Children and Young People? Assessing the Use of Alternative Regulatory Instruments in the Area of Social Networks

Eva Lievens

Introduction

Policies aimed at a safer Internet for children, with a view to minimising risks and maximising opportunities, have over the past 15 years put significant emphasis on the use of alternative regulatory instruments such as self- and co-regulation (McLaughlin, 2013). This was again confirmed in the Commission Communication on a European Strategy for a Better Internet for Children of May 2012, which stated that, '[l]egislation will not be discarded, but preference will be given to self-regulation, which remains the most flexible framework for achieving tangible results in this area' (European Commission, 2012, p. 6).

Self-regulation[1] does seem better adapted than traditional legislation to fast-changing, complex environments (Cave, Marsden & Simmons, 2008), and could thus at first sight help achieve important policy goals in the social networking services (SNS) environment. Advantages of self-regulation that are often mentioned are flexibility, the capacity to adapt quickly to fast-developing technologies and increasingly global issues, the high degree of expertise of the players that are involved and a lower cost (de Haan, van der Hof, Bekkers & Pijpers, 2013; Lievens and Valcke, 2012; McLaughlin, 2013; Mifsud Bonnici, 2008). However, next to these assets, there are also a number of drawbacks such as the lack of effective enforcement and the often mild sanctions. Other criticisms are limited transparency, a lack of accountability and a lack of legal certainty, all of which result in a decrease in democratic quality of regulation (de Haan et al., 2013; Latzer, Just & Saurwein, 2012). Furthermore, earlier research has found that self-regulation does not always protect fundamental rights of users and citizens in the same adequate way as traditional government legislation does, as private interests may be put before the public interest (Lievens, 2010; Price & Verhulst, 2000).

This chapter discusses the implementation of self-regulation to protect children and young people on social networks, and identifies the implications of non-compliance by SNS providers from a children's rights perspective. In addition, the chapter considers how evolving insights into Corporate Social Responsibility and its interplay with human rights can provide a framework for devising strategies that benefit both SNS providers and children and young people in their daily engagement with these networks.

Self-Regulation to Protect Children in the Social Networking Environment

In complex environments, such as those offering online and social networking services, it has been considered crucial that industry actors are involved to protect children, since they have the expertise and technical possibilities to offer users certain tools (O'Neill & Staksrud, 2012). Industry has, over the past years, taken up responsibility in this area. Examples of 'ongoing' industry self-regulation related to the online and social networking environment are the Safer Social Networking Principles (SSNPS) for the EU,[2] the CEO Coalition[3] and the ICT Coalition for Children Online[4] (formerly known as the ICT Principles Coalition or ICT Coalition for the Safer Use of Connected Devices and Online Services by Children and Young People in the EU); three 'coalitions' that consist of different constellations of companies.[5,6] They put forward largely similar principles, albeit with different emphases, to make the Internet in general, or SNS in particular, safer for children. Examples of these principles are promoting privacy-friendly default settings, encouraging age-appropriate content, offering reporting mechanisms, implementing content classification and providing parental controls.

In February 2009, a number of SNS providers subscribed to a self-regulatory[7] charter titled Safer Social Networking Principles for the EU following a public consultation on online social networking by the European Commission (European Commission, 2008).[8] The pan-European principles have been developed by SNS providers in cooperation with the Commission and a number of NGOs 'to provide good practice recommendations for the providers of social networking and other user interactive sites, to enhance the safety of children and young people using their services' (European Social Networking Task Force, 2009). In order to achieve this goal, one of the core elements of the SSNPs is multi-stakeholder collaboration (including SNS providers, parents, teachers and other carers, governments and public bodies, police and other law enforcement bodies, civil society and users themselves). The seven principles that were put forward are the following:

Principle 1: *Raise awareness of safety education messages and acceptable use policies to users, parents, teachers and carers in a prominent, clear and age-appropriate manner.*

Principle 2: *Work towards ensuring that services are age-appropriate for the intended audience.*

Principle 3: *Empower users through tools and technology.*

Principle 4: *Provide easy-to-use mechanisms to report conduct or content that violates the Terms of Service.*

Principle 5: *Respond to notifications of illegal content or conduct.*

Principle 6: *Enable and encourage users to employ a safe approach to personal information and privacy.*

Principle 7: *Assess the means for reviewing illegal or prohibited content/ conduct.*

In February 2010, the results of an independent evaluation of the implementation of the SSNPs were made public (Staksrud & Lobe, 2010). This evaluation analysed the self-declaration statements of the signatories to the charter and evaluated a number of services offered by them (Lobe & Staksrud, 2010). Overall, the report showed that there was (significant) room for improvement. With regard to reporting mechanisms, the evaluation showed that only 9 out of 22 sites responded to complaints submitted by minors asking for help.

In June and September 2011, the results of a second assessment of the SSNPs proved also disappointing, for instance with regard to the principle of ensuring that minors' profiles be accessible only to their approved contacts by default, which only four SNS providers were found to comply with (Donoso, 2011a; Donoso, 2011b; European Commission, 2011a). Whereas this evaluation found that almost all services offer age-appropriate, user-friendly, easily accessible and always available reporting mechanisms, still only 17 out of 23 services responded to complaints or reports,[9] sometimes taking up to 10 days to do so (Donoso, 2011a; Donoso, 2011b). According to the report, these responses ranged from 'personalised emails explaining to minors how to delete the offending content themselves and giving minors concrete tips on how to deal with this type of situation to replies mentioning that the offending content had been / would be reviewed and eventually removed from the site' (Donoso, 2011a, pp. 10–11).

The results of these evaluations raise the question of the effectiveness of this type of regulatory initiative: although the commitment of the SNS providers to take steps to make their services safer is to be applauded, the concrete implementation of such safety measures is of course crucial in order to achieve actual protection. The text of the SSNPs mentions '[t]hese Principles are aspirational and not prescriptive or legally binding, but are offered to service providers with a strong recommendation for their use'. This does not provide a solid base for enforcement, nor a compelling incentive for compliance. Since 2011, the SSNPs have not been evaluated anymore and calls to the Commission to undertake a third evaluation remain unanswered. If yearly evaluations are no longer undertaken, incentives to comply for industry will decrease significantly, and the SSNPs may, very soon, lose all importance.

In December 2011, 28 companies voluntarily formed the Coalition to make the Internet a better place for kids and published a Statement of Purpose (Coalition to make the Internet a better place for kids, 2011). This self-regulatory initiative was an answer to a call for action from the European Commission and has been endorsed by Commissioner Kroes (European Commission, 2011d). Social network providers such as Facebook and Netlog have also joined this coalition. In order to achieve their goal the coalition drafted a work plan which ran from December 2011 until December 2012, and focuses on five concrete action points: simple and robust reporting tools for users, age-appropriate privacy settings, wider use of content classification, wider availability and use of parental controls and effective takedown of child abuse material.

In July 2012, for the first time, the Coalition presented the progress that was made after the first six months. The general conclusion was that progress could be established, but that more needed to be done to realise the promises that had been made (*Report of mid-term review*, 2012). In February 2013 again a state of affairs was proposed. The various working groups drew up a report on their work and formulated a number of recommendations, but really tangible results remained limited (European Commission, 2013a). In June 2013 (European Commission, 2013b), the companies that are involved in the Coalition reaffirmed, in a meeting with Commissioner Kroes, their commitment to cooperate to improve the Internet for kids. However, in what form this cooperation would be continued or how and when the further implementation of the principles would be evaluated remained very unclear.

In January 2012 another industry initiative was launched. 25 companies, including Facebook and Google, formed the ICT Coalition for a Safer Internet for Children and Young People, and issued the *Principles for the Safer Use of Connected Devices and Online Services by Children and Young People in the EU*. Their focus is on 'content, parental controls, dealing with abuse/misuse, child sexual abuse content or illegal contact, privacy and control, education and awareness'. In December 2014, the name of the Coalition was changed to the 'ICT Coalition for Children Online'.

These principles are meant to function as a best practice and provide a long-term roadmap for the member companies (ICT Coalition for a Safer Internet for Children and Young People, 2012). Commitments that are assumed by companies in the framework of the ICT Coalition are rather detailed, but companies self-report on their progress. However, in June 2013 an independent assessor was appointed to evaluate the implementation of the principles.[10] An extensive report was published in April 2014 (O'Neill, 2014). The assessment of mechanisms in place to address the prioritised topics claimed that improvements have been made by members of the coalition, for instance with regard to internal procedures to deal with reports and parental control solutions. The latter, however, are not yet adapted to mobile use of Internet and mobile devices. Improvements can also be made with regard to labelling and classification of content, also on mobile apps and for user-generated content. In addition, interpretation of the broadly formulated principles appears to be quite different in practice. Whereas the Coalition provides for a 'forum for knowledge exchange and sharing of experience between industry partners on Internet safety developments', O'Neill recommended extending membership and developing areas (e.g., gaming) and that actors (e.g., device manufacturers) should be included (O'Neill, 2014, p. 7).

The Failure of Self-Regulation?

Doubts can be raised as to the implementation of processes and the realisation of commitments by the current self-regulatory initiatives (de Haan et al., 2013).

As mentioned above, independent assessments of the implementation of the SSNPs have shown that the promises that were made by SNS providers have not been complied with in a satisfactory manner.[11] Moreover, the organisational processes of the CEO Coalition have been opaque to outsiders and the results are unclear, to say the least. Although it has been claimed that regular meetings are held, companies engage in research and realisation of new ideas and actual progress is being made, transparent information is lacking, reports are brief and unclear and communication by the Commission has remained superficial. It is also not clear whether the new Commissioner for Digital Economy and Society Oettinger will support the CEO Coalition to the same extent as the previous Commissioner Kroes has done. So far, the ICT Coalition for children online seems to be the association that undertakes a greater effort to be transparent and assesses its own impact. However, the first evaluation in 2014 was largely based on self-reporting and did not carry out actual tests, for instance as to the actual reaction or feedback users get when they have reported something.

In any case, doubts remain. We could wonder whether it would not be more productive and efficient to combine the efforts of all companies in one single over-arching initiative, instead of fragmenting the commitment in various coalitions. In addition, transparency about the organisation of these initiatives is acutely lacking. It is not clear how members are elected, who is in charge of management of the coalitions, or whether there is funding for communal purposes. Finally, even though efforts are undertaken, issues such as privacy policies and settings offered by social networking providers remain deeply problematic, as has been demonstrated by Facebook's latest policy changes in February 2015 (ICRI and SMIT, 2015).

Children's Rights

Of course, it would be possible to argue that social networking platforms are hosted by private companies, that it is their right to conduct their business in the way they see fit (See also, Article 16 of the EU Charter of Fundamental Rights) and that they are not obliged to take up responsibility to protect children in the online environment.

This raises the question of the validity of this policy goal (which has been relevant since the first emergence of mass media), children's rights and the responsibility for the protection and realisation of these rights.

Since the creation of the United Nations Convention on the Rights of the Child it has been accepted across the globe that children are entitled to a number of fundamental rights, such as the right to freedom of expression (Article 13) and the right to privacy (Article 16). At the same time, children sometimes need to be protected, for instance, against harmful content (Article 17). Overall, children's rights have increasingly been awarded a significant place on the international as well as the supranational (Council of Europe and European Union) policy agenda. Aside from the possible application of the European Convention on Human Rights (Article 8 – privacy and Article 10 – freedom of expression) to children, the Council of Europe has, over the past decade, issued various documents concerning human rights in general, and children's rights in particular, also specifically with respect to the protection of these rights in the information society.[12] The EU has been active in this field as well, laying down a legal basis for the protection of children's rights in the Charter of Fundamental Rights (Article 24)[13] as well as the Lisbon Treaty, and developing a conscious EU strategy on the rights of the child.[14] A similar theme runs through the various documents at all levels: on the one hand, children are active subjects of rights who can invoke a number of fundamental rights, but, on the other hand, this also entails that sometimes they need to be safeguarded from harmful influences.

Social Networks, Children's Rights and Responsible Actors

It is undeniable that the use of SNS by children is closely linked not only to their fundamental right to freedom of expression and their right to privacy but also to their right to be protected in certain circumstances. As the Council of Europe's *Recommendation on the protection of human rights with regard to social networking services* has articulated:

> This complexity gives operators of SNS or platforms a great potential to promote the exercise and enjoyment of human rights and fundamental freedoms, in particular the freedom to express, to create and to exchange content and ideas, and the freedom of assembly. SNS can assist the wider public to receive and impart information. […]
>
> Social networking services play an increasingly important role in the life of children and young people, as part of the development of their own personality and identity, and as part of their participation in debates and social activities.
>
> Against this background, children and young people should be protected because of the inherent vulnerability that their age implies. (Council of Europe, 2012)

As regards the question who is responsible for this protection the Recommendation not only points to parents, carers and educators[15] but also to the private sector - *SNS providers* -,[16] civil society and member States. This exemplifies a multi-stakeholder type of involvement, in which each of these actors is thought to have a specific responsibility to contribute to a safe, positive, and creative online experience for young Internet users.

The Recommendation also points to and promotes the use of self- and co-regulation for upholding certain standards for the use of social networks, but emphasises that it 'is important that procedural safeguards are respected by these mechanisms, in line with the right to be heard and to review or appeal against decisions, including in appropriate cases the right to a fair trial, within a reasonable time, and starting with the presumption of innocence' (Council of Europe, 2012).

The EU Strategy for a better Internet for kids (European Commission, 2012) starts from a multi-stakeholder perspective as well and states that '[r]egulation remains an option, but, where appropriate, it should preferably be avoided, in favour of more adaptable self-regulatory tools, and of education and empowerment'. However, the Strategy does clarify, for instance with regard to the development of simple and robust reporting tools for users and the promotion of a wider use of age rating and content classification, that if industry self-regulation fails to deliver, legislative or regulatory measures will be considered by the Commission.

It is clear that many actors are involved in putting the protection of fundamental rights into practice: governments, civil society organisations, industry and media organisations as well citizens. In this context, in 2011, the United Nations issued the *Guiding principles on business and human rights* (United Nations, 2011). These principles, which are part of the larger United Nations 'Protect, Respect and Remedy' framework (Ruggie, 2008), highlight the responsibility of States to 'protect against human rights abuse within their territory and/or jurisdiction by third parties, including business enterprises. This requires taking appropriate steps to prevent, investigate, punish and redress such abuse through effective policies, legislation, regulations and adjudication' (United Nations, 2011, p. 3). On the other hand, '[b]usiness enterprises should respect human rights. This means that they should avoid infringing on the human rights of others and should address adverse human rights impacts with which they are involved' (United Nations, 2011, p. 13). This includes the obligation for businesses to carry out human rights due diligence and track the effectiveness of their response to verify whether adverse human rights impacts are being addressed.

Specifically tailored to children's rights are the *Children's rights and business principles*, drafted by the UN Global Compact, Unicef and Save the Children in 2013 (Unicef, 2013). According to these principles 'respecting and supporting children's rights requires business to both prevent harm and actively safeguard children's interests' (Unicef, 2013, p. 3). Businesses are called upon to guarantee that products and services are safe and aim to support children's rights through them. This includes, for instance, '[r]estricting access to products and services that are not suitable for children or that may cause them harm, while ensuring that all such actions align with international standards, including non-discrimination, freedom of expression and access to information' (Unicef, 2013, p. 24).

Additionally, in 2013 the Committee on the Rights of the Child published a *General comment on State obligations regarding the impact of the business sector on children's rights* (United Nations Committee on the Rights of the Child, 2013). This General Comment is addressed at States to provide guidance on how they can create a facilitating environment for businesses to respect children's rights. It is explicitly recognised that 'duties and responsibilities to respect the rights of children extend in practice beyond the State and State-controlled services and institutions and apply to private actors and business enterprises' and that both parties, States and business enterprises, must take up these responsibilities. Businesses can take active steps toward this goal by undertaking child-rights due diligence and States should carry out child-rights impact assessments (United Nations Committee on the Rights of the Child, 2013, p. 17, 20). With regard to transnational companies that operate on a global scale (as SNS most often do), the Committee clarifies that States must ensure that the companies that operate within their borders are adequately regulated within a legal and institutional framework that guarantees that children's rights are respected (United Nations Committee on the Rights of the Child, 2013). In addition, the legislation in question should be clear and predictable (United Nations Committee on the Rights of the Child, 2013). We can wonder whether, at the moment, in the digital environment this is not an area where significant improvements are urgently needed. Internet service providers that operate globally are not only subject to many different legislative obligations, they are also confronted with varying degrees of legal uncertainty in different parts of the world because legal frameworks are not adapted to or are challenged by the nature of online activities. This is also the case with regard to issues that are linked to the protection of human rights. The 2014 judgment of the European Court of Justice in the *Google Spain* case is an illustration thereof.[17] In that case, the Court decided that 'the operator of a search engine is obliged to remove from the list of results displayed following a search made on the basis of a person's name links to web pages, published by third parties and containing information relating to that person, also in a case where that name or information is not erased beforehand or simultaneously from those web pages, and even, as the case may be, when its publication in itself on those pages is lawful'. The judgement, which addresses questions related to the balance of the right to freedom of expression and the right to information with the right to privacy and reputation (Ausloos, 2014), is very controversial and seems to imply that a significant extra burden will be put on search engine operators. On the other hand, the case also illustrates that globally operating companies that have their origins in the United States, will increasingly be expected to respect and uphold European human rights standards.

We can frame the question related to the responsibility of the ICT industry in general, and SNS providers in particular, within the general debate on Corporate Social Responsibility (CSR).[18] In 1953, Howard Bowen defined 'the social responsibilities of the businessman' as 'the obligations of businessmen to pursue those policies, to make those decisions, or to follow those lines of action which are desirable in terms of the objectives and values of our society' (p. 6). Davis (1973) proposed that social responsibility is 'a firm's acceptance of a social obligation beyond the requirements of the law' (p. 313). Along the same lines, according to the European Commission

(2011c, p. 3) the notion CSR refers to 'actions by companies over and above their legal obligations towards society and the environment'. Cohen-Almagor (2012) has, in relation to Internet Service Providers and web hosting services, argued that upholding norms of CSR has advantages both for the companies and the society in which they operate. Potential benefits of CSR that have been articulated are linked to risk management, cost savings, attracting customers and improving customer relationships, employee commitment and innovation capacity (Crane & Matten, 2004; Davis, 1973; European Commission, 2011c).[19]

In 2011, the Commission adopted 'A renewed EU strategy 2011–14 for Corporate Social Responsibility' (European Commission, 2011c). In this strategy is it emphasised that human rights are an increasingly significant element in CSR and that companies should implement 'a process to integrate social, environmental, ethical, human rights and consumer concerns into their business operations and core strategy in close collaboration with their stakeholders, with the aim of: maximising the creation of shared value for their owners/shareholders and for their other stakeholders and society at large; and identifying, preventing and mitigating their possible adverse impacts' (European Commission, 2011c, p. 6). The strategy also refers to the *UN Guiding principles on business and human rights* (United Nations, 2011) and recommends a better implementation. As one of the steps in achieving this goal, the general principles were translated to specific sectors. For the ICT sector, the drafting of the *ICT Sector Guide on implementing the UN Guiding principles on business and human rights* (Shift and the Institute for Human Rights and Business, 2013) was commissioned by the European Commission.[20] In this guide, the six core elements[21] for CSR to respect human rights are elaborated and specifically applied to activities carried out by companies in the ICT sector.

Child safety online is one of the topics that is addressed in the ICT sector guide under the element of 'Integrating and acting on potential impacts'. Detailed measures are proposed for ICT companies to consider, such as providing direct links and information on ways for users to report abusive images or behaviours such as bullying, implementing effective age and identity verification mechanisms at the level of individual users, implementing appropriately heightened security measures for personal information that has been collected from children, seeking parental consent before using or disclosing information collected from children, considering any unintended consequences of decisions on child safety and engaging with child safety and children's rights experts to provide ongoing feedback and guidance on the company's policy in this area (Shift and the Institute for Human Rights and Business, 2013).

Along the same lines, the *Council of Europe Guide to human rights for Internet users* encourages a genuine dialogue between the private sector and relevant state authorities and civil society regarding the implementation of their CSR, with a specific focus on transparency and accountability,[22] in line with the *Guiding Principles on Business and Human Rights* (Council of Europe, 2014). The Appendix to this recommendation contains an actual guide which aims to raise users' awareness of the corporate responsibilities of Internet service providers and providers of online content and services.[23] It is mentioned explicitly, for instance, that these companies should inform users about their rights, freedoms, possible remedies and how to obtain them, including '*easily accessible information on how to report and complain about interferences with your rights and how to seek redress*' (Council of Europe, 2014, Appendix).

Traditional justifications for companies to adopt a clear CSR strategy are, amongst others, moral obligations, sustainability, license to operate[24] and reputation (Porter and Kramer, 2006 and Unicef, 2013). Porter and Kramer have argued that these justifications have significant limitations because of their emphasis on the tension between business and society, instead of on their interdependence. Hence, they advocate focusing on shared value, and making choices that benefit both sides. According to them, 'the essential test that should guide CSR is not that a cause is worthy but whether it presents an opportunity to create shared value – that is, a meaningful benefit for society that is also valuable to the business' (Porter & Kramer, 2006, p. 6). And while Porter and Kramer were aware of the fact that this requires radically different thinking in business, they were also convinced that CSR is increasingly significant to competitive success. Transposing this way of thinking about CSR to the domain of children's rights in the digital environment it is necessary to consider the fact that whereas CSR activities in this field are definitely beneficial for society, they may also be '*valuable for businesses in supporting the emergence of knowledgeable and responsible future users and developing and maintaining trust towards their services and brands*' (Ságvári & Máder, 2013, p. 161). Trust and confidence in services is an increasingly important factor for businesses in the ICT sector (O'Neill, 2014), argued to be able to sustain, among other goals, a competitive knowledge economy and a digitally skilled labour force (Livingstone & O'Neill, 2014). In its *Strategy for a better Internet for children*, the European Commission also pointed to the fact that 'analyses show that a better and wider use of the Internet by children is opening the door for intensive business development in innovative online content and services' (European Commission, 2012, p. 2).[25] Along the same lines, the *Children's rights and business principles* indicate how considering how products and services can better meet children's needs can also be a source of innovation and create new markets (Unicef, 2013). The focus of ICT companies, such as SNS providers, in developing their CSR strategy, should hence be on the fact that children are a target audience worth investing in, instead of concentrating on the idea that incorporating protection and empowerment mechanisms into services is an additional cost (European Commission, 2012). For SNS providers this would mean in practice that a mutually beneficial CSR strategy should include a conscious and substantial investment of resources (financial, personnel, etc.) in putting the rights laid down in Articles 13, 16 and 17 UNCRC into practice. This could for instance entail the (further) development of reporting mechanisms with a fast and supportive follow-up, the provision of clear and age-appropriate information in a transparent manner through innovatively designed Terms of Use and privacy policies (Wauters, Lievens & Valcke, 2014) or participatory strategies to involve young users in the improvement and identification of elements that should be included in the CSR strategy.

Another action included in the Commission strategy for Corporate Social Responsibility (European Commission, 2011c) related specifically to developing Principles for Better self- and co-regulation and establishing a Community of Practice gathering stakeholders interested in self- and co-regulation. (Newsroom Editor, 2013) The principles were adopted in 2013 as the result of a process of public consultation and focus on the concept of self- and co-regulation on the one hand and the implementation thereof on the other. The latter part includes recommendations with respect to iterative improvements, monitoring and evaluation. According to the principles, participants in such regulatory schemes should, for instance, regularly and collectively evaluate performance both against output commitments, and with regard to impact. This remains rather abstract, and lacks clarity on how to implement such evaluations in practice as well as guidance as on which actions could be taken if these evaluations show that the systems in place do not reach their objectives. Although these principles could thus be strengthened. In a 2014 public consultation on the Commission's CSR strategy (European Commission, 2011c) 71% of the respondents also perceived 'Improving self- and co-regulation processes' as an important means to promote responsible business conduct (European Commission, 2014).

Conclusion: The Way Forward?

At the moment, SNS providers have committed themselves to self-regulatory mechanisms such as the SSNPs for the EU, the CEO Coalition and the ICT Coalition. This engagement fits within their responsibility to respect and support children's fundamental rights and must be encouraged. At the same time, there still are many doubts about the concrete implementation of the commitments that have been taken up as well as the opaqueness of the initiatives. Success factors for self-regulation have been identified by Latzer, Just, Saurwein and Slominski (2003) as operational objectives and clearly defined responsibilities, transparent regulatory processes and measurable results, defined fall-back scenarios in case of malfunction, adequate sanction powers, periodical reviews and external control by the general public and the state, and participation possibilities for interested stakeholders. It is clear that many of these success factors are not included in the current organisation of the self-regulatory initiatives with regard to SNS.

Increasingly detailed insights into CSR and fundamental (children's) rights could be combined with empirical research into children's use of SNS to achieve a well-considered, detailed development and elaboration of policy in this area by SNS providers. The principles detailed in the *ICT Sector Guide on implementing the UN Guiding principles on business and human rights* are useful to carefully consider a CSR policy with regard to children's rights, not only with regard to (further) putting in place measures to lower risks, but also with a view to integrating tools and strategies that enable children to make the most of the opportunities that SNS offer them. Creating a corporate social agenda which, according to Porter and Kramer (2006), goes beyond best practices, should be a priority. Already existing initiatives, such as the ICT (Principles) Coalition and the European Commission's Community of Practice for Self- and Co-regulation, that aim to share best practices may be helpful, but SNS providers must also be encouraged to go one step further in devising pioneering CSR strategies that are tailored to their specific features and advance the rights of a significant proportion of their current and future users: children.

In its 2012 strategy the European Commission itself refers to the fact that regulatory measures will be considered if industry initiatives fail to deliver. Such a conclusion can only be drawn if the existing initiatives are regularly and independently assessed. Taking up its own responsibility to ensure that children's needs (both positive and negative) are addressed in the online and social networking environment, the Commission has an important role to play in encouraging such evaluations, and, consequently, based on sound evidence, considering whether implementation is satisfactory or whether a shift towards co-regulation is necessary. The fact that the European Commission is an important actor in the field of CSR and that the Commission could do more to fulfil its potential role in this area was confirmed by a large majority of the respondents to the 2014 public consultation on the Commission's CSR strategy (European Commission, 2014). As the new European Commission headed by Jean-Claude Juncker has placed 'better regulation' among the top priorities of its mandate (Juncker, 2014), we can only hope that the use of self- and co-regulatory mechanisms in areas where important goals of public interest and fundamental rights are at stake will be evaluated and clarified.

Notes

1. Self-regulation entails the creation, implementation and enforcement of rules by a group of actors, from industry in particular, with minimal or no intervention by the state (Lievens, 2010).
2. http://ec.europa.eu/information_society/activities/social_networking/docs/sn_principles.pdf.
3. http://ec.europa.eu/information_society/activities/sip/docs/ceo_coalition_statement.pdf.
4. http://www.ictcoalition.eu/.

Is Self-Regulation Failing Children and Young People? 89

5. But, for instance, Facebook is part of all three coalitions.
6. The three initiatives have recently been included in LSE & EU Kids Online's overview: Children's safety on the Internet: a guide to stakeholders (Chernyavskaya & Livingstone, 2015).
7. De Haan et al. (2013, p. 118) argue: 'Basically, the principles are a hybrid form of self-regulation, given the involvement of the European Commission in initiating and evaluating the implementation of the regulatory initiative. Since the adoption of the principles by the industry is voluntary and, because there is no legislative force behind the principles, this is not a form of co-regulation (see Cave et al., 2008)'.
8. In the United States in 2008 the *Joint statement on key principles of social networking safety* was adopted.
9. The reporting mechanisms were tested by 'creating a realistic bullying situation on the SNS where a fake 'bullied child' contacted the provider asking for help to remove offending content posted on her profile' (Donoso, 2011a, p. 10).
10. Regular evaluations are important given the pace with which social networks and their terms of services and privacy settings change. Mid October 2013, for instance, Facebook adapted the privacy settings for their users between 13 and 18 years of age. Although the adapted default setting is now 'friends only', it is now possible for this category of users to share posts publicly, which was not possible before. The fact that public sharing was impossible was at the time mentioned in the self-report of Facebook in the framework of the ICT Principles as one of the means of fulfilling their commitments.
11. For instance: European Commission, 2011b.
12. See, for instance: Council of Europe, 2009.
13. Article 24: 1. Children shall have the right to such protection and care as is necessary for their well-being. They may express their views freely. Such views shall be taken into consideration on matters which concern them in accordance with their age and maturity. 2. In all actions relating to children, whether taken by public authorities or private institutions, the child's best interests must be a primary consideration. 3. Every child shall have the right to maintain on a regular basis a personal relationship and direct contact with both his or her parents, unless that is contrary to his or her interests.
14. Cf. http://europa.eu/legislation_summaries/human_rights/fundamental_rights_within_european_union/r12555_en.htm.
15. Council of Europe (2012): 'Parents, carers and educators should play a primary role in working with children and young people to ensure that they use these services in an appropriate manner (...)'.
16. For instance, Council of Europe (2012): 'While not being required to control, supervise and/or rate all content uploaded by its users, SNS providers may be required to adopt certain precautionary measures (for example, comparable to 'adult content' rules applicable in certain member States) or take diligent action in response to complaints (ex-post moderation)'.
17. European Court of Justice, *Google Spain v. AEPD*, C-131/12, 13 May 2014.
18. For a broader contrasting conceptualisation of CSR, see Laidlaw, 2012. For an extensive overview of CSR definitions and practice, see Carroll, 2008.
19. For an elaborate discussion of criticisms of corporate responsibility, see Blowfield & Murray, 2008, pp. 338–361.
20. The Human Rights Guidelines on Freedom of Expression Online and Offline, adopted by the Council of the European Union in May 2014 specifically

emphasise that 'the EU will promote the implementation of the guidance for ICT/telecommunications companies on business and human rights, developed by the Commission on the basis of the UN Guiding Principles on Business and Human Rights' (Council of the European Union, 2014, p. 15).
21. 1/ Developing a policy commitment and embedding respect for human rights; 2/ Assessing human rights impact; 3/ Integrating and acting; 4/ Tracking performance; 5/ Communicating performance; and 6/ Remediation and operational-level grievance mechanisms (Shift and the Institute for Human Rights and Business, 2013).
22. On media accountability, see McQuail, 2003.
23. For example, 'your Internet service provider and your provider of online content and services have corporate responsibilities to respect your human rights and provide mechanisms to respond to your claims. You should be aware, however, that online service providers, such as social networks, may restrict certain types of content and behaviour due to their content policies. You should be informed of possible restrictions so that you are able to take an informed decision as to whether to use the service or not. This includes specific information on what the online service provider considers as illegal or inappropriate content and behaviour when using the service and how it is dealt with by the provider' (Council of Europe, 2014, Appendix).
24. According to Porter and Kramer, the notion of 'licence to operate' 'derives from the fact that every company needs tacit or explicit permission from governments, communities, and numerous other stakeholders to do business' (Porter & Kramer, 2006, p. 3).
25. Also: 'With the wide proliferation of tablets, smart phones and laptops that children use heavily, the potential market for interactive creative and educational online content for both young children and teenagers is substantial. Online and mobile apps and games provide unprecedented opportunities for business development, in particular for SMEs and creators, as they allow for direct contact with potential users/clients. Children themselves could become online creators and start up businesses' (p. 4).

References

Ausloos, J. (2014, 13 May). European Court rules against Google, in favour of right to be forgotten. [Weblog]. Retrieved from http://blogs.lse.ac.uk/media-policyproject/2014/05/13/european-court-rules-against-google-in-favour-of-right-to-be-forgotten/.

Blowfield, M., & Murray, A. (2008). *Corporate responsibility: A critical introduction*. Oxford: Oxford University Press.

Bowen, H. (1953). *Social responsibilities of the businessman*. New York: Harper and Row.

Carroll, A. (2008). A history of corporate social responsibility: Concepts and practices. In A. Crane, A. Williams, D. Matten, J. Moon & D. Siegel (Eds.), *The Oxford handbook of corporate social responsibility* (pp. 19–46). Oxford: Oxford University Press.

Cave, J., Marsden, C., & Simmons, S. (2008). *Options for and effectiveness of Internet self- and co-regulation*. Retrieved from http://www.rand.org/pubs/technical_reports/TR566.html.

Chernyavskaya, A., & Livingstone, S. (2015, 31 March). Children's safety on the Internet: A guide to stakeholders. [Weblog]. Retrieved from http://blogs.lse.ac.uk/mediapolicyproject/2015/03/31/childrens-safety-on-the-internet-a-guide-to-stakeholders/.

Coalition to make the Internet a better place for kids. (2011). *Statement of purpose*. Retrieved from https://ec.europa.eu/digital-agenda/sites/digital-agenda/files/ceo_coalition_statement.pdf.

Cohen-Almagor, R. (2012). Freedom of expression, Internet responsibility and business ethics: The Yahoo! saga and its implications. *Journal of Business Ethics, 106*(3), 353–365. doi: 10.1007/s10551-011-1001-z.

Council of Europe. (2009). Recommendation CM/Rec(2009)5 of the Committee of Ministers to member states on measures to protect children against harmful content and behaviour and to promote their active participation in the new information and communications environment. Retrieved from https://wcd.coe.int/ViewDoc.jsp?id=1470045.

Council of Europe. (2012). Recommendation CM/Rec(2012)4 of the Committee of Ministers to member States on the protection of human rights with regard to social networking services. Retrieved from https://wcd.coe.int/ViewDoc.jsp?id=1929453.

Council of Europe. (2014). Recommendation CM/Rec(2014)6 of the Committee of Ministers to member States on a Guide to human rights for Internet users. Retrieved from https://wcd.coe.int/ViewDoc.jsp?id=2184807.

Council of the European Union. (2014). EU human rights guidelines on freedom of expression online and offline. Retrieved from http://www.consilium.europa.eu/uedocs/cms_data/docs/pressdata/EN/foraff/142549.pdf.

Crane, A., & Matten, D. (2004). *Business ethics*. Oxford: Oxford University Press.

Davis, K. (1973). The case for and against business assumption of social responsibilities. *The Academy of Management Journal, 16*(2), 312–322.

De Haan, J., van der Hof, S., Bekkers, W., & Pijpers, R. (2013). Self-regulation. In B. O'Neill, E. Staksrud, & S. McLaughlin, *Towards a better Internet for children? Policy pillars, players and paradoxes* (pp. 111–129). Gothenborg, Sweden: Nordicom.

Donoso, V. (2011a). *Assessment of the implementation of the Safer Social Networking Principles for the EU on 14 websites: Summary report*. Luxembourg: European Commission.

Donoso, V. (2011b). *Assessment of the implementation of the Safer Social Networking Principles for the EU on 9 services: Summary report*. Luxembourg: European Commission.

European Commission. (2008). Public consultation on online social networking. Retrieved from http://ec.europa.eu/information_society/activities/sip/docs/pub_consult_age_rating_sns/summaryreport.pdf.

European Commission. (2011a, 21 June). Digital agenda: Only two social networking sites protect privacy of minors' profiles by default; Retrieved from http://europa.eu/rapid/press-release_IP-11-762_en.htm?locale=en.

European Commission. (2011b, 30 September). Digital agenda: social networks can do much more to protect minors' privacy. Retrieved from http://europa.eu/rapid/press-release_IP-11-1124_en.htm.

European Commission. (2011c). *A renewed EU strategy 2011–14 for corporate social responsibility*. COM (2011) 681. Retrieved from http://ec.europa.eu/

information_society/activities/sip/docs/pub_consult_age_rating_sns/summaryreport.pdf.
European Commission. (2011d, 1 December). Digital Agenda: Coalition of top tech & media companies to make Internet better place for our kids. Retrieved from http://europa.eu/rapid/press-release_IP-11-1485_en.htm.
European Commission. (2012). Communication from the Commission to the European Parliament, the Council, the European Economic and Social Committee and the Committee of the Regions. *European strategy for a better Internet for children*. COM(2012) 196. Retrieved from http://eur-lex.europa.eu/LexUriServ/LexUriServ.do?uri=COM:2012:0196:FIN:EN:PDF.
European Commission. (2013a). Better Internet for kids: CEO coalition 1 year on. Retrieved from http://ec.europa.eu/information_society/newsroom/cf/itemdetail.cfm?item_id=9574.
European Commission. (2013b). Europe's top tech executives and Commission affirm commitment to collaborate, not compete, to improve the internet for kids. Retrieved from http://europa.eu/rapid/press-release_MEMO-13-504_en.htm.
European Commission. (2014). The corporate social responsibility strategy of the European Commission: Results of the public consultation. Retrieved from http://ec.europa.eu/newsroom/dae/document.cfm?doc_id=8313.
European Social Networking Task Force. (2009). *Safer social networking principles for the EU*. Retrieved from https://ec.europa.eu/digital-agenda/sites/digital-agenda/files/sn_principles.pdf.
Interdisciplinary Centre for Law and ICT (ICRI) and Studies Media Information Telecommunication SMIT. (2015). From social media service to advertising network: A critical evaluation of Facebook's revised Policies and Terms, Retrieved from http://www.law.kuleuven.be/icri/en/news/item/facebooks-revised-policies-and-terms-v1-2.pdf.
ICT Coalition for a Safer Internet for Children and Young People. (2012). *Principles for the safer use of connected devices and online services by children and young people in the EU*. Retrieved from http://www.egba.eu/pdf/ICTPrinciples.pdf.
Juncker, J.-C. (2014). A new start for Europe: My agenda for jobs, growth, fairness and democratic change. Retrieved from http://ec.europa.eu/priorities/docs/pg_en.pdf.
Laidlaw, E. (2012). *Internet gatekeepers, human rights and corporate social responsibilities* [PhD thesis]. The London School of Economics and Political Science, London. Retrieved from http://etheses.lse.ac.uk/317/.
Latzer, M., Just, N., & Saurwein, F. (2012). Self- and co-regulation: Evidence, legitimacy and governance choice. In M. Price & S. Verhulst (Eds.), *Routledge handbook of media law* (pp. 373–397). Oxford: Routledge.
Latzer, M., Just, N., Saurwein, F., & Slominski, P. (2003). Regulation remixed: institutional change through self and co-regulation in the mediamatics sector. *Communications & Strategies, 50*(2), 127–157.
Lievens, E. (2010). *Protecting children in the digital era: The use of alternative regulatory instruments*. Leiden, Netherlands/Boston: Martinus Nijhoff Publishers.
Lievens, E., & Valcke, P. (2012). Regulatory trends in a social media context. In M. Price, & S. Verhulst (Eds.), *Routledge handbook of media law* (pp. 557–580). Oxford: Routledge.
Livingstone, S., & O'Neill, B. (2014). Children's rights online: Challenges, dilemmas and emerging directions. In S. van der Hof, B. van den Berg, & B. Schermer, *Minding minors wandering the web: Regulating online child safety* (pp. 19–38). The Hague: T.M.C. Asser Press/Springer.

Lobe, B., & Staksrud, E. (Eds.). (2010). Evaluation of the implementation of the Safer Social Networking Principles for the EU, Part 2: Testing of 20 social networks in Europe. Retrieved from http://ec.europa.eu/danmark/documents/alle_emner/information/100209_4part_ii_individual_results_en.pdf.

McLaughlin, S. (2013). Regulation and legislation. In B. O'Neill, E. Staksrud & S. McLaughlin, *Towards a better Internet for children? Policy pillars, players and paradoxes* (pp. 77–91). Gothenborg, Sweden: Nordicom.

McQuail, D. (2003). *Media accountability and freedom of publication*. Oxford: Oxford University Press.

Mifsud Bonnici, J. (2008). *Self-regulation in cyberspace*. The Hague: T.M.C. Asser Press.

Newsroom Editor. (2013, November 2). Principles for a better self- and co-regulation and establishment of a community of practice. Retrieved from http://ec.europa.eu/digital-agenda/en/news/principles-better-self-and-co-regulation-and-establishment-community-practice.

O'Neill, B. (2014). *First report on the implementation of the ICT principles*. Retrieved from http://www.ictcoalition.eu/gallery/75/ICT_REPORT.pdf.

O'Neill, B., & Staksrud, E. (2012). Policy implications and recommendations: Now what? In S. Livingstone, L. Haddon & A. Görzig, *Children, risk and safety on the Internet: Research and policy challenges in comparative perspective* (pp. 339–354). Bristol: The Policy Press.

Porter, M., & Kramer, M. (2006, December). Strategy and society: The link between competitive advantage and corporate social responsibility. *Harvard Business Review*. Retrieved from https://hbr.org/2006/12/strategy-and-society-the-link-between-competitive-advantage-and-corporate-social-responsibility.

Price, M., & Verhulst, S. (2000). In search of the self: Charting the course of self-regulation on the Internet in a global environment. In C. Marsden, *Regulating the global information society* (pp. 57–78). London: Routledge.

Report of mid-term review meeting of the CEO coalition to make the Internet a better place for kids. (2012). Retrieved from http://www.consumersforum.it/files/report_11_july.pdf.

Ruggie, J. (2008). *Promotion and protection of all human rights, civil, political, economic, social and cultural rights, including the right to development. Protect, respect and remedy: A Framework for business and human rights*. Retrieved from http://www.reports-and-materials.org/Ruggie-report-7-Apr-2008.pdf?3e3ea140.

Ságvári, B., & Máder, M. (2013). Industry. Towards the socially responsible Internet. Industry CSR practices across Europe. In B. O'Neill, E. Staksrud & S. McLaughlin, *Towards a better Internet for children? Policy pillars, players and paradoxes* (pp. 153–172). Gothenborg, Sweden: Nordicom.

Shift, & The Institute for Human Rights and Business. (2013). *ICT sector guide on implementing the UN guiding principles on business and human rights*. Retrieved from http://bookshop.europa.eu/en/ict-sector-guide-on-implementing-the-un-guiding-principles-on-business-and-human-rights-pbNB0413165/.

Staksrud, E., & Lobe, B. (2010). *Evaluation of the implementation of the Safer Social Networking Principles for the EU, Part 1: General report*. Retrieved from https://www.duo.uio.no/bitstream/handle/10852/27216/Safer-Social-Networking-part1.pdf?sequence=2.

Unicef .(2013). Children's rights and business principles, Retrieved from http://www.unglobalcompact.org/docs/issues_doc/human_rights/CRBP/Childrens_Rights_and_Business_Principles.pdf.

United Nations. (2011). *Guiding principles on business and human rights. Implementing the United Nations 'Protect, respect and remedy' framework*. Retrieved from http://www.ohchr.org/Documents/Publications/GuidingPrinciplesBusinessHR_EN.pdf.

United Nations Children's Fund. (2013). *Children's rights and business principles*. Retrieved from http://www.unglobalcompact.org/docs/issues_doc/human_rights/CRBP/Childrens_Rights_and_Business_Principles.pdf.

United Nations Committee on the Rights of the Child. (2013). *General comment No. 16 (2013) on State obligations regarding the impact of the business sector on children's rights*. Retrieved from http://tbinternet.ohchr.org/_layouts/treatybodyexternal/Download.aspx?symbolno=CRC%2fC%2fGC%2f16&Lang=en.

Wauters, E., Donoso, V., Lievens, E., & Valcke, P. (2014). D1.2.5: Re-designing & re-modeling social network terms, policies, community guidelines and charters: Towards a user-centric approach. Retrieved from http://emsoc.be/wp-content/uploads/2014/04/D-1.2.5_Re-designing-and-re-modeling-Social-Network-terms-policies-community-guidelines-and-charters_Towards-a-user-centric-approach.pdf.

6 Media Policy and Regulation in Times of Crisis

Corinna Wenzel, Stefan Gadringer and Josef Trappel

Introduction

Both private commercial media companies and public service media organisations are exposed to structural and technological transformations and the implications of the economic recession. Audience fragmentation and decreasing advertising revenues lead to the erosion of traditional business models. Recent studies show that aspects of media performance, such as quality and diversity, are under threat (Fenton, 2010; Meier, 2011b; Meier, 2012). Policy reactions to these undesired effects of the crisis include not only establishing public service institutions or granting subsidies but also relying on forms of self-regulation or governance – allowing the industries to find their own solutions. Yet another policy reaction is to let unregulated markets prevail. Within recent media policy research and practice, governance concepts (self- or co-regulation) have been high on the agenda to solve problems concerning media accountability and performance (Donges, 2007; Kleinsteuber, 2011; McQuail, 2003; Meier, 2011a; Rossi & Meier, 2012). These concepts focus on the participation of private, public and civil society stakeholders within media policy processes. Governance concepts have been not only praised for being more flexible, faster and more transparent but also criticised for lacking democratic legitimation (Rossi & Meier, 2012) and being toothless and thus ineffective (Freedman, 2008; Iosifidis, 2011). Moreover, lack of monitoring and sanctioning are additional weaknesses of self- and co-regulation, while it has been argued that inclusion of civil society in the media policy process serves to legitimise neo-liberal media policy (Karppinen & Moe, 2013).

Regarding these current weaknesses of media performance (see Fenton 2010; Meier, Bonfadelli, & Trappel, 2012), the question arises whether concepts of self- and co-regulation are still appropriate for addressing this problem or if the state should re-regulate the media sector (Braithwaite, 2008). Therefore, the main research questions in this chapter are:

- How has media policy makers' commitment to enforce self-, co-, or state-regulation changed during times of crisis?
- Which interests (private-commercial or civil society) are favoured by establishing self-regulatory regimes in the media field?
- What are the reasons for the heavy reliance on media self-regulation?

We assume that media policy pursues the goal of alleviating the current neo-liberal media order, which includes favouring private-commercial industries and leaving them to negotiate important issues among themselves. The research questions have been addressed by conducting a qualitative document analysis focusing on legal and judicial actions in media policy, as well as semi-structured interviews with media policy makers and stakeholders in five countries (Austria, Canada, Germany, Switzerland and the United Kingdom [UK]).

The purpose of this chapter is *not* to assess the effectiveness or efficiency of self-regulation or its contribution to democratic goals. The potential advantages and disadvantages of any forms of governance, instead, are deducted from previous assessments and studies in the field. The goal is to assess types and forms of regulatory mechanisms, their realisation and occurrence as well as their initialisation (e.g., whether initiated by the state or by media organisations), and not to evaluate benefits or threats.

The Current Media Environment

Related scientific literature suggests that the media are in a current structural 'crisis' or at least experiencing a form of 'structural change'. The changes specifically refer to technologies (digitalisation) (Schneider, 2012), media usage and processes of socialisation (fragmentation) (Seufert, 2012) which are leading to the erosion of business models in the daily newspaper sector (Jarren, 2012) and other 'core media' (Meier, 2012, p. 33). Other authors suggest that the financial crisis has affected advertising revenues and enforced the 'Financialization' of media organisations (Winseck, 2010, p. 366). Therefore, there is no doubt that media business models and their funding principles are changing. However, it seems important to keep in mind that these developments have severe implications for media performance such as quality, diversity and accountability (Altmeppen, 2012). Structural and financial crises have reduced the resources and investments of the media industries, adversely affecting content quality (Fenton, 2010). Liberalisation and market concentration have led to commercialisation, lower editorial quality and lack of professionalism (Altmeppen, 2012; McChesney, 2013; Meier, 2012; Ruhrmann & Göbbel, 2007). However, some media organisations have managed to cope with these developments and continue to deliver services to their respective publics that support democracy (Freedman, 2014, p. 18). The structural changes of the media therefore refer to funding, legitimacy, but also media performance, either of the entire media industry or a single media organisation. Whereas some scholars think that these changes still are not severe enough for initiating media policy change and innovations (Meier, 2012), others believe that the 'media crisis' requires immediate media policy actions (Trappel, 2012).

However, in the end it seems specifically important to analyse these changes with regard to their specific circumstances, their political and cultural contexts, actors, states and industries and reflect these differences as part of the analysis.

Media Governance: Definitions and Assessments

From a political-economic perspective, the democratic significance of media policy values, the media policy process and the influence of stakeholders need to be addressed. Media policy has been dominated by neo-liberal values over recent decades (Freedman, 2008; Iosifidis, 2011). Neo-liberalism can be understood in a strict sense as an economic agenda, or, in a wider sense, as a political or even cultural programme (Chomsky, 1998). According to Chomsky, neo-liberalism has achieved worldwide hegemony since the governments of Ronald Reagan (U.S.) and Margaret Thatcher (UK). Consequently, large corporations have ruled not only the economy but also the policy process. Moreover, the free market does not lead to economically and socially fair distribution of welfare benefits. Instead, neo-liberal ideology has expanded to everyday life and gained cultural hegemony (Castells, Caraça & Cardoso, 2012, p. 13; Iosifidis, 2011, p. 70; McChesney, 2000, p. 6). Neo-liberal media policy heavily relies on market forces and favours private-commercial stakeholders. Media policy makers seek to maintain their power and gain votes and expertise. Strong and powerful networks of media lobby groups and corporations are able to deliver these resources; their knowledge about markets and media products is profound. Therefore, media lobby groups are able to frame politics positively in their reporting. However, they only do so in exchange for favourable regulation (which can be deregulation, but also more regulation to restrict market competitors, such as public service broadcasters) (see Freedman, 2008; Freedman, 2014; Marsh, 1998; McChesney, 2013; Niechoj, 2003; Stigler, 1971). One essential feature of this neo-liberal media policy paradigm is the importance of state-initiated self-regulation. In this case, governments refrain from active intervention, thereby leaving policy issues in the hands of industrial stakeholders and encourage them to solve these issues on their own.

Dimensions of Governance

Over the years, the governance concept has gained prominence in communication studies (Donges, 2007; Kleinsteuber, 2011). In its strict meaning, governance can be described as an institutional and geographic expansion of regulation (Meier, 2011a, p. 37). Puppis (2010, pp. 59–62) identifies a vertical and a horizontal extension of media regulation. Media governance is therefore not just self- and co-regulation, but also describes politics on a supranational level and leads to a renaissance of structures and institutions (Freedman, 2008, p. 14; Mayntz, 2005, p. 11; Schuppert, 2007, p. 35).

Freedman, contrary to our understanding, uses governance as an 'umbrella term':

> [It is the] sum of total mechanisms, both formal and informal, national and supranational, centralized and dispersed, that aim to organize media systems according to the resolution of media policy debates (2008, p. 14).

In turn, self-regulation describes a situation 'in which a group of persons or organisations perform a regulating function with regard to themselves and others, who accept their authority' (Donges, 2002, p. 96). In most cases, self-regulation is realised through the monitoring and enforcement of an external, non-state organisation (Baldwin & Cave, 1999, p. 39). Other than 'government', 'governance' acknowledges the state, market and society as complementary actors (Benz, 2004, p. 126). It regards state actions as embedded in geographic and content-wise interdependent relations; Schuppert (2007, p. 28) calls the 'blurring borderlines between sectors' and the organisational 'halfway houses' between public and private sectors the 'hybridisation of governance'. McQuail (2003, p. 98) identifies different types of governance. Whereas *internal governance* refers to self- or co-regulation of a single organisation (for example, work routines in newsrooms), *external governance* means self- or co-regulation of the whole industry. Whereas informal regulation does not consist of written rules and happens in a rather ad hoc fashion, formal governance comprises written structures (such as an industry code). Apart from these forms of industry self-regulation, Puppis (2010, p. 60) describes 'self-organization' as the 'process of rule-setting, rule-enforcement and sanctioning of non-compliance by a private organization within the branch'. Self-organization therefore means self-regulation of one, single organisation. Co-regulation or 'state-regulated self-regulation' accepts state intervention only if self-regulation is not working. According to Palzer (2003, p. 33), the difference between co-regulation and self-regulation is the voluntariness of the latter. Whereas self-regulation is industry-initiated, co-regulation is a product of intentional state intervention.

Governance represents a solution to the classic dilemma of media policy, the contradiction between state intervention and media freedom (Puppis, 2007, p. 332). However, there are several downsides of self-regulation: the lack of efficiency, democratic legitimacy and transparency, as well as the domination of private interests (Rossi & Meier, 2012, pp. 385–387). Moreover, self- and co-regulation merely concern the industries, whereas civil society is rarely included (Rossi & Meier, 2012, pp. 385–388).[1] Voluntary or state-initiated self-regulation and self-organisation enforce media policy goals successfully only under specific circumstances (Wenzel, 2012). Private-commercial and public service media organisations use governance to 'escape' state regulation, whereas civil society is neglected (Campbell, 1999; Hemels, 2005; Rossi & Meier, 2012, p. 383; Russ-Mohl, 1992).

Karppinen and Moe (2013, p. 8) argue that governance is ideologically abused in many cases to favour private industry interests, not reflecting its downsides, such as the lack of legitimacy, transparency and accountability. Neo-liberal approaches use the concept for promoting the distinction between 'good governance' and 'bad government', again not reflecting its limited potential to provide remedies against threats to democratic media performance. Moreover, self-regulation is most prominent in states where a culture of journalistic professionalism already exists (Eberwein, Leppik-Bork, & Lönnendonker, 2013). Therefore, state regulation still seems to be central when it comes to ensuring democratic media performance (Iosifidis, 2011, p. 107).

However, one should note the distinction between state-initiated regulation, co-regulation and industry-initiated governance (self-regulation). Co-regulation does not necessarily go along with initiatives of the state, but can also be self-regulation that was later recognized by the state. Because we focus on media policy actions during times of media crisis, our main research question is whether delegated regulatory responsibilities of state actors to media industries, organisations or markets gain importance during times of media crisis. What is relevant to us is government-initiated self-regulation, in terms of an active, intentional delegation of power from political to industry actors. What counts is the initiative to establish self-regulation. Therefore, government-initiated self-regulation is broadly defined, describing any case where the state empowers industry actors, such as institutions (e.g., press or advertising councils), single organisations ('self-organisation') or just market forces to regulate themselves.

Method

In order to analyse government-initiated self-regulation, we conducted a qualitative analysis of media policy documents published from 1999 to 2012 in five countries (Austria, Canada, Germany, Switzerland and the UK). In each country, we selected media policy documents that were capable of breaking with media policy traditions and guiding the entire media system towards a new direction (Brantner, Dohle, Haas & Vowe, 2013, p. 222). The chosen documents have either established new media policy actors, altered power relations (Vowe, Opitz, & Dohle, 2008, p. 161), sorted conflicts or competitions, answered crucial media policy questions or have had a fundamental rather than an incremental character. The selection was not tied to a certain quality and consisted of documents ranging from constitutional laws to informal or non-binding reports. The research was conducted by using databases like IRIS MERLIN, as well as the data archives of ministries or regulation authorities. In total, we selected 102 policy documents, among them 39 laws and treaties, 16 additional notes, 36 orders and regulations, 10 reports and statements as well as 3 judicial documents. However, it must be borne in mind that the characteristics and significance of the document types (such as laws or regulations) differ significantly from nation to nation. Whereas, for example, media policy in Canada mainly consists of actions by the central regulatory authority (the Canadian Radio-television and Telecommunications Commission), most of the policy documents in Germany are treaties drawn up by the regional *Bundesländer*.

Table 6.1 Media Policy Documents

	Austria	Canada	Germany	Switzerland	UK	Total count
Laws and Treaties	10	0	13	10	6	39
Additional Notes on Laws and Treaties	0	0	16	0	0	16
Orders and Regulations	1	24	4	4	3	36
Reports and Statements	0	1	0	4	3	8
Judgements	3	0	0	0	0	3
Total Count	14	25	33	18	12	102

Source: [ADD].

Additionally, we conducted 28 semi-structured, face-to-face interviews with media policy makers and stakeholders (public, private-commercial and non-commercial service) to assess their goals, motives and reasons for their media policy actions.

Results

The qualitative analysis of the media policy documents showed that government-initiated self-regulation was prominent during times of economic crisis, specifically, in 2001, 2008, 2009 and 2010. Government-initiated self-regulation mainly concerned advertising regulation in public service broadcasting, accountability issues (participation of the industries in policy boards), content regulation issues (e.g., youth protection), trade agreements, local programming, accessibility rules for people with disabilities, inclusion of independent producers and monitoring issues (soft dispute settlement instead of hard regulatory sanctions).

Canada

In Canada, government-initiated self-regulation has been constantly present during the 1999–2012 period; however, it has taken different forms, compared to the other countries. In most cases, however, it did not refer to institutionalised forms of governance. The *Ethnic Broadcasting Policy* in 1999 (Canadian Radio-television and Telecommunications Commission

[CRTC] (1999) indicated an early enforcement of self-regulation, in which co-regulatory rules were implemented with regard to minority programmes, together with advisory councils within media organisations (see paras. 58, 66).

> In Public Notice 1997–25, the Commission determined that it would no longer require cable companies to provide a community channel for local expression. It considered that cable companies have an incentive to provide these services without regulatory intervention given that they operate in an increasingly competitive environment (CRTC, 1999, para. 58).

Moreover, an advisory board was established to stimulate self-regulation in response to comments and demands of third parties. This board's tasks were to monitor the reflection of multicultural content, help ethnic communities become more involved in broadcasting and ensure that ethnic broadcasters would provide programming in an appropriate number of languages (CRTC 1999, para. 66). However, the decision whether or not to include minority members in these advisory councils was left to the organisations: 'The Commission encourages broadcasters who have not already done so to establish advisory councils incorporating representatives of the ethnic communities in their service areas' (CRTC, 1999, para. 67). The CRTC also established a broadcast standards council for the industry within the *Policy Framework for Community Media* 2002:

> The Commission encourages low-power radio licensees to become members of the Canadian Broadcast Standards Council, and expects such licensees to adhere to the following industry codes: The CAB's *Sex-role portrayal code for television and radio programming* [...], [and] the CAB's *Broadcast code for advertising to children* [...] (CRTC, 2002, para. 154).

The *Policy Framework for Broadcasting Distribution Undertakings* (CRTC, 2008a) initiated self-regulatory regimes for dispute settling and programming rights, which should be left to industry negotiations (by establishing a so-called 'Commission staff-assisted mediation' and the mechanism of 'final offer arbitration'). Thereby, the Commission, as an arbitrator, should not impose a solution other than that put forward by one of the parties: 'As such, the result should lead each party to suggest a moderate position for fear that an extreme position would lead to that of the other side being selected by the arbitrator' (CRTC, 2008a, para. 163–164). Further co-regulation was implemented by the Regulatory Policy *Diversity of Voices*, 2008, which turned over trade agreements with independent producers to the commercial industries:

> The Commission reiterates the expectation [...] that licensees provide draft or signed terms of trade agreements with independent

producers as part of their upcoming licence renewal applications. If, at licence renewal time, this expectation has not been fulfilled, the Commission may choose to arbitrate the negotiations to develop terms of trade agreements with independent producers (CRTC, 2008b, para. 149, 150).

The *Policy determinations to the local programming improvement fund* 2009 (CRTC, 2009) promoted industry-negotiated trade agreements, as well as quotas for regional programmes (the definition of the latter was left to the industries). 'It is the Commission's view that ... the establishment of appropriate terms of trade agreements is best directly negotiated by the parties involved without Commission intervention by way of mediation or otherwise' (CRTC, 2009, para. 83). Moreover, in 2010, *Reporting Requirements* in new media were filed (Broadcasting Regulatory Policy CRTC, 2010), leaving the definition of revenues and expenditures to the industries. For this purpose, a working group, with the participation of the industries, was established: 'Accordingly, the Commission determines that New Media Broadcasting Undertakings (NMBUs) that are affiliates of licensed broadcasting undertakings will be required to report to the Commission their revenues and expenditures' (CRTC, 2010).

In addition to the findings of the document analysis, the results of the interviews confirmed that Canadian media policy makers trust self-regulation during media crisis. State-initiated self-regulation in Canada means trusting market mechanisms, without establishing institutions responsible for setting rules and monitoring compliance. A representative of the regulatory authority admitted that the primary goal was to allow the companies to react and become more efficient. Instead of establishing some kind of code or rules, media policy makers trusted market forces. The *Community TV Policy* in 2010 was forwarded as an example, which established a best-practice code of access. A member of the Canadian labour association stated that media policy would mainly be about monitoring an industry regulating itself. Most of the interviewees shared the opinion that the regulator would have to adapt itself to the market. A reason for the delegation of responsibilities seemed to be the lack of time and personal resources. Regulatory authorities furthermore rejected dealing with civil society complaints because it would take a lot of time and energy, as claimed by one representative of the Canadian community media association.

United Kingdom

In the UK, the willingness of media policy makers to delegate power to the industry was particularly evident in two cases. The first one was the Communications Act of 2003 (UK Parliament, 2003), which obliged the Office of Communications (Ofcom) to 'promote and facilitate the development and use of effective forms of self-regulation' (Part 1, Art. 3). The addressed goals were more competition, 'light touch' regulation, reliance on the market, greater flexibility and more innovation (Doyle & Vick, 2005, p. 77).

> The intention is to move away from a reliance on detailed and prescriptive licence requirements and a so-called culture of 'box ticking' towards a more transparent and liberal regime in which 'co- and self-regulation' are to play a more important role.
> (Doyle & Vick, 2005, p. 79)

The core of the reform was a three-tier regulatory structure, which indicated more quality and diversity obligations for the public service broadcasters (Independent Television – ITV, Channel 4 and Channel 5), specifically in the areas of education or minority programmes, while the broadcasters without such obligations were merely left out of the regulations. However, the public service broadcasters should implement these obligations by themselves, <u>because</u> they were assigned to be difficult to quantify. Elements of this kind of self-regulation were detailed programme statements and reports, as well as regular evaluations (Doyle & Vick, 2005, p. 81).

> The Act is fundamentally deregulatory in nature and that Ofcom must further reduce regulatory burdens whenever a communications market seems sufficiently strong that competition would thrive without them; and that as markets become more competitive, Ofcom should use industry-specific powers less and general competition powers more.
> (Doyle & Vick, 2005, p. 87)

Ofcom kept its regulatory policy according to the Act, as shown in the guidelines on self- and co-regulation from 2004 (Office of Communications, 2004) and a statement from 2008:

> Since Ofcom's inception, our preference has been to work in partnership with stakeholders to develop regulation. We recognise that self- and co-regulation can, in the right circumstances, provide an effective means to address citizens' and consumers' interests, in line with our statutory duties and obligations. The fast moving and technologically complex nature of the communications markets can also, under some circumstances, make statutory regulation insufficiently flexible (Office of Communications, 2008).

Ofcom had conducted a consultation where it proposed that self-regulation was most efficient when it would be implemented 'aligned with those [interests] of the public'. It developed five steps to assess the industry's incentives to deliver effective self- or co-regulation and proposed a set of criteria for best practice in self-regulation. Most of the stakeholders supported those proposals. The consultation resulted in the establishment of criteria for effective self-regulation, which referred to the industry acting collectively in solving issues; the existence of clear objectives; the matching of industry solutions with the legitimate needs of citizens and consumers, 'public awareness transparency, significant industry participation, adequate resources, clarity of processes, ability to enforce codes, audits of performance, the involvement of independent members, regular review of objectives, and non-collusive behaviour' (Office of Communications, 2008).

The second case where media policy relied heavily on self-regulation involved its reactions to the *Leveson Inquiry* in 2011 (UK Government, 2013a), set up by Prime Minister David Cameron to examine work routines and failures of the press, specifically in response to the phone-hacking scandal of *News of the World*. As a result, Lord Justice Leveson made recommendations on the future of press regulation ('Press "need to act"', 2012), which included a law for the press, additional self-regulation, independence of serving editors, government and business, and a clear separation between the press and politicians ('Leveson report', 2012). The report recommended an independent regulatory body for the press, which 'should take an active role in promoting high standards, including having the power to investigate serious breaches and sanction newspapers' ('Leveson report', 2012). The government's legal duty to protect press freedom should be established, backed by an arbitration system. Furthermore, it proposed the establishment of a whistle-blowing hotline for journalists ('Leveson report', 2012). The report specifically criticised the work of the current self-regulatory body, the Press Complaints Commission (PCC).

However, the *Leveson Inquiry* (Leveson, 2012a) resulted in political authorities promoting more self-regulation of the media. Media policy did not enforce the inquiry's recommendations; instead, it recommended a new self-regulator that had to seek recognition by the ministries. Although Prime Minister Cameron had initially promised to implement the recommendations, he stated that a law for press regulation was not his favourite solution. He basically urged the press to improve its own self-regulatory system: 'That means million-pound fines, proper investigation of complaints, prominent apologies' ('Press "need to act" after Leveson', 2012). The report also proposed a second phase of examination: 'Looking at the extent of unlawful or improper conduct within *News International* and other media organisations, and how the police investigated allegations'. To date, this second phase has not yet been started. Lord Justice Leveson (2012b) released a statement questioning what would be gained from issuing Part 2 of the report, given the 'enormous cost'. the fact that the materials would be years out of date by then and that it could take longer than the first inquiry. In 2013, the government proposed a regulation deal that should contain a Royal Charter for the press. In turn, the newspapers proposed their own rival version of a Royal Charter, which the government turned down. Then the newspapers urged a judicial review, which was rejected (O'Carroll, 2014). Instead, the Privy Council officially approved the government version in October 2013

(Conlan, 2013; Mason, 2013). The Royal Charter on Self-regulation of the Press (UK Government, 2013a) set up 'a body corporate known as the Recognition Panel' (Article 1), assigned to recognise new self-regulatory bodies. The organisation and management of the panel were left to the panel itself: 'the Board shall determine and regulate its own procedures for conducting its business and discharging its functions under this Charter' (Article 6.1). An amendment of the charter would need an agreement between the parliament and the panel:

> Politicians cannot amend the Charter without the unanimous agreement of the Board of the Recognition Panel. This is in addition to the requirement that an amendment may only be made if approved by both Houses of Parliament with at least a two-thirds majority in both Houses. (UK Government, 2013a, 2013b, Article 9).

The Recognition Panel started its work on 3 November 2014 (Greenslade, 2014b). In September 2014, the PCC was closed (Conlan, 2014c). In its place, two new regulatory bodies were created, the Independent Press Standards Organisation (IPSO) and The Impress Project (Impress). Many newspaper groups have already signed up with IPSO, although so far, *The Guardian*, *The Independent* and the *Financial Times* have not yet done so. However, none of these new regulators has sought recognition under the Royal Charter yet (O'Carroll, 2014). As of January 2015, a new investigation of the House of Lords Communications Committee has been set up to examine the current situation of press self-regulation. The goal is to find out 'if the public knows what to do if they want to complain about the press and establish what the system of press regulation is in the UK' (O'Carroll, 2014). These developments, which have emerged from the *Leveson Inquiry*, show that the press industry is still not unanimous about its own self-regulation and to a certain extent, confirm the risky nature of the government's decision to leave regulation up to the industry. The government's solution in response to the *Leveson Inquiry* was clearly a co-regulatory regime, which on the one hand, included a state authority's recognition of the self-regulatory bodies. On the other hand, organisation and management, even by the Recognition Panel, remain in the hands of its board members.

The willingness to delegate powers to the industries was also confirmed in the interviews, where media policy makers admitted trying to avoid more state regulation and instead, defending the continuance of self-regulation where appropriate. Media policy would wait for the appropriate time to intervene. However, there was also a certain kind of awareness that self-regulation would bear some risks. A member of the regulatory body, Ofcom, acknowledged the suitability of self-regulation when the incentives of the industry and public purposes would be totally aligned (e.g., preventing child abuse on the Internet). However, he admitted that realistically, total alignment between the state and the industry would be quite rare. The regulator's representative confirmed the weakness of self-regulation if public policy differed from industry incentives. Similar problems would result from co-regulation. Therefore, self-regulation would depend heavily on each party's willingness to cooperate – a rare characteristic, as one representative admitted. According to the representatives, the only alternative would be statutory regulation.

Germany

In Germany, state-initiated self-regulation has gained importance over the last decade as well; however, it was implemented in institutionalised forms. Moreover, the analysis of these changes did not confirm a clear relationship to the media crisis. The starting point was 2003, when the commission for protection of young adults (Kommission für Jugendmedienschutz [KJM]) recognised the voluntary self-control body, *Freiwillige Selbstkontrolle Fernsehen* (FSF) (KJM, 2003). The latter is a non-profit organisation of private-commercial broadcasters ('Geschichte der FSF', 2014) that publishes information, hosts events and promotes awareness and reflections about the duties and tasks of broadcasting. By 2003, it was assigned to monitor and judge the programmes of the broadcasters as an officially recognised, self-regulatory body. The FSF has a *Kuratorium*, a board that selects and assigns the examiners who have to be independent from the broadcasters. For a long time, the respective legal roles of the German *Landesmedienanstalten* (federal state regulatory authority) and the FSF were not clear. The *Landesmedienanstalten* were obliged to take into account the FSF reports in their decisions. However, they were free to decide on regulatory sanctions on their own. The FSF reports required a compulsory reaction of the media organisation only when the *Landesmedienanstalten* approved them. The reform of the youth protection laws in 2003 tried to solve this problem; a system of 'regulated self-regulation' was introduced, which should have summarized several youth protection rules in the *Jugendschutzgesetz* (JuSchG) for offline media and the *Jugendmedienschutz-Staatsvertrag* (JMStV) for online media. A further goal was to not only align the youth protection rules for TV and the Internet (see 'Geschichte der FSF', 2014), but also to strengthen the self-regulatory body. The JMStV 2003 recognised and extended the FSF responsibilities to *Telemedien*.[2] The 14th *Rundfunkänderungsstaatsvertrag* (RFÄndStV – German legal framework for electronic media) 2010 went beyond this scope and implemented new self-regulatory rules concerning child and youth protection, while the FSF was to monitor the classification of the programmes (§ 5 (2), § 19 (4) RFÄndStV). In 2012, the KJM further extended the responsibilities of the voluntary self-control in broadcasting (FSF) (Medienanstalten, 2012). Specifically, the FSF was recognised officially as a self-regulatory body for TV-like content in new media services (*Telemedien*), concerning movies, TV series or documentaries normally aired on TV, but also available on the Internet.

Similar to the other countries, the interviews in Germany showed media policy's positive judgement on self-regulation. Media policy makers were convinced that it would be the most important instrument of media policy during times of crisis. Although they did not confirm that the crisis of media funding and performance was the reason for these changes, they nevertheless admitted that self-regulation of the industries would be the best solution. Their view was that industry participants would know best where their problems were, if there were any at all. The reason for this positive stance might be resignation and insecurity when it came to the increasing complexity of media markets. However, media policy makers in Germany tried to maintain their position as decision makers. The interviewees confirmed that no compliance would be possible in the absence of an institution that would intervene in case of an emergency. Pure self-regulation would always lead to competition, which in turn would cause monopolies. Thus, self-regulation would need legal backing, as stated by a representative of the regulation authority. Self-regulation is used to include industries and make cooperation possible. The specific goal is to build alliances against major international players such as Google or Facebook. This openness of politicians in terms of self-regulation was recognised by the industry stakeholders as well, as a representative of the private-commercial sector admitted.

Austria

In Austria, state-initiated self-regulation took place mainly in connection with the autonomy of the public service broadcaster *Österreichischer Rundfunk* (ORF) and its relationship to the press association. In 2010, the Press Publishers' Association *Verband Österreichischer Zeitungen* (VÖZ) and the ORF itself were assigned to negotiate on the new rules for online activities of the public ORF. Their proposed agreement and the related actions were implemented without any modifications. These negotiations were not kept secret; instead, media policy actively promoted them. The main point of the negotiations was the tightening of rules for the ORF's online advertising. The ORF's intention was to maintain the two per cent limit[3], whereas the VÖZ wanted to tighten it further. The ORF proposed a deal in April 2010, which would have obliged the ORF to focus on posting images and videos on the Internet, while text messages would only be allowed when they referred to a TV or radio programme ('Für Onlinedeal', 2010). This would have secured the existence of the radio programme oe3.at, while the ORF would have given up ownership of the online portal futurezone.orf.at. Another key point of the negotiations was the prohibition of regional advertising in the ORF's TV and national radio programmes. The VÖZ insisted on maintaining this prohibition; if it was lifted, the VÖZ threatened to challenge the licence fee funding scheme altogether. In the end, media policy implemented the proposals of the stakeholders ('ORF-Gesetz', 2010): the ORF maintained the two per cent online advertising limit and the prohibition of regional advertising and sold the online portal futurezone.orf.at ('ORF-Direktor Grasl', 2010; Parlamentskorrespondenz, 2010; Baumgartner, 2010). On the other hand, media policy agreed on the *Gebührenrefundierung* (licence fee restitution).

Furthermore, the press council was re-introduced in 2010, which was initiated by the government and the financial market authority (see also Gottwald, 2006); the latter criticised the reporting of the press during the financial crisis. It had not been active since 2002 as a consequence of a dispute with the newspaper *Kronen Zeitung* (Warzilek, 2013).

The interviews did not confirm a trend in the direction of state-initiated self-regulation due to the crisis. However, it was mentioned that the 'importance of media policy as such' would decrease in times of crisis. A representative of the community media organisation added that self-regulation was increasing because politicians would appreciate delegating responsibilities. In contrast, the other interviewees noted the decrease in self-regulation and autonomy of public service broadcasting in Austria, specifically with the enactment of ORF Law 2010. Until then, the *Stiftungsrat* (control board) was obliged to approve licence fees. Now it is no longer the sole decision maker; the *KommAustria* (regulation authority) has to issue the approval. Otherwise, the board has to deal with the issue again. Moreover, the ORF is not allowed to decide on the approval of public value tests, mentioned as another evidence for its declining self-regulatory capacities.

Switzerland

The most prominent case of state-initiated self-regulation in Switzerland was the report of the *Bundesrat* (Swiss Federal Council) in response to the parliamentary proposition of left-wing parliament member (MP) Hans-Jürg Fehr (Social Democrat) (Schweizerische Eidgenossenschaft, 2011). It indicated the government's commitment to promoting more self-regulation of the press in order to manage the ongoing structural changes. Hans-Jürg Fehr and several other MPs submitted a *Postulat* (parliamentary motion [Switzerland]) in June 2009, requesting the government to publish a report on press diversity being allegedly threatened by market monopolies. In its response, the government referred to constitutional constraints for regulating the press but commissioned several scientific studies on the situation (see Kamber & Imhof, 2011; Keel, Wyss, Stoffel & Saner, 2011; Kraldorfer, Custer & Künzler, 2010; Meier, 2011a; von Rimscha & Russi, 2010). These studies provided empirical evidence for the negative implications of the increasing media concentration on quality and diversity of press content.

However, in its final report in 2011, the government proposed that the industry should solve the problem itself (in other words more self-regulation of the press). In a sense, this was an 'active non-intervention' by the government. The industry itself was to find ways to cope with structural changes, including the search for new business models for online content, improvement of journalistic working conditions and safeguarding online and offline qualitative content. Furthermore, the government announced that it would monitor developments and industry activities and publish a report about this within four years (Eidgenössisches Departement für Umwelt, Verkehr, Energie und Kommunikation[4] [UVEK], 2011, p. ii).

One of the studies' recommendations was the amendment or replacement of the indirect press subsidies scheme, which consisted of lower fees for postal services and a reduced VAT. Nonetheless, the government insisted on maintaining the indirect subsidy model, because it remained unconvinced of the effectiveness of the proposed new subsidy scheme in order to improve training and education of journalists.

The interviews showed that in most cases, self-regulation in Switzerland did not refer to institutionalised industry rules but (similar to the Canadian situation) to reliance on market mechanisms (which media policy confirmed by laws, regulations and reports). One Swiss media policy maker stated that both self-regulation and state regulation were declining and that the few regulatory measures had almost disappeared. Institutionalised participation in decision-making processes within the media organisations would decrease as well. However, he also admitted being unaware of any efforts within the industry that could replace or avoid state regulation. In this sense, *self-regulation* disappeared without new state regulation being implemented. He described the situation as a laissez-faire approach, which was a concession to economic pressures.

The Rising Significance of State-Initiated Self-Regulation

The results of this study and previous findings in media policy research support the conclusion that media policy is characterised by strong interrelations between policy makers and media organisations is appropriate (see also Blumler and Gurevitch, 1995, p. 12; Ciaglia, 2013, p. 4; Schulz, 2004, p. 88). These circumstances force media organisations to comply with government rules, whereas media organisations deliver audiences to political actors, set the political agenda and increase trust in politics and its reliability. Media organisations contribute to the timing of political events and situations of crisis:

> [...] to which politicians are obliged to react, requiring comment on issues that media personnel have emphasized as important, injecting new personalities into the political dialogue (such as television interviewers) and stimulating the growth of new communication agencies (such as public relation firms, opinion-poll agencies, and political advertising and campaign management specialists).
> (Blumler & Gurevitch, 1995, p. 13)

These facts imply tensions between media reporting about media policy and their own interest in certain media policy outcomes (Freedman, 2008, p. 88).

If revenue creation and subsequently media performance are in trouble, media organisations will try to influence media policy outcomes in their own favour. They will use their power to deliver audiences and agenda-setters enforcing their interests.

Moreover, in a digital, convergent and complex media environment, media policy actors lose self-confidence regarding their actual competence and responsibility (see Crouch, 2009, p. 58). Specifically, they act like private enterprises, as they rely increasingly on consultancies and deny their ability to recognize problems which private firms cannot see. They believe in the expertise of private media organisations about media markets and performance. Crouch accordingly describes politicians as 'shopkeepers', whose only interest is 'to stay in business' (2009, p. 58).

Problems have to be solved faster in times of crisis, making self-regulation more attractive. Moreover, crises alter the lobbying capacities of interest groups:

> Once a bust produces a wave of regulatory reform, during the long period of expansion that mostly follows in developed economies, companies and investors again become more interested in wealth creation than in regulation that secures retention of wealth (and the legal use of it). Everyone is happy to make money without enquiring too deeply into how they are making it.
>
> (Braithwaite, 2008, p. 35)

Additionally, Ribstein states:

> In normal and boom times, new regulation would not help any distinct group enough to motivate the group to push for it. Regulated entities therefore have enough clout to defeat significant increases in liability or regulation. Those who might shift the balance, such as consumers or investors, do not see a need for new regulation while they are riding a rising market (2003, p. 79).

Consequently, powerful policy networks might seize the opportunity to achieve favourable policy outcomes. Because the industries have an interest in enforcing self-regulation in order to avoid state regulation, it seems likely that media policy actors will delegate power in times of crisis, given their lack of expertise and self-confidence.

Conclusion

However, the analysis has made clear that the connection between the media crisis and the enforcement of self-regulation by media policy actors does not pertain in any cases. Therefore, one conclusion is that media crisis might enforce the commitment of media policy to rely on self-regulation, but that in many cases several other factors, like media policy cultures and traditions play their role.

Overall, the qualitative document analysis has shown that during times of media crisis, media policy makers indeed tend to rely on self-regulation more heavily than in times of prosperity. However, there were other reasons for this development as well. Thus, significant differences between the states got evident. In Germany and Canada, for example, the crisis seemed not to be the main reason for media policymakers to rely on self-regulation. Instead, state-initiated self-regulation is generally promoted, rather independent from the crisis. For example, when self-regulation emerged as prominent in Germany with the establishment of the FSF in 2003, there still was no media crisis on the way. In Canada, trusting in the media market is a general tradition which creates kind of a path-dependency. In Austria, state-initiated self-regulation mainly referred to the public service broadcaster and its relationship to the Newspaper Association, whereas the private-commercial sector mainly still is left out of the self-regulatory regime. Furthermore, the rules for the public ORF as such have tightened, while there is less self-organization.

We have furthermore found evidence that reactions to the crisis focus rather widely on self-regulation of industries, markets but also on organisations. In Canada, the reliance on self-regulation has taken rather informal forms and became evident when media policy makers just relied on market forces, but also when soft forms of dispute settlements or industry negotiations about trade agreements were implemented. In Austria and Switzerland, government-initiated self-regulation mainly concerns the promotion of and support for stakeholder negotiations involving advertising regulations in public service broadcasting. In Germany, the issue took rather formalised forms by delegating responsibilities to the industry-organised KJM.

Furthermore, one important result of this study is that media policy makers are not really convinced about the effectiveness of interventions in media markets (as shown in the discussions about the direct press subsidies in Switzerland and the reactions to the *Leveson Report* in the UK). The interviews have made clear that crises at least help to strengthen the politicians' commitment to self-regulation. Therefore, media policy makers do not share the concerns about governance of media industries, specifically referring to their lack of effectiveness, transparency and democratic legitimacy (as described in Chapter 3, this volume). One reason for this might be the rapidly increasing complexity of the media sector. Media policy makers delegate responsibilities to industries because they recognise their own lack of expertise and have confidence in the quick solutions provided by industry self-regulation; they also suffer from the lack of time and personal resources in dealing with complex, media policy issues. Consequently, the relative importance of media policy as such is declining – which probably again is not a consequence of the crisis, but a development that gains importance if the media are in trouble.

As media organisations play a pivotal role in establishing a democratic public sphere, the growing popularity of state-initiated self-regulation in the media sector seems problematic – particularly when considering its deficits in democratic legitimacy and transparency, as well as the supremacy of vested industry interests.

Notes

1. The idea of *participatory media governance* places civil society at the heart of the media policy decision-making process (Rossi & Meier, 2012, p. 389), whereby the state stabilises the institutions necessary to ensure civil society participation, thus delegating decision-making powers to decentralised organisations.
2. This is a legal term for ICT-services in Germany.
3. ORF's upper limit for total online advertising is regulated by two per cent of total licence fee revenues.
4. Department for Environment, Infrastructure, Energy and Communication.

References

Altmeppen, K. (2012). Einseitige Tauschgeschäfte: Kriterien der Beschränkung journalistischer Autonomie durch kommerziellen Druck. In W.A. Meier, H. Bonfadelli & J. Trappel (Eds.), *Gehen in den Leuchttürmen die Lichter aus? Was aus den Schweizer Leitmedien wird* (pp. 37–53). Berlin: LIT-Verlag.
Baldwin, R., & Cave, M. (1999). *Understanding regulation*. Oxford: Oxford University Press.
Baumgartner, Bernhard. (2010). Einigung bei ORF-Gesetz: Behörde prüft, ORF spart. *Wiener Zeitung Online*. Retrieved January 20, 2015 from http://www.wienerzeitung.at/nachrichten/kultur/medien/43457_Einigung-bei-ORF-Gesetz-Behoerde-prueft-ORF-spart.html.
Benz, A. (2004). Multilevel governance – Governance in Mehrebenensystemen. In A. Benz (Ed.), *Governance – Regieren in komplexen Regelsystemen* (pp. 125–146). Wiesbaden, Germany: Springer VS.
Blumler, J.G., & Gurevitch, M. (1995). *The crisis of public communication*. London: Routledge.
Braithwaite, J. (2008). *Regulatory capitalism. How it works, ideas for making it work better*. Northampton, MA: Edward Elgar Publishing.
Brantner, C., Dohle, M., Haas, H., & Vowe, G. (2013). Medienpolitische Weichenstellungen in der Retro- und Prospektive. Ergebnisse von Delphi-Erhebungen in Österreich und Deutschland. In W. Seufert, & F. Sattelberger (Eds.), *Langfristiger Wandel von Medienstrukturen. Theorie, Methoden, Befunde* (pp. 221–239). Baden-Baden, Germany: Nomos.
Campbell, A (1999). Self-regulation and the media. *Federal Communications Law Journal, 51*(3), 712–772.
Canadian Radio-television and Communications Commission [CRTC]. (1999). Public Notice CRTC 1999–117. Retrieved January 30, 2015 from http://www.crtc.gc.ca/eng/archive/1999/pb99-117.htm.
CRTC. (2002). Broadcasting Public Notice CRTC 2002–61. Retrieved January 30, 2015 from http://www.crtc.gc.ca/eng/archive/2002/pb2002-61.htm.

CRTC. (2008a). Broadcasting Public Notice CRTC 2008–100. Retrieved January 30, 2015 from http://www.crtc.gc.ca/eng/archive/2008/pb2008-100.htm.
CRTC. (2008b). Broadcasting Public Notice CRTC 2008–4. Retrieved January 30, 2015 from http://www.crtc.gc.ca/eng/archive/2008/pb2008-4.htm.
CRTC. (2009). Broadcasting Regulatory Policy CRTC 2009–406. Retrieved January 20, 2015 from http://www.crtc.gc.ca/eng/archive/2009/2009-406.htm.
CRTC. (2010). Broadcasting Regulatory Policy CRTC 2010–582. Retrieved January 21, 2015 from http://www.crtc.gc.ca/eng/archive/2010/2010-582.htm.
Castells, M., Caraça, J., & Cardoso, G. (2012). The cultures of the economic crisis: Introduction. In M. Castells, J. Caraça, & G. Cardoso (Eds.), *Aftermath. The cultures of the economic crisis* (pp. 1–17). Oxford: Oxford University Press.
Chomsky, N. (1998). *Profit over people – Neoliberalism and global order*. New York: Seven Stories Press.
Ciaglia, A. (2013). Politics in the media and the media in politics: A comparative study of the relationship between the media and political systems in three European countries. *European Journal of Communication, 28*(5), 541–555.
Conlan, Tara. (2014c). Press regulators invited to give evidence to Lords committee. *The Guardian Online*. Retrieved January 20, 2015 from http://www.theguardian.com/media/2014/dec/15/press-regulators-evidence-lords-committee-ipso-impress-hacked-off.
Crouch, C. (2009). *Postdemokratie*. Frankfurt am Main, Germany: Suhrkamp.
Donders, K., & Van den Bulck, H. (2013). Flemish media policies in an age of globalization: A three case diachronic analysis [Presentation]. *ECREA Law and Policy Workshop*. Manchester, 26 October 2013.
Donges, P. (2002). *Rundfunkpolitik zwischen Wollen, Sollen und Können*. Wiesbaden, Germany: Westdeutscher Verlag.
Donges, P. (2007). Governance und Steuerung – zwei Theorieansätze im Vergleich. In P. Donges (Ed.), *Von der Medienpolitik zur Media Governance?* (pp. 67–85). Cologne, Germany: Herbert von Halem.
Doyle, G., & Vick, D. (2005). The Communications Act 2003: A new regulatory framework in the UK. *Convergence, 11*(3), 75–94.
Eberwein, T., Leppik-Bork, T., & Lönnendonker, J. (2013). Participatory media regulation: International perspectives on the structural deficits of media self-regulation and the potentials of web-based accountability processes. In M. Puppis, M. Künzler & O. Jarren (Eds.), *Media structures and media performance*. (Relation: No. N.F.4) (pp. 135–159). Vienna, Austria: Austrian Academy of Sciences Press.
Eidgenössisches Departement für Umwelt, Verkehr, Energie und Kommunikation (UVEK). (2011). Bundesrat setzt auf Selbstregulierung der Medien. Retrieved from http://www.uvek.admin.ch/dokumentation/00474/00492/index.html?lang=de&msg-id=39886.
Fenton (Ed.), *New media, old news. Journalism and democracy in the digital age* (pp. 3–17). London: Sage.
Fenton, N. (2010). *New Media, Old News. Journalism and Democracy in the Digital Age*. Los Angeles: SAGE.
Freedman, D. (2008). *The politics of media policy*. Cambridge, MA: Polity Press.
Freedman, D. (2014). *The contradictions of media power*. London: Bloomsbury.
Für Onlinedeal will ORF 'Futurezone' opfern. (2010, 11 March). *DerStandard*. Retrieved January 20, 2015 from http://derstandard.at/1267743745879/.

Geschichte der FSF – Ein Überblick. (2014). *Freiwillige Selbstkontrolle Fernsehen.* Retrieved December 17, 2014 from http://fsf.de/die-fsf/geschichte/.

Gottwald, F. (2006). *Medienselbstregulierung zwischen Ökonomie und Ethik: Erfolgsfaktoren für ein österreichisches Modell.* Vienna, Austria: LIT-Verlag.

Greenslade, Roy. (2014b). Royal charter's 'press recognition panel' recruits five board members. *The Guardian Online.* Retrieved January 20, 2015 from http://www.theguardian.com/media/greenslade/2014/oct/31/press-regulation-leveson-report.

Hemels, J. (2005). *Regulierung, Selbstregulierung und Medienkompetenz in den Niederlanden: die Entwicklung und die öffentliche Debatte.* Hilversum, Netherlands: Netherlands Institute for the Classification of Audio-Visual Media (NICAM).

Iosifidis, P. (2011). *Global media and communication policy: An international perspective.* London: Palgrave Macmillan.

Jarren, O. (2012). Kommentar: Medienkrise oder Tageszeitungsfinanzierungskrise? In O. Jarren, M. Künzler & M. Puppis (Eds.), *Medienwandel oder Medienkrise? Folgen für Medienstrukturen und ihre Erforschung* (pp. 165–175). Baden-Baden, Germany: Nomos.

Kamber, E., & Imhof, K. (2011). Medienkonzentration und Meinungsvielfalt. Informations- und Meinungsvielfalt in der Presse unter Bedingungen dominanter und crossmedial tätiger Medienunternehmen. Retrieved from http://www.bakom.admin.ch/dokumentation/gesetzgebung/00909/03627/index.html?lang=de.

Karppinen, K., & Moe, H. (2013). A critique of media governance. In M. Löblich & S. Pfaff-Rüdiger (Eds.), *Communication and media policy in the era of digitization and the Internet* (pp. 69–80). Baden-Baden, Germany: Nomos.

Keel, G., Wyss, V., Stoffel, A., & Saner, M. (2011). Auswirkungen des Internets auf die journalistische Praxis und berufskulturelle Normen. Retrieved from http://www.bakom.admin.ch/dokumentation/gesetzgebung/00909/03627/index.html?lang=de.

Kleinsteuber, H.J. (2011). *Media governance in Europa. Regulierung – Partizipation – Mitbestimmung.* Wiesbaden: Springer VS.

Kommission für Jugendmedienschutz (KJM). (2003). Übersicht. Retrieved January 20, 2015 from http://www.kjm-online.de/de/pub/aktuelles/pressemitteilungen/pressemitteilungen_2003/pm_022003.cfm.

Kradolfer, E., Custer, U., & Künzler, M. (2010). Die wirtschaftliche Entwicklungen der Medien in der Schweiz 2000–2010. Strukturen und Perspektiven. Retrieved from http://www.bakom.admin.ch/dokumentation/gesetzgebung/00909/03627/index.html?lang=de&download=NHzLpZeg7t,lnp6I0NTU04212Z6ln1a-cy4Zn4Z2qZpnO2Yuq2Z6gpJCDeoB,gGym162epYbg2c_JjKbNoKSn6A.

Leveson, Brian (Lord Justice). (2012a). An inquiry into the culture, practices and ethics of the press. Retrieved January 20, 2015 from https://www.gov.uk/government/publications/leveson-inquiry-report-into-the-culture-practices-and-ethics-of-the-press.

Leveson, Brian (Lord Justice). (2012b). Application of Rule 13 of the Inquiry Rules 2006. Retrieved from http://www.levesoninquiry.org.uk/wp-content/uploads/2011/11/Application-of-Rule-13-of-the-Inquiry-Rules-2006.pdf.

Leveson report: At a glance. (2012, 29 November). *British Broadcasting Corporation News Online.* Retrieved December 16, 2014 from http://www.bbc.com/news/uk-20543133.

Marsh, D. (1998). *Comparing policy networks.* Buckingham, PA: Open University Press.

Mason, Rowena. (2013). Leveson deal: MPs debate press regulation: As it happened. *The Telegraph Online*. Retrieved January 20, 2015 from http://www.telegraph.co.uk/news/uknews/leveson-inquiry/9937228/Leveson-deal-MPs-debate-press-regulation-as-it-happened.html.

Mayntz, R. (2005). Governance theory als fortentwickelte Steuerungstheorie? In G. F. Schuppert (Ed.), *Governance-Forschung. Vergewisserung über Stand und Entwicklungslinien* (pp. 11–20). Baden-Baden, Germany: Nomos.

McChesney, R.W. (2000). *Rich media, poor democracy*. New York: The New Press.

McChesney, R.W. (2013). *Digital disconnect: How capitalism is turning the Internet against democracy*. New York: The New Press.

McQuail, D. (2003). *Media accountability and freedom of publication*. New York: Oxford University Press.

Medienanstalten. (2012). Mehr Selbstkontrolle für fernsehähnliche Inhalte im Netz: KJM beschließt Erweiterung der FSF-Anerkennung. Retrieved January 20, 2015 from http://www.die-medienanstalten.de/presse/pressemitteilungen/kommission-fuer-jugendmedienschutz/detailansicht/article/kjm-pressemitteilung-042012-mehr-selbstkontrolle-fuer-fernsehaehnliche-inhalte-im-netz-kjm-beschl.html.

Meier, W.A. (2011a). Demokratie und media governance in Europa. In H.J. Kleinsteuber (Ed.), *Media governance in Europa: Regulierung – Partizipation – Mitbestimmung* (pp. 37–55). Wiesbaden, Germany: Springer VS.

Meier, W.A. (2011b). Pluralismus und Vielfalt in Regionalzeitungen. Auswirkungen von Medienkonzentration und Medienkrise auf die Lokalberichterstattung in ausgewählten Regionen in der Schweiz. Retrieved from http://www.bakom.admin.ch/dokumentation/gesetzgebung/00909/03627/index.html?lang=de&download=NHzLpZeg7t,lnp6I0NTU042l2Z6ln1acy4Zn4Z2qZpnO2Yuq2Z6gpJCDeoB,-f2ym162epYbg2c_JjKbNoKSn6A.

Meier, W.A. (2012). Die Medienkrise als Forschungsprogramm. In W.A. Meier, H. Bonfadelli & J. Trappel (Eds.), *Gehen in den Leuchttürmen die Lichter aus? Was aus den Schweizer Leitmedien wird* (pp. 11–42). Berlin, Germany: LIT-Verlag.

Meier, W.A., Bonfadelli, H., & Trappel, J. (Eds.). (2012). *Gehen in den Leuchttürmen die Lichter aus? Was aus den Schweizer Leitmedien wird*. Berlin, Germany: LIT-Verlag.

Niechoj, T. (2003). *Kollektive Akteure zwischen Wettbewerb und Steuerung: Effizienz und Effektivität von Verhandlungssystemen aus ökonomischer und politikwissenschaftlicher Sicht*. Marburg, Germany: Metropolis-Verlag.

O'Carroll, L. (2014). Press regulation: Newspapers lose court of appeal battle over rival royal charter. *The Guardian Online*. Retrieved January 20, 2015 from http://www.theguardian.com/media/2014/may/01/press-regulation-newspaper-court-appeal-royal-charter.

Office of Communications. (2004). Criteria for promoting effective co- and self-regulation. Retrieved from http://stakeholders.ofcom.org.uk/binaries/consultations/co-reg/statement/co_self_reg.pdf.

Office of Communications. (2008). Identifying appropriate regulatory solutions: Principles for analysing self- and co-regulation. Retrieved December 16, 2014 from http://stakeholders.ofcom.org.uk/consultations/coregulation/statement/.

ORF-Direktor Grasl: 'Schließen keine Maßnahme aus'. (2010, 19 April). *Diepresse.com*. Retrieved January 27, 2015 from http://diepresse.com/home/kultur/medien/559298/.

ORF-Gesetz: Einstimmiger Beschluss im Nationalrat möglich Offener Punkt Online-Werbung soll noch geklärt werden. (2010). *APA–OTS*. Retrieved January 20, 2015, from http://www.ots.at/presseaussendung/OTS_20100610_OTS0250/orf-gesetz-einstimmiger-beschluss-im-nationalrat-moeglich-offener-punkt-online-werbung-soll-noch-geklaert-werden.

Parlamentskorrespondenz. (2010). Lissabon-Begleitgesetz soll noch vor dem Sommer beschlossen werden. Retrieved January 20, 2015 from http://www.parlament.gv.at/PAKT/PR/JAHR_2010/PK0317/.

Palzer, C. (2003). Selbstkontrolle oder Selbstregulierung oder Co-Regulierung. In European Audiovisual Observatory (Ed.), *Co-Regulierung der Medien in Europa* (pp. 27–36). Strasbourg: Nomos.

Press 'need to act' after Leveson. (2012, 5 December). *British Broadcasting Corporation News Online*. Retrieved December 16, 2014 from http://www.bbc.com/news/uk-15686679.

Puppis, M. (2007). Media governance as a horizontal extension of media regulation: The importance of self- and co-regulation. *Communications*, 32(3), 330–336.

Puppis, M. (2010). Media governance: A new concept for the analysis of media policy and regulation. *Communication, Culture and Critique*, 3(2), 134–149.

Ribstein, L. (2003). Bubble laws. *Houston Law Review*, 40(1), 77–97.

Rossi, P., & Meier, W.A. (2012). Civil society and media governance: A participatory approach. In N. Just & M. Puppis (Eds.), *Trends in communication policy research. New theories, methods and subjects* (pp. 381–400). Bristol, UK: Intellect Books.

Ruhrmann, G., & Göbbel, R. (2007). Veränderung der Nachrichtenfaktoren und Auswirkungen auf die journalistische Praxis in Deutschland. Retrieved from http://www.netzwerkrecherche.de/files/nr-studie-nachrichtenfaktoren.pdf.

Russ-Mohl, S. (1992). *Regulating self-regulation: The neglected case of journalism policies: Securing quality in journalism and building media infrastructures on a European scale* (European University Institute [EUI] working papers in political and social sciences). San Domenico di Fiesole, Italy: European University Institute.

Schneider, N. (2012). Krise der Medien, Krise des Journalismus, Krise der Demokratie?. In O. Jarren, M. Künzler & M. Puppis (Eds.), *Medienwandel oder Medienkrise? Folgen für Medienstrukturen und ihre Erforschung* (pp. 25–37). Baden-Baden, Germany: Nomos.

Schulz, W. (2004). Reconstructing mediatization as an analytical concept. *European Journal of Communication*, 19(1), 87–101.

Schuppert, G.F. (2007). Governance reflected in political science and jurisprudence. In D. Jansen (Ed.), *New forms of governance in research organisations. Disciplinary approaches, interfaces and integration* (pp. 33–57). Dordrecht, Netherlands: Springer.

Schweizerische Eidgenossenschaft. (2011). Pressevielfalt sichern. Bericht des Bundesrates in Erfüllung des Postulats Fehr 09.3629 und des Postulats der Staats-politischen Kommission des Nationalrates (SPK-NR) 09.3980. Retrieved from http://www.news.admin.ch/NSBSubscriber/message/attachments/23504.pdf.

Seufert, W. (2012). Auswirkungen des Medienwandels auf die Struktur des marktfinanzierten Medienangebots. In O. Jarren, M. Künzler & M. Puppis (Eds.), *Medienwandel oder Medienkrise? Folgen für Medienstrukturen und ihre Erforschung* (pp. 145–165). Baden-Baden, Germany: Nomos.

Stigler, G. (1971). The theory of economic regulation. *The Bell Journal of Economics and Management Science*, 2(1), 3–21.

Trappel, J. (2012). Baustellen der Medienpolitik: Die Krisenfolgen im Medienpolitikdiskurs. In W.A. Meier, H. Bonfadelli & J. Trappel (Eds.), *Gehen in den Leuchttürmen die Lichter aus? Was aus den Schweizer Leitmedien wird* (pp. 277–297). Berlin, Germany: LIT-Verlag.

UK Government. (2013a). Royal Charter on Self-Regulation of the Press. Retrieved from https://www.gov.uk/government/uploads/system/uploads/attachment_data/file/254116/Final_Royal_Charter_25_October_2013_clean__Final_.pdf.

UK Government. (2013b). Explanatory note on amendments to the final version Royal Charter on Self-Regulation of the Press. Retrieved from https://www.gov.uk/government/uploads/system/uploads/attachment_data/file/254119/EN_on_11_Oct_changes_final_version.pdf.

UK Parliament. (2003). Communications Act 2003. Retrieved from http://www.legislation.gov.uk/ukpga/2003/21/pdfs/ukpga_20030021_en.pdf.

Von Rimscha, B., & Russi, L. (2010). Die Schweizer Medienbranche 2015 – Rechnerische und narrative Szenarien der Medienzukunft. Forschungsbericht zuhanden des Bundesamtes für Kommunikation BAKOM. Retrieved from http://www.bakom.admin.ch/dokumentation/gesetzgebung/00909/03627/index.html?lang=de&download=NHzLpZeg7t,lnp6I0NTU04212Z6ln1acy4Zn4Z2qZpnO2Yuq2Z6gpJCDeoB,fmym162epYbg2c_JjKbNoKSn6A.

Vowe, G., Opitz, S., & Dohle, M. (2008). Medienpolitische Weichenstellungen in Deutschland – Rückblick und Vorausschau. *Medien- und Kommunikationswissenschaft*, 56(2), 159–186.

Warzilek, A. (2013). Der wieder gegründete Österreichische Presserat – eine erste Bilanz und ein Blick in die Zukunft. In H. Koziol, J. Seethaler, & T. Thiede (Eds.), *Medienpolitik und Recht II* (pp. 39–50). Vienna, Austria: Jan Sramek Verlag.

Wenzel, C. (2012). *Selbstorganisation und Public Value. Die Zulässigkeit einer externen Regulierung des öffentlich-rechtlichen Rundfunks*. Wiesbaden, Germany: Springer VS.

Winseck, D. (2010). Financialization and the 'crisis of the media': The rise and fall of (some) media conglomerates in Canada. *Canadian Journal of Communication*, 35(3), 365–393.

7 Digital Switchover
EU State Aid, Public Subsidies and Enlargement

Mark Wheeler

Introduction

This chapter focuses on the European Union's (EU) Competition Directorate's approach concerning the application of the State Aid mechanism with regard to those Member States who used public subsidies for digital switchover. This analysis will show how the European Commission (EC) deployed its competition rules to pursue a normative view founded upon the liberalization of services and the enhancement of consumer needs to ensure economic opportunities. However, it was further required to deliver a framework for social accountability to allow for an equitable delivery of services across a range of different platforms. Therefore, this analysis considers not only how the Directorate's approach was governed by a market-driven set of rules but also discusses whether it proved to be adaptable enough to encompass the specific requirements of Member States.

For national television markets, the introduction of digital services facilitated a range of technological, economic and social reforms. Most especially, digital television (DTV) operations carried many more channels than their analogue predecessors. Through the compression of data in which eight digital channels used the amount of spectrum previously taken up by one analogue station, consumers could benefit by enjoying a wider degree of choice; improved picture quality and better sound; and a greater amount of flexibility through portable and mobile reception, on-demand and enhanced information services (European Commission, 2005a). In tandem, business opportunities allowed for new market suppliers, a rise in competition, first-mover advantage, alternative forms of delivery and convergence (European Commission, 2005a). In this respect, digitalization became a major pillar in the EU's i2010 Initiative and within the Lisbon Agenda adopted in 2000.

Moreover, the freeing up of the analogue transmission spectrum meant that a 'digital dividend' would be effected as business contractors could buy the channels to pursue commercial gains. In particular, the switching off of analogue broadcasts left a surplus of radio frequencies to be divided into three sub-bands on the available Ultra High Frequency (UHF) band 470–862 MHZ for other applications. These included opportunities for mobile and high definition television alongside the release of 800 MHZ bandwidths for transnational mobile telephony including 3G, 4G and WiMAX (ITU, 2012).

Consequently, between 2003 until 2013, the EU promoted digital switchover for economic gain and consumer benefits. It harmonized digital switchover throughout the range of EU Member States while maintaining the principles of subsidiarity and derogation. Thus, the EC recognised the importance of digital switchover in its 2005 Action Plan eEurope and in three related communications. In particular, the Commission committed itself to the goal of analogue switch-off / digital switchover by 2012. This was problematic, as at the beginning of the switchover process in 2003, 43% of all European households were still only in receipt of analogue-based terrestrial services (Matteucci 2008, p. 3). In the event, a number of Member States (Poland, Hungary, Bulgaria, Greece, Romania) could not achieve switchover by the 2012 deadline (Starks, 2013, p. 92).

Moreover, the EU was confronted by the problem that the exponential take-up by Member States of Digital Terrestrial Television (DTT), Digital Satellite Television (DST) and Digital Cable Television (DCT) services had been differentiated due to specific national governmental frameworks, regulatory structures and market demand (Iosifidis 2011b, p. 162). Most especially, despite the mandatory requirement of technological neutrality, it became apparent that the market-leading DTT platform's penetration on an EU-wide level was inconsistent and problematic. Such variability within take-up led to questions of potential market failure and the need to affect public subsidies to ensure complete take-up by 2012.

Therefore, Member State governments, regulators and audio-visual actors sought financial support through public subsidies to facilitate analogue switch-off / digital switchover (Wheeler, 2010). This usage of public subsidies triggered the employment of the EU State Aid mechanism to determine whether such an employment of funds was competitive or had unfairly distorted the market between public and commercial television suppliers. Further, there was an underlying concern that such an employment of state monies would lead to 'mission creep' in which the values of the market might be absorbed into a wider array of public service provisions (Donders & Pauwels, 2008, p. 295). This chapter will provide a review of these concerns with reference to EC legislation and policy provisions to consider how several State Aid cases concerning digital switchover were considered by the Directorate:

> The EU ... was particularly hawk-eyed on the subject of State Aid for the digital terrestrial platform, where, of course, rival platforms were quick to complain. While national governments could promote a specific digital television technology if this was justified by 'well-defined general interests', e.g., to achieve a fast and efficient switchover, 'policy interventions should be transparent, justified, proportionate and timely to minimize the risk of market distortion'.
>
> (Starks, 2013, pp. 76–77)

The Principles of the EU State Aid Action Plan and Digital Switchover: Market Failure, Competitive Practices and the Facilitation of the Digital Economy

The Commission contends that a State Aid is an appropriate measure if it may stem a market failure (European Commission, 2001). To determine the legitimacy of a State Aid, the EU employs a well-established legal framework which is embedded in the EU Treaty. The Commission has contended that if a societal gain cannot be shown to have been maximized, even in cases where market efficiency has been demonstrated, there are grounds for the use of public subsidies to enhance specific social outcomes (European Commission, 2009). However:

> Very clearly, [the EU's] approach [to State Aid] is underscored by strong normative assumptions of the superiority of the market. ... Overall, the EU's approach is underpinned by two key ideas – maintaining the primacy of market based competition, where State Aid is viewed as distortive, though necessary, and ensuring appropriate returns (value) for any state resources which are invested.
>
> (Simpson 2014, p. 8)

Therefore, it is the EU's general belief that public assistance should not replace the market provision of digital services. However, a key factor in deciding whether public subsidies should be employed concerning digital switchover was determined by the requirement to accelerate take-up by 2012. It remained the Commission's view that, if left to the market, there was the risk that switchover could be slowed down, which might prove fatal for the expansion of the digital economy (Norlander & Melin 2006, p. 257).

Moreover, according to the EC, such a form of switchover had 'positive externalities', which referred not only to a more efficient usage of the frequency spectrum but also to the concern that the extension of channels had a social benefit for consumer demands and citizens' rights. Yet, from the EU perspective such a 'common good' function could often exceed the private interests of the incumbent broadcasters. For instance, it was contended that a commercial broadcaster who does not anticipate a significant increase in audience share and a rise in advertising revenues might be reluctant to participate in switchover. Consequently, the Commission believed that the acceleration of the analogue switch-off process to reap the benefits of the freed-up spectrum was a valid justification for public intervention and possible exemption from an unfettered marketplace (European Commission, 2005b).

In addition, the 2005 State Aid Action Plan commented that Member States could employ State Aid to overcome specific market failures in the transference from analogue to digital services to ensure social cohesion. As María Trinidad García Leiva and Michael Starks comment, two distinct patterns of analogue switch-off / digital switchover occurred (García Leiva & Starks, 2009, p. 790). First, in countries with extensive cable and satellite reception (Germany, the Netherlands, Luxembourg, Switzerland), analogue switch-off was sustainable, as only a small section of the population had been dependent on terrestrial reception. However, in a second model of transference, in states such as the United Kingdom (UK), France, Spain and Italy, the majority of households received terrestrial-based forms of analogue transmissions. For example, in Italy 19 million out of its 22 million households (84.2%) were serviced by terrestrial forms of distribution (Santamato & Salto, 2006, p. 96).

Moreover, there were significant variations in DTV take-up between Northern, Southern and Eastern European countries. In 2010, DTV household adoption in Finland, Norway and Sweden stood well above 70%, with the UK having the highest rate of penetration standing at 92%. Conversely, in Mediterranean states such as Italy, Spain and Greece, take-up levels were well below 50% and in these Member States there was limited awareness of the process of analogue switch-off / digital switchover (Iosifidis, 2011b, p. 162). This meant that the process of transfer was problematized by the variation in different states of digital penetration and the greater amount of time required for switchover. Further, there remained significant danger that only a limited section of the population would benefit from the advantages of digital television (García Leiva & Starks, 2009, p. 790–791). These problems are made more acute due to the expenses incurred by the parallel forms of 'simulcasting' between analogue and digital transmissions which were necessitated to smooth the course of switchover.

Across Member States, terrestrial networks had been employed to fulfill Universal Service Obligations (USO) (Starks, 2007, p. 55). This meant that a high percentage of the population had to be covered by digital transmissions before a government could contemplate analogue switch-off. Therefore, the Commission acknowledged that a cohesive switchover could have been undermined by several types of market failure concerning the coordination of technological reforms; by the danger that incumbent broadcasters might gain a competitive advantage by delaying switchover and by the fact that problems associated with audience uncertainty undermined USOs (European Commission, 2005b) .

Conversely, the Competition Directorate required that the Member States abide by State Aid instruments to address switchover to stem any distortion of competition and to ensure that the level of subsidy remains limited to an absolute minimum. Therefore, of greater concern for the Directorate than market failure has been how the EU State Aid Action Plan might be employed to support sustainable growth and competitiveness. Thus, the EC required that the given State Aid scheme for the digital switchover must be proportionate to the public service obligations. It is only when these conditions were met that State Aid schemes could be approved under Article 87(3) (c) of the EU Treaty (Wheeler 2010, p. 57).

The Commission contended this approach provided a fairer assessment of the investigated measures as only well-targeted forms of aid could meet the overall objective of promoting competitiveness and technological development across Europe (Schoser & Santamato, 2006, p. 23). Therefore, the Directorate examined the impact of market failures on the switchover process, with reference to whether these perceived failures prevented the market from achieving full economic efficiency.

Similarly, the EC contended that there should be technological neutrality to the extent that there is competition among platform providers and that no one platform – terrestrial, cable or satellite – should be favoured by a national authority (European Commission, 2005b). In principle, each network was required to compete on its own strengths and Member States could not be discriminatory. While public support for one particular option was not excluded, it had to be justified by well-defined general interests and be implemented in a proportionate manner. However, due to market demand, DTT has become the most diffused platform across the EU. The Commission was concerned that with the different levels of DTT penetration across national markets, there became a further pressure to employ public subsidies for DTT switchover to ensure USOs.

Finally, public subsidies could be used to sustain the EU's central goal of efficient digitalization for the benefit of media plurality and consumer choice. This meant that not all measures constituted State Aid. For example, in one ruling the Commission decided that the UK regulator Office of Communication's (OfCom) decision to replace existing analogue licences with Digital Replacement Licences (DRLs) for terrestrial broadcasters, including Independent Television (ITV), Channel 4, Channel 5 and Public Teletext was appropriate, as the DRL's contained obligations related to the digital switchover (European Commission, 2006). In view of these obligations and of the diminished 'scarcity' value of the broadcasting licences, the regulator reduced the costs associated with broadcasting licence fees – the so-called 'additional payments'.

However, in spite of such exemptions, the EC remained concerned with how 'to seize this potential in our digital economy', through facilitating the opportunities for competitive market supply, claiming that:

> Europe will need to create the right framework for ensuring effective competition and sound regulatory conditions in a well-functioning single market as well as incentives for innovation. In view of the commitment to the social market economy, we also need to make sure that, in the end, consumers benefit from the digital economy.
>
> (Reding, 2009, p. 2)

State Aid and Digital Switchover Cases

It has been with these values in mind that the Competition Directorate has considered a range of cases within Member States concerning the utilization of public subsidies to extend the possibilities of analogue switch-off / digital switchover. The assessment of a State Aid case occurred as a two-stage process. First, the Commission investigated whether a measure could be considered as a form of State Aid. Second, if the measure was defined as a State Aid, the Commission investigated if any exception or derogation might be deemed as being appropriate. A State Aid had to receive the Commission's approval prior to implementation; otherwise the recipient could be liable for the repayment of the subsidy.

In applying these measures, the EC noted that in many European countries, governments have reserved monies to support consumers, broadcasters and network operators to affect digital switchover. However, there have been significant controversies concerning the character of these subsidies. This led to the Directorate considering whether these forms of State Aid were illegitimate due to an unfair distortion of the competitive marketplace. Yet, the EC's response was further conditioned by the specific nature of the national broadcasting market, political interests, matters of technological neutrality and interoperability, questions of market failure and concerns about whether incumbent players benefited at the expense of their competitors (Wheeler, 2010).

Germany: The Berlin-Brandenburg Case – Social Cohesion Versus Competition

The Commission ruled on several German State Aid measures regarding digital switchover. The most important of these cases occurred in 2005, when it had to decide whether the regional funding awarded by the Media Council of the Media Authority for Berlin-Brandenburg (MABB) for promoting switchover to the European standard terrestrial digital video broadcasting (DVB-T) network out of licence fees was commensurate with State Aid rulings.[1] The MABB investigation indicated how the two of the German Lander had employed public subsidies to affect a cohesive transfer for analogue switch-off / digitalswitchover (Garcia Leiva & Starks, 2009, p. 791).

On 13 February 2002, to ensure the smooth digitization of broadcasting, MABB had concluded a 'switchover agreement' with the public service broadcasters (PSBs) including Arbeitsgemeinschaft der öffentlich-rechtlichen Rundfunkanstalten der Bundesrepublik Deutschland (ARD) and the Zweites Deutsches Fernsehen (ZDF) and commercial players such as Radio Television Luxemburg (RTL) and ProSiebenSat.1, which contained schedules for switchover and the allocation of programme channels. In this respect, MABB received binding agreements from all parties and enacted a comprehensive public communications campaign deemed to be socially acceptable (Iosifidis, 2006, p. 261). The Berlin-Brandenburg case was praised as a model for switchover, as the region had the appropriate technical and commercial infrastructure to allow for a relatively short phase of simulcasting and had completed the switchover by 2003.

Therefore, MABB contended these grants had offset market failures and had ensured media diversity by safeguarding infrastructure competition for digital modes of transmission. In particular, it argued that subsidies allowed the players to remove those barriers which could undermine the expedition of a speedy process for switchover. Further, MABB claimed the €4 million granted to the broadcasting groups was proportionate as it reflected how the transmission costs of a multiplex (consisting of several bundled programming channels) were 50% more expensive than those accrued through broadcasting programmes on an analogue service. In addition, the German Federal Government argued that as the financial assistance had not been selective it did not distort competition, as any broadcaster or network operator could have benefited from the funding (García Leiva & Starks, 2009, p. 792).

Yet, following complaints from cable operators, the Competition Directorate decided MABB had unfairly employed public subsidies for the advantages of the incumbent commercial broadcasters RTL and ProSiebenSat.1. Most especially, in exchange for undertakings with these groups to transmit via DTT for five years, it contended MABB had inequitably allocated entire multiplexes to each organisation regardless of audience figures. The EC contended that RTL enjoyed an annual level of grant of €265,000 per annum at a rate of €66,250 per programme channel, while ProSiebenSat.1 received a subsidy of €330,000 a year working out to €82,500 for each channel. Moreover, the financial assistance granted to the commercial broadcasters indirectly benefited the network operator T-Systems, as it would enjoy guaranteed income from the two major German broadcasting groups for a minimum of five years. In turn, the Commission commented that such financial assistance also enabled T-Systems to charge higher transmission prices (European Commission, 2005c).

Therefore, for the EU, MABB's use of public funds was felt to be anti-competitive as it had skewed the German broadcasting system by favouring incumbent commercial players and had undermined an open and transparent tendering process. Moreover, the EU noted that while MABB's use of state intervention achieved beneficial forms of cohesion, in this case such a use of State Aid breached the principles of technological neutrality as it forced consumers to use T-Systems infrastructure to access the digital platform.[2] Further, in terms of MABB arguments concerning the need for coordination to stem market failures, the Directorate concluded:

> State Aid to reduce the burden of transmission costs is not the appropriate instrument to address the problem of coordination between market players. Limiting the duration of the simulcast phase and achieving a simultaneous switchover may instead be attained by, for example, setting a common expiry date for all analogue licences.
>
> (Norlander & Merlin, 2006, p. 260)

The MABB decision proved to be a test case and had implications for the application of State Aid concerning digital switchover in other Member States. Principally, the EC decided that the specific indications of acceptable forms of public subsidy included:

- Funding for the roll-out of a transmission network in areas where otherwise there would be insufficient television coverage.
- Financial compensation to PSBs for the cost of broadcasting via all transmission platforms in order to reach the entire population, provided this forms part of the public service mandate.
- Subsidies to consumers for the purchase of digital decoders as long as they are technologically neutral, especially if they encourage the use of open standards for interactivity.
- Financial compensation to broadcasters which are required to discontinue analogue transmission before the expiry of their licences, provided this takes account of granted digital transmission capacity (European Commission, 2005c).

Italy: Competition as a Form of Corporate War – *Sky Italia V. Mediaset*

The precedent of MABB would be an important determinant for other State Aid cases, most especially with regard to the digitization of the Italian broadcasting system. In Italy, the television market was dominated by two major incumbents: Radiotelevisone Italiana (RAI), the public broadcaster, and the commercial media monopoly Mediaset, owned by the broadcasting mogul and former Italian Prime Minister Silvio Berlusconi (European Commission, 2007, p. 1). As both suppliers operated through terrestrial networks, digital switchover was not welcomed by either the Italian media or the political elites. Most specifically, the inclusion of a wider spectrum of airwaves meant that more channels could be broadcast, thereby leading to the potential growth of new or alternative competitors. Consequently, the European rules for switchover were implemented at a painfully slow rate and the abolition of the analogue signal was postponed on several occasions.

However, this process was radically altered when Rupert Murdoch's News Corporation established a competitive satellite broadcaster monopoly from its acquisition of the existing Telepiu stations (owned by Vivendi) which were renamed Sky Italia in 2002. From then on, the Italian government (led by Berlusconi on a second occasion from 2001–2006) argued that since the terrestrial delivery of broadcasting signals was the major means of receiving television in Italy, a subsidized programme for DTT switchover was necessary. It claimed that such a use of State Aid would ensure that the commercial applications of digitization could be maximized for the public's social benefit (European Commission, 2007, p. 2).

Therefore, from 2004 to 2005, Berlusconi's government distributed over €200 million in grants to enable consumers to purchase or rent interactive digital decoders capable of receiving only DTT and DCT transmissions (European Commission, 2007, p. 1). In effect, these subsidies awarded each buyer of digital terrestrial decoders with a sum of €150 per person in 2004 and €70 in 2005. In 2006, Italy provided notification of a further measure which subsidized the purchase by Sardinian and Valle d'Aosta DTT consumers of interactive decoders that included an open application programming interface (API) (Santamato & Salto, 2006, p. 98).

Thus, at a formal level, Italy defended the scheme by citing DTT's benefits including an improved use of frequencies to promote pluralism, economic development, information technologies and e-society services. However, these measures reflected the ongoing war which was occurring between the Berlusconi and Murdoch empires. They were part of a process through which the Italian government, in an outrageous conflict of interest, sought to rid Silvio Berlusconi's Mediaset corporation of its major DST pay TV competitor. This approach protected Mediaset's revenues, as 88% of its digital services were funded by subscription monies by undermining the economic opportunities for Sky Italia (Santamato & Salto, 2006, p. 99). Moreover, in applying these public subsidies, Berlusconi's government failed to notify the Commission and by only supporting the purchase of terrestrial decoders undermined the EU principles of technological neutrality. Such a lack of interoperability was evidenced in the exclusion of Sky Italia's customers (who used alternative satellite DVB-S decoders) from receiving financial support in buying the kit required to receive digital satellite services.

It was within this economic, political and regulatory context that Sky Italia's lawyers filed a complaint with the Competition Directorate contending that the Italian state's financial contributions unfairly distorted the Italian pay TV market. In turn, the Commission opened a formal State Aid investigation into the 2004–2005 subsidies, while simultaneously providing an analysis of the 2006 measures, about which it had also received complaints from satellite television operators. In 2007, after consulting with the market operators, the Commission concluded that both the 2004–2005 and the 2006 round of subsidies provided an indirect advantage to the incumbent terrestrial television broadcasters by unfairly allowing them to develop their digital audience – a crucial revenue base for subscription television services (European Commission, 2007).

In making this judgement, the EC contended that even those measures that supported an objective of common interest (like digitalization) must be proportional. The Italian explanation that the subsidy could be excused under those rules regarding the social character of State Aid was not accepted. Further, the utilization of public subsidies not only benefited some consumers over others but aided the incumbent companies and discriminated against other operators who had to provide their consumers with decoding equipment at their own expense. Concurrently, the Commission rejected the argument that the aid was only part of delivering services of general economic interest and required Mediaset to pay back the subsidies it had received (Renzi, 2010).

Subsequently, when Mediaset appealed the decision, the Court of Justice of the European Union backed the EC in 2011 by ruling that the Italian government's use of subsidies infringed the European State Aid rules (case T-177/07). The court expressed agreement with the Commission's assertion that the grant did not have the required technology neutrality and that:

> [o]n one hand it gave consumers an incentive to move from an analogue system to a digital terrestrial system, thus limiting expense for digital terrestrial television broadcasters, and on the other it had allowed these same broadcasters to consolidate their position in the market compared to new competitors, in terms of brand image and reinforcing the loyalty of their clientele (Court of Justice of the European Union, 2011).

In effect, the Commission's decision and the Court's backing tipped the balance of power in the Italian pay TV market to Sky Italia, who immediately sought the further removal of a 2003 clause that barred it from to entering the DTT market.

Spain: Digital Service Obligations Against Commercial Interests

From 2005 to 2008, Spain enacted a set of regulatory recommendations to achieve analogue switch-off / digital switchover. For the DTT network to operate effectively there needed to be an upgrade and a building of new transmission centres resulting in the Spanish digital television sector being divided into three distinct areas of delivery. In Area I, which represented the major Spanish cities and towns and accounted for 95% of the national population, the costs could be covered by the broadcasters. For Area II, which was composed from the rural and poorly populated regions, the Spanish authorities believed that the broadcasters would have little or no commercial interest in providing services and established a State Aid scheme worth €260 million to ensure USOs for 2.5% of the population. However, in making this decision, the Spanish government failed to notify the EU. Finally, in Area III, the mountainous topography of the regions being covered meant that a DST platform was chosen to provide digital television channels (European Commission, 2010a).

With reference to employment of public subsidies in Area II, Europe's first private satellite provider, SES Astra, complained to the EC that the Spanish government's use of State Aid had unfairly distorted the market. SES Astra's lawyers contended that it had enabled the incumbent DTT platform operator (Abertis SA) to become a de facto monopoly player. It was argued that the employment of public subsidies violated the principles of technological neutrality and would jeopardize the survival of the digital satellite operators.

Following this complaint, in 2010 the Commission opened an in-depth investigation into the public financing of the DTT infrastructure (case C23/2010). On 19 June 2013, the Competition Directorate's investigation concluded that the State Aid measure had exclusively funded the digitization of terrestrial transmission technology to the detriment of others. The investigation demonstrated that alternative transmission platforms, like satellite, cable or the Internet, would not effectively benefit from the subsidies. Consequently, the EU decided that the public financing for the digitization and extension of the terrestrial television networks in the remote areas of Spain was incompatible with EU State Aid rules. Subsequently, those terrestrial platform operators who had enjoyed a selective advantage over their satellite-based competitors were required to pay the monies back to Spanish taxpayers.

> In short, Spain was held to have not carried out the digital switchover in a technology neutral way. This decision follows precedents set in previous cases concerned with public subsidies to assist the process of digital switchover (e.g., Cases T-8/06, T-21/06 and T-24/06, *Berlin-Brandenburg* and Case T-177/07, *Mediaset*) (EBU, 2013).

Apart from this case, the Commission opened two further investigations into the digitization of television services in Spain. One concerned the implementation of the transition plan in the region of Castilla–La Mancha where, in addition to possible technological discrimination, there had been further discrimination against regional and local terrestrial platform operators. The second case concerned the aid granted to broadcasters for the change of bandwidth (JOCE C/213/2012). This looked at how the Spanish government had planned to compensate DTT broadcasters for the extra costs of parallel broadcasting while services were re-allocated to other frequencies to free up the digital dividend. Again doubts were expressed about the necessity, proportionality and technological neutrality of this measure (European Commission, 2010a).

Eastern European States, Economic Malaise and the European Project

With regard to the German, Italian and Spanish cases, the Commission enforced a liberalizing agenda towards its employment of State Aid rules. It argued that public subsidies for switchover could only be applied if they did not distort the competitive nature of the specific digital marketplaces. However, the EC faced greater pressures to allow for public forms of financial intervention in those Eastern European Member States which required greater rates of investment either due to the demand to bring in new technical standards, their long-standing reliance on traditional terrestrial forms of transmission or because of the financial weaknesses of their broadcasting industries. Further, 'analogue switch-off in ... [Eastern] Europe [was] hampered by political issues, governments' lack of political priority and the lack of political consensus that [made] it difficult to reach an agreement (Iosifidis, 2011a, p. 8).

For instance, on 17 November 2010 the European Commission approved Slovakia's €7 million aid scheme, which supported parallel analogue and digital broadcasting during a period of the transition between analogue switch-off to digital switchover (European Commission, 2010b). According to the Slovakian authorities, broadcasters would not be able to switch to digital broadcasting in advance of the 2012 deadline due to the public's unwillingness to acquire digital decoders. Therefore, to avoid a 'last-minute' panic as well as the danger of creating blank signal reception spots, they decided there should be a year-long simulcast period of parallel transmission from 2010–2011. This would provide viewers with the time to purchase digital decoders (or new digital TV receivers) so that the broadcasters could switch to digital technology in advance of the legal deadline. Therefore, the Slovakian government publicly funded the broadcasters and network operators with a 50% contribution to the costs related to analogue signal transmission, and the purchase or rental of temporary mobile analogue transmitters during the period of parallel broadcasting (European Commission, 2010b, p. 2).

The Competition Directorate decided the scheme was commensurate with State Aid rules as it provided funds related to the additional costs triggered by the simulcast and that it did not favour one technology over another. The beneficiaries were selected in open and non-discriminatory procedure founded on pre-defined criteria, and the Slovakian authorities were required to provide annual reports upon the allocation of the funds to the Commission. Therefore, the EC contended that the measure facilitated digital switchover without unduly distorting competition. Then EC vice-president in charge of competition policy, Joaquín Almunia, commented, 'I commend the Slovak authorities for supporting the parallel analogue operation without unduly distorting competition. This is a further step towards the digitisation of broadcasting in Europe' (European Commission, 2010b).

Moreover, across those Eastern European states who had joined the European Union in 2004 within the process of Enlargement, concerns were raised about the ability of their citizens to afford the purchase of the new hardware required for DTV reception. In 2010, the EC decided that Slovakia's €11 million scheme to support the purchase of decoders for socially vulnerable groups did not infringe the State Aid rules. This meant that those members of the Slovakian public who were on a low income, received an old-age pension or were in receipt of benefits became entitled to claim a voucher with a maximum value of €20 for the purchase of digital television equipment. This measure was especially important as Slovakia had planned to switch from analogue to digital television by the end of 2012, and without upgraded devices, these citizens would have been excluded from this information source. Therefore, such a use of funds for switchover affected the competitive structures of national media markets over a long period and in unforeseen ways (European Commission, 2010c).

As Marko Milosavljević and Sally Broughton Micova have shown, the EU Competition Directorate continued to show a greater flexibility to those South Eastern European States delivering digital services for poor or disadvantaged households (Milosavljević & Broughton Micova, 2013). In Croatia, the authorities offered a subsidy to all households and made equipment available through the post office. Additionally, in Slovenia, Macedonia, Serbia and Montenegro there was the direct use of public money for the construction of the networks by public companies.

> Far from objecting to this intervention in the market for transmission on competition grounds, the EU is also investing in both Serbia and Montenegro through the IPA funds within the context of accession. This can be seen less as a compromise on EU competition policy and more so as a recognition that without such assistance and significant efforts by the states to push the process, there were no forces to drive digitalization or assurance that these countries would meet the required deadlines.
> (Milosavljević & Broughton Micova, 2013, p. 273)

Further, because of the general economic malaise that has affected the European Union since the Banking Crisis of 2008, there was an acceleration within the processes of digital switchover. For the EC, any slowdown could have had a disastrous consequence in terms of the commercial imperatives to use up the digital dividend from the freed-up analogue spectrum (EurActive, 2010a). It estimated that the incremental value of the spectrum for wireless broadband across the EU stood at a figure of between €150 and €200 billion. Most especially, the 'Europe 2020' strategy for new jobs and sustainable growth (which has replaced the Lisbon Agenda) placed the availability of high-speed Internet, to be rolled out from freed-up spectrum, as being crucial in the formation of the EU's Knowledge Economy. Therefore, it contended that an appropriate coordination of Member States was required to affect the digital dividend so that its potential economic impact would raise an additional €50 billion from 2010 to 2015. This was particularly attractive to the EC, as it was cost-free to taxpayers and would be available for all Member States as a means of raising further revenues (Reding, 2009, p. 4).

Consequently, the Directorate remained mindful that any barriers that it imposed over the use of public subsides might detrimentally impact the development of digital services (European Commission, 2010c). Paradoxically, by pursuing the values of competition, the EU could have undermined the commercial benefits to be drawn from the digital switchover process.

Therefore, the application of these measures on a national case-by-case basis led to a wider range of outcomes as the Competition Directorate became less committed to the explicit rules of competition.

This change in attitude focused attention on several divisions which existed in the Competition Directorate between its neo-liberal values and the Member States' normative objectives to maximize the potential for the digital market along with an effective delivery of services with a pronounced social character. Further, all of the cases indicated that a wider tension was apparent with regard to the integrationist 'European Project' in relation to cultural policies, as the inherent:

> [e]conomic and liberalizing concepts designed to ensure the functioning of an internal market as a key pillar of integration established in the Treaty are not always easily aligned to the historical policy framework that has evolved in individual Member States and they are not in themselves sufficient to ensure public interest objectives are achieved in this vital sector for European societies and economies ... The complexities are further increased by the architecture of the EU itself as it is composed of policy-making processes whose design, all things being equal, is inextricably stamped with a trade-off between the terms of the EC Treaty and national interests.
>
> (Ward, 2008, p. 2)

Thus, throughout the process of employing State Aid measures to aid analogue switch-off and digital switchover, a growing division existed between the principles of supra-nationalism and inter-governmentalism (Iosifidis, 2011a). On the one hand, Member States were concerned that their sovereign powers had been undermined by the EU as the Competition Directorate had exercised too much control in determining the use of public subsidies. Further, it was a concern that the EU's normative liberalizing agenda conflicted with the need for a coordinated form of switchover to allow for the commercial benefits and demand for social cohesion to be realized in relation to digitization (Norlander & Melin, 2006, p. 267).

Conversely, the Directorate was concerned that Member States had abused their rights of derogation under the European Treaty to expand the digital public service remit in unauthorized ways, such as financing commercial digital activities. Moreover, questions of market fragmentation continued to be related to the DTV take-up rates and the utilization of the digital dividend made available from the freed-up analogue spectrum (Kroes, 2010). Therefore, these tensions indicated how the questions of subsidiarity and complexities of cultural practices increasingly came to the fore in the period of digital switchover. As reflected in many areas of EU audio-visual policies, they demonstrated that media and communications reform was as much determined by political and social interests as by the technocratic, legalistic and economic demands of Competition Policy.

Conclusion

This chapter has discussed how the provision of a competition policy with regard to the State Aid Action Plan for switchover has been defined by three significant factors. First, State Aid was targeted to stem the potential market failures concerning the pace of take-up and cohesion due to universal service obligations, but only in a proportionate manner as to remain competitive. Second, any intervention had to respect the principles of technological neutrality and interoperability among the different digital platforms as confirmed by the Regulatory Framework. Third, the regulation governing the access to public funds was required to facilitate the EU's central goal of sustainable digitalization for the benefit of media plurality and consumer choice.

The chapter has shown how these ideological, regulatory and policy frameworks were utilized to define State Aid decisions in relation to digital switchover cases in Germany, Italy and Spain. In each of these State Aid cases there was an interface between the liberalizing principles of the Directorate and the economic, political and cultural/historical trajectories of the Member State's broadcasting ecology. For instance, in Germany switchover related to greater concerns about the coordination of public and commercial interests to ensure social cohesion, whereas the Italian case was determined by the economic and political interests of Silvio Berlusconi's Mediaset as against Rupert Murdoch's Sky Italia. In Spain, the questions about USOs and poorly resourced areas came to the fore in relation to the use of public subsidies. In each case, the State Aid mechanism had been seen to be violated and digital suppliers were required to pay back the subsidized monies they had received.

In relation to the changing nature of and complexities associated with digitization, this analysis concludes that there has been a more relaxed employment of State Aid in relation to digital switchover with reference to Eastern and Southern European Member States. This has occurred due to the disadvantages in terms of finances, information infrastructures, consumer take-up and developed broadcasting markets that have emerged in smaller European States. Thus, the chapter has shown how the EU had supported the employment of public finances for switchover in newer Member States such as Slovakia and how the Competition Directorate realized that these subsidies were necessary in light of USO obligations. At the same time, the economic crisis within the EU confirmed fears that the respective commercial and democratic gains of switchover could be fatally compromised.

Moreover, these financial considerations brought attention toward the wider debates concerning the EU's integrationist, neo-liberal agenda as against Member States' rights of derogation. While the regulatory environment was shaped by the EU's concern to liberalize services for market opportunities, national governments have sought to use public subsidies for digitization to maintain social cohesion and consumer protection. Therefore, these fissures have facilitated tensions between the EU's 'macro' liberalizing tendencies to ensure an internal market and 'micro' interests within Member States concerning their sovereignty over the regulation of communications industries (Iosifidis, 2011a; Iosifidis, 2011b, p. 162).

Notes

1. There has been a standardization of DTV transmission and reception technology into three main international families denoted by their acronyms – the DVB in Europe, ATSC in the United States, and ISDB in Japan. A fourth group of standards has been formulated in China.
2. Accordingly, the EU would employ this form of reasoning when it considered whether there had been an imposition of specific platforms of distribution in other switchover cases in other German regions including North Rhine–Westphalia and Bavaria, along with Sweden and Austria and concluded that they had breached State Aid rules.

References

Court of Justice of the European Union. (2011). The Court confirms that the Italian subsidies for the purchase of digital terrestrial decoders in 2004 and 2005 constitute State aid which is incompatible with the common market. Retrieved from http://curia.europa.eu/jcms/upload/docs/application/pdf/2011-07/cp110077en.pdf.

Donders, K., & Pauwels, C. (2008). Does EU policy challenge the digital future of public service broadcasting? An analysis of the commission's State Aid approach to digitization and the public service remit of public broadcasting organizations. *Convergence: The International Journal of Research in New Media Technologies*, 14(3), 295–311. doi: 10.1177/1354856508091082.

EurActive. (2010a, 9 March). 2020 plan pins hopes on 'Digital Agenda'. *EurActive.com*. Retrieved from http://www.euractiv.com/priorities/2020-plan-pins-hopes-digital-agenda-news-286500.

EurActive. (2010b, 4 June). Italy: Digital dividend sparks media tycoon battle. *EurActive.com*. Retrieved from http://www.euractiv.com/infosociety/digital-dividend-sparks-media-tycoons-battle-italy-news-494769.

European Broadcasting Union. (2013, 18 June). EU Commission: Spain in breach of state aid rules during digital switchover. Retrieved from https://www3.ebu.ch/contents/news/2013/06/eu-commission-spain-in-breach-of.html.

European Commission. (2001). *Communication from the Commission on the application of state aid rules to public service broadcasters*. Retrieved from http://ec.europa.eu/competition/state_aid/legislation/broadcasting_communication_en.pdf.

European Commission. (2005a). Switchover from analogue to digital broadcasting. Retrieved from http://europa.eu/legislation_summaries/audiovisual_and_media/l24223a_en.htm.

European Commission. (2005b). Competition policy in the media sector (compiled 2005). Retrieved from http://ec.europa.eu/competition/sectors/media/documents/media_decisions_2005.pdf.

European Commission. (2005c, 9 November). State Aid: Commission rules subsidy for digital terrestrial TV (DVB-T) in Berlin-Brandenburg illegal; Explains how digital TV can be supported. Retrieved from http://europa.eu/rapid/press-release_IP-05-1394_en.htm.

European Commission. (2006, 25 January). *State aid NN 64/2005 – United Kingdom digital replacement licences*. Brussels, Belgium: European Commission.
European Commission. (2007, 24 January). State Aid: Commission endorses subsidies for digital decoders in Italy, but only where technology-neutral. Retrieved from http://europa.eu/rapid/press-release_IP-07-73_en.htm.
European Commission. (2009, 19 May). *Community guidelines for the application of state aid rules in relation to the rapid deployment of broadband networks*. Brussels: European Commission.
European Commission. (2010a, 29 November). State Aid: Commission opens two investigations on Spanish National Transition Plan for digitization and extension of terrestrial television network. Retrieved from http://europa.eu/rapid/press-release_IP-10-1195_en.htm.
European Commission. (2010b, 17 November). State aid: Commission authorises €7 million aid to support digital switch-over in Slovakia. http://europa.eu/rapid/press-release_IP-10-1519_en.htm.
European Commission. (2010c, 15 September). State aid: Commission authorises a Slovak aid of €11 million towards the purchase of digital TV decoders by socially vulnerable persons. Retrieved from http://europa.eu/rapid/press-release_IP-10-1128_en.htm.
García Leiva, M.T., & Starks, M. (2009). Digital switchover across the globe: The emergence of complex regional patterns. *Media, Culture and Society, 31*(5), 787–806. doi: 10.1177/0163443709339465.
International Telecommunication Union. (2012). *Digital dividend insights for spectrum decisions. August 2012*. Retrieved from http://www.itu.int/ITU-D/tech/digital_broadcasting/Reports/DigitalDividend.pdf.
Iosifidis, P. (2006). Digital switchover in Europe. *The International Communications Gazette, 68*(3), 249–268. doi: 10.1177/1748048506063764.
Iosifidis, P. (2011a). Growing pains? The transition to digital television in Europe. *European Journal of Communication, 26*(1), 1–15. doi: 10.1177/0267323110394562.
Iosifidis, P. (2011b). *Global media and communications policy*. Basingstoke, UK: Palgrave Macmillan.
Kroes, N. (2010, 15 February). The Digital Agenda: challenges for Europe and the mobile industry. Retrieved from http://europa.eu/rapid/press-release_SPEECH-10-28_en.htm?locale=en.
Matteucci, N. (2008). Multiplatform competition and state aid in EU digital TV: A comparative assessment. *Proceedings of the 2008 EUCPR conference*. Seville, Spain: ITPS-JRC. Retrieved from http://works.bepress.com/cgi/viewcontent.cgi?article=1005&context=nicola_matteucci.
Milosavljević, M., & Broughton Micova, S. (2013). Because we have to: Digitalization of terrestrial television in South East Europe. *International Journal of Digital Television, 4*(3), 261–277. doi: 10.1386/jdtv.4.3.261_1.
Nordlander, K., & Melin, H. (2006). Switching to action: Commission applies state aid action plan to digital switchover. *European State Aid Law Quarterly, 5*(2), 11–15.
Office of Communications. (2009). *Ofcom's second public service review: Putting viewers first*. Retrieved from http://stakeholders.ofcom.org.uk/binaries/consultations/psb2_phase2/statement/psb2statement.pdf.
Reding V. (2009, 9 July). Digital Europe – Europe's fast track to economic recovery. Retrieved from http://europa.eu/rapid/press-release_SPEECH-09-336_en.htm.

Renzi, S. (2010, 11 August). Sky versus Mediaset: The battle comes to Europe. *TheEuros.eu*. Retrieved from http://www.theeuros.eu/spip.php?page=print&id_article=3950&lang=fr.
Santomato, S., & Salso, M. (2006). State Aid to digital decoders: Proportionality is needed to meet common interest. *Competition Policy Newsletter, 2006*(1), 97–99. Retrieved from http://ec.europa.eu/competition/publications/cpn/2006_1_97.pdf.
Schoser, C. (2006). Commission rules subsidy for digital terrestrial television (DVB-T) in Berlin Brandenburg illegal. *Competition Policy Newsletter, 2006*(1), 93–96. Retrieved from http://ec.europa.eu/competition/publications/cpn/2006_1_93.pdf.
Schoser, C., & Santamato, S. (2006). The Commission's state aid policy on digital switchover. *Competition Policy Newsletter, 2006*(1), 23–27. Retrieved from http://ec.europa.eu/competition/publications/cpn/2006_1_23.pdf.
Simpson, S. (2014). Next generation network environments in Europe – The significance of the EU as a policy actor. *Government Information Quarterly, 31*(1), 100–107. doi: 10.1016/j.giq.2012.08.008.
Starks, M. (2007). *Digital television: UK public policy and the market*. Bristol, UK: Intellect Books.
Starks, M. (2013). *The digital television revolution: Origins to outcomes*. Basingstoke, UK: Palgrave.
United Kingdom. Department of Culture, Media and Sport, & Department for Business Enterprise and Regulatory Reform. (2009). *Digital Britain: The Interim Report*. Retrieved from https://www.gov.uk/government/uploads/system/uploads/attachment_data/file/238653/7548.pdf.
University of Edinburgh School of Law. (2010, 12 November). Digital switchover: State aid rules switched off? [Weblog]. Retrieved from http://www2.law.ed.ac.uk/courses/blogs/medialaw/blogentry.aspx?blogentryref=8482.
Ward, D. (Ed.). (2008). *The European Union and the culture industries: Regulation and the public interest*. Aldershot, UK: Ashgate.
Wheeler, M. (2010). The European Union's competition directorate: State aids and public service broadcasting. In P. Iosifidis (Ed.), *Reinventing public service communication: European broadcasters and beyond*. Basingstoke, UK: Palgrave Macmillan.

Section III
Regulatory Policy Issues in Advanced Communication Network Environments

8 New Networks, Old Market Structures? The Race to Next Generation Networks in the EU and Calls for a New Regulatory Paradigm

Maria Michalis

Introduction

Around the world, there is a race to roll out advanced broadband communication infrastructure that allows very fast Internet connections. This infrastructure is believed to be vital for stimulating economic growth and competitiveness and for promoting greater social cohesion. Since the 2000s, the focus has been more specifically on so-called next generation (access) networks (NGNs), that is, fibre optic and Internet Protocol networks. Outside the EU, countries like Japan and South Korea have achieved near-universal broadband access, but in the EU, the question is if – and if yes, how – national governments and regulators can spur investment in such networks.

This chapter examines the EU policy debate on such superfast NGNs. It begins by assessing the rising importance of Information and Communication Technology (ICT) in pursuit of economic growth and identifies two implicit theoretical underpinnings, based on neo-classical and Hayekian ideas and Schumpeterian thinking respectively, with differing assumptions about the relationship between market and state intervention. Next, the chapter charts the move from Hayekian to Schumpeterian thought, which has disturbed, though not eliminated, conflicts in policy aims. It argues that since the 2000s there has been evidence of a new policy paradigm which has gradually become stronger and recognisably dominant in the aftermath of the 2008 financial crisis. This new paradigm prioritises innovation in a Schumpeterian sense, emphasises related monopoly rents and is therefore not immediately consistent with open competitive markers. As such, it is at odds with the earlier policy paradigm that guided the progressive liberalisation of telecommunications markets since the mid 1980s and was largely inspired by neo-classical and Hayekian thought, positing a pro-market response to address the failings of state monopolies. The chapter ends with a summary of the key arguments.

ICT and Economic Growth

From as early as the late 1950s, it is possible to trace the origins of explicit preoccupation with a distinct 'information sector' and of the rising perception that ICT is a key determinant of economic growth and competitiveness (Preston, 2001, p. 43). New explanations of the drivers of economic growth became imperative in response to mounting concern about economic development following the monetary crises and subsequent international turmoil. These new explanations came at a time when the fields of information and communications, in particular electronics, were experiencing fast technological change. Economic development came to be closely associated with these fields as a consequence. Besides, it was becoming increasingly apparent that neo-classical economic growth theory, dominant in the immediate postwar period, could not fully explain why an economy grows (e.g., Solow, 1956). Changes in output could not be attributed to changes in the two key inputs of labour and capital. The theory could account for the effects of technological progress but not its causes. Technology was considered an exogenous driver of growth, the crucial implication being that intervention by governments, firms or individuals could do little to influence it. Gradually since the mid 1960s, technological progress, 'knowledge, education, research and development' became progressively identified as major parameters to economic wealth and were referred to as "investment in human resources' and the 'third' or 'residual' factor' (see Organisation for Economic Co-operation and Development [OECD], 1964 p. 5).

During the recessionary 1970s, Japan, the U.S. and Western Europe gradually turned their attention to the 'information sector'. This mutually reinforcing preoccupation arose from concern about falling rates of productivity and growth, and belief that the application of information technology was instrumental to socio-economic development and competitiveness. From the start, most studies centred on perceived changes in the U.S., a core theme being how quantitative shifts, such as the growing percentage of the workforce in the services sector, automatically engendered broader and far-reaching qualitative socio-economic transformations (e.g., Bell, 1976; Machlup, 1962). By the late 1970s and early 1980s, the 'information society' notion encapsulating these ideas had become commonplace (Preston, 2001, pp. 63–64). Attention turned to the revolutionary technological changes underway, in particular the plethora of new services coming out of the merging of data processing and telecommunications and the high growth potential of the nascent telematic sector. In 1979, EU political leaders endorsed the 'information society' as the answer to Europe's socio-economic challenges (European Commission, 1979). It is also in this period that Europe's preoccupation with the technology gap can be traced. The risk of technological dependency on the U.S. becoming permanent and the associated serious implications for the economic, political and strategic interests of Western Europe pushed some analysts to call for common European solutions (Layton, 1969; Servan-Schreiber, (1968 [1967]).

In the course of the 1980s, new economic growth and trade theories reinforced the link between technology, public policy and economic growth. These theories were instrumental in justifying policy intervention in high technology sectors and, in turn, with their emphasis on economies of scale, in lending support to the European single market project.

Elaborating on earlier insights concerning the 'residual factor', endogenous (or 'new') growth theory developed as a critique to the dominant neo-classical theory mentioned above. Whereas for the neo-classical model growth was exogenous and so there is little, if anything, policies can do to accelerate its rate, for the new theory, growth was driven by endogenous factors such as technological innovation and human capital. The logical consequence is that government policies are important and may play a role in enhancing growth (Lucas, 1998). Competitive advantage is not given but instead created (Porter, 1990).

However, there is no universal agreement on what policies should do. Rather, differing understandings of the relationship between states and markets are reflected in policy responses (see Garnham, 2005). These understandings are not stated as such but can be inferred from the policy discourse used to describe the problem(s) in hand and the recommended solutions. The key argument put forward in this chapter is that, within an overall neo-liberal context, the policy paradigm has changed from one inspired by neo-classical economics and Hayekian thinking at the beginning of pro-competitive telecommunications market restructuring (from sometime in the 1980s to the early 2000s) to one more aligned to Schumpeterian thinking since the 2000s, with the advent of the Internet, technological convergence and growing emphasis on broadband communications. This new policy paradigm has become more visible since the 2008 economic crisis. Originally, in the 1980s, Hayekian ideas served to highlight the failings of state monopolies and to justify market liberalisation. At the heart of Hayekian thought is strong support for the market and opposition to state intervention. It views state intervention as ill-conceived and considers free markets as crucial in delivering equilibrium and underpinning social welfare. In policy terms, this understanding contributed to the dismantling of bureaucratic, inefficient and unresponsive national monopolies, as was the case of telecommunications, exemplified in the work of the Thatcher administration in Britain between 1979 and 1991.

Hayekian thought only supports state intervention in so far as it is circumscribed to enable the free functioning of the market. Similar to neo-classical economic growth theory, Hayekian ideas fail to account for market failure and tend to assume that perfect competition exists, an assumption that does not correspond with the oligopolistic market structures evident in many markets today, and which are arguably the norm in the field of ICT (see Ernst & O'Connor, 1992, p. 40). Despite these similarities, there is a key difference in emphasis between neo-classical economics and Hayekian ideas. For the former, the competitive market (with many firms, free market entry and price competition) will automatically result in efficient resource allocation and maximise benefits for society. But, for Hayekian thought, the free market is desirable not so much because it promotes efficiencies but principally because of the positive correlation between unconstrained markets and personal liberty and its function, through price competition, as a signalling mechanism that allows consumers and producers to exchange information, plan and make informed decisions (Hayek, 1945). The expectation is that opening up markets by breaking down barriers will not only result in economic and productivity gains but, by minimizing state involvement, will at the same time maximise personal liberty, because the market left to its own devices can respond to individual consumer needs better (see Webster, 2014, pp. 263–268).

With regard to innovation, in stark contrast to Schumpeterian thinking discussed below, the starting point of the Hayekian thought is the imperfect knowledge and limited capabilities economic actors possess to make rational decisions. It purports that incentives to spur innovation will not come from state intervention in the form of, for example, research and development (R&D) spending, but it is rather the free market itself that will act as an incentive: the more firms that exist in a market, the higher the chances for innovation to occur. Thus the policy objective, from a Hayekian point of view, is to nurture market competition and encourage as large a number of firms as possible, thereby increasing the overall potential for innovation (see Lee, 2012). Developing this point further, Wu (2005) has examined the role that Intellectual Property Rights (IPRs) can play in industry structure, economic decision-making, innovation and market entry. Wu critiques strong IPRs (aligned with Schumpeterian thinking) which engender centralised use of information and decision-making. Using Hayekian analysis, Wu argues in favour of lighter IPRs which will create decentralised structures and will not act as barriers to market entry aiming to maximise economic rents for the first mover. Instead, they will open and facilitate market entry by encouraging more firms to make use of IPRs and in so doing will simultaneously increase the chances for further innovation.

Unlike Hayekian thought, the starting point of the Schumpeterian view of innovation is the need to provide incentives. A competitive market is not a precondition. Schumpeter himself stressed the role of large, even monopolistic, companies in promoting innovation as opposed to the role of new and smaller companies (Schumpeter, 2010 [1943]). What matters is not inter-firm competition but the nurturing of an innovation-friendly environment through measures that influence the behaviour and motives of economic agents to innovate, such as R&D subsidies or legal encouragement in the form of strong IPRs that will allow innovators to capture greater market returns. The two examples of incentives (R & D subsidies and strong IPRs) confirm Godin's remarks that innovation is understood as applied invention, as bringing a new technology to the market which, in turn, assumes that innovation is a linear process that starts with scientific research and ends with commercialisation. It has come to mean primarily *'technological* innovation', a term that Godin attributes to the work of MIT economic historian Rupert W. Maclaurin in the late 1940s to the early 1950s (Godin,

2014 emphasis added). Godin explains that gradually since the 1960s '[h]igh technology rapidly came to be viewed as the solution to [improving a country's competitiveness and position in world trade], and statistics were developed to document the case' (Godin, 2004, p. 1218). These statistics reflect recognition of the fact that a country's growth is not narrowly down to its own resources (labour and capital) but rather other factors are important too such as technology, science, R&D expenditures and volumes of patents issued. Indeed, terms such as 'structural' or 'systemic competitiveness' and the 'competitive advantage' of nations underscore precisely the significance of such additional factors deemed previously 'non-economic' (Jessop, 2002, pp. 119–125). The availability of statistical data has accentuated the policy fixation on narrow technological innovation, overlooking aspects which are not as readily quantifiable, such as Schumpeter's notion of secondary waves of innovation and innovation in processes. At the heart of the Schumpeterian long-wave cyclical perspective of economic and social development is the view that primary innovations trigger other secondary innovations and give rise to supporting social and organisational structures (European Commission, industrial structures, division of labour) (see Preston, 2001, pp. 107–133). The majority of the available statistical data fails to capture these developments.

If economic growth and competitiveness depend on innovation, the problem is that the benefits of innovation are temporary. Flamm, drawing on Schumpeter, explains competition in the computer industry as 'continuous investments in technology creating a sequence of temporary monopolies on new products, with rents [high profits] earned on current products financing the investments in the next round of innovation' (1988, p. 13).

The same applies to the broader ICT field. This process creates a vicious circle whereby the targeting of oligopolistic industries creates strong incentives for first-mover advantage and measures that will sustain, if not strengthen, the oligopolistic characteristics on which government intervention and international competitiveness are based. The picture that emerges is not one of free markets and free trade but one of oligopolies trying to stymie competitive pressures.

Complementing the emphasis of new growth theories on the pivotal role of public policy, new trade theory, originating in the 1970s, critiques international free trade and draws attention to the role of economies of scale, increasing returns and imperfect competition (Krugman, 1990, pp. 1–10). For new trade theory, some industries matter more than others in maximizing a country's welfare. Industrialised countries, facing mounting competition from low-wage economies, cannot compete in labour intensive sectors. The solution is for them to move up the value-added chain and specialise in technology-intensive sectors where competition is based on innovation, not lower cost (McGuire, 1999, pp. 76–77). This is precisely the rationale behind the growing policy emphasis on the electronic communications sector and in particular the rapid roll-out of superfast NGNs. The emphasis on technology-intensive industries combined in international trade relations with a focus on sectors that exhibit significant economies of scale which governments can help cultivate to gain competitive advantage, resembles what Cerny calls the 'competition state', a state increasingly concerned with international competitiveness, with 'promoting the competitive advantages of particular production and service sectors in a more open and integrated world economy' (2000, p. 22). Jessop takes this point further and talks of the emergence of a specifically Schumpeterian version of the competition state 'because of its concern with technological change, innovation and enterprise' (2002, p. 96).

These developments give rise to two important paradoxes. First, the relation between market and industry structure and the pace of innovation is as perplexing now as it has ever been. As Scherer concludes, theoretical and empirical economic research 'provides at best meagre support' for Schumpeter's claim that large companies drive innovation (1992, p. 1425). Yet, and here lies the paradox, the findings of such research are at odds with national and European policies. Beginning in the 1960s at the national level and since the late 1970s increasingly evident in European policy circles, it has been strongly argued that firm size matters in international competitiveness and that European national markets and companies are too small to lead in technological innovation and be competitive on the world stage. What matters is high-technology industries, overcoming fragmented national markets to create a single European one, consolidation on a European scale, and cooperative European R&D programmes.

The second paradox concerns the problematic notion of 'competitiveness'. Krugman maintains that concerns about competitiveness are empirically unfounded and attributes the obsession with competitiveness to three factors (1994, pp. 39–41). First, competitive images among nations are easy to understand and associate with. Second, the notion that a country's economic problems have to do with external, as opposed to domestic, factors gives the impression that these problems are somehow easier to address. Finally, competitiveness is a useful political construct in that in can legitimate unpopular policies or, by contrast, avoid them. 'Competitiveness', therefore, can be dangerous when applied to national economies, because it implies that countries compete with each other the way firms do and assumes that countries, like corporations, are rivals. It portrays economic growth and trade as a zero-sum game whereby one country's gains are another country's losses and as such carries the risk of fuelling trade conflicts and calls for protectionism. 'Competitiveness' also lacks meaning, because it has at its core improvements of living standards and thus turns out to mean domestic productivity, another concept that has been difficult to define and measure (Michalis, 2007, pp. 195–196). Most studies refer to labour productivity, which is the output per worker. A second more accurate, but complex, measure is multi-factor productivity, which captures the efficiency with which capital and labour inputs are combined ('A productive primer', 2004, p. 93).

Measuring productivity and defining its determinants is as controversial today as it has ever been. Paul Strassmann (1997), a consistent sceptic of the contribution of information technology to productivity improvements, maintains that investment in better machines and equipment will increase labour productivity but for benefits to the economy as a whole one needs also to take into account the additional capital spending that this investment implies, as well as the increasingly rapid depreciation cycles of information technology products and the fact that each wave of investment is bigger than the last. He argues that productivity gains are firm, not sector, specific and it is thus wrong to make generalisations.

The link between ICT and economic growth and these two main analytical understandings based on neo-classical and Hayekian ideas and Schumpeterian thinking clearly are grounded on differing assumptions about the state-market relationship. The remainder of this chapter illustrates how these understandings have been manifest in EU telecommunications policy.

Innovation Trumps All Else? The Rise of Schumpeterian Ideas Since the Early 2000s

A European Commission official has defined three telecommunications policy strands or, put another way, in Garnham's terms, definitions of the problems that EU telecommunications policy has been called upon to address (Garnham, 2005, p. 9; Johnston, 2005, p. 44). The first of these is the *industrial policy strand* evident since before the start of the market liberalisation process of the 1980s and beyond. The policy problem here was one of small fragmented markets in Europe seen to be depriving telecommunications operators and equipment manufacturers from needed economies of scale that would allow them to compete globally. Market consolidation and the creation of big European, as opposed to national, companies is another element of this strand. This perspective does not necessarily favour market competition whilst it arguably supports supply-led initiatives. The second strand is *consumer welfare policies* which view competitive and cross-border supply of networks and services as central to increasing corporate efficiency, in the first instance, and wider consumer welfare, as a consequence. This is achieved through increased choice, better networks and services offered at competitive prices (e.g., cost-oriented prices that squeeze profit margins) and low market entry barriers. To deliver this, the twin pronged strategy of pro-competitive market restructuring and harmonised European rules has been the preferred policy response. The third policy strand emphasises *innovation*. Originally, the issue was innovation in the telecommunications field as part of the broader ICT sector but this was soon succeeded by strong calls for innovation in both telecommunications and ICT distinctly. Such activity was viewed as a precondition for sustainable rates of economic growth and often even as the answer to social development (e.g., European Commission, 1994). It is this innovation strand that is associated with various information society visions. Such visions, although reincarnated under differing names, prioritise network and service innovation. This policy perspective explains the emphasis on creating superfast broadband networks in recent years perceived as essential for economic and social rejuvenation. Increasingly, innovation is thus understood along Schumpeterian ideas which stress that monopoly rents can increase the chances for it to occur. However, crucially, this is not compatible with market competition and does not necessarily deliver enhanced consumer welfare.

These three policy strands are used for analytical purposes. They are not mutually exclusive but, equally, they are not linked unproblematically. Rather, the three strands are based on divergent problem definitions and result in different, even contradictory, media policy solutions to co-exist. This is not surprising. Policy is not a linear, rational and methodical process in pursuit of a single universally agreed objective (Garnham, 2005; Bauer, 2005). Policy is a field of contestation. It tries to address various issues at the same time on the basis of limited knowledge. It can even have unintended consequences as one line of action can create new – or aggravate existing – problems. Path dependencies and established power structures further limit policy responses (Mansell, 2014). Policy then resembles what Charles Lindblom (1959) has called 'muddling through' with small incremental adaptations and can even be accidental (Kingdon, 1995).

Progressively since the 2000s, there has been a change of paradigm in EU electronic communications policy. The first phase of telecommunications market restructuring (roughly from the 1980s to the early 2000s) was characterised by the gradual shift from monopolistic to liberalised markets in order to facilitate the modernisation of networks and services, ease market entry, improve corporate efficiency and indirectly consumer welfare through lower prices and more choice whilst at the same time supporting industrial policy aims by allowing European ICT manufacturers to benefit from a bigger European harmonised market. With the rise of the Internet since the mid 1990s, there has been a progressive change in the policy paradigm. Increasingly, in line with Schumpeterian thinking, the primary policy objective is no longer market liberalisation, lower market entry barriers, corporate efficiency and consumer welfare but rather the emphasis has moved to innovation and associated monopoly rents and is therefore inconsistent with open markets. This transformation refers to changes in policy priorities since, as noted, policy is neither linear nor rational. Perhaps the most representative early debates illustrating the growing calls to upset the established policy paradigm of market liberalisation and endorse innovation more openly were those leading to the EU's Regulation on local loop unbundling in December 2000, obliging incumbent operators to allow competitors to access their access networks in an effort to promote competition and accelerate the rollout of broadband Internet services, and the European Commission Recommendation on relevant product and service markets in 2003 setting out the markets that may warrant regulatory intervention, with a focus on the nascent broadband market (see Michalis, 1997, pp. 203–205). Arguably, the consumer imperative of competition won in these two cases, but calls for policy to prioritise innovation were evidently growing stronger and their influence has become progressively more visible especially after the 2008 economic collapse. The two visions of liberalisation and innovation are still present and, as explained above, are not necessarily opposites but are rather based on differing understandings of the relationship between innovation and market structure. Indeed, policy debates reflect the presence of both visions, as will be now discussed.

If Broadband Is the Answer, What Is the Question?

The Schumpeterian inspired policy paradigm views regulatory intervention, especially of a sector specific kind, as restrictive. Public policy has only a general enabling role to play. This role refers in particular to the nurturing of an investment- and innovation-friendly environment that, for this model, means no regulation, except for financial support and the, at least temporary, support of oligopolies and even monopolies, as necessary incentives for innovation (for the application of state aid rules to broadband networks see Simpson, 2012).

In the latter part of the 1990s, several studies established a link between ICT, especially the Internet, and strong economic performance. Although most of the data concerned the U.S. and its so-called productivity miracle of that decade, comparative studies concluded that, despite differences in economic growth, other countries too benefited from investment in ICT and warned that failure to accelerate the transition toward an information society and deploy broadband communications, would adversely impact on economic and productivity gains (Schreyer, 2000; Ferguson, 2002). Insufficient ICT spending and use was accepted as the root cause of the gap between U.S. and European productivity and growth (European Commission, 2002, pp. 4–5). Like in the 1960s and 1970s, the technology gap was once again the key explanatory variable for the economic gap with the U.S.

Yet other studies suggested caution over the interpretation of the data. In particular, they drew attention to the inconclusive evidence as to whether the perceived gains were confined to the firm or sectoral level, or whether they concerned entire national economies (OECD, 2000, pp. 208–209). The OECD challenged the very notion that ICT was the single most important contributor to U.S. productivity whilst, for Gordon, the reason for its growth, perceived to be cyclical, was simply economic recovery (Gordon, 2000; OECD, 2001).

Despite diverging interpretations, at the turn of the millennium, the issue of competitiveness reached the highest political level of the EU which culminated in its endorsement as a newly declared strategic goal at the Lisbon summit in 2000. EU political leaders committed to transform Europe into the 'most competitive and dynamic knowledge-based economy in the world, capable of sustainable economic growth with more and better jobs and greater social cohesion' by 2010 (EU, 2000, para. 5). Ten years later, with Europe facing the same, and in many cases intensified, problems, this commitment was renewed under a different name.

In May 2010, the European Commission adopted the Digital Agenda with the main objective to create a digital single market and support Europe's 2020 strategy 'for smart, sustainable and inclusive growth' for the next decade (European Commission, 2010). The picture presented was familiar: Europe lagged behind its major trading partners in ICT investment, research and innovation. The Commission reported that the ICT sector accounted for 5 percent of European GDP but contributed to 50 percent of overall productivity growth (European Commission, 2010, p. 4). Investment in R&D in ICT in Europe continued to be below that of its major trading partners and was less than half of what the U.S. spent.

The Digital Agenda put forward Internet penetration and, importantly, take-up targets: all European citizens were to get access to Internet speeds of at least 30 megabits per second (mbps) with half of them subscribing to connections of 100 mbps or higher by 2020. The Commission opined that 'We need very fast Internet for the economy to grow strongly and to create jobs and prosperity' (European Commission, 2010, p. 18).

In September 2013, the European Commission announced the 'Connected Continent' initiative, a series of legislative reforms aiming to 'reduce consumer charges, simplify red tape faced by companies, and bring a range of new rights for both users and service providers, so that Europe can once again be a global digital leader' (European Commission, 2013a, p. 1). By May 2015, the European Commission was now expecting that its new more ambitious Digital Single Market Strategy – covering a broad set of issues including, for instance, courier and parcel delivery rates, and copyright rules – could increase EU GDP by up to €415 billion a year (European Commission, 2015, p. 3).

Three policy areas demonstrate the pre-eminence of Schumpeterian thinking in recent EU policies on telecommunications: roaming, network neutrality and network access regulation and competition. All three issues are prominent in the Telecommunications Single Market policy proposals and complement the more recent Digital Market Strategy.

Roaming

The European Commission proposed to remove mobile phone charges for incoming calls when travelling within the EU with a view to abolish roaming charges fully by 2018 (European Commission, 2013c). Mobile operators who failed to do this would be forced to allow their customers to use temporarily a rival operator when travelling to take advantage of lower prices. These proposals had a clear potential consumer benefit in squeezing profit margins and resulting in lower prices.

The industry's reaction has been strong. It has warned that lower roaming charges would result in lower revenues and cost the industry around €7 billion by 2020 at a time when it was called to rollout out 4G infrastructure, that is next generation mobile networks (Fontanella-Khan & Thomas, 2013). In other words, the Commission's proposals would promote consumer welfare but harm innovation significantly.

In March 2015, European governments tabled another proposal, departing significantly from the European Commission's original plan subsequently strengthened by the European Parliament (European Parliament, 2014). Siding with the industry and prioritizing innovation, European governments asked for the continuation of roaming charges up until at least 2018 when the European Commission would be asked to reconsider the issue with any subsequent changes to be adopted around 2020, due to the lengthy EU legislative process. EU Member State governments through the Council of Ministers have called for a basic roaming allowance from mid 2016, that is a basic quantity of voice, text, and data traffic to which all European citizens would be entitled. If they exceed this allowance, then users would incur roaming surcharges which, however, could not be higher than the wholesale charge that mobile operators paid for using the networks in other EU countries. The Council's proposals are not final at the time of writing. Given their differences, the three institutions (the European Commission, the European Parliament and the European Council) have started so-called trialogue negotiations to try to agree on a common position. But it is clear that the Council's proposals favour big mobile operators and aim to protect their financial stability because they allow them to recover any possible losses in roaming charges from increases in domestic tariffs while smaller or alternative mobile operators will find it hard to compete if wholesale access prices remain high and thus competition might suffer as a result (Genna, 2015). It seems therefore that, despite the proclaimed aim of the proposals to create a single telecommunications market, fragmented European markets is the preferred business model for mobile operators.

In sum, whereas the European Parliament and the European Commission seem more aligned to Hayekian thinking in that they appear to prioritise consumer welfare in the form of market competition and in particular lower retail prices through the lowering and eventual dismantling of roaming charges, European governments appear to follow Schumpeterian ideas and wish to allow mobile network operators to continue to benefit from roaming charges and associated greater market returns in the hope that these will lead to innovation in the form of investment in next generation mobile networks which are in turn expected to boost economic growth.

Network Neutrality

In general, network neutrality refers to reasonable Internet traffic management, beyond the blocking of illegal content such as child pornography and harmful content such as viruses and spam. In particular, it is the idea that similar types of traffic (for example, video) should be treated equally on the Internet. Huge economic interests are at stake because traffic flows translate into money flows. The network neutrality debate is currently for the most part about how value (and money) is distributed in the Internet value chain and about 'who pays' for NGNs, content and services (Michalis, 2014, p. 81). Critically though, network neutrality is more than money flows because traffic management turns ISPs into content regulators essentially and can therefore have 'potentially enormous consequences for free speech, free competition and individual expression' (Marsden, 2010, p. 235).

In response to pressure from established telecommunications operators, the original proposals of the European Commission put forward in September 2013 allowed for price differentiation and service discrimination (paid prioritisation) which effectively means that some content providers get priority over others (European Commission, 2013b, Art. 23). Telecommunications operators in their role as ISPs would thus be able to ask so-called over-the-top[1] players (e.g., Netflix, Facebook) to pay them for faster and reliable delivery of their content, the expectation being that this extra revenue would feed back into network investment.

The proposals did not prohibit so-called zero rating (positive discrimination) either. ISPs would be in a position to cap bandwidth and choose to privilege certain own or affiliated services by providing them 'free' to end-subscribers (while getting payment from the providers of these affiliated specialised services) and not subject them to usage caps. Mobile subscribers would still be able to access alternative services not included in this basic 'free' package but such use would be taken out of their agreed network usage level and they could incur additional charges if they exceeded it, a realistic scenario with music or video streaming services. In short, the European Commission's proposals on network neutrality supported the interests of established telecommunications operators and prioritised innovation and investment in next generation mobile networks at the expense of consumer benefit.

In 2014, the European Parliament, the only directly elected EU institution and thus arguably closer to citizens' concerns, strongly opposed the European Commission's proposals and, once again, came out in support of an open Internet which respects the fundamental freedoms of Europeans. By contrast, the European Council's proposals, representing EU Member States, are more aligned to the original Commission proposals favouring established telecommunications operators (European Council, 2015). These would not prohibit specialised services and zero rating practices. Striking a compromise between the majority of countries which are against strong network neutrality rules (e.g., Britain) and the two countries (Slovenia and the Netherlands) which have adopted legislation domestically in support of network neutrality prohibiting the above practices, the Council essentially advocated leaving the issue of network neutrality in the hands of national regulators.

The Junker European Commission (2014–2019) appears divided on the issue. On the one hand, Günther Oettinger, the German Commissioner for Digital Economy and Society, has come out opposing (strong) network neutrality and called it a 'Taliban-like issue' (Reda, 2015). On the other hand, the Estonian Andrus Ansip, European Commission Vice President for the Digital Single Market, supports 'strong net neutrality rules' and described the Council's proposals on roaming 'a joke' (Ansip, 2015).

Strong network neutrality rules would follow Hayekian ideas: if greater innovation in the field of electronic communications is the aim, the role of policy is to enable the functioning of an open and competitive market in the belief that the higher the number of firms in the market, the greater are the chances for innovation and in turn economic and productivity gains.

In contrast, the absence of (strong) network neutrality rules, supported by many national governments and big industry players, is in line with Schumpeterian thinking. Again the aim is the same (the promotion of innovation in the electronic communications sector to unleash economic growth) but the means are different. An open and competitive market is not a requirement for innovation. Policy should aim at creating an innovation-friendly environment by shaping the behaviour and motives of ISPs. Governments, by refraining from introducing (strong) net neutrality regulation, and in doing so allowing (big) ISPs to capture greater market returns (higher profits), hope that these will spur investment in fast NGNs which in turn will translate into economic growth. Innovation understood as investment in NGNs might indeed produce benefits, but market competition and consumer benefit could also suffer. Additionally, innovation from start-up firms might also be disadvantaged. For example, the inclusion of certain services in the usage caps would steer users towards these services and away from competitors' services which would count toward data usage and very likely result in additional charges.

Network Access Regulation and Competition

The European Telecommunications Network Operators' (ETNO) Association, representing mainly ex-monopolist telecommunications operators, has argued that market 'fragmentation' is about too many players in the market and too many rules. The policy objective as a corollary should be no longer liberalisation but rather innovation and investment in super-fast broadband networks because market fragmentation hinders investment. ETNO maintains that '[i]nvestment in better, faster and more pervasive networks should be at the heart of new EU policies' (European Telecommunications Network Operators [ETNO], 2015, p. 5). It argues that a pro-investment strategy needs to be premised on two elements: deregulation and market consolidation. Deregulation will get rid of rules which are considered obsolete for telecommunications incumbents. It has called for a complete rethink and a major reform of the regulatory framework in order to get rid of existing 'rigid and prescriptive rules' which favour infrastructure renters as opposed to investors. This would include network neutrality rules on network traffic management, network access obligations, and price regulation, in particular cost-orientation requirements (2015, pp. 18, 21). This is precisely what telecommunications operators' demands for so-called regulatory holidays are about. Regulatory holidays refer to an initial period of no regulation to encourage investment in new network infrastructure. Perhaps the most debated case is that concerning the amendment to the German Telecommunications Act in 2006 allowing Deutsche Telekom to be exempted from regulation for an initial period in return for investing in a NGN. In 2009, the European Court condemned Germany for doing so and ordered that competitors should be allowed to access Deutsche Telekom's high-speed network (*European Commission v. Federal Republic of Germany*, 2009). In turn, requiring incumbent operators to allow competitors to access their networks raises the question of the terms of, and in particular the price for, such access.[2] The terms of access have sparked heated policy debates with incumbent operators arguing that the cost and risk involved in NGN investment is very high and that they need as a result monopoly rents if they are to undertake it and contribute to Europe's growth.

For ETNO, the second essential element for the creation of a telecommunications single market is scale even if, again, it comes at the expense of competition. ETNO explains that '[s]cale can support the development of stronger companies, who will in turn deliver better services' (2015, p. 5). Freed from regulatory requirements obliging them to share their investment with competitors and allowing them to benefit from economies of scale through market consolidation will energise telecommunications incumbents to proceed with the needed investment, the argument goes.

This idea is familiar in the history of communication policy which supports European market consolidation in order to create European champions. It is based on the unsubstantiated belief that scale matters and it is large companies that drive innovation. ETNO has thus pleaded for what is in effect industrial consolidation to occur: 'There are more than 100 mobile operators across the EU, whereas in the United States there are only four and three in China' (Thomas, 2013); 'Why is it a necessity [...] that two million Slovenians have more operators than one billion Chinese?' (ETNO ThinkDigital, 2015).

The position of established mobile operators is rather different. For them market fragmentation is welcome as their business model is premised on it, as noted above. They favour consolidation within national markets but do not see major benefits in consolidating across countries (Gordon, 2014).[3] Nevertheless, mobile operators support the single market in the area of spectrum harmonisation as concerted action across the EU will allow them to reap some economies of scale. To this end, they have argued for more spectrum to be released from terrestrial television. Again, and this time similar to fixed operators, they maintain that this is crucial for them to invest in future generation mobile networks (see ETNO, 2015, pp. 18–19; Groupe Spéciale Mobile Association, 2015).

In short, whilst the EU's current regulatory proposals aim to create a telecommunications single market, there is no consensus over what such a market will look like (for instance, can indicators be used to determine how 'common' it is?) and indeed market players perceive it differently, with mobile operators even opposing the idea in the case of roaming. Woolcock's (1996) remark that a 'constructive ambiguity' runs through the single market project applies to telecommunications. This allows some to view it as a lever to promote liberalisation by removing market barriers. It allows others to view it as premised on industrial policy aims, with the EU and national governments working to encourage innovation in the form of investment in new technologies (such as NGNs) even if this implies market protection. Both visions have their own strong supporters within the industry, the European institutions and among national governments. The argument of this chapter is that, in particular since the 2008 economic crisis, Schumpeterian perspectives on innovation on the back of greater market returns, not necessarily market competition, have become recognizably dominant.

National telecommunications regulators, through the pan-European regulatory Body of European Regulators in Electronic Communications (Berec), have been vociferous in opposing the European Commission's original Telecommunications Single Market regulation proposals tabled in September 2013. They saw them as a rushed and unnecessary move by the then outgoing Commission and, more importantly, they argued that the proposals represented 'a significant shift in policy orientation' (Body of European Regulators in Electronic Communications, 2013, p. 2). Echoing the argument of this chapter, Berec argued that by adding 'the promotion of global competitiveness of the EU' as a new regulatory objective, the proposals represented a move away from pro-competitive regulation to market consolidation, jeopardising the goals of promoting competition and efficient investment and, by extension, undermining consumer benefit.

Whereas the link between ICT and economic growth is as intriguing today as it has ever been, demand for fixed and mobile superfast connections remains uncertain, and the over-optimistic traffic projections put forward by equipment manufacturers and dominant telecommunications operators which stand to benefit from such projections are increasingly questioned. Policy makers nevertheless seem to accept uncritically the need for NGNs and rather ponder whether these should be offered on a competitive basis or through a reversion to old market structures (monopolies/duopolies). There is strong evidence which demonstrates that policy makers around the world are increasingly favouring the second option.

In 2003, the Federal Communications Commission in the U.S. deregulated the market for high-speed Internet access and ruled that fibre optic networks would be exempted from unbundling requirements. Regulatory forbearance meant that telecommunications operators investing in such networks would not be required to let competitors access (parts of) their networks for the purposes of offering services to end-customers themselves (unbundling). This absence of regulation has resulted in market consolidation – effectively duopolies in both the wired and wireless markets – and higher prices for U.S. Internet users for less speedy service (Crawford, 2013). In 2009, the Labour government in Australia announced the renationalisation of the telecommunications infrastructure through the creation of the National Broadband Network company, 90% owned by the state, with the objective to invest in a Fibre to the Premises network. Within the EU, in another case where investment in new technologies has trumped competition, the British National Audit Office (NAO) in its latest report reiterated concerns about the lack of competition in rural broadband and the fact that the scheme has effectively re-established a British Telecom monopoly on the back of £1.7 billion of public funding (NAO, 2015). Similarly, in EU policy circles, Günther Oettinger, European Commissioner for Digital Economy and Society, appears to support the views of established telecommunications operators about the creation of big European champions. In a recent blog, he suggested that in order to incentivise investment in rural broadband, consumer choice could be sacrificed by locking in customers to longer contracts and/or by exempting investing broadband providers from regulation (Oettinger, 2014).

Conclusion: From Liberalisation to Innovation?

The belief that ICT can drive economic growth and productivity gains has been constant in EU telecommunications policy, as this chapter explained. The information society vision, under various guises, has moved at the forefront of economic development planning and even social policies. Both competition and innovation are integral and fundamental parts of this vision. This follows a conceptualisation of policy not as a mechanical, linear and rational process in pursuit of a single objective (either competition or innovation) but rather as a field of contestation with various concurrent problem definitions, often with conflicting aims and associated interventions, based in turn on different analytical understandings, and shaped by path dependencies and power structures. The argument put forward in this chapter is that the relative emphasis between these two parts (competition and innovation) has changed over the years in EU telecommunications policy thinking and that this, in turn, is premised on differing perceptions of the state-market relationship and the notion of innovation.

From from the 1980s to the early 2000s policy was closer to neo-classical economics and Hayekian thinking. The belief was that free markets, not state involvement, would rejuvenate the economy. These ideas contributed to the gradual breaking down of national telecommunications state monopolies, seen as inefficient and unresponsive. The benefits from better networks and services, greater choice, and cost-oriented prices would trickle down from the corporate world to ordinary end users, bolstering individual consumer sovereignty and personal freedom. Innovation was not absent from this period. But the belief was that the unconstrained market, by supporting as large a number of firms as possible, would maximise the chances for innovation and would, at the same time, enhance economic and consumer welfare. Free markets and competition would take care of everything.

Since the 2000s and, in particular, in the aftermath of the 2008 economic crisis, innovation in telecommunications and ICT has moved to be the central policy priority overshadowing, and often side-lining completely, the pursuit of market competition. This is because innovation is increasingly understood along Schumpeterian lines. Prioritised no longer is inter-firm competition and the free market but rather the enabling role of public policy in nurturing an innovation-friendly environment by shaping the behaviour and motives of economic agents. This Schumpeterian understanding emphasises innovation and related monopoly rents and is therefore not consistent with open competitive markets.

Big telecommunications market players maintain that rules which prioritise competition (such as European Commission existing and planned network access obligations, proposed roaming and network neutrality regulations) are investment- and innovation-unfriendly. They further contend that European markets are fragmented and that, lacking needed economies of scale, they cannot compete globally. Hence, the argument goes, the European telecommunications industry needs to consolidate. To stimulate investment in next generation (access) networks, drive innovation and support the objective of the Europe 2020 strategy requires a potentially dangerous combination of deregulation and the re-establishment (at least temporarily) of monopolistic (at best oligopolistic) market structures, preferably on a pan-European scale.

This chapter has provided evidence that various institutional, political and economic actors have capitalised on the political saliency of superfast broadband networks and the rise of a Schumpeterian understanding of innovation in an attempt to promote their own narrow interests overlooking, in the process, broader consumer and social welfare. The outcome of the Digital Single Market policy proposals will determine whether the emphasis on innovation in a Schumpeterian sense will remain. At the moment, and especially in view of the persistent economic downturn, it looks likely that the prioritisation of innovation, possibly with a bit of watering down ('muddling through') by use of vague language in order to accommodate aspects of competition and consumer welfare, will win. Schumpeterian and Hayekian ideas have strong supporters within different parts of the EU institutions, national governments and industry stakeholders. Any concrete policy proposals will have to satisfy to an extent both perspectives. The final judgement concerning the balance between innovation and competition will tend to fall on the shoulders of national regulators, which will assume responsibility for the detailed implementation of any agreed-upon policies.

It will be interesting to see to what extent regulators will be able to balance the economic-industrial imperative of innovation with the consumer imperative of competition, taking into account the specific national circumstances they face within overall EU policy constraints.

Notes

1. Over-The-Top (OTT) refers to delivery over the open Internet, via a browser or an application.
2. Space limitations do not allow this chapter to examine these in detail. For the latest compromise see European Commission, 2013d.
3. Two recent developments concern the British market. In March 2015, Hutchinson, the smallest mobile operator, which owns Three, agreed to buy O2 for £10 billion to become the largest domestic operator, whilst the ex-fixed monopolist British Telecom will buy EE (co-owned by Orange and Deutsche Telekom following an earlier merger) for £12.5 billion in order to enter the mobile market. If these deals are approved, then the British mobile market will go from four down to three network operators. Similar consolidation has taken place in other markets, such as in Germany, when, following the approval in 2014 of the merger between Telefonica and E-Plus for €11.8 billion by the European Commission, the mobile market was reduced from four to three network operators.

References

A productivity primer. (1994, 6 November). *Economist*, p. 93.
Ansip, A. (2015, 24 March). Telecoms: the backbone of the Digital Single Market. Retrieved from http://europa.eu/rapid/press-release_SPEECH-15-4659_en.htm.
Bauer, J. (2005). Mechanical to adaptive policy. In P. Verhoest (Ed.) *Contradiction, confusion and hubris. A critical review of European information society policy* (pp. 27–30). Brussels, Belgium: ENCIP.
Bell, D. (1976). *The coming of the post-industrial society: A venture in social forecasting*. Harmondsworth, UK: Penguin.
Body of European Regulators for Electronic Communication. (2013). *BEREC views on the proposal for a regulation 'laying down measures to complete the European single market for electronic communications and to achieve a Connected Continent'*. Retrieved from http://berec.europa.eu/eng/document_register/subject_matter/berec/download/0/2922-berec-views-on-the-proposal-for-a-regula_0.pdf.
Cerny, P. (2000). Structuring the political arena. Public goods, states and governance in a globalizing world. In R. Palan (Ed.), *Global political economy: Contemporary theories* (pp. 23–35). London and New York: Routledge.
Crawford, S. (2013). *Captive audience: The telecom industry and monopoly power in the new gilded age*. New Haven, CT: Yale University Press.
European Commission. (1979, 26 November). *European society faced with the challenge of new information technologies: A community response*. COM(79) 650. Retrieved from http://aei.pitt.edu/3806/1/3806.pdf.
European Commission. (1994). *Europe and the global information society. Bangemann report recommendations to the European Council*. Retrieved from https://docs.google.com/file/d/0B2vWhkwcw_1MZDA4Y2U0NGYtM2I2Ny00NTczLTg4YTUtZDIyZDYxMGJjYmFm/edit?hl=en.

European Commission. (2002, 21 May). *Productivity: The key to competitiveness of European economies and enterprises.* COM(2002) 262. Retrieved from http://aei.pitt.edu/45432/1/COM_(2002)_262.pdf.
European Commission. (2010, 19 May). *A digital agenda for Europe.* COM(2010) 245. Retrieved from http://eur-lex.europa.eu/legal-content/EN/TXT/PDF/?uri=CELEX:52010DC0245&from=EN.
European Commission. (2013a, 11 September). *Commission proposes major step forward for telecoms single market.* IP 13-828. Retrieved from http://europa.eu/rapid/press-release_IP-13-828_en.doc.
European Commission. (2013b, 11 September). Proposal for a regulation laying down measures concerning the European single market for electronic communications and to achieve a Connected Continent. Retrieved from https://ec.europa.eu/digital-agenda/en/news/regulation-european-parliament-and-council-laying-down-measures-concerning-european-single.
European Commission. (2013c, 11 September). *Communication on the telecommunications single market.* COM(2013) 634. Retrieved from http://ec.europa.eu/information_society/newsroom/cf/dae/document.cfm?doc_id=2733.
European Commission. (2013d, 11 September). *Commission recommendation of 11.9.2013 on consistent non-discrimination obligations and costing methodologies to promote competition and enhance the broadband investment environment.* COM(2013) 5761. Retrieved from http://ec.europa.eu/information_society/newsroom/cf/dae/document.cfm?doc_id=2735.
European Commission. (2015, 6 May). *A digital single market strategy for Europe.* COM(2015) 192. Retrieved from http://ec.europa.eu/priorities/digital-single-market/docs/dsm-communication_en.pdf.
European Commission v. Federal Republic of Germany [2009] C-424/07. Retrieved from http://curia.europa.eu/juris/document/document.jsf?text=&docid=73876&pageIndex=0&doclang=EN&mode=lst&dir=&occ=first&part=1&cid=236653.
European Council. (2015, 4 March). Roaming and open internet: Council ready for talks with EP. Retrieved from http://www.consilium.europa.eu/en/press/press-releases/2015/03/150304-roaming-and-open-internet-council-ready-for-talks-with-ep/.
European Parliament. (2014). European Parliament legislative resolution of 3 April 2014 on the proposal for a regulation of the European Parliament and of the Council laying down measures concerning the European single market for electronic communications and to achieve a Connected Continent. Retrieved from http://www.europarl.europa.eu/sides/getDoc.do?pubRef=-//EP//TEXT+TA+P7-TA-2014-0281+0+DOC+XML+V0//EN.
European Telecommunications Network Operators. (2015a). *Achieving a stronger digital union. ETNO contribution to the digital single market strategy.* Retrieved from https://etno.eu/datas/publications/studies/DIGITAL%20STRATEGY-72dpi_website.pdf.
European Telecommunications Network Operators. (2015b, 5 May). ETNO Think-Digital Interview – Aiming for a stronger Europe with less national division. Retrieved from http://www.think-digital.eu/?n=2015/283.
European Union. (2000). Lisbon European Council 23 and 24 March 2000 Presidency conclusions. Retrieved from http://www.europarl.europa.eu/summits/lis1_en.htm.
Ernst, D., & O'Connor, D. (1992). *Competing in the electronics industry – The experience of newly industrializing economies.* Paris: OECD.

Ferguson, C. (2002). *The United States broadband problem: Analysis and recommendations.* Washington, DC: Brookings Institution.

Flamm, K. (1988). *Targeting the computer: Government support and international competition.* Washington, DC: Brookings Institution.

Fontanella-Khan, J., & Thomas, D. (2013, 10 July). Telecoms groups warn over end to EU roaming. *Financial Times.* Retrieved from http://www.ft.com/intl/cms/s/0/ecd7ada6-e978-11e2-9f11-00144feabdc0.html#axzz3fnqw9Aaj.

Garnham, N. (2005). Contradiction, confusion and hubris: A critical review of European information society policy. In P. Verhoest (Ed.), *Contradiction, confusion and hubris. A critical review of European information society policy* (pp. 6–18). Brussels, Belgium: ENCIP.

Genna, I. (2015, 4 March). The European governments find a deal on roaming and net neutrality: a low-level compromise. [Weblog]. Retrieved from https://radiobruxelleslibera.wordpress.com/2015/03/04/the-european-governments-find-a-deal-on-roaming-and-net-neutrality-a-low-level-compromise.

Godin, B. (2004). The obsession for competitiveness and its impact on statistics: the construction of high-technology indicators. *Research Policy, 33*(8), 1217–1229. doi: 10.1016/j.respol.2004.07.005.

Godin, B. (2014). *The vocabulary of innovation* (Project on the Intellectual History of Innovation Working Paper, 20). Retrieved from http://www.csiic.ca/PDF/LexiconPaperNo20.pdf.

Gordon, R. (2000). Does the 'New Economy' measure up to the Great inventions of the past? *Journal of Economic Perspectives, 14*(4), 49–74. doi: 10.3386/w7833.

Gordon, S. (2014, 25 March). No winners in Europe's fragmenting telecoms market. *Financial Times.* Retrieved from http://www.ft.com/cms/s/0/3c2b1b24-b41f-11e3-a09a-00144feabdc0.html#axzz3fnqw9Aaj.

Groupe Spéciale Mobile Association. (2015, 6 May). GSMA calls for urgent telecoms rule changes to support EU industry investment. Retrieved from http://www.gsma.com/newsroom/press-release/gsma-calls-for-urgent-telecom-rule-changes-to-support-eu-industry-investment.

Hayek, F.A. (1945). The use of knowledge in society. *The American Economic Review, 35*(4), 519–530.

Jessop, B. (2002). *The future of the capitalist state.* Cambridge, MA: Polity Press.

Johnston, P. (2005). European research and telecommunications policy: An evaluation perspective. In P. Verhoest (Ed.), *Contradiction, confusion and hubris. A critical review of European information society policy* (pp. 43–46). Brussels, Belgium: European Network in Communication & Information Perspectives.

Kingdon, J. (1985). *Agendas, alternatives, and public policy* (2nd Ed.). New York: HarperCollins.

Krugman, P. (1990). *Rethinking international trade.* Cambridge, MA: MIT Press.

Krugman, P. (1994). Competitiveness: A dangerous obsession. *Foreign Affairs, 73*(2), 28–44.

Layton, C. (1969). *European advanced technology: A programme for integration.* London: Allen & Unwin.

Lee, T.B. (2012, 27 May). Two views of innovation. *Forbes.* Retrieved from http://www.forbes.com/sites/timothylee/2012/05/27/two-views-of-innovation.

Lindblom, C. E. (1959). The science of 'muddling through'. *Public Administration, 19*(2), 79–88. Retrieved from http://www.jstor.org/stable/973677.

Lucas, R. E., Jr. (1998). On the mechanics of economic development. *Journal of Monetary Economics, 22*(1), pp. 3–42. doi: 10.1016/0304-3932(88)90168-7.
Machlup, F. (1962). *The production and distribution of knowledge in the United States*. Princeton, NJ: Princeton University Press.
Mansell, R. (2014). Here comes the revolution – The European digital agenda. In K. Donders, C. Pauwels & J. Loisen (Eds.), *The Palgrave handbook of European media policy* (pp. 202–217). Basingstoke and New York: Palgrave Macmillan.
Marsden, C. (2010). *Net neutrality. Towards a co-regulatory solution*. London: Bloomsbury Academic.
McGuire, S. (1999). Trade tools: Holding the fort or declaring open house? In T. Lawton (Ed.), *European industrial policy and competitiveness* (pp. 72–92). London: Macmillan.
Michalis, M. (2007). *Governing European communications*. Lanham, MD: Lexington.
Michalis, M. (2014). Infrastructure as a content issue and the convergence between television and broadband internet: Insights from the British market. *International Journal of Digital Television, 5*(1), 75–90. doi: 10.1386/jdtv.5.1.75_1.
NAO [National Audit Office, UK] (2015). *The Superfast (Rural) Broadband Programme: update*. http://data.parliament.uk/writtenevidence/committeeevidence.svc/evidencedocument/public-accounts-committee/rural-broadband-progress-update/written/17767.pdf (25 March 2015).
Oettinger, G.H. (2014, 14 November). Connected Europe? Broadband for all is the answer. [Weblog]. Retrieved from http://ec.europa.eu/commission/2014-2019/oettinger/blog/connected-europe-broadband-all-answer_en.
Organisation for Economic Co-operation and Development [OECD] (1964). *The residual factor and economic growth*. Paris: OECD.
OECD. (2000). *OECD Economic outlook No. 67*. Paris: OECD. doi: 10.1787/data-00099-en.
OECD. (2001). *The new economy: Beyond the hype*. Paris: OECD. doi: 10.1787/9789264033856-en.
Porter, M. (1990). *The competitive advantage of nations*. London: Macmillan.
Preston, P. (2001). *Reshaping communications: Technology, information and social change*. London: Sage.
Reda, J. (2105). Net neutrality is 'Taliban-like issue', says Europe's top digital policymaker [Weblog]. Retrieved from https://juliareda.eu/2015/03/oettinger-net-neutrality-taliban-like.
Scherer, F. M. (1992). Schumpeter and plausible capitalism. *Journal of Economic Literature, 30*(3), 1416–1433.
Schreyer, P. (2000). *The contribution of information and communication technology to output growth: A study of the G7 countries* (OECD STI Working Paper no. 2000/2). Retrieved from http://www.oecd.org/internet/ieconomy/1826375.pdf.
Schumpeter, J. (2010). *Capitalism, socialism, and democracy*. London: Routledge. (Original work published 1943).
Servan-Schreiber, J.-J. (1968). *The American challenge* (R. Steel, Trans.). New York: Atheneum. (Original work published 1967).
Simpson, S. (2012). New approaches to the development of telecommunications infrastructures in Europe? The evolution of European Union policy for next generation networks. In N. Just, & M. Puppis (Eds.), *Trends in communication policy research* (pp. 335–351). Bristol: Intellect Books.

Solow, R. (1956). A contribution to the theory of economic growth. *Quarterly Journal of Economics, 70*(1), 65–94. doi: 10.2307/1884513.
Strassmann, P. (1997). Facts and fantasies about productivity. Retrieved from http://www.strassmann.com/pubs/fnf/factnfantasy.shtml.
Thomas, D. (2013, 11 September). EU regulators adopt measures to reform telecoms market. *Financial Times*. Retrieved from http://www.ft.com/cms/s/0/41958a7e-1aee-11e3-a605-00144feab7de.html#ixzz3VDcjQgvd.
Webster, F. (2014). *Theories of the information society*. Abingdon, UK: Routledge.
Woolcock, S. (1996). Competition among rules in the single European market. In W. Bratton, J. McCahery, S. Picciotto, & C. Scott (Eds.), *International regulatory competition and coordination. Perspectives on economic regulation in Europe and the United States* (pp. 289–321). Oxford: Clarendon Press.
Wu, T. (2005). Intellectual property, innovation, and decentralized decisions. *Virginia Law Review, 92*(1), 101–127. Retrieved from http://www.jstor.org/stable/4144999.

9 The Net Neutrality Debate from a Public Sphere Perspective[1]

Francesca Musiani and Maria Löblich

Introduction

The Internet impacts social communication and the public sphere, and this impact has consequences for the political shape of the communication order and therefore, for society as a whole. One important question in this regard is which regulatory framework is being developed for the Internet, and how this framework enables and at the same time restricts communication in the public sphere. The debate on net neutrality – originally the idea according to which all data packets circulating on the Internet should be treated equally, without discrimination between users, types of content, sites, platforms, applications, equipment or modes of communication – is at the very core of this question. Indeed, it questions the extent to which the Internet, as a set of distribution channels, can be used to discriminate, control, prevent access and otherwise interfere in communication processes. In other words, content and user behavior can be controlled through the architecture of the physical layer and the 'code' layer of the Internet. The discussion on net neutrality touches fundamental values (diversity, freedom of expression and free flow of information), that communications policy authorities in liberal democracies have been appealing to in order to legitimise their interventions in communication systems. The implementation of these values, from a normative point of view, is seen as a pre-condition to create the public sphere – be it online or offline – and thus fulfill its function in society (Napoli, 2001).

This chapter explores the implications of the net neutrality debate for communication research and the public sphere in Europe. We adopt a public sphere theory framework to discuss areas of net neutrality that are relevant for communication studies, and we highlight the contributions of communication scholarship to their analysis. Peter Dahlgren's three-dimensional framework – structure, representation and interaction – serves as an entry point into the field (Dahlgren, 1995). We draw upon literature from a heterogeneous field to which different disciplines contribute.

Although other disciplines, such as law and economics, have played a more active role in the net neutrality debate so far, this chapter demonstrates that communication scholars have fundamental contributions to offer in illuminating core issues in the net neutrality debate. First, communication scholars can inform and advance the debate by means of the public sphere concept. Our paper highlights how this perspective can complement the frameworks offered in the economic and legal traditions. A public sphere perspective sheds light on the effects of Internet infrastructure on online communication spaces. Second, some of the issues that are now regrouped under the pervasive label of net neutrality – such as the effect of network bottlenecks on freedom of speech, the extent of user control and the diversity of media ownership – have been under consideration by communication policy scholars under different labels before the 'net neutrality' label became so prominent. These cognate issues are now crystallised in new ways, thanks to evolutions in both technologies and power balances. As a result, the study of net neutrality may benefit from more effective connections between the research conducted on these issues within communication scholarship – even if this research often does not explicitly refer to net neutrality – and those bodies of work that explicitly include research on net neutrality. We illustrate this by means of several examples.

The term neutrality can itself be a source of ambiguity. In journalism, neutrality is related to the idea of neutral reporting, implying a balance of viewpoints surrounding a topic and, more generally, a balance of discourses in the public media. However, the neutrality that Tim Wu, a law professor at Columbia Law School, referred to in his 2003 seminal article, 'Network Neutrality, Broadband Discrimination', did not entail balanced viewpoints on Internet-hosted documents nor the relation between content producers and their readers or users. Wu was concerned with the underlying infrastructure of the Web, the so-called transport layer of the Internet, in particular the ways in which data packets circulate in the network and the preservation of the principle that these packets of information, regardless of their source and recipient, should be treated equally (Wu, 2003). Several measures and arrangements related to network management have, in recent years, breached net neutrality (Krämer, Wieviorra & Weinhardt, 2012, p. 6), often because of technical necessity: for instance, the incessant fight against spam; the existence of services such as virtual private networks or television over IP, which 'borrow' the Internet as a channel but remain independent from it. The core question is to know whether the deliberate choice to distinguish between different kinds of data packets and route them to their destination in a more or less rapid fashion should be entirely left to the different Internet operators and to the commercial negotiations between them or if active regulatory measures are needed to preserve the neutrality of the global Internet as much as possible. Thus, net neutrality concerns both 'the extent to which providers of Internet services should be allowed to favour some traffic or users over others, perhaps affecting what content, applications or devices are used on the providers network' (Peha, Lehr & Wilkie, 2007, p. 709) and the equal treatment of content providers and users (Blevins & Shade, 2010).

As the Internet has become the central nervous system of our societies, it has undergone profound changes. Entire industrial sectors participate in the shaping of the 'network of networks': computer networking industries, data centres, content industries (media, video producers), service companies (social networking, electronic commerce), telecommunication industries and even companies providing the energy needed to operate computing equipment. By 2012, the number of Internet users had reached two billion (ITU, 2012), and these users are becoming central actors in the Internet value chain, both as content producers and participants in many services whose 'value' and usefulness increases with the number of people using them. These evolutions of the network and its global economic value are transforming this network into a central actor in economic, political and geopolitical relations and a centre of attention for political actors and law makers.

Europe is, in this regard, an especially peculiar policy arena. Less than a year after the European Parliament voted to enshrine net neutrality in law, approving former Digital Agenda Commissioner Neelie Kroes's reform package, which included strong safeguards for the principle, net neutrality has come under attack from the European Commission. In March 2015, the Parliament expressed itself in favour of the prioritisation of some 'specialised' services requiring high quality internet access to function effectively (Geere, 2015). It is unlikely that this will be the last important change for European net neutrality, highlighting, once more, the extent to which economic, political and technical issues as well as actors converge around many of the issues highlighted below.

A Public Sphere Framework

The debate on net neutrality has made visible a number of diverse – and intertwined – political, economic and social concerns. Despite its 'inherently technical character' (Yoo, 2012), the debate has implications for users and content providers, be they bloggers, media organisations or social networking sites. European media policy scholars can situate themselves in the field of net neutrality research by addressing relevant issues from a public sphere perspective.

Differing concepts of the public sphere are present in the work of several authors (Calhoun, 1992; Habermas, 1989; Lunt & Livingstone, 2013; Splichal, 2012). However, the concept developed by Habernas is widely recognised as being the most influential. According to Habermas, the public sphere links citizens and power holders. It is 'a realm of our social life in which something approaching public opinion can be formed'. Habermas's concept of the public sphere centres on deliberation. Functioning deliberation requires that 'access is guaranteed to all citizens' (Habermas, 1984, p. 49). This emphasis on access makes this concept of the public sphere particularly useful for an investigation of the net neutrality debate. Peter Dahlgren (1995, 2005, 2010) developed Habermas's notion of the public sphere into an analytic tool in order to study the role of the media and the Internet vis-à-vis the public sphere. According to Dahlgren, the public sphere is 'a constellation of communicative spaces in society that permit the circulation of information, ideas, debates – ideally in an unfettered manner – and also the formation of political will' (Dahlgren, 2005, p. 148). Traditional media and online media play an important role in these spaces or 'public spheres', as there are distinct, sometimes overlapping social spaces that constitute different public spheres (Dahlgren, 2010, p. 21).

Dahlgren (1995) distinguishes three analytical dimensions of the public sphere: the structural, the representational and the interactional. The structural dimension refers to the organisation of communicative spaces 'in terms of legal, social, economic, cultural, technical and even Web-architectural features' (Dahlgren, 2005, p. 149). These patterns impact Internet access. The representational dimension directs attention to media output and raises questions concerning fairness, pluralism of views, agenda setting, ideological biases and other evaluation criteria for media content. According to Dahlgren, representation remains highly relevant for online contexts of the public sphere. The interactional dimension focuses on the ways users interact with the media and with each other in particular online sites and spaces. In these 'micro-contexts of everyday life', users deliberate on meaning, identity, opinions or entertain themselves (Dahlgren, 2005, p. 149).

We use these analytical dimensions as a heuristic framework to identify net neutrality areas that are relevant for media policy. Each dimension serves as an entry point into a particular set of net neutrality issues. The structural dimension is an analytical starting point for examining the bundle of net neutrality issues that are related to access to the Internet infrastructure for individuals and collective entities. The representational dimension leads to the question of how net neutrality relates to online content. We refer to content 'accessible in the public Internet', as opposed to secure or closed private networks (Marsden, 2010, p. 29). The related issues are content diversity, control and censorship of social communication, although of course net neutrality is just one aspect of these debates. The interactional dimension directs attention to the modes, cultures and spaces of social communication online and whether they are affected by net neutrality. Closed systems, or 'walled gardens', will illustrate the extent to which the potential benefits of online interaction and deliberation can be impeded or lost.

Dahlgren outlined these dimensions before the Internet became so widely diffused; thus, there is some overlap when they are applied to online spaces. Content control carried out by Deep Packet Inspection (DPI) – packet filtering techniques examining the data and the header of a packet as it passes an inspection point in the network – may affect interacting users as much as media organisations. While Dahlgren pointed to the blurring of the representation and interaction dimensions in relation to the Internet, traditional mass communication categories such as 'one-to-many' versus 'one-to-one' can no longer be separated as clearly (Dahlgren, 2005, pp. 149–150). However, by distinguishing access to Internet infrastructure, diversity of content transmitted via Internet infrastructure and user interaction enabled through Internet infrastructure, these dimensions provide important analytical tools.

The Structural Dimension: Access to the Network for Content Producers

Architectural, economic and other structures shape the organisation of communicative spaces and constitute the framework for different actors' access to Internet infrastructure. Net neutrality bears technical implications and economic consequences for audiovisual content producers, news media outlets and other corporate content providers. These implications influence the definition and the implementation of the quality of service principle. This principle is essential for audiovisual service providers, because video on demand needs to be delivered by strict technical deadlines ('real-time' traffic). Delays severely and negatively affect the viewing experience (van Eijk, 2011, p. 9). By contrast, an email 'just needs to get there as soon as (and as fast as) possible (so-called 'best-effort' traffic)' (Clark, 2007, p. 705). Therefore, some authors make the point that network management can benefit content providers and consumers by making the flow of traffic more balanced, or smoother (Yoo, 2012, p. 542).

In order to prevent network overload at times of peak usage, corporate content providers make quality of service one of their priorities. Google has built its own infrastructure of server farms and fibre optic networks in order to store content and get it more quickly to end-users (Levy, 2012). Economists have argued that producers of the next generation of online video, who depend 'critically' on the prioritisation of data, need a legal or quasi-legal assurance of its delivery (Hahn & Litan, 2007, p. 605). Proponents of net neutrality, however, emphasise that the priority should be to keep the costs of market entry as low as possible for the 'lowest-end market entrants – application companies' (Wu & Yoo, 2007, p. 591). As the Internet becomes an increasingly important distribution channel for traditional media, the boundaries of old business models, such as those of broadcasting and telecommunications, blur. Problems arise with the interaction of content and networks (Vogelsang, 2010, pp. 8–9). In the view of some scholars, deviations from network neutrality do not necessarily harm users and media organisations. However, these scholars generally acknowledge that situations where Internet service providers become content providers may favour the implementation of network management techniques in order to discriminate against competitors. Providers can exclude competitor content, distribute it poorly or make competitors pay for using high-speed networks (Marsden, 2010, p. 30; van Eijk, 2011, p. 10). Critics fear the dominance of a similar model to that of the cable TV industry, where cable providers 'charge a termination fee to those who wish to get access to the user' (Marsden, 2010, p. 18). In particular, this would mean a burden for new media businesses and non-commercial services, such as citizens' media and blogs. Whereas large content providers are able to negotiate free or even profitable access, smaller content providers with less contracting power are forced to pay cable TV operators for access. As a result, net neutrality might be easily circumvented both by large content providers and Internet service providers

(ISPs) (Marsden, 2010, pp. 18, 101). Whereas some scholars argue that antitrust and competition laws are sufficient to protect upstart content providers from negative consequences of vertical integration and concentration (Hahn & Litan, 2007, p. 606), others argue that there are limits to competition in the access network market due to high fixed costs that restrict market entry (Vogelsang, 2010, p. 7).

In Europe, the debate on competition and net neutrality has become particularly controversial in political terms. In November 2014, the Council of the European Union affirmed it wanted 'compromise' on the issue of net neutrality and fostered a position that included both the rejection of discriminatory practices and the rejection of an 'anti-competitive' Internet. This left uncertainty about how competition could express itself without allowing for differentiated services offering a range of speeds of functionality (Barrie, 2015). More broadly, a historical net neutrality concern for Europe has been public service broadcasting. Many scholars demand open and non-discriminatory access to distribution for this service. Several German authors, for instance, regard must-carry rules as a suitable instrument to secure the circulation of online services: They suggest introducing a classification of online services that fulfil indispensable functions for public sphere, contribute to the diversity of opinions and that, therefore, should enjoy the privilege of must-carry rules. They classify public service broadcasting as such an indispensable service (Holznagel, 2010, p. 95; Libertus & Wiesner, 2011, p. 88). The question of who decides which services should get this privilege remains alongside whether net neutrality will only apply to public service broadcasting (directing other content into the slow lane) or to all content providers (Marsden, 2010, pp. 83, 98).

The Representational Dimension: Diversity and Control of Content

A functioning public sphere is based on the representation of the diversity of information, ideas and opinions (Dahlgren, 2005, p. 149). Different technical practices of inspection or prioritisation of data packets, for political or law enforcement purposes, shape net neutrality in various ways. They condition access and circulation of content and restrict the variety and diversity of such content.

A number of technical practices are currently available to governments and the information technology industry to control or restrict content. Examples are bandwidth throttling (the intentional slowing down of Internet service by an Internet Service Provider), blocking of websites, prioritisation of certain services to the detriment of others and DPI. The latter has several implications, beyond net neutrality, for privacy, copyright and other issues. DPI may be implemented for a variety of reasons, including the search for protocol non-compliance, virus, spam and intrusions; the setting of criteria to decide whether a packet may go through or if it needs to be routed to a different destination; and the collection of statistical information (Bendrath & Mueller, 2011; Mueller & Asghari, 2012).

As a technology capable of enabling advanced network management and user service and security functions potentially intrusive or harmful to user privacy – such as data mining, eavesdropping and censorship – DPI has been framed in a predominantly negative way. This is due to the fact that, even though this technology has been used for Internet management for many years already, some net neutrality proponents fear that DPI may be used to prevent economic competition and to reduce the openness of the Internet. Indeed, this has already happened. For example, in April 2008, Bell Canada was accused of using DPI technology to block peer-to-peer traffic generated not only by clients of its service Sympatico but also by other consumers relying on independent ISPs (Bendrath & Mueller, 2011, p. 1153). Thus, net neutrality proponents argue that the purpose of DPI deployment is crucial and should be made as transparent as possible (Ufer, 2010). Furthermore, emphasis is put on the need to reflect further on the extent to which the employment of filtering techniques is bound to specific cultures. Blocking of content sometimes takes place in specific contexts where it is regarded as harmful to the public or to some segment of the public, as is the case for hate speech. Some researchers warn that the role played by local values and cultures in the deployment of such measures should not be underestimated (Goldsmith & Wu, 2006; Palfrey & Rogoyski, 2006, p. 33). However, others emphasise instead that the implementation of these techniques, especially if bent to the requirements of political actors, may lead to biases in the content of online communications, or blocking and/or censorship of it. These scholars emphasise the power that ISPs have to 'control access to vast expanse of information, entertainment and expression on the Internet' (Blevins & Barrow, 2009, p. 41; see also Elkin-Koren, 2006).

The intermediaries of the Internet economy have the technical means to implement traffic shaping practices, as well as a number of measures that are susceptible to affecting diversity of content on the Internet, such as DPI or filtering. So far, the directive or mandate to shape traffic has often come from governments. The literature identifies two central motivations for political actors adopting these practices. First, they can be used by authorities as an investigation tool. ISPs are sometimes used as 'sheriffs' of the Internet, when they are placed in the position of enforcing the rules of the regime in which they are doing business (Palfrey & Rogoyski, 2006). The use of these measures is also attributed to security purposes such as the fight against terrorism, child pornography and online piracy – with all the controversies this raises in terms of setting critical precedents (Marsden, 2010, pp. 19, 67, 81) or to bolster and sustain largely shared values such as the protection of minors or the fight against hate speech (Marsden, p. 102). These techniques are also used for law enforcement in the area of intellectual property protection. For example, in the infamous Comcast controversy of 2007, one of the first controversies labelled as net neutrality-related, the

U.S. broadband Internet provider started blocking P2P applications, such as BitTorrent. The stated rationale was that P2P is used to share illegal content and the provider's infrastructure was not designed to deal with the high-bandwidth traffic caused by these exchanges. Accordingly, the cinema and music recording industry have repeatedly taken positions against net neutrality in their fight against 'digital piracy' (Bendrath & Mueller, 2011, p. 1152; Palfrey & Rogoyski, 2006, p. 45). Civil society organisations and some political actors have vocally opposed both these sets of motivations, deemed as inadequate to justify an increased control of data and the invasion of freedom of speech rights (Libertus & Wiesner, 2011, p. 87).

The Interactional Dimension: 'Walled Gardens'

Net neutrality breaches also have effects on the interactional dimension of the public sphere. The formation, in the landscape of information and communication technologies, of so-called 'walled gardens' – where the carrier offers service without access to the wider Internet, controls applications and restricts non-approved content – has important implications for online interaction. It illustrates the extent to which the potential advantages leveraged through online interaction and deliberation can be short-circuited by restrictions on software and content (Marsden, 2010, p. 88).

The debate over the neutrality of the Internet is – perhaps surprisingly – often separated from a reflection on the attacks on the universality of the Web. However, the two largely overlap in the economic strategies of content providers and application designers on the Web and their effects on the network (Dulong de Rosnay, 2011). The tendency to create walled gardens is perhaps the best illustration of this phenomenon. For example, social networking services harness users' personal data to provide them with value-added services, but exclusively and specifically on their own sites. In doing so, they contribute to the creation of sealed 'silos' of information, and they do not allow users to export or recover data easily. The 'giants' of digital services manifest, more and more frequently, their intention to become broad social platforms underpinning the entire spectrum of web services using these strategies. In fact, their goal is oftentimes to direct users to specific commercial services, closed economic systems and stores that control not only the software that can be installed on users' devices but also the content (Zittrain, 2008).

This is an issue of both application discrimination and content discrimination (Marsden, 2010, p. 88). The ways in which content providers rely on applications that depend on major social networking players reinforces this logic of partition and gate-keeping. The walled gardens phenomenon has also been described as 'balkanisation' or 'gilded cages'. Hardware manufacturers also seek to ensure a 'captive audience': The model proposed by Apple, notably, forbids providers of content and media from proposing applications directly to users and prevents them from buying paid goods, such as music or digital books, outside of the Apple ecosystem (which includes among others a partnership with Amazon).

Breaches of neutrality also affect the application layer itself. Carriers 'offer exclusive, preferential treatment to one application provider', thereby creating walled gardens of preferred suppliers (Marsden, 2010, p. 88). Search engines choose their answers to queries based on advertising revenue, whereas endorsement systems such as 'Like' on Facebook and '+1' on Google, and social networking/recommendation systems such as the now-defunct Ping for iTunes, form a set of competing systems that affect the entire value chain of the Internet. The issue of 'exclusivities' – especially in the mobile Internet – and of the mergers between communication operators and other stakeholders, such as Deezer and Orange, are further symptoms of the emergence of vertical conglomerates.

The walled gardens phenomenon, as an illustration of the interactional dimension of the public sphere, bridges the structural and representational dimensions by revealing the close connection between the diversity of content and the 'diversity of stakeholders who have editorial control over that content' (Herman, 2006, p. 116). The policy implemented by Apple in relation to applications developed by external actors is seen as a possible way to downplay unwelcome political and cultural ideas. Preventing an application from running on Apple devices may have immediate implications for diversity of political views. Similarly, an ISP may or may not allow users to select some of the Web sites contained or barred from the garden, thus hindering expressions of political and social significance with network management choices (Nunziato, 2009, pp. 5–8). The isolation of content on specific networks or services from other content on the wider Internet, preventing broader interaction between them, is reinforced by the 'cumulative effect' of walled gardens. If a sufficient number of people join a service, and the service is able to reach a critical mass of users, it becomes self-reinforcing. The companies managing such services are thus able to move toward a quasi-monopoly (Marsden, 2010, pp. 67, 186–194).

The issue of walled gardens and net neutrality is further compounded (and complicated) by the advent of the mobile Internet, for which the allotted bandwidth remains scarce. At the same time, mobile networks increasingly constitute the first 'entry point' into the Internet for several regions in the world – first and foremost, Africa. Access restrictions on mobiles to certain protocols, such as Voice over IP (VoIP), and other limits are officially justified by a poor allocation of band frequency. But they are often attributable, behind the scenes, to industrial battles. The model fostered by Apple's iPhone (and its 'cousins', such as Amazon's Kindle tablet) contributes to the change in the market's power relations by contributing to the shift of power from the operator to the hardware manufacturer (Curien & Maxwell, 2011, p. 64).

Communication Research and the Net Neutrality Debate

In addition to providing a way to organise the net neutrality literature, a public sphere framework illuminates how communication research – even if this research often does not explicitly refer to net neutrality – can inform the net neutrality debate. We want to illustrate this through three examples.

1. The issue of access to the network for content producers can be linked to media policy research on 'bottleneck regulation' in broadcasting. Standard setting and the resulting control over distribution platforms and facilities have been a constant concern in the processes of adjustment of broadcast regulation to new communication technologies, such as cable and satellite television. Digitisation and the Internet have led to a new wave of research on gatekeepers of information flows and the potential for distribution system owners to restrict access to certain types of content (Michalis, 2007; Simpson, 2004). Systems of standardisation, encryption techniques and new selection interfaces could all be used as market control mechanisms. The discussion about bottleneck regulation in broadcasting and instruments used in the past to ensure diversity intersects with the net neutrality debate. The earlier-mentioned must-carry-rules in cable TV are one such instrument in Europe (Storsul & Syvertsen, 2007). Media and communication policy research has examined this modification of regulatory structures and, in part, also developed justifications for a media regulation framework that aims at ensuring 'that all programs are treated on equal, adequate and non-discriminatory terms' (Schweizer, 2013, p. 109).

2. The application of the neutrality principle has not only been limited to platform regulation. The regulation of press distribution in Germany also contains the neutrality principle. Germany is divided into areas in each of which only one press wholesaler (*Pressegrossist*) distributes newspapers and journals (with the exception of a few areas where two wholesalers share the business). These regional monopolies are tolerated because the press wholesalers have forced themselves to distribute the products of all publishing houses in a non-discriminatory way and under conditions which are the same for all publishing houses (Beck, 2012, p. 128).

3. The net neutrality debate can also benefit from Internet usage research, which would place net neutrality in the context of the broader discussion on digital inclusion. Broader conceptualisations of access to communications go beyond technical infrastructures and understand access as multifaceted, 'encompassing an overlapping mixture of technical, economic and social infrastructures' (Shade, 2010, p. 137). Access to economic and social infrastructures includes having access to online resources related to jobs, education, entertainment and health, as well as the ability to produce and use online content. From this perspective, the use of a communication infrastructure in which data packages are not discriminated is one part of the issue of access. Specific sectors of the world's population do not access that infrastructure at all, for reasons of socioeconomic status, culture or geographical location. As a result,

the current net neutrality debate is limited to those who already are participating online; those who, in general, have higher income, higher education and live in densely populated areas in the Northern Hemisphere (Ball-Rokeach & Jung, 2008; Shade, 2010). Broadening the concept of access points to what is excluded when net neutrality scholars discuss the issues of access.

Conclusion

A public sphere perspective applied to net neutrality sheds light on the infrastructure of the online public sphere, as well as its contentions. It underlines the issue of access to communicative spaces and the conditions under which the circulation of information and opinions takes place on the Internet.

Net neutrality is concerned with the organisation of the online public sphere infrastructure, in particular its technical – and especially its economic and power – structures. At the same time, net neutrality takes into account the interests of old and new content providers and of Internet users and Internet service providers. Large content providers such as Google and Facebook are not the only 'gatekeepers' in the Internet. Internet service providers, perhaps more than any other entity, enable and constrain online communication. Net neutrality research takes their position into consideration, exploring how diverse interests can be balanced in the light of increased bandwidth usage, quality of service demands and limited mobile Internet capacities.

A functioning public sphere is based on the representation of the diversity of information, ideas and opinions. Traffic shaping and filtering measures are applied for economic reasons, but also for political and law enforcement ones. These measures can be fostered by other actors than Internet service providers.

The existence of walled gardens points to the fact that interaction in the online public sphere can be impeded by restrictions on software and content. In closed platforms, providers decide which applications, content and information are allowed and which are not allowed within the service. Proprietary, closed systems set limits for connecting to the Web and pose limits to the user's individual capacity to refine or develop new applications based on existing ones. Users, when confronted with the net neutrality debates, are equipped with diverse and uneven tools. Not all users have the technical knowledge enabling them to make informed choices; these are therefore, out of necessity, often left outside the realm of political intervention and to the exclusive authority of the market. Thus, actors with large and multifaceted stakes in the Internet value chain are constantly on the verge of monopolizing a debate with underlying impacts on social architecture, fundamental freedoms and the conditions for democratic expression.

There is some overlapping and interrelation between the dimensions, due to the blurring of categories in an online public sphere. However, the three analytical dimensions – access to Internet infrastructure, diversity of content transmitted via Internet infrastructure and user interaction enabled through Internet infrastructure – highlight how a perspective grounded in communication studies can complement the frameworks offered in the economic and legal traditions, thereby offering a more robust basis for an informed media policy debate on the issues raised by the highly contested issue of net neutrality. The public sphere perspective connects, for example, scholars interested by freedom of expression and speech with those concerned by issues of economic advantage, monopoly and concentration. Net neutrality affects and relates to a number of issues central to media policy, which have been re-labelled as net neutrality. These include bottleneck regulation, user rights, competition and public service values which reappear in new forms in the Internet environment.

Note

1. An earlier and longer version of this piece appeared in *Communication Yearbook 38* (Löblich & Musiani, 2014). A previous version of the present paper was published in the first report of the Internet Governance Forum Dynamic Coalition on Net Neutrality and is freely available at http://networkneutrality.info/sources.html.

References

Ball-Rokeach, S.J., & Jung, J.-Y. (2008). Digital divide. Retrieved from www.communicationencyclopedia.com.

Barrie, J. (2015, 6 March). A lot of powerful lobbyists are trying to get rid of net neutrality in Europe. *Business Insider*. Retrieved from: http://uk.businessinsider.com/explanation-of-net-neutrality-in-europe-2015-3?r=US.

Beck, K. (2012). *Das Mediensystem in Deutschland*. Wiesbaden, Germany: VS Verlag.

Bendrath, R., & Mueller, M. (2011). The end of the net as we know it? Deep packet inspection and Internet governance. *New Media & Society, 13*(7), 1142–1160. doi: 10.1177/1461444811398031.

Blevins, J., & Barrow, S. (2009).The political economy of free speech and network neutrality: A critical analysis. *Journal of Media Law & Ethics, 1*(1/2), 27–48.

Blevins, J., & Shade, L.R. (2010). Editorial: International perspectives on network neutrality. Exploring the politics of Internet traffic management and policy implications for Canada and the U.S. *Global Media Journal – Canadian Edition, 3*(1), 1–8.

Calhoun, C. (1992). *Habermas and the public sphere*. Cambridge, MA: MIT Press.

Clark, D. (2007). Network neutrality: Words of power and 800-pound gorillas. *International Journal of Communication, 1*, 701–708.

Curien, N., & Maxwell, W. (2011). La neutralité d'Internet. Paris: La Découverte.

Dahlgren, P. (1995). Television and the public sphere. London: Sage.

Dahlgren, P. (2005). The Internet, public spheres and political communication: Dispersion and deliberation. *Political Communication, 22*(2), 147–162. doi: 10.1080/10584600590933160.

Dahlgren, P. (2010). Public spheres, societal shifts and media modulations. In J. Gripsrud, & L. Weibull (Eds.), *Media, markets & public spheres. European media at the crossroads* (pp. 17–36). Bristol: Intellect.

Dulong de Rosnay, M. (2011). Réappropriation des données et droit à la rediffusion. *Hermès, La Revue, 59*(1), 65–66.

Elkin-Koren, N. (2006). Making technology visible: Liability of Internet service providers for peer-to-peer traffic. *New York University Journal of Legislation & Public Policy, 9*(1), 15–76.

Geere, D. (2015, 6 March). Europe reverses course on net neutrality legislation. *Wired*. Retrieved from: http://www.wired.co.uk/news/archive/2015-03/06/europe-reverses-on-net-neutrality.

Goldsmith, J., & Wu, T. (2006). *Who controls the Internet? Illusions of a borderless world*. Oxford: Oxford University Press.

Habermas, J. (1984). *The theory of communicative action* (Vols. I & II). Cambridge, MA: Polity Press.

Habermas, J. (1989). The structural transformation of the public sphere. Boston: MIT Press.

Hahn, R., & Litan, R. E. (2007). The myth of network neutrality and what we should do about it. *International Journal of Communication, 1*, 595–606.

Herman, B.D. (2006): Opening bottlenecks: On behalf of mandated network neutrality. *Federal Communications Law Journal, 59*(1), 107–159.

Holznagel, B. (2010). Netzneutralität als auf gabeder Vielfaltssicherung. *Kommunikation & Recht, 13*(2), 95–100.

International Telecommunication Union. (2012). Key statistical highlights: ITU data release June 2012. Retrieved from www.itu.int/ITU-D/ict/index.html.

Krämer, J., Wiewiorra, L., & Weinhardt, C. (2012). Net neutrality: A progress report. *Telecommunications Policy, 37*(9), 794–813. doi: 10.1016/j.telpol.2012.08.005.

Levy, S. (2012, November). Power House. Deep inside a Google data center. *Wired*, pp. 174–181.

Löblich, M. & Musiani, F. (2014). Net neutrality and communication research: The implications of Internet infrastructure for the public sphere. *Communication Yearbook, 38*, 339–367.

Libertus, M., & Wiesner, J. (2011). Netzneutralität, offenes Internet und kommunikative Grundversorgung. *Media Perspektiven, 2*, 80–90.

Lunt, P., & Livingstone, S. (2013). Media studies' fascination with the concept of the public sphere: Critical reflections and emerging debates. *Media Culture & Society, 35*(1), 87–96. doi: 10.1177/0163443712464562.

Marsden, C. (2010). *Net neutrality. Towards a co-regulatory solution*. London: Bloomsbury Academy.

Michalis, M. (2007). *Governing European communications: From unification to coordination*. Lanham, MD: Lexington Books.

Mueller, M., & Asghari, H. (2012). Deep packet inspection and bandwidth management: Battles over BitTorrent in Canada and the United States. *Telecommunications Policy, 36*(6), 462–475. doi: 10.1016/j.telpol.2012.04.003.

Napoli, P. (2001). *Foundations of communications policy: Principles and process in the regulation of electronic media*. Cresskill, NJ: Hampton Press.

Nunziato, D. (2009). *Virtual freedom: Net neutrality and free speech in the Internet age*. Stanford, CA: Stanford University Press.

Palfrey, J., & Rogoyski, R. (2006). The move to the middle: The enduring threat of 'harmful' speech to network neutrality. *Washington University Journal of Law and Policy, 21*, 31–65.

Peha, J., Lehr, W., & Wilkie, S. (2007). Introduction: The state of the debate on network neutrality. *International Journal of Communication, 1*, 709–716.

Schweizer, C. (2013). Regulating new bottlenecks of digital television distribution. An analysis of the policy making process in Switzerland. In M. Löblich, & S. Pfaff-Rüdiger (Eds.), Communication and media policy in the era of digitization and the Internet (pp. 107–118). Baden-Baden, Germany: Nomos.

Shade, L.R. (2010). Access. In M. Raboy, & J. Shtern (Eds.), *Media divides: Communication rights and the right to communicate in Canada* (pp. 120–144). Vancouver: UBC Press.

Simpson, S. (2004). Universal service issues in converging communications environments: The case of the UK. *Telecommunications Policy, 28*(3–4), 233–248. doi: 10.1016/j.telpol.2003.09.001.

Splichal, S. (2012). *Transnationalization of the public sphere and the fate of the public.* New York: Hampton Press.

Storsul, T., & Syvertsen, T. (2007). The impact of convergence on European television policy: Pressures for change. *Convergence: The International Journal of Research into New Media Technologies, 13*(3), 275–291. doi: 10.1177/1354856507079177.

Ufer, F. (2010). Der Kampf um die Netzneutralität oder die Frage, warum ein Netz neutral sein muss. *Kommunikation & Recht, 13*(6), 383–389.

Van Eijk, N. (2011). Net neutrality and audiovisual services. *IRIS plus, 2011*(5), 7–19.

Vogelsang, I. (2010). Die Debatte um Netzneutralität und Quality of Service. In D. Klumpp, H. Kubicek, A. Roßnagel, & W. Schulz (Eds.), *Netzwelt – Wege – Werte – Wandel* (pp. 5–14). Berlin: Springer. doi: 10.1007/978-3-642-05054-1_1.

Wu, T. (2003). Network neutrality, broadband discrimination. *Journal of Telecommunications and High Technology Law, 2*(1), 141–176.

Wu, T., & Yoo, C. S. (2007). Keeping the Internet neutral?: Tim Wu and Christopher Yoo debate. *Federal Communications Law Journal, 59*(3), 575–592.

Yoo, C. S. (2005). Beyond network neutrality. *Harvard Journal of Law & Technology, 19*(1), 1–77.

Yoo, C. S. (2012). Network neutrality and the need for a technological turn in Internet scholarship. In M.E. Price, S.G. Verhulst & L. Morgan (Eds.), *Routledge handbook of media law* (pp. 539–555). New York: Routledge.

Zittrain, J. (2008). The future of the Internet and how to stop it. New Haven & London: Yale University Press.

10 Access to the Network as a Universal Service Concept for the European Information Society

Olga Batura

Introduction

The omnipresence and impact of information and communications technologies (ICTs) on all spheres of life and their increased utility for economic activity (both business and working), political participation and organisation of leisure have become characteristic of the society we live in. The revolutionary technological processes of digitalisation and convergence have become so common that users are not aware of them most of the time. In this new Information Society (Webster, 2001) they expect instant communication at any time, at any location and over any type of network – satellite, cellular, radio, copper wire, cable, fibre or powerline. Consumers ignore the technological and regulatory difference between the functionally similar services of audio (traditional voice telephony versus VoIP) or video (video-streaming versus broadcast) transmission, but pay attention to the performance and capacity of their Internet connection to be able to enjoy ever-richer converged communication services.

In this 'media-saturated environment' (Webster, 2003) we learn to deal with the newly acquired freedom from limitations of time and space and with the blurring boundaries between different spheres of living (van Dijk, 2006). Interpersonal (horizontal) interactive communication dominates the landscape by contrast to unidirectional mass communication, which prevailed before (Castells, 2011). The concept of citizenship is changing as ICT has become essential for participation in social and economic life and in government. The minimum of information necessary to survive in such a society is growing so that information – and the means and ways to access and transmit it – can be considered primary goods (Rawls, 1971).

In such an environment, the digital divide is felt all the more sharply and affects the disadvantaged disproportionately. The digital divide can be understood as a gap between those who can access and use ICT services and those who cannot.[1] In the European Union (EU), notwithstanding the successes of market liberalisation and technological advances in the form of ever-increasing choice of – and falling prices for – electronic communication devices and services, there is a more or less stable proportion of three per cent of the population that has no access even to the plain old voice telephony. The respective risk group can be profiled as rural dwellers over 65 residing alone and to a large extent residents of the new EU Member States, where the number of phoneless people is even higher (see TNS Opinion and Social network, 2012; 2013; 2014).

The EU has recognised both the significance of ICTs for its social and economic development and the dangers of the gap in access to them. The EU's *A Digital Agenda for Europe* (European Commission, 2010) aims 'to maximise the social and economic potential of ICT', but also to enhance inclusiveness of ICT usage, proclaiming that 'the benefits of the digital society should be available to all'. These objectives are to be achieved through swift and consistent implementation of the regulatory framework on electronic communications with Directive 2002/22 on Universal service and users' rights relating to electronic communications networks and services (Universal Service Directive: USD) (European Parliament and Council, 2002a) addressing, in particular, the issue of inclusiveness. However, the current EU regulatory framework for universal service was conceptualised in 1990s, when monopolistic telecommunications provision via PTT system (post, telephone and telegraph administration) was the norm and the variety of telecommunications services began and ended with voice telephony.

Against this backdrop, the question raised in this chapter is whether the current scope of universal service is still adequate considering the increased importance of ICTs in people's lives, the contemporary ICT environment and the Information Society goals of the EU. After outlining the main elements of the current universal service scope, this chapter discusses discrepancies between it and the changing information and communications environment. It then discusses the potential and the nature of possible changes based on the legal analysis of the current mechanism for the review of the scope of universal service. Considering the limitations of the construction of the review mechanism as well as the shortcomings of its application practice, in Section 5 a concept for reform of the EU-wide universal service is suggested. Drawing upon the analytical framework discussed by Milne (1998) and insights from other (tele)communications scholars, the chapter advocates the idea of individual access to the network as a core (and potentially the only) element of a revised articulation of universal service.

The chapter argues that the concept of access to the network would better correspond to the level of development of ICT markets and is a more user-oriented concept by comparison to the current one because it would take into account expectations and communication needs of end-users. It would be better aligned with the objectives and possibilities of electronic communications policy. Focusing on access at the EU level would allow for more flexibility for the EU-28 and would keep regulatory intervention at the supranational level to the minimum. A precise definition of access to the network and its characteristics can only be introduced in the legislation after additional research aiming at a deeper understanding of social

Deficits of the Current Legal Framework for Universal Service

The EU universal service concept has four main elements (European Parliament and Council, 2002b: Art. 2 (j)): It comprises (1) minimum scope of services; (2) of specified quality; (3) available and affordable and (4) able to be provided by a designated undertaking where the competitive market has failed to do so. Harmonisation of universal service rules at the EU level is extensive, especially with regard to the scope of universal service. Member States shall ensure that the following services are available to all end-users in their territory, independent of their geographical location (European Parliament and Council, 2002a, Article 3(1)):

1 A connection to the public communications network at a fixed location
2 Voice telephony over this connection and payphones
3 Accessory services (directory and directory enquiry)
4 Social obligations

Little flexibility to circumvent these stipulations is allowed at the national level. A Member State may exclude one of the elements from national scope only if – and as long as – it is provided by the market on a ubiquitous basis and in fulfilment of all requirements of the USD. In addition to the services listed, a Member State may decide to make other electronic communications services universally available within its own territory if it wishes to enhance and improve the communications environment for its citizens and assumes that the markets do not fulfil the emerged communications needs. However, it is important to note that such services do not constitute part of universal service (Eur. Parl., 2002a: Recital 25) and are called additional mandatory services. This means that compensation mechanisms which are used to finance universal service obligations may not be applied to them (Eur. Parl., 2002a: Article 32). Member States are not permitted to impose on electronic communications operators or providers any financial contributions in relation to measures which are not part of universal service obligations (Eur. Parl., 2002a: Recital 25). Thus, for these services, the only funding route is the national budget (Cawley, 2001) which must be done in compliance with European State aid rules. The above said effectively means that universal service scope set out at the EU level is both a minimum and a maximum.

Both the content of the universal service scope at the EU level and the lack of flexibility in this regard at the national level represent critical shortcomings when viewed against the backdrop of the changing information and communication environment as described in Section 1. The legacy of the twentieth-century mindset about means of telecommunications lives forth in the minimum EU-wide set of services to be provided on a universal service basis. As it was thirty years ago (European Commission, 1987), universal service is still centred on voice telephony and consists of a telephone service at a fixed location, directory and directory enquiry services and public payphones. No other (electronic) communications services, especially no information society services, are included in the scope. Connection to a public communications network – seemingly a separate service – is in fact coupled with access to services, and as a part of the service provided it can be understood as one of the characteristics of the telephone service (Batura, 2014). However, the connection is bound to voice telephony in that it shall be provided only at a fixed location and shall be able to support voice, facsimile and functional access to the Internet as a rather modest single narrowband network connection of 56 kbps (Eur. Parl., 2002a: Recital 8; Bohlin & Teppayayon, 2009).

In a clarification of the position on universal service, the EU's Communication Committee (COCOM, 2011) emphasised that at the national level Member States can 'take due account of specific circumstances in national markets' and increase the connection speeds (Eur. Parl., 2009: Recital 5). However, flexibility at the national level is nothing new and is characteristic of the harmonisation instrument: within their jurisdiction, Member States may go beyond the minimum requirements. Yet, this does not alter the EU-wide definition of functional *access* to the Internet and does not enhance the requirements for the connection.

An important additional limitation of the USD (Eur. Parl., 2002a: Art. 4(1)) is that connection and telephone services are to be provided only at a fixed location. Member States are even allowed to restrict the provision of the service to the end-user's primary location or residence (Eur. Parl., 2002a: Recital 8). This approach clearly ignores the well established practice of using mobile communications and the wish of many consumers to be connected everywhere and most of the time. Taking into account technological convergence and bearing in mind the regulatory principle of technological neutrality (Eur. Parl., 2002b: Recital 18 and Article 8 (1)), it can be argued that this clause reveals technological bias as it does not adequately account for convergence in the markets for fixed and mobile telephony and for the developments in Voice over IP.

Affordability and quality are obligatory and interdependent elements of EU-level universal service (Eur. Parl., 2002a: Art. 1 (2)). Geographic availability is directly linked to the affordability requirement. Obviously, ubiquitous geographic coverage is of little use if consumers cannot purchase the service due to high market prices. If a universal service at an affordable price is required, but a quality requirement is absent, there is a danger that providers would offer the lowest possible quality of service. In such a case, end-users would be unable to fulfil their communication needs and the digital divide between user groups could conceivably deepen.

Current requirements in respect of quality of service can also be considered problematic in the context of the information society (Batura, 2015). Member States shall ensure that, in the context of universal service provision, quality of service is the same for all end-users, disregarding their geographical location (Eur. Parl., 2002a: Art. 3 (1)). In the absence of a legal definition of quality of service, the Universal Service Directive refers to its content, based on the parameters, definitions and measurements set out in Annex III of the USD (Eur. Parl., 2002a: Art. 11 (1)). These parameters address mainly non-network related criteria, not the substantive quality of service ones. For example, the quality parameters for connection to a public communications network are symmetry of the connection, jitter, latency and the like.[2] Next to data transfer rates (speed), they allow determination of whether functional internet access is possible. However, Annex III of the USD does not mention them at all and uses instead such parameters as supply time for initial connection, fault rate per access line, fault repair time for connection, call set up time, bill correctness complaints and unsuccessful call ratio for voice telephony.

Clearly, non-network related parameters are easier to measure and depend on fewer factors. They are also easier to ensure EU-wide because national differences in infrastructure development and in network architecture play a lesser role. Yet, from the perspective of the completion of the single electronic communications market and European competitiveness, the lack of European network-related standards may be disadvantageous as interoperability is indispensable for further development of ICTs and for smooth functioning of the internal market (European Commission, 2011a). It also undermines the universal service rationale: divergence in quality of service impacts the quality of participation in the information society and thus contributes to the digital divide.

The current universal service framework at the EU level is arguably too rigid for the large and multifarious EU-28 since it leaves Member States no room for shaping the content of their national universal service (Feijóo González, Gómez Barroso, González Laguía & Rojo Alonso, 2004). As noted above, Member States do not have the possibility of adding services to the national universal service scope or to change it according their needs. Under current EU legislation, if in a Member State the specified kind of voice telephony is provided by the market at an affordable price with blanket coverage and imposition of special universal service obligations on telecommunications providers is not necessary, such a Member State still cannot support other communications services via the universal service instrument, even if there is a public interest in them. Promotion of other communications infrastructure and services, like broadband deployment, must be done through measures other than universal service. These measures are also subject to EU rules on State aid and are, therefore, more complicated to adopt and more restricted in their application sphere.

Besides accommodating national differences in economic, technological and infrastructural developments, the EU-wide framework needs to be flexible enough to account for national cultural specificities manifest in different market behaviour. For instance, in some countries people prefer mobile phones for texting (SMS) instead of voice telephony, which is explained by the national custom that private and business communications are not to be held in public ('The Apparatgeist calls', 2009). Last but not least, the current universal service framework as a policy instrument is deficient with regard to promoting ICTs along the lines of the European information society policies (Batura, 2014). The universal service concept consisting, at the EU level, practically only of voice telephony is obviously insufficient to deliver ambitious Information Society objectives set therein and cannot contribute in a meaningful way to the achievement of broad coverage of the EU population with fast and ultra fast internet by 2020 as envisaged by the Digital Agenda for Europe (European Commission, 2010). In this context, the European Commission some time ago indirectly undermined the meaning of universal service in its current form by quite correctly stating that the internet is nowadays much more than a plain telephone connection (European Commission, 2011b). The relevance of the current universal service concept for a Single Information Space initiative (European Commission, 2005) is weak since, as noted above, the requirement of mobility to achieve it is not encompassed in universal service's scope.

Universal Service Concept and Electronic Communications Reality

The established shortcomings of the legal and regulatory framework are exacerbated by the fact that the universal service concept used in the EU does not fully correspond to the level of development of the information and communication environment. Arguably, there is a discrepancy between, on the one hand, a very high level of market development in terms of technological quality and innovation, take-up rate of landlines and mobile phones (combined) and level of competition, and, on the other hand, the universal service concept. For instance, according to the Eurobarometer survey (TNS Opinion and Social network, 2014), in 2014 the take-up rate of households for landlines and mobile (combined) was about 98%, with some countries exceeding the 100% rate. There were no data about take-up rates of businesses, but one can assume that they reach at least the same high numbers because businesses are traditionally early adopters of technology. The European single market for electronic communications services, while still being developed, is clearly becoming a competitive one. Although incumbents still dominate national markets for landline telecommunications services, their market shares have been slowly diminishing. Major competitors in mobile services have more or less similar market shares and are active simultaneously in several national markets.[3] At the same time, fixed-to-mobile convergence and substitution redefines the product markets and competition patterns (BEREC, 2011). Observing the development of ICT, as early as

1997 Mueller argued that a new generation of universal service policy was necessary because the old one focusing on two or three particular services and access in a fixed location did not correspond to the heterogeneous and mobile character of an emerging communications environment.

According to the analytical framework proposed by Milne (1998), a proper corresponding communications policy for this level of market development should aim at provision of 'service to individuals', and the universal service concept should pursue the objective of ensuring the individual right to communicate. By contrast, current universal service at the EU level is a 'safety net' (European Commission, 2011c) enacted to provide voice telephony to those who cannot afford it under market conditions. The significance of the correspondence between the universal service policy objectives and telecommunications development was studied by Milne empirically. On the basis of comparative analytical studies, she established that each country passes through five stages of policy development, and that the nature of ICT development requires constant change of universal service. Policy is defined through developments in communications infrastructure and technology and through the economic and social transformations accompanying this. A universal service concept lagging behind network, technology and market developments may, ironically, exacerbate the digital divide because, due to the universal service mechanism, disadvantaged end-users are provided with basic services which do not correspond to the state of the art and the demands of the economy. This keeps these end-users trapped in their disadvantaged environment. An outdated universal service could therefore slow down the development of electronic communications more broadly.

Similar views are expressed by other scholars. For instance, Xavier (2008) argues that, having achieved today's universal service objectives, countries should develop a universal choice or universal access concept, which would mean the right of end-users to choose freely between providers (and services). Falch and Henten (2009) argue for universal access because in a new generation networks (NGNs) environment, the current universal service concept is not sustainable and actually disregards the specific features and opportunities offered by NGNs, not least the user choice of any electronic communications service if there is a connection to any network. Noam (2010) describes a new 'Telecom 3.0' environment as requiring greater investments, changing economies of scale and causing convergence as well as instability in ICT sectors. Such significant changes require a new regulatory framework with universal service focusing on universal connectivity.

The Universal Service Directive employs a dynamic concept of universal service meaning that the scope of universal service can be modified according to the changing technological and social environment. However a key question concerns whether allows for the necessary adjustment of the universal service concept at the EU level.

Would a Revision of the Scope of Universal Service Help?

Every three years, the Commission is obliged to review the scope of universal service in the light of social, economic and technological developments and paying special attention to mobility and data rates in view of the prevailing technology used by the majority of subscribers (Eur. Parl., 2002a: Art. 15). The review procedure (Eur. Parl., 2002a: Annex V) consists of two steps. First, the Commission has to determine whether there are any grounds for a review. For this it has to analyse the economic and social environment in order to investigate whether the context for universal service has changed. It shall take into consideration social and market developments, services used by consumers, availability and choice of services and technological developments regarding the way services are provided to consumers.

Second, if the Commission concludes that revisions to the directive are necessary, it shall examine any possible alterations by applying a twin test consisting of a majority use test and market failure test (Eur. Parl., 2002a: Recital 25). First, it shall identify possible new services to be included in the universal service scope. These need to be available to and used by a substantial majority of consumers. Second, the Commission has to determine whether the lack of availability or non-use by a minority of consumers results in their social exclusion. Additionally, it has to make an assessment of possible implications of the intended extension or re-definition of the universal service scope because the expansion of universal service scope shall convey 'general net benefit to all consumers such that public intervention is warranted in circumstances where the specific services are not provided to the public under normal commercial conditions' (Eur. Parl., 2002a: Annex V para. 2). The Commission must ensure that the existing technological neutrality shall not be endangered and natural technological evolution shall not be hindered through artificial promotion of particular technologies above others. Competition and innovation in the market shall not be distorted by imposing a disproportionate financial burden on undertakings. Consumer security and protection, especially of consumers with lower income, shall not be endangered by any financial burden unfairly imposed on them as a result of any change to universal service (Eur. Parl., 2002a: Recital 25).

The construction of the review mechanism exhibits a number of flaws that, in combination with the experience of its application, raise doubts whether it can bring about necessary reforms to the scope of universal service. To begin with, although the two parts of the examination are complementary and obligatory, the wording of the Universal Service Directive does not clearly state whether both of them must be satisfied in order to alter the universal service scope. Rather, it suggests that all these issues shall be merely addressed and taken into account by the Commission during the examination and in the report to the European Parliament and to the Council, but no decisive value is ascribed to them.

The use of a substantial majority test for evaluation of candidate services is questionable because it is by definition a quantitative test and cannot take into account the non economic value of an individual service for the society and economy. There is no possibility to assess a candidate service on its merit and in comparison to other services, including those already part of the universal service scope. The majority criterion would always favour established existing services and not allow extending the universal service scope, for instance, to elements which fail a majority test, but are of immense social benefit (like broadband connection). Moreover, the threshold of a substantial majority is not specified in the Universal Service Directive. It refers to the whole EU population, and without additional mechanisms cannot account for specific national developments and needs so that it is unlikely to take into account digital divides between the countries.

The practice of the reviews (European Commission, 2006; 2008; 2011c) demonstrates that disproportionate importance has been given by the Commission to the majority test, while other criteria are largely neglected. If the majority test was not satisfied, no other criteria were considered beyond it. In all three reviews to date, the Commission thoroughly carried out the majority test, but did not properly examine the risk of social exclusion, for instance, in the case of mobile communications. Wide-spread provision of the service in question by the market and lowering prices were considered indicative of affordability and inclusiveness. The evaluation of services in the reviews was limited to their physical availability and affordability (in terms of average prices), and a full comparison of candidate services to the services that are already included in the universal service scope or to other services on the market was not undertaken.

In practice, the reviews were used only as an instrument to explore extension of the universal service scope to new service. They did not consider whether the services already included in the scope of universal service complied with the criteria of Annex V of the USD and should be still provided on a universal service basis. Only the first review pointed out the necessity to examine payphones, directory and directory enquiry services in the future, but this work was not followed up in the second and third reviews which were solely focused on the possibility of adding broadband and mobile communications to the universal service scope.

The wording, but also the vagueness, of legal provisions leaves a significant leeway for the Commission to decide on the future of universal service scope. However, it shall be recalled that the Commission is a gatekeeper, but not the final decision taker on this question. The results of the review are to be reported to the European Parliament and to the Council. (Eur. Parl., 2002a: Art. 15) If the Commission deems necessary a modification or re-definition of the scope of universal service, it makes a respective legislative proposal to both legislators in compliance with the ordinary legislative procedure (Articles 289 (1) and 294 of the Treaty on the Functioning of the European Union). Such a proposal may be examined and discussed in the Parliament and in the Council, in theory, on completely different grounds than the criteria of the review used by the Commission.

In these circumstances, the expressly political nature of universal service as a concept and a policy becomes evident (Nihoul & Rodford, 2004), and an assumption can be made that a review is unlikely to result in dramatic changes to adjust the universal service scope to the requirements of the information society. The identified deficits and shortcomings of the universal service scope can be rectified by a revision only partially through this means. Rather, in order to adequately meet the technological challenges and respond to market and societal transformation, a fundamental reform of the concept is necessary.

Concluding Remarks: Access as a Core of the Universal Service Concept

A reform of the universal service concept should be based on the realities of the new information and communications environment, technological possibilities and economic and social requirements. In the information society, the process of communication and access to means of communication have become disproportionately decisive for all societal activities. Communication can be carried out in different forms and with the help of different services. Voice telephony is not even the most preferable option at times. An electronic communications service can be chosen among the variety on offer depending on the type and purpose of a communicative action and on the type of information that needs to be transferred.

Against this background, with more services provided electronically and more activities being carried out electronically, it is not a particular electronic communications service, but rather access to communications networks, which has become a *conditio sine qua non* (Falch & Henten, 2009; Gómez Barroso & Pérez Martínez, 2004). Hence, respective regulation should primarily deal with the promotion and development of networks of an appropriately high quality, while efforts at the transnational level, policy effort could be directed at equalising the state of national networks and their interconnection. In this context, the universal service instrument would focus on availability and affordability of access to the networks for everybody (Feijóo González et al., 2004; Nagy, 2013), while access as a core element of universal service would be interpreted as physical and material access to the network (Sarrocco, 2002).

A defining feature of access to the network is that it shall be clearly decoupled from any electronic communications service and focused on provision of sufficient connectivity for users (Feijóo González Gómez Barroso, González Laguía & Rojo Alonso, 2005). Access to the network shall be the basis that enables users to enjoy any service they prefer or consider necessary to fulfil their communication needs. Yet, it is important to understand and conceive of access to the network as a minimum requirement to satisfy citizens' needs in the information society. Werbach (2009) uses the terms 'floor' and 'ceiling' to communicate this idea. Here, the flexible EU-wide universal service instrument can provide the 'floor': access to the network in order to use essential services or necessities.

The question of what services can be considered essential in the information society is highly complicated and under-researched. There is only a handful of empirical studies devoted to this problem (Kreutzmann-Gallash, Cadman, Harker & Waddams, 2013; Mack, Lansley, Nandy & Pantazis, 2013; TNS Opinion and Social network, 2010). They heavily focus on products perceived to be necessities in general and do not take into consideration the information society context and the role of ICTs as an enabler to enjoy rights, opportunities or resources that allow a person to participate fully in a particular society.

The capability framework developed by Sen (1992; 1999) can add a necessary normative dimension to empirical studies of poverty and social exclusion and provides a more holistic, but also precise and forward-looking, approach to the determination of necessities and of ICT means that can contribute to user satisfaction. The framework has already been applied to ICTs in developmental contexts (Birdsall, 2011; Oosterlaken, 2011), but not within the framework of universal service and not to the EU or its Member States. Drawing on this approach, there is a need to identify, first, what experiences and affordances people value (for instance, health, education, social communication or political freedom) and what the specific features of these might be in the information society. Second, a consideration is needed of how these capabilities can be provided for and/or enhanced by means of ICTs. For example, it is arguable that social network communication is ensured and enhanced within various networks, like Facebook, and that education has a wider reach in terms of territory and number of students due to the Massive Open Online Courses. In these two examples, knowing this can help determine what electronic communications services are essential to receive these information society services, and, thus, to define technical and other characteristics of the access to the network that should be able to support them.

Sen's framework presupposes a complex approach in order to enhance human capabilities and development and, therefore, requires a joint action in several policy fields. Universal service being an instrument of electronic communications policy is only one of the enablers and should be used to solve the tasks it can capably solve. Being an instrument of communications infrastructure development for the most part of its history (Mueller, 1997), universal service can remain in its role. The main difference between its role now and older concepts of its role is that it will now serve individual not collective needs. With this in mind, the concept of universal service as access to the network should acquire completely different qualities than it has before.

Access should be characterised as being simultaneously uniform and heterogeneous. Uniformity of access shall ensure that access to *any* given network grants access to the whole infrastructure of converged networks (for example, NGNs). Heterogeneity refers to access to the network that can be established by the use of various technologies and devices (for instance, over a phone, a computer, a PlayStation, etc., and with the help of different technologies) (Birke, 2009). Therefore, for the user, the value of a predetermined set of services due to be provided on a universal basis is reduced, while relevance of separate access and connection to the network increases. Subscribing to an NGN in the information society, users may be more interested in certain features of the connection in order to be able to choose from a multiplicity of functionally similar services (for example, VoIP or conventional voice telephony) according to their own criteria, as well as choosing the services they value more than voice telephony (Sawhney & Jayakar, 2007). They may even be able to choose from different service operators for the same service, as they do now, using special dial-codes for long-distance calls. Heterogeneous uniform access would signify the definitive renunciation of the infrastructural differentiation in broadcasting, telecommunications and computer networks. It would promote network convergence and interconnection between networks, while network neutrality in the sense of tolerance and interplay of various physical and logical connection solutions would be enhanced (Werbach, 2007). This feature of access to the network could be guaranteed in countries with different levels of infrastructure development thanks to the current state of technology.

Separation of the element of access from service enhances technological neutrality of regulation, helping to overcome further the division of networks along technology lines. Thus, access to the network shall be described in a technologically neutral manner, that is, avoiding where possible references to any particular kind of network or service. Technological neutrality and the reality of the information society should be more strongly accentuated by introducing greater mobility in the universal service concept (Goggin, 2008; Leith, 2012). This can be done by declaring as an objective of universal service regulation that access to the network shall be provided at any location, in contrast to the current fixed location. This would correspond to the user's wish for a connection at any location and at any time. Countries with well-developed, multiple-network infrastructure can outline a goal of nomadic access at any time aiming for the development of a ubiquitous network which users can effectively access at will. Countries lacking infrastructure can employ the universal access solution, meaning that at any location a person should be within a certain distance from the network. Practically, this can mean the existence of public access points similar to pay phones. Although smart phones and commercial cybercafés supply part of the market demand for communications services other than voice telephony, one could argue that these arrangements do not suffice to meet the needs of low-income users. For these cases, free-of-charge public communication points could be established in the locations where their instalment would be reasonable and necessary (for example, hospitals and train stations).

Introduction of access to the network as a part of universal service allows for a more precise and effective regulation of quality of service, which actually refers to quality of connection. The determination of a 'basket' of essential services that the access shall be able to support will be indicative of what substantial characteristics of the access need to be regulated and for determination of necessary 'floor' and 'ceiling' values. In such a case, a defined quality of access would benefit not only one service, but would provide a foundation for various enhanced services a user might want over the same connection. This could help solve current problems with technical quality of service parameters being confused with service-to-customer quality standards. However, a detailed definition and monitoring of quality of access is a technically demanding and sophisticated task requiring expertise and knowledge of the market and might be difficult at the European level. Therefore, such questions as precise bandwidth, symmetry of data transfer rates, latent time of data transfer, security of data transfer rates and parameters for direct and constant data transfer shall be left to national legislation, or even regulators (Birke, 2009). For harmonisation purposes, the EU level legislation could, however, refer to the relevant European Telecommunications Standards Institute specifications to agree the necessary parameters.

Considering the fact that access quality would be introduced as a minimum requirement, a periodic review process could ensure that this overall minimum level is sufficient over time. The review criteria should put a greater emphasis on the social exclusion criteria and include analysis of technological and market development with the aim to determine the changes in the information environment and the new services and applications that access to the network shall support so that users can fully realise their capabilities. Hence, besides majority usage, such criteria as economic growth, future orientation and usefulness should be included (Wirzenius, 2008).

When considering a reform of the universal service concept along the suggested lines and in accordance with economic, technological and societal developments, timeliness is of utmost importance. A too ambitious universal service would be unbearable for an economy, distort further technological and market developments and might not be carried by society. Against this background, is the introduction of access as a core of the universal service concept at the EU level premature?

The introduction of access to the network as an individual element of universal service at all is preconditioned by whether or not access to the network can be effectively decoupled from the service. Thus, European legislators would closely follow technological and market evolution. While at the moment the technology does not leave any doubts in this respect, it needs to be examined to what extent access to the network and service are available and affordable on the markets (Lie, 2007) in the future. Currently, markets are not ripe for an 'access only' solution because infrastructure competition is not advanced yet, with incumbents enjoying dominant positions and therefore being able to serve bundled offers of connection to the network and services (Lie, 2007). Aiming at an eventual 'access only' universal service, European legislators could consider a gradual phasing-in of an access requirement as a separate part of the universal service scope. The provision describing the scope of universal service in the current regulatory framework (Eur. Parl., 2002a: Art. 3) could be considered a starting point. However, it should be optimised in order to include a proper definition of connection as an element separate from telephone service, and its features should be properly described.

Access to the network in the suggested form shall guarantee a certain level of connectivity for all citizens, sufficient to enjoy electronic communications services of their choice that allow them to satisfy their information and communications needs and to participate fully in all societal activities. Such a shift of the universal service concept not only allows technological and economic challenges to be accounted for and addressed but also can ensure a greater social embeddedness of the electronic communications services market by putting citizens' needs and concerns at the heart of the policy.

Notes

1. Over the years, the digital divide phenomenon has become a complex issue that also refers to ICT skills and impact of use (see Fink and Kenny 2003; Norris 2001). This chapter focuses solely on those aspects of the digital divide that can be tackled with the means of electronic communications policy, namely availability and affordability of infrastructure and services.
2. For other parameters see ETSI EG 202 057-2, ETSI EG 202 057-3, ETSI EG 202 057-4 and other standards.
3. For instance, Vodafone, Telefónica, T-Mobile, KPN and some others are present in several EU Member States. A short overview on mobile markets development can be found at http://ec.europa.eu/competition/sectors/telecommunications/mobile_en.html.

References

Batura, O. (2014). Universal service in the EU information society policy. *info*, 16(6), 24–34. doi: 1.0.1108/info-06-2014-0025.

Batura, O. (2015). *Liberalisation and social regulation of telecommunications services markets: Approaches of the WTO and the EU to universal service*. The Hague: T.M.C. Asser Press (forthcoming).

Body of European Regulators for Electronic Communication BEREC (2011). *Report on impact of fixed-mobile substitution in market definition*. BoR(11) 54. Retrieved from http://berec.europa.eu/doc/berec/bor/bor11_54_FMS.pdf.

Birdsall, W. F. (2011). Human capabilities and information and communication technology: the communicative connection. *Ethics and Information Technology*, 13(2), 93–106. doi: 10.1007/s10676-010-9260-4.

Birke, F. (2009). *Zum Wandel des Universaldienstes in der Telekommunikation: Eine netzökonomische Analyse*. Baden-Baden: Nomos.

Bohlin, E., & Teppayayon, O. (2009). Broadband universal service: A future path for Europe? *International Journal of Management and Network Economies*, 1(3), 275–298. doi: 10.1504/IJMNE.2009.030592.

Castells, M. (2011). *Communication power*. Oxford: Oxford University Press.
Cawley, R. (2001). *Universal service: Specific services on generic networks – Some logic begins to emerge in the policy area*. Paper presented at the 29th Telecommunications Policy Research Conference, Alexandria, VA, United States. Retrieved from http://arxiv.org/ftp/cs/papers/0109/0109063.pdf.
Communications Committee COCOM. (2011). *Implementation of the revised Universal Service Directive: internet-related aspects of Article 4*, COCOM 10–31 final, Brussels.
European Commission. (1987). *Towards a dynamic European economy – Green paper on the development of a common market for telecommunications services and equipment*. COM(87) 290. Retrieved from http://ec.europa.eu/green-papers/pdf/green_paper_telecom_services__common_market_com_87_290.pdf.
European Commission. (2005, 1 June). *i2012 - A European information society for growth and development*. COM(2005) 229. Retrieved from http://eur-lex.europa.eu/LexUriServ/LexUriServ.do?uri=COM:2005:0229:FIN:EN:PDF.
European Commission. (2006). *Report regarding the outcome of the review of the scope of universal service in accordance with Article 15 (2) of Directive 2002/22/EC*. COM(2006) 163. Retrieved from http://eur-lex.europa.eu/LexUriServ/LexUriServ.do?uri=COM:2006:0163:FIN:EN:PDF.
European Commission. (2008). *Second periodic review of the scope of universal service in electronic communications networks and services in accordance with Article 15 of Directive 2002/22/EC*. COM(2008) 572. Retrieved from http://eur-lex.europa.eu/LexUriServ/LexUriServ.do?uri=COM:2008:0572:FIN:EN:PDF.
European Commission. (2010, 19 May). *A digital agenda for Europe*. COM(2010) 245. Retrieved from http://eur-lex.europa.eu/legal-content/EN/TXT/PDF/?uri=CELEX:52010DC0245&from=EN.
European Commission. (2011a, 1 June). *A strategic vision for European standards: Moving forward to enhance and accelerate the sustainable growth in European economy by 2020*. COM(2011) 311. Retrieved from http://eur-lex.europa.eu/LexUriServ/LexUriServ.do?uri=COM:2011:0311:FIN:EN:PDF.
European Commission. (2011b, 19 April). *The open Internet and net neutrality in Europe*. COM(2011) 222. Retrieved from http://eur-lex.europa.eu/LexUriServ/LexUriServ.do?uri=COM:2011:0222:FIN:ES:PDF.
European Commission. (2011c, 23 November). *Universal service in e-communications: Report on the outcome of the public consultation and the third periodic review of the scope of in accordance with Article 15 of Directive 2002/22/EC*. COM(2011) 795. Retrieved from http://eur-lex.europa.eu/LexUriServ/LexUriServ.do?uri=COM:2011:0795:FIN:EN:PDF.
European Parliament and the Council. (2002a). Directive 2002/22 on Universal service and users' rights relating to electronic communications networks and services [Universal Service Directive]. (OJ L 108 of 24.04.2002).
European Parliament and Council. (2002b). Directive 2002/21/EC of the European Parliament and of the Council of 7 March 2002 on a common regulatory framework for electronic communications networks and services, OJ L 108/33 of 24.04.2002, Brussels.
European Parliament and the Council. (2009). Directive 2009/136/EC of the European Parliament and of the Council of 25 November 2009 amending Directive 2002/22/EC of the European Parliament and of the Council of 7 March

2002 on universal service and users' rights relating to electronic communications networks and services, Directive 2002/58/EC of the European Parliament and of the Council of 12 July 2002 concerning the processing of personal data and the protection of privacy in the electronic communications sector and Regulation (EC) No 2006/2004 on cooperation between national authorities responsible for the enforcement of consumer protection laws, OJ L 337 of 18.12.2009, Brussels.

European Union. (2012). Consolidated version of the Treaty on the Functioning of the European Union, signed on 13 December 2007, OJ C 326 of 26.10.2012, Brussels.

Falch, M., & Henten, A. (2009). Achieving universal access to broadband. *Informatica Economică, 13*(2), 166–174.

Feijóo González, C., Gómez Barroso, J. L., González Laguía, A., & Rojo Alonso, D. (2004). *Service universalisation versus universal service*. Paper presented at the conference 'ITCs and Inequalities: The Digital Divides'. Paris, France. Retrieved from http://irene.asso.free.fr/digitaldivides/papers/gomezbarroso.pdf.

Feijóo González, C., Gómez Barroso, J.L., Ramos Villaverde, S., & Rojo Alonso, D. (2005). *Public policies for broadband development in the European Union: New trends for universalisation of services*. In E. Ferro, Y.K. Dwivedi, J.R. Gil-García & M.D. Williams (Eds.), *Handbook of research on overcoming digital divides: Constructing an equitable and competitive information society* (pp. 409–421). IGI Global. doi: 10.4018/978-1-60566-699-0.ch022.

Fink, C., & Kenny, C. J. (2003). W(h)ither the Digital Divide? *Info, 5*(6), 15–24. doi: 10.1108/14636690310507180.

Goggin, G. (2008). The mobile turn in universal service: Prosaic lessons and new ideals. *Info, 10*(5/6), 46–58. doi: 10.1108/14636690810904706.

Gómez Barroso, J. L., & Pérez Martínez, J. (2004). *Should advanced telecommunication services be considered a global public good?* Paper presented at the conference 'ICTs and inequalities: the digital divide', Paris, France. Retrieved from http://irene.asso.free.fr/digitaldivides/papers/barroso2.doc.

Kreutzmann-Gallash, A., Cadman, R., Harker, M., & Waddams, C. (2013). *Criteria to define essential telecoms services. Report by the ESRC Centre for Competition Policy*. Retrieved from http://competitionpolicy.ac.uk/documents/107435/107584/Ofcom+Lit+Review+Essential+Services_final_updated+title.pdf/c3852606-2b8b-4044-8986-b924cc8159dc.

Leith, P. (2012). Europe's information society project and digital inclusion: Universal service obligations or social solidarity? *International Journal of Law and Information Technology 20*(2), 102–123. doi: 10.1093/ijlit/eas004.

Lie, E. (2007, February). *Next Generation Networks and Universal Access: The Challenges Ahead*. Discussion paper at the Global Symposium for Regulators, Dubai, United Arab Emirates. Retrieved from http://www.itu.int/ITU-D/treg/Events/Seminars/GSR/GSR07/discussion_papers/Eric_Lie_universal_service.pdf.

Mack, J., Lansley, S., Nandy, S., & Pantazis, C. (2013). *Attitudes to necessities in the PSE 2012 survey: Are minimum standards becoming less generous?* (Poverty and Social Exclusion in the UK Working Paper, Analysis Series No. 4). Retrieved from http://www.poverty.ac.uk/working-papers-analysisl/attitudes-necessities-pse-2012-survey.

Milne, C. (1998). Stages of universal service policy. *Telecommunications Policy, 22*(9), 775–780. doi: 1.0.1016/S0308-5961(98)00045-7.

Mueller, M. (1997). Telecommunications access in the age of electronic commerce: Toward a third-generation universal service policy. *Federal Communications Law Journal, 49*(3), 655–673.

Nagy, C.I. (2013). The metamorphoses of universal service in the European telecommunications and energy sector: A trans-sectoral perspective. *German Law Journal, 14*(9), 1731–1756.

Nihoul, P.L., & Rodford, P.B. (2004). *EU electronic communications law: Competition and regulation in the European telecommunications market*. Oxford: Oxford University Press.

Noam, E.M. (2010). Regulation 3.0 for Telecom 3.0. *Telecommunications Policy 34*(1/2), 4–10. doi: 1.0.1016/j.telpol.2009.11.004

Norris, P. (2001). *Digital divide: Civic engagement, information poverty, and the Internet worldwide*. New York: Cambridge University Press.

Oosterlaken, I. (2011). Inserting technology in the relational ontology of Sen's capability approach. *Journal of Human Development and Capabilities: A Multi-Disciplinary Journal for People-Centered Development 12*(3), 425–432. doi: 10.1080/19452829.2011.576661.

Rawls, J. (1971). *Theory of justice*. Cambridge, MA: Harvard University Press.

Sawhney, H., & Jayakar, K.P. (2007). *Universal access in the information economy: Tracking policy innovations abroad*. Benton Foundation universal service report. Retrieved from http://www.indiana.edu/~telecom/people/faculty/sawhney/Jayakar_Sawhney.doc.

Sarrocco, C. (2002). *Elements and principles of the information society*. Paper prepared for the ITU World Summit on the Information Society. Retrieved from http://www.itu.int/osg/spu/wsis-themes/access/backgroundpaper/IS%20Principles.pdf.

Sen, A. (1992). *Inequality reexamined*. New York: Russel Sage Foundation.

Sen, A. (1999). *Development as freedom*. New York: Anchor Books.

The Apparatgeist calls. (2009, 30 December). *Economist*. Retrieved from http://www.economist.com/node/15172850.

TNS Opinion and Social network. Special Eurobarometer 355. (2010). *Poverty and social exclusion report*. Retrieved from http://ec.europa.eu/public_opinion/archives/ebs/ebs_355_en.pdf.

TNS Opinion and Social network. (2012). *E-Communications household survey. Special Eurobarometer 381*. Retrieved from http://ec.europa.eu/public_opinion/archives/ebs/ebs_381_en.pdf.

TNS Opinion and Social network. (2013). *E-Communications household survey report. Special Eurobarometer 396*. Retrieved from http://ec.europa.eu/public_opinion/archives/ebs/ebs_396_en.pdf.

TNS Opinion and Social network. (2014). *E-communications and telecom single market survey. Special Eurobarometer 414*. Retrieved from http://ec.europa.eu/public_opinion/archives/ebs/ebs_414_en.pdf.

Van Dijk, J.A.G.M. (2006). *The network society: Social aspects of new media*. Thousand Oaks, CA: Sage.

Webster, F. (2001). *The information society revisited. Handbook of the new media*. London: Sage.

Webster, F. (2003). *Theories of the information society*. London: Routledge.

Werbach, K. (2007). Only connect. *Berkeley Technology Law Journal, 22*(4), 1234–1301.

Werbach, K. (2009). Connections: Beyond universal service in the digital age. *Journal on Telecommunications and High Technology Law, 7*(1), 67–94.

Wirzenius, A. (2008). Telecommunications universal service in Finland. *info, 10*(5/6), 107–120. doi: 1.0.1108/14636690810904751.

Xavier, P. (2008). From universal service to universal network access? *info, 10*(5/6), 20–32. doi: 1.0.1108/14636690810904689.

Section IV

Lessons for European Media Policy from Cases beyond the EU

11 Between Norms and Accomplishment
Lessons for EU Media Policy from EU Enlargements

Beata Klimkiewicz

Introduction: Polyvalent Media, Polyvalent Media Policies

This chapter explores the relationship between EU media policy and its external environment in the specific context of the EU's enlargement processes and the effects that these have had on the shape of the EU media policy. The chapter focuses on the accession of a selected number of states from the Central and Eastern Europe (CEE) region. Both media policy and EU enlargements are approached in the chapter as dynamic processes which mutually influence each other. The chapter shows how some aspects of the media policy harmonisation inevitably entailed in the processes have been successful in the light of what are landmark important geopolitical changes, whereas others can be regarded as policy lessons learned for the future.

The communication media have been seen as one of the most challenging subjects of regulation in the EU, because of diverse functions the media play in societies. In normative terms, one of the leading justifications for media policies has been the recognition of their *specific* functions in a society. In other words, communication media are so *specific* that they seem to be conducive and indispensable to the operation of other social fields, such as the political system, economy, culture, education and technology. Hence, the media–as objects of public policies–represent polyvalent phenomena: they are not only rooted in multiple sets of values, but also function as a means to various societal ends. Consequently, justifications for media freedom, independence and autonomy–as leading policy rationales–are derived from a shared sense of importance by the media and agreement on the roles the media generally play in other areas of social life (Craig, 2004; Crowley & Mitchell, 1994; McQuail, 1992; Schulz, 2004; Voltmer, 2013). Ideally, media policies seek to respond to these polyvalent expectations by balancing desired media functions. In practice, though, policy responses are conditioned by many other factors, such as rapid and elusive transformation of media environments, growing institutional interdependence of policy actors, growing complexities of decision-making, functional convergence and others.

The EU media policy field has displayed these accommodating traits while at the same time pursuing a widening of its scope. Distinct strands in EU media and communication policy have developed: in particular phases (connected also with technological change), in thematic clusters (for example, media pluralism, electronic communication, EU support for media production, public service and community media, media literacy and the digital agenda for Europe and the digital divide) and in media levels (structural, content and performance-related policies). Setting priorities by the EU institutions in terms of dealing with economic, technological, political, cultural and educational functions of the media, has spawned much scholarly interest. A number of scholars have argued that there has been a fundamental prevalence of economic arguments about and a technocratic approach to the EU media policy regarding the consideration of communication needs based on cultural, political (democratic) and social values (Harcourt, 2005; Humphreys, 2008; Kaitatzi-Whitlock, 2005; Psychogiopoulou, 2012; Venturelli, 1998; Ward, 2002). Yet, conceptualising the media as a policy object from the economic and single-market perspective has been prompted to a great extent by the legal confines of the EU Treaties, the specific EU mandate in the area of media and communication, conflicting national interests and approaches and politically sensitive media questions. Thus, EU media policy has been exercised quite carefully through the least contentious terrain, leaving the predominant portion of competence at the level of the Member State. David Ward (2008, p. 4) has argued that the EU's complex architecture, together with a restricted mandate based on the EC Treaty, form quite difficult foundations for the regulation of media and communication environments. Moreover, scholars have frequently pointed out the limitations generated by the EU decision-making system and EU's complex structure that has stimulated a 'democratic deficit' and remoteness from its citizens (Fossum & Schlesinger, 2007; Kaitatzi-Whitlock, 2005; Siedentop, 2001; Sükösd & Jakubowicz, 2011; Ward, 2002).

Yet, with the evolution and enlargement of the European Union and its competencies, the mandate of EU institutions – and in particular the European Commission – in the area of electronic and audiovisual media grew extensively. Some authors even argue that over the last 20 years, EU policy initiatives have steadily increased in number and expanded to cover a wide range of issues, effectively limiting the capacity of member states to frame their national cultural and media policies (Ariño, 2011, p. 328). This refers in particular to the efforts of the EU institutions to accomplish synchronized standards and implementation procedures in such areas as the internal market, common rules on audiovisual media services, support schemes for EU audiovisual production and for pan-European media projects (Ariño, 2011; Boyer & Sükösd, 2011; Graham, 2011; Humphreys, 2008; Jakubowicz, 2011; McGoonagle, 2008; Varga, 2011). At the same time, however, nationally specific approaches have thwarted EU initiatives when it comes to media pluralism, the independence of media regulatory authorities, support to other media sectors such as the print press or community and minority media and a more complex approach towards the PSM (Centre for Media Pluralism and Media Freedom, 2013; Humphreys, 2008;

Jakubowicz, 2010; Just, 2009; Sarikakis, 2004; Schulz, Valcke & Irion, 2013; Ward, 2008). Often, the difficult task of harmonising supra-national versus national policy-making thus results in an enthusiastic promotion of the least contentious policy options, such as the recently used concept of the digital agenda. The use of the term 'agenda' is not accidental. It demonstrates the seriousness and principal place of digital communication in the hierarchy of post-Lisbon EU policies, and is also a dominant vector for redirecting media policies diffused across various thematic fields (Klimkiewicz, 2014).

EU enlargement and its associated processes are one of the most interesting yet under-addressed of EU media and communication policy. The enlargement process provided a procedural set up for transposition of EU standards in many areas (including media-related issues) to the national level. The process also offered a condensed framework of conditions that could potentially verify normative integrity and balance of values, media policy choices, as well as responsiveness to communication needs and rights (Klimkiewicz, 2014). The EU has undergone several waves of enlargement since its creation. However, particularly the fifth enlargement–which the EU underwent in 2004–has been considered most significant not least because the highest number of countries ever joined the Union (including the Czech Republic, Estonia, Cyprus, Latvia, Lithuania, Hungary, Malta, Poland, Slovakia and Slovenia), but also because it was seen as an important act of political will signifying the re-unification of Europe after decades of geopolitical disjuncture. On the one hand, the process of accession has involved a policy of conditionality, sharply applied through bargaining strategies, monitoring and technocratic procedures of alignment. On the other, more informal integration has been in place, with its roots in earlier political change in the region, and subsequent absorption of the CEE countries by other international governance organisations, such as the Council of Europe (CoE), the Organisation for the Economic Co-operation and Development (OECD) and the World Trade Organisation (WTO).

The 2004 EU Enlargement: Conditionality and Assessment

EU enlargement has emerged as product of specific historical circumstances. The fifth EU enlargement and pre-accession process followed political and economic transformation in the CEE, in which communication media were largely seen both as catalysts for the process of democratic consolidation as well as objectives of desired policy change. The catalytic role in democratic consolidation does not simply result from the mere fact of providing communication, but from particular norms in the institutional structure and the quality of performance of media (Voltmer, 2013, p. 23). These include in particular a watchdog function over the abuse of power and state wrongdoings, a civic forum function and an agenda-setting function, all strengthening government responsiveness to social problems (Norris, 2006; Norris

& Odugbemi, 2009). Many new media emerging in the CEE at the end of 1980s and afterwards played some of these functions. On the other hand, media change in post-communist CEE countries was expected 'to mirror the general process of democratic development and create an 'enabling environment' for media freedom and independence' (Price & Krug, 2000; qtd in Jakubowicz, 2012, p. 19). In this sense, the communication media became, quite obviously, shaped by democratising public policies and choices made by policy makers. CEE media environments were not a *tabula rasa* on which completely new media structures could be built from scratch. New ones were created as a form of reaction to the old, though something of a hybrid process developed, even though external and exogenous impetus (in particular for legal and policy change) dominated over the internal pressures, especially during the initial period of transformation. It is important to note that this exogenous influence was generally welcome as an antidote to the 'old system'.

Less formalised media policy change usually implies adopting some institutional arrangements, legal rules, regulatory models and mechanisms. A more formalised approach (as was the case of EU enlargement) follows technocratic procedures that start with setting norms and standards, and continues with transposition of legal rules, institutional design and regulatory mechanisms, each marked by clear yardsticks and tested through monitoring or other forms of evaluation. Yet, any such attempt will always be adjusted to the specific historical, cultural and political circumstances on ground. Although some authors criticized copying Western and European policy models by the CEE countries (Jakubowicz, 2007; Splichal, 2001), and others noticed that such policies have been adopted on paper only (Harcourt, 2012, p. 138), policy diffusion and adoption hardly resembles mechanic cloning, as it is always distilled through cultural precepts, social values and norms, historical background and political performance. Thus, the meanings of policy outcomes and institutions change as they move from one place to another (Voltmer, 2013, p. 21).

Two important external influences on domestic media and communication policy had been present in the CEE region since the mid 1980s. The U.S. option favoured extensive media deregulation with a primary focus on privatisation of a sector which was once the property of the state and the general liberalisation of audiovisual media services (Downey & Mihelj, 2012; Hume, 2011). On the other hand, the European option, promoted through the CoE and the EU, foresaw the 'cultural' protection of European audiovisual works and public support for the PSM (Council of Europe, 1989). The joining by CEE countries of the CoE marked an important move towards adopting the 'European' model. Hungary became a member in 1990, and Poland, the Czech Republic and Slovakia in 1991. The CoE's objectives concerning media and communication were historically linked to the democratisation of media systems in the CEE. It assisted the CEE with the implementation of its crucial legal instrument in the field of media and communication, the European Convention on Transfrontier Television (ECTT) (Council of Europe, 1989). Consequently, the signatories needed to implement rules on freedom of expression, reception and retransmission, transmission of European works, protection of minors, prohibition of pornography, prohibition of incitement of racial hatred, anti-Semitism and xenophobia, 'right of reply' and advertising standards, among other issues. In parallel to the EU's Television without Frontiers (TWF) Directive (1989), the ECTT underwent revision prompted by technological and economic changes in audiovisual landscapes. Ironically, the ECTT's legal significance started to diminish as, in 2011, the Committee of Ministers of the CoE decided to discontinue work on transfrontier television following a deadlock in negotiations with the European Union. Despite a renewed attempt to return to revisions addressed by the CoE's Parliamentary Assembly in its Resolution 1978 (2014), the CoE's Committee of Ministers expressed no willingness to continue the work on ECTT. The CoE's phasing-out from the field of media policy has been marked by tension around setting boundaries regulatory competencies. The EU has maintained a stance that most issues covered by the ECTT fall under the exclusive external competences of the EU and that as a consequence, it will not become party to the ECTT (Ó Fathaigh, 2015).

Historically however, the CoE's involvement in the setting of standards and promoting policy solutions in the CEE has proved useful for the EU as it provided an important normative basis for the EU to build on, especially in terms of defining the EU's own membership conditions for new candidate states. Unlike in the current pre-accession monitoring process, media-related issues and media policy were not distinguished as an independent category for systematic assessment of the fulfilment of membership criteria before the 2004 accession. The EU's principal monitoring instrument – annual Regular Reports – addressed media conditions with respect of human rights and audiovisual policies. In other words, media-related issues were monitored mainly under the Copenhagen political criteria (with reference to freedom of expression) and the *acquis communautaire* (mainly in the section on culture and audiovisual policy).

The Copenhagen criteria stipulate that the candidate country must have achieved 'stability of institutions guaranteeing democracy, the rule of law, human rights and respect for and protection of minorities' (European Council, 1993, p. 13). The Community *acquis* comprises the evolving body of the EU law, common rights and obligations which bind all Member States together within the European Union.[1] As the Copenhagen criteria were not based on the *acquis* as such, the Commission had to conduct its monitoring and assessment following a set of values and standards derived from non-EU documents, such as the European Convention on Human Rights (Sasse, 2004).

This chapter addresses EU enlargement as a specific set of conditions for development and implementation of a polyvalent media policy, in which rationales are derived from political, economic, technological, cultural and educational media functions. To this extent, the chapter shows how priorities were shaped by the EU institutions in terms of assessing media-related issues during the 5th enlargement, and post-accession period. In principal, the analysis sought to answer the question, What aspects of media functions were most frequently reflected in the process of transposing EU norms and standards at the national level of the CEE countries and how these changed over time in post-accession period? This naturally involved the difficult task of balancing and harmonising various functions in the process of polyvalent media policy-making. Understandably, evidence is provided of various interests and levels of political commitment in policy-making.

In the case of the Regular, Strategy and Comprehensive Reports[2] and assessment of the candidate countries during the 5th enlargement, various aspects of freedom of expression were covered between 1998 and 2003. SIn this exercise, structural concerns were mixed with the questions of content, media portrayals and legal policies. Thus, on the one hand, the Reports were attentive to the development of robust media markets and presence of foreign media ownership, yet, on the other, they highlighted such issues as biased reporting by Public Service Media (PSM) or the use of libel and defamation laws. In the area of the *acquis*, monitoring focused on legislative alignment with the principal legal instrument of the day – the TWF Directive. Given that most of the CEE countries have ratified and enforced the ECTT and had been involved in the ratification of its amending protocol before the monitoring of the audiovisual *acquis* started, the CEE were able to fulfil the EU's conditions in this matter. The EU has considered ratification of the ECTT by the candidate countries as one of the main benchmarks of progress towards full transposition of the audiovisual *acquis*.

In general, analysis of the pre-2004 position reveals a number of inconsistencies between proclaimed norms and values and actual achievements realized. EU conditionality certainly influenced domestic media policies in the CEE more than rhetorically but it was, at the same time, essentially complementary and arguably superficial in a process which was dominated by domestic policy priorities (Klimkiewicz, 2014). Under the surface of the official EU rhetoric there was an absence of solid anchoring of expected norms and solutions in the practices of the older EU member states. Many problematic issues indicated in the Reports (most notably insufficient political independence of media regulatory authorities and the PSM) have continued to define the reality of media landscapes, not only in the CEE countries but also those of the established EU members (e.g., political control over the media regulatory authorities; crisis of public service television in Spain, Portugal and Greece. See Hans Bredow Institute for Media Research et al., 2011; Iosifides, 2010; Open Society Institute, 2005).

The monitoring reports also illustrated how the quality of technocratic assessment had been subordinated to political goals of integration. A domestic adjustment to supra-national policies always entails a calculation of the risk and cost of domestic resistance. In addition, policy alignment implies a specific domestic 'translation' of common policy principles. While conditionality can impose some adjustment to these principles, if the conditions are not succinctly defined, there is a danger that in the post-accession period, practices and old mechanisms will quickly re-emerge. Thus, for example, standards addressing the problems of 'insufficient independence or political control over Media Regulatory Authorities and PSM', as observed repeatedly by the Regulatory Reports,[3] have not been clearly defined. This provided a room for political manoeuvre at the national level. Another thorny issue concerns what might be described as a 'double standard' in terms of what is required from the new member (or candidate) states on the one hand, and tolerated in the case of the established Member States on the other (Klimkiewicz, 2014).

Post-Accession Developments in Freedom of the Media

The 2004 post-accession period has tested the depth of media system and policy reforms in CEE countries. Interestingly, the issues related to media performance and policies have not been systematically analysed or monitored by the European Commission after accession, with the exception of some areas tackled in the EU Network of Independent Experts Reports on Fundamental Rights (published for the years 2002–2005), annual reports to the EU on the application of the EU Charter of Fundamental Rights (published since 2010) and the European Agency for Fundamental Rights annual reports (published since 2009). Although quite different in nature, the reports approach media-related issues from the perspective of human rights, and freedom of expression in particular, describing usually selective cases that serve to illustrate either some problematic developments or good practice. None of the set of reports, however, provides a comparative, long-term tool for tracking and monitoring media conditions at various levels, including structural developments (in respect of pluralism, in particular), performance, policies and media access and use. In the absence of a systematic means of assessment from inside the EU, an indication of evolving media conditions in the region can be derived from the *Freedom of the Press* reports compiled systematically across the world since 1980 by Freedom House and the *Press Freedom Index* produced by RWB since 2002. The measurements of media freedom in these two indexes show signs of weaknesses, especially in terms of methodologies, excessive reliance on experts' views and a Western bias (Burgess, 2010). However, it does provide a useful mechanism for comparison of countries in respect of freedom and pluralism of the media, conditions in which journalism operates and the overall media environment with regard to the political function of the media. Table 11.1 and Figure 11.1 show the ranking of the CEE countries in the *Freedom of the Press* index by Freedom House in the years following the EU accession.

Table 11.1 Freedom of the Press Rankings by Freedom House (2005–2013) for the Czech Republic, Hungary, Poland and Slovakia.

	2005	2006	2007	2008	2009	2010	2011	2012	2013	2014
Czech Republic	22	20	18	18	18	18	19	19	19	20
Hungary	21	21	21	21	21	23	30	36*	36*	35*
Poland	20	21	22	24	24	24	25	25	26	27
Slovakia	21	20	20	22	23	23	22	21	22	23

Source: Freedom House: Freedom of the Press (2005–2014).
*Only Hungary was evaluated as 'partly free' in 2012 and 2013; other CEE countries were perceived as 'free' in 2005–2014.

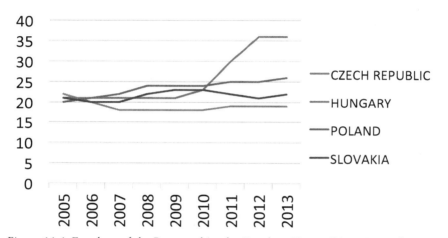

Figure 11.1 Freedom of the Press ranking by Freedom House (2005–2013) for the Czech Republic, Hungary, Poland and Slovakia.
Source: Elaborated on the basis of Freedom House: Freedom of the Press (2005–2013) (available at: http://www.freedomhouse.org/report-types/freedom-press; retrieved 19.09.2013).

In the Freedom of the Press methodology, zero (or the lowest score) signals the highest level of media freedom. A score of 0 to 30 means that the country has a 'free' media, while 31 to 60 signals 'partly free', and 61 to 100 'not free' (Burgess, 2010, p. 9). As can be seen in Table 11.1 and Figure 11.1, the trends observed in the CEE countries do not indicate straightforward and unequivocal progress towards freedom of the media after EU accession. For some countries (Poland – until 2014, Slovakia 2005–2010), the score indicates a gradual decrease in freedom of the press, actually reaching its lowest level in 2014. The most striking developments were registered in the case of Hungary, which moved from a score of 23 in 2010 to 30 in 2011 and 36 in 2012 and 2013, and 35 in 2014. This led to a change in the Hungarian media's status from 'free' to partly in 2012, mostly due to Freedom House's critical account of a new Hungarian media law (passed in 2010) which put strong controls over the media in the hands of a new regulatory authority. Thus, Hungary found itself among other EU countries assessed in 2014 as 'partly free' by Freedom House, which also included Bulgaria (39), Croatia (40), Greece (46), Italy (31) and Romania (41). Notably, Intriguingly, the boundaries between 'free' and 'partly free' media in the EU demonstrate patterns of proximity between 'old' and 'new' EU Member States. In addition to Hungary, a slight rise in score increased in the case of Slovakia (from 20 in 2007 to 23 in 2010). It stemmed from an enactment of the controversial 2008 Press Act which, among other problematic provisions, required publishers to print responses to any 'statement of fact that impinges on the honor, dignity, or privacy of a natural person, or the name or good reputation of a legal entity', regardless of whether the statement in question were accurate (Freedom House, 2011). The law was subsequently amended, although the controversial framing of the 'right of reply' intensified a widespread practice of civil defamation cases where judges, politicians or business elites could claim excessive damages and were often successful in collecting over-proportional financial compensation. This has not only severely affected the financial capacity of the Slovak media, but, in some cases, also prevented the publication of journalistic material (Klimkiewicz, 2014).

Table 11.2 and Figure 11.2 show the rankings of the CEE countries in *Press Freedom Index* by Reporters Without Borders (RWB) in the years following EU accession.

Table 11.2 'Press Freedom Index' by Reporters Without Borders (2005–2014) for Czech Republic, Hungary, Poland and Slovakia

	2005	2006	2007	2008	2009	2010/2011	2012	2013	2014*
Czech Republic	9	5	14	16	24	24	14	16	10
Hungary	12	10	17	23	26	23	40	56	27
Poland	55	60	57	48	37	32	24	22	11
Slovakia	8	8	4	10	45	35	27	23	11

Source: Reporters Without Borders: Press Freedom Index (2005–2014).
*In 2013, there took place a major change in the method used for calculation of the index. Thus the data from the last column (for 2014) are not directly comparable with the data compiled for 2005–2013.

Similar to the Freedom of the Press methodology, in RWB's Press Freedom Index, an overall low score for a country is indicative of the existence of strong press freedom. The calculation undertaken represents scores for controversial matters, such as killed, illegally detained, kidnapped and tortured journalists, censorship and self-censorship. Trends observed in the CEE countries indicate a fluctuating pattern rather than a steady improvement of media freedom after EU accession. Developments in Hungary were similarly reflected compared to Freedom House's analysis: scores were 23

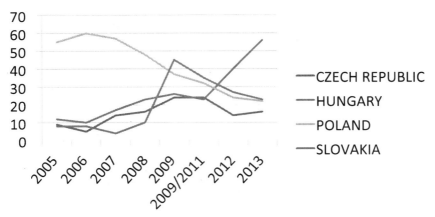

Figure 11.2 Press Freedom Index by Reporters Without Borders (2005–2013) for the Czech Republic, Hungary, Poland and Slovakia.
Source: Reporters Without Borders: Press Freedom Index (2005–2013). Retrieved from http://en.rsf.org/press-freedom-index-2013,1054.html

in 2010/2011, 40 in 2012 and 56 in 2013. The 2013 Report concluded: 'Hungary is still paying the price of repressive legislation that has had a palpable effect on how journalism is practiced' (Reporters without Borders, 2013). In the case of Slovakia, the Press Freedom Index score rose more sharply than in the analysis done by Freedom House. In 2009, the score increased from 10 to 45. Yet just two years earlier, in 2007, Slovakia, with a score of 4 occupied one of top positions in the RWB's ranking on a global scale. This dramatic deterioration stemmed from the enactment of the controversial press law discussed briefly above. The RWB's Press Freedom Index also paid more prominent attention than the Freedom House's index to surveillance of journalists. In the case of Poland, this contributed to the assignment of a score of 55 in 2005, 60 in 2006 and 57 in 2007 (Klimkiewicz, 2014).

In 2013, a new methodological design was implemented by RWB, including the use of a new questionnaire and new quantitative and qualitative measurement techniques. The new methodology also brought new categories, including: 'good situation', 'satisfactory situation', 'noticeable problems', 'difficult situation', and 'very serious situation'. Interestingly, in 2014, the Czech Republic, Poland and Slovakia were placed under the first category—'good situation', together with Germany and the Scandinavian countries. Hungary fell under the category 'noticeable problems' together with Greece, Bulgaria and Croatia, while many well-established EU members were assessed as having a 'satisfactory situation', including France, Spain, Italy, UK, Romania, Lithuania, and Latvia.

This analysis shows that mapping freedom of the media does not produce a coherent regional pattern. In essence, a fluctuation of ranking positions, and sometimes even sharp deviations has occurred in respect of scores assigned to CEE countries after the EU accession, though the reasons behind these differ. The section below examines in detail two cases that manifest a stark dissonance between norms and implementation in media policies, and also a lack of leverage at the EU level to achieve compatibility between these norms and implementation.

The 'Silent' Case of Slovakia and the 'Loud' Case of Hungary

In recent years, the national courts have acted as principal players in determining journalistic performance, exercising in the process significant leverage in media policy and regulatory decisions. Andrej Školkay and Mária Ondruchová-Hong (2012, p. 195) have pointed out that the courts are the final arbiter in defining the limits of freedom of speech and the press (especially regarding libel, defamation, privacy and breaking the law by disclosure of government secrets). The role of the courts has intensified with the passing of the controversial Press Act of 10 April 2008. The Act, widely criticised by international organisations (including RWB, Freedom House and OSCE—Organisation for Security and Co-operation in Europe), legalised an automatic 'right of reply' to anyone regardless of whether defamation or insult occurred. The Act was amended in September 2011 to disqualify the use of 'right of reply' by officials when disputed facts pertain to their public lives. Yet, an extensive use of civil defamation suits resulted in the penalisation of critical coverage of state officials and business elites, and what amounted to minor inaccuracies in otherwise solid investigative journalism have served as arguments for high financial compensations (see, e.g., Freedom House, 2011).

The corruption scandal called the 'Gorilla Affair' illustrates to some extent this role of the courts. The scandal exploded in December 2011, when a file coded 'Gorilla' was uploaded on a U.S.-based server. The file was presented as a wiretap document produced by the Slovak Intelligence Service (*Slovenská Informačná Služba*; SIS)[4] in 2005–2006. The document contained operational transcripts of the conversations allegedly held in 2005 and 2006 between the representatives of Penta (a finance and investment company) and leaders of some Slovak political parties about deals on large privatisation projects. Tom Nicholson, an investigative journalist of Canadian origin, associated formerly with the daily Slovak newspaper *SME*, wrote the book *Gorilla* (Nicholson, 2012), analysing the Gorilla Affair and explaining corruption practices and intricate links between Slovak business and politics. In February 2012, a court in Bratislava delayed the publication of the book for several months based on injunctions brought by a co-owner of the Penta group. Nicholson has since been sued several times for libel. The revelation of the scandal spurred citizen demonstrations in January 2012, the first such significant event of public disapproval against the way politics have been played in Slovakia since the Velvet Revolution in 1989. A quite ironic consequence of the scandal was the recent sale of a 50% stake in the Slovak publishing company Petit Press by the German group *Rheinisch-Bergische Verlagsgesellschaft* to the Penta group. Petit Press is the publisher of its the flagship newspaper, *SME*, which reported extensively about the Gorilla scandal and published a blog by Tom Nicholson. Under a wave of criticism and serious concerns raised by journalists, Penta agreed to withdraw to a 45% minority share in Petit Press, and tp leave the controlling 55% package to the *Prvá Slovenská Investičná Skupina* (PSIS), the original founder of the publishing house.[5] Despite the initiation of an official investigation into the Gorilla Affair in 2012, publicly available information has not, so far, offered any clear-cut explanations. Perhaps one of the reasons has been the relatively low profile of the case on the international arena, due to its 'complicated' and 'ambiguous' character. The EU paid little attention to the case, and the critical tone of international press freedom index organizations did not translate into a significant voice that was able to change the status quo (Klimkiewicz, 2014).

By contrast, controversy about Hungary's new media laws that were passed in 2010 and amended in 2011 and 2013 received high international exposure, particularly at the EU level. When Hungary adopted its 2010 Press and Media Act[6] and the 2010 Mass Media Act,[7] critics emphasized three points: first, the system for media content regulation (including Internet and ICT media content) reaches beyond the needs of a democratic system of social communication; second, a highly centralized and politically controlled regulatory institution and regulatory system may have a serious chilling effect on media freedom and independence (OSCE, 2010, p. 5–6); and third, the inclusion in the legislation of a requirement of 'balanced reporting' might lead to the abuse of regulatory power. A focal point of the criticism was the newly created body, the National Media and Communications Authority (*Nemzeti Média és Hírközlési Hatóság*; NMHH), and, in particular, its competencies, appointment procedure and mechanisms of accountability. Although the Hungarian government maintained that its legislation conformed to EU standards and that its elements are drawn from existing regulations in other European and EU Member States (CMCS, 2012), critical accounts of other supra-national actors, particularly the CoE, European Parliament and European Commission, have been repeatedly evident in policy documents and statements issued since 2011. These clearly demonstrate a determination by supra-national European actors to influence media law developments in Hungary and change the status quo (Klimkiewicz, 2014).

One of such soft measures was the *Resolution of 10 March 2011 on media law in Hungary* adopted by the European Parliament in 2011 (European Parliament, 2011). The Resolution expressed concerns about undermining of media pluralism by the new legislation, in particular pervasive and centralized governmental and political control over all media through the operation of the Media Regulatory Authority and Media Council. Interestingly, the Parliament linked the problematic legislative developments in

Hungary with EU membership criteria: 'Copenhagen criteria for EU membership, as established in June 1993 at the Copenhagen European Council, relating to freedom of the press and freedom of expression should be upheld by all EU Member States and enforced through relevant EU legislation' (European Parliament, 2011). The European Parliament also called for revisions to the Hungarian law in order to ensure that it is fully 'in conformity with EU law and European values and standards on media freedom, pluralism and independent media governance' (European Parliament, 2011). In 2013, the law was amended such that the President of the NMHH is no longer appointed by the Prime Minister but by the President of the Republic on recommendation of the Prime Minister. The Amendment also empowered professional interest groups and self-regulatory interest organizations to make proposals as part of the appointment procedure.

The debate about Hungarian media laws evoked a broader discussion about the norms of media freedom and pluralism in the EU, particularly in relation to its neighbours, EU enlargement policy and surrounding international environment. The Resolution of the European Parliament on *Freedom of press and media in the world* synthesized this approach by stating that 'the EU can only be credible on the global stage if press and media freedoms are safeguarded and respected within the Union itself' (European Parliament, 2013a). The EP also acknowledged 'the general downward trend in the grading of the press and media freedom environments in various countries both within and outside Europe' and observed that 'in recent years some media, notably in the EU, have come under scrutiny themselves for unethical and allegedly illegal behavior' (European Parliament, 2013a). The Resolution also noticed that, while the EU addresses press and media freedom through several policies and programmes, it lacks a specific overall focus on the issue, as well as a coherent driving vision (European Parliament, 2013a). The Commission's DG Connect in response to this claim launched an initiative on *Increased involvement of the European Commission in ensuring respect towards media freedom and pluralism*. This was premised ona follow-up action after several consultation processes in the area of media freedom and pluralism through 2014.[8] Both the EP's resolutions enacted in 2013 urged the EU to play a more significant role in the candidate countries, as well as in relation to its immediate southern and eastern neighbourhood. The Resolution of 3 July 2013 specifically argued that similar obligations that are imposed on candidate countries under the Copenhagen criteria continue to apply to Member States once accession has occurred and should therefore be assessed on a regular basis (European Parliament, 2013b).

Both cases demonstrate the issue of political or institutional control over the media. The Hungarian case caused almost immediate reaction from the EU institutions due to its high political resonance and exposure. In the Slovak case, the involvement of the courts in the defence of political and business elites against media investigation, led to dispersed responsibility for influence on media performance. As already mentioned, the issue of political and institutional control over the media was covered under the political Copenhagen criteria during the 5th enlargement process. The second important aspect of media monitoring provided more detailed assessment as part of the EU's audiovisual *acquis*, arising from responsibilities as part of the transposition of the TWF Directive. The next part of this chapter briefly examines the implementation of the Audiovisual Media Services (AVMS) Directive, the successor to the TWF, by the CEE countries.

Implementation of the AVMSD: Protection of European Works and Free Circulation of Audiovisual Media Services

The post-accession 'Europeanising' effect on the CEE communication and media environments cannot be examined fully without a consideration of the transposition and implementation on CEE states of the of the AVMS Directive in 2007 (European Parliament & the Council, 2010). The AVMSD was drafted between 2005–2007 When during the pre-accession monitoring, the EU's Regular Reports referred to above underlined repeatedly the institutional weakness of regulatory bodies responsible for implementation and monitoring of the Directive in the CEE candidate countries. Insufficient capacities of the regulatory bodies, political pressures and a communication deficit led to serious delays in the implementation of the AVMS Directive in the case of Poland (which required until the end of 2012) and Slovakia (which required until the beginning of 2013). In in the case of Hungary, concerns were raised by the Commission, about the political control begin exercised by the government over its National Media and Communications Authority.

Despite covering a broad variety of issues, the AVMSD principally addresses two audiovisual policy axes: on the one hand, free circulation of audiovisual media services within the EU internal market; and, on the other, cultural protection of the EU audiovisual media services. European quotas constitute a key element of cultural-protection in the AVMS Directive. With the exception of the Czech Republic, the other Central European countries introduced provisions on European works in their media or broadcasting laws before the formal start of pre-accession monitoring in 1997. Currently, legal provision in all CEE countries protects European works, although there is variety in how the AVMSD was implemented nationally in this respect. In general, the CEE countries have implemented more prescriptive rules than is required by the AVMSD. The most flexible rules were introduced in the Czech Republic where the lack of schedule time requirements, no protection of national works, a choice of obligation in the definition of the 'independent producer', a relatively low quota threshold for the share of recent works, a choice of obligations applicable to providers of on-demands services are stand out features (Klimkiewicz, 2014).

Analysis of the dynamics of the average share of transmission time devoted to European works in the CEE countries on the basis of AVMSD implementation reports (European Commission, 2008, 2012a, 2012b, 2012c),

Between Norms and Accomplishment 209

indicates a stable picture among the CEE states between 2005 and 2010. Two countries, Slovakia and Hungary, witnessed a growth of transmission time devoted to European works, while Poland experienced a slight drop and the Czech Republic a more visible decrease. In comparison to the average EU-27 figure for 2009 and 2010, all CEE countries demonstrated a higher share bar the Czech Republic.

Table 11.3 The average share of transmission time devoted to European works in the CEE Member States between 2005 and 2010

	2005	2006	2007	2008	2009	2010
Czech Republic	62.95	79.92	64.3	65.9	64.1	58.1
Hungary	71.95	76.93	68.5	75.3	83.0	81.0
Poland	80.18	81.08	85	83.1	78.4	78.4
Slovakia	63.8	62.27	66.5	67.3	71.7	68.2

Source: European Commission (2008; 2012c).

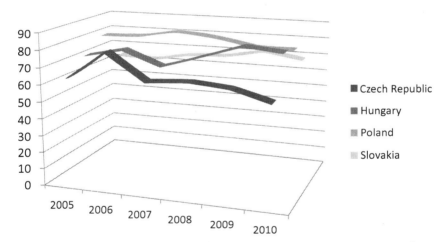

Figure 11.3 The average share of transmission time devoted to European works in the CEE Member States between 2005 and 2010.
Source: Elaborated on the basis of the European Commission (2008, 2012c).

The high and relatively stable share of European works especially in Poland and Hungary (around 75–80 %) indicates that a crucial portion of audiovisual production offered by the channels originates in the EU countries (European Commission, 2008; 2012a; 2012b; 2012c). However, a consideration of provisions concerning promotion of national works in the CEE countries provides an alternative picture. Both Poland and Hungary apply a fairly similar quota system to promote national works.

Broadcasters are obliged to reserve one third of their transmission time to national works in Hungary,[9] while 33% in Poland.[10] Differences can be observed, however, with regard to the definition of 'Hungarian works' in Hungary which may also include works produced in other languages provided that they concern the life and culture of nationalities in Hungary[11] whereas 'programmes originally produced in the Polish language' refer to 'European works' originally registered in the Polish language and produced on basis of the script in the Polish language.[12] Although implying a direct causal link between the legal promotion of national works and significant share of European works may be too far-reaching, the statistical data show that the largest share of European works between 2005 and 2010 was achieved in Poland and Hungary. These are states which used the quota system to promote their *national* works as well as other European originated ones.

Interestingly, in most of the CEE countries, the proportion of channels targeting non-domestic markets is very small – 0.7% in Hungary; 0,9% in Poland and lack of such channels in Slovakia. The largest number of channels targeting other countries was registered in the Czech Republic (33.7%). Many of these, are however, not part of EU broadcasting/media groups, but belong to US corporations. Examples are *Cinemax HBO* (25 channels); *CBS Action* (3 channels); *Comedy MTV* (3 channels); *Disney Children's* (8 channels); *HBO 2 and 3* (10 channels); *HBO Comedy* (13 channels); *HBO HD* (9 channels); *MTV* (4 channels).[13] As can be seen from these examples, the most represented group is *HBO*, a subsidiary of Time Warner, the owner of *TV Nova* and *TV Markíza* with a controlling share on the market of commercial terrestrial television in the Czech Republic and Slovakia. The Czech Republic was the first CEE country to attract US TV inward investment in the beginning of the 1990s and, around then, developed into a 'regional center' of the US-based television industry, at that time owned mainly by CME (Central European Media Enterprises) and later acquired by Time Warner. The EU accession and transposition of the *aquis* in the area of audiovisual policy has not fundamentally changed this setting.

All this evidence leads to a return to the initial questions of the chapter about transposition of EU standards and Europeanisation of national media policies among the new EU Member States. There seems to be a fundamental difference between national responses to two goals set by the AVMS Directive. Why do countries performing well in the area of protection of European production not employ structures supporting the free circulation of audiovisual media services? Conversely, why do countries supporting more open audiovisual landscapes achieve lower shares of European works? The answer is that in both cases (the protection of European production and free circulation of audiovisual services) the evidence doesnot refer primarily to the *European* dimension: countries attracting transnational broadcasters with channels targeting other countries and linguistic communities (for example, the Czech Republic) actually appeal to US-based corporations. Likewise, countries achieving the highest share of European production and demonstrating the most supportive legal implementation in this regard (in this case Hungary and Poland) mostly protect national works.

Conclusion

EU enlargement has brought a demanding test for media and communication policy. In particular, it spurred the debate about consistency of norms and standards to be achieved before joining the EU, and the accomplishment of and adherence to norms by both new and old members. The polyvalent character of EU media and communication policy implies harmonising political, economic, cultural, technological and educational functions of the media, to achieve meaningful policy balance. The monitoring of media-related issues during the 5th enlargement addressed in this chapter shows greater focus on economic media functions (emphasised both under the audiovisual *acquis* as well political Copenhagen criteria) and cultural functions (covered mainly under the audiovisual *acquis* with reference to European quotas). The political functions lacked more profound anchoring in non-negotiable standards, especially with regard to political control over the media, independence of Media Regulatory Authorities and PSM.

In 2013, the European Commission admitted that previous enlargements offered valuable lessons, especially when it comes to the need to address policy fundamentals (European Commission, 2013b). The lessons include the poorly developed nature of benchmarks in the area of freedom of expression and the media, but also a quite passive stance of EU institutions largely accepting the prescribed and imagined course of action towards the accession process. Post-accession developments, however, proved that the EU found itself in a more turbulent environment challenged by instances of excessive concentration of political and media business power (European Parliament, 2004) unethical media behaviour (European Parliament, 2013a) and also some regressive developments in the new EU member states (European Parliament, 2013b).

Certainly, freedom of expression and the media has been more explicitly and intensely recognized by the Commission and other EU institutions in the recent enlargement policy as a right and quality through which the political functions of the media can be fulfilled. The geopolitical scope is now potentially even more challenging than with the previous enlargements as the EU attempts to incorporate Turkey and the countries of the Western Balkans (including Albania, Bosnia and Herzegovina, Kosovo, Montenegro, Serbia, and the Former Yugoslav Republic of Macedonia) to complete the Stabilisation and Association Process. Independent and healthy media have been seen as vital watchdogs of political systems that are expected in turn to create the right conditions for operation of such media.

Analysis of the *Enlargement Strategy* documents (European Commission, 2011, 2012d, 2013) provides a richer perspective of the EU's assessment of freedom of expression and media-related issues. One of the central pillars of these assessments is the institutional blueprint conceived through the values of impartiality and independence of the Media Regulatory Authorities (MRA). In the previous monitoring exercise, the Commission paid attention mainly to the effectiveness, strength and capacities of the MRA which was closely connected with the implementation of its audiovisual *acquis*. Various instances observed by the Commission in the region resulted in close scrutiny of the MRA's status, appointment procedures, and forms of political control and values that justify the MRA's special status among state institutions.

Whilst defamation and libel laws were monitored also before the 2004 enlargement, greater attention was paid to legal measures and provisions themselves than the practice of the courts. In the current assessments, DG Enlargement has created an expectation that judges do not use state or political power to silence journalists as has already been the case in some countries, including Slovakia. The reform of the PSM in transitional and post-transitional media systems has been a central theme in the EU and pan-European media policies since the 1990s, while in the newest enlargement strategy greater importance is attributed to transfer of the best practices and solutions, in particular financial autonomy and sustainability. An interesting development in comparison with previous enlargement assessments can be observed in the area of the economic performance of the media. While pre-2004 reports focused on the robustness of media landscapes, number of actors, and instruments encouraging foreign investments, the new approach emphasises challenges of informal economic pressure that can possibly silence the media and spread self-censorship (European Commission, 2013; DG Enlargement, 2013). These include lack of media ownership transparency and lack of effective competition (Klimkiewicz, 2014).

In general, it can be argued that the basic norms of freedom and pluralism of the media, as well as principles of audiovisual policy under the AVMSD have exhibited considerable stability over a long period of time in EU media policy. What has changed is a more clear focus on the political and pro-democratic functions of the media, and, where other values are tested (such as the economic competitiveness of the media), these are approached through the logic of the performance of the political system in which the communication media are seen to play a fundamental role (Klimkiewicz, 2014). Yet, there is an open question how, consequently, the accomplishment and implementation of standards will be assessed and politically used by the EU institutions. Even more important is a consideration of how deeply resonant will be the perception of freedom of the media as a fundamental norm that needs constantly to be upheld and developed through self-reflection among EU Member States and modified as necessary through policy adjustments.

Notes

1. European Commission (2015) *European Commission–Enlargement–Acquis*. Retrieved from http://ec.europa.eu/enlargement/policy/glossary/terms/acquis_en.htm; 20 April 2015.
2. Following Regular Reports of the European Commission were analysed for this chapter: 1998, 1999, 2001, 2002 Regular Report on Czech Republic's Progress Towards Accession; 1998, 1999, 2001, 2002 Regular Report on Hungary's Progress Towards Accession; 1998, 1999, 2001, 2002 Regular Report on Poland's Progress Towards Accession; 1998, 1999, 2001, 2002 Regular Report on Slovakia's Progress Towards Accession. In addition, the 2003 EC Comprehensive Monitoring Reports on the Candidate Countries' Preparations for Membership were analysed in the case of: the Czech Republic, Hungary, Poland, Slovakia. Finally, two Composite Reports of the European Commission on Progress towards Accession by each of the Candidate Countries were analysed for 1998 and 1999. Since 2000, these reports were restructured into: Enlargement Strategy Papers of the European Commission on Progress towards Accession by each of the Candidate Countries. The four such strategy papers were analysed for: 2000, 2001, 2002 and 2003 (available at: http://ec.europa.eu/enlargement/archives/key_documents/reports_2000_en.htm;.
3. See the Regular Report on the Czech Republic (2000, 2001, 2002), the Regular Report on Hungary (1999, 2001), the Regular Report on Slovakia (1999, 2000).
4. SIS (Slovak Information Agency) is a state body with the mandate to defend the constitutional structure, public order and security of the state.
5. Penta to withdraw to minority (2014, November 10) *Spectator*. Retrieved from http://spectator.sme.sk/articles/view/55825/2/penta_to_withdraw_to_minority.html.
6. Act CIV of 2010 on the freedom of the press and the fundamental rules on media content published on 9 November in Magyar Közlöny (Official Journal) 2010 and amended in March 2011. The Act has been notoriously referred as the 'Press Freedom Act', although the official translation of the Act establishes the abbreviated version: Press and Media Act.
7. Act CLXXXV of 2010 on media services and mass media published on 31 December 2010 in Magyar Közlöny (Official Journal) and amended in March 2011.
8. DG Connect (2013) *Media policy, media pluralism and media freedom* (available at: http://ec.europa.eu/dgs/connect/en/content/media-policy-media-pluralism-media-freedom; 30.12. 2014).
9. Article 20 (1) Act CLXXXV of 2010 on Media Services and Mass Media.
10. Article 15 (1) 1992 Broadcasting Act adopted on 29 December, 1992, as amended.
11. Article 203 (37) Act CLXXXV of 2010 on Media Services and Mass Media.
12. Article 4 (14) 1992 Broadcasting Act.
13. Elaborated on the basis of European Audiovisual Observatory (2013) The MAVISE database: mavise.obs.coe.int.

References

Ariño, M. (2011). Which frontiers for EU media policy? An assessment in the context of the European project. In M. Sükösd, & K. Jakubowicz (Eds.), *Media, Nationalism and European Identities* (pp. 321–344). Budapest, Hungary/New York: CEU Press.

Boyer, D., & Sükösd, M. (2011). European media and culture of Europeaness. In M. Sükösd, & K. Jakubowicz (Eds.), *Media, nationalism and European identities* (pp. 223–246). Budapest, Hungary/New York: CEU Press.

Brouillette, A., & Van Beek, J. (2012). *Hungarian media laws in Europe: An assessment of consistency of Hungary's media laws with European practices and norms.* Retrieved from http://homepage.univie.ac.at/katharine.sarikakis/wp-content/uploads/2012/09/Hungarian_Media_Laws_in_Europe.pdf.

Burgess, John. (2010). *Evaluating the evaluators: Media freedom indexes and what they measure.* Washington, DC: Center for International Media Assistance. Retrieved from http://www.cima.ned.org/resource/evaluating-the-evaluators-media-freedom-indexes-and-what-they-measure/.

Center for Media and Communication Studies. (2012). Hungarian Media Laws in Europe: An Assessment of Consistency of Hungary's Media Laws with European Practices and Norms. Budapest: CMCS.

Centre for Media Pluralism and Media Freedom. (2013). *European Union competencies in respect of media pluralism.* Retrieved from http://cmpf.eui.eu/Documents/CMPFPolicyReport2013.pdf.

Council of Europe. (1989) *Recommendation 1098 (1989) of the Parliamentary Assembly on East-West audiovisual co-operation* Strasbourg: Council of Europe. http://www.coe.int/t/dghl/standardsetting/media/themes/radiotv_en.asp?/.

Craig, G. (2004). *The media, politics and public life.* Crows Nest, Australia: Allen & Unwin.

Crowley, D., & Mitchell, D. (Eds.). (1994). *Communication theory today.* Stanford, CA: Stanford University Press.

Directorate General Enlargement. (2013). *EU Enlargement: Speaking out: The EU supports freedom of expression in enlargement countries.* Retrieved from http://ec.europa.eu/enlargement/pdf/publication/20130617_speaking_out_the_eu_supports_freedom_of_expresion.pdf.

Downey, J., & Mihelj, S. (Eds.). (2012). *Central and Eastern European media in comparative perspective: Politics, economy and culture.* London: Ashgate.

European Commission. (2008, 22 July). *Eight communication on the application of Articles 4 and 5 of the Directive 89/552/EEC 'Television without Frontiers', as amended by Directive 97/36/EC, for the period 2005–2006.* SEC (2008) 2310. Retrieved from http://www.ipex.eu/IPEXL-WEB/dossier/files/download/082dbcc530b1bf490130bc8e277b6502.do.

European Commission. (2011, 12 October). *Enlargement Strategy and Main Challenges 2011–2012.* COM (2011) 666. Retrieved from http://eur-lex.europa.eu/LexUriServ/LexUriServ.do?uri=COM:2011:0666:FIN:EN:PDF.

European Commission. (2012a, 4 May). *Audiovisual Media Services and Connected Devices: Past and Future Perspectives. First Report from the Commission to the European Parliament, the Council, the European Economic and Social Committee and the Committee of the Regions on the application of Directive 2010/13/EU 'Audiovisual Media Service Directive'.* Retrieved from http://eur-lex.europa.eu/legal-content/EN/TXT/PDF/?uri=CELEX:52012DC0203&from=EN.

European Commission. (2012b, 24 September). *Promotion of European works in EU scheduled and on-demand audiovisual media services. Report from the Commission to the European Parliament, the Council, the European Economic and Social Committee and the Committee of the Regions: First Report on the*

Application of Articles 13, 16 and 17 of Directive 2010/13/EU for the period 2009–2010. COM(2012) 522. Retrieved from http://eur-lex.europa.eu/LexUriServ/LexUriServ.do?uri=COM:2012:0522:FIN:EN:PDF.
European Commission. (2012c, 24 September). *Promotion of European works in EU scheduled and on-demand Audiovisual Media Services – PART II – On the application of Articles 16 and 17 of Directive 2010/13/EU for the period 2009–2010*. SWD (2012) 269. Retrieved from http://eur-lex.europa.eu/legal-content/EN/TXT/PDF/?uri=CELEX:52012DC0522&from=EN.
European Commission. (2012d, 10 October). *Enlargement Strategy and Main Challenges 2012–2013*. COM (2012) 600. Retrieved from http://eur-lex.europa.eu/LexUriServ/LexUriServ.do?uri=COM:2012:0600:FIN:EN:PDF.
European Commission. (2013, 16 October). *Enlargement Strategy and Main Challenges 2013–2014*. COM (2013) 700. Retrieved from http://eur-lex.europa.eu/legal-content/EN/TXT/PDF/?uri=CELEX:52013DC0700&from=EN.
European Council. (1993). *European Council in Copenhagen 21–22 June 1993. Conclusions of the Presidency*. SN 180/1/93 REV 1. Retrieved http://www.consilium.europa.eu/uedocs/cms_data/docs/pressdata/en/ec/72921.pdf.
European Parliament. (2004, 22 April). *European Parliament Resolution on the risks of violation, in the EU and especially in Italy, of freedom of expression and information (Article 11(2) of the Charter of Fundamental Rights)*. P5_TA(2004)0373. Retrieved from http://www.europarl.europa.eu/sides/getDoc.do?pubRef=-//EP//TEXT+TA+P5-TA-2004-0373+0+DOC+XML+V0//EN.
European Parliament. (2011, 10 March). *Media law in Hungary*. P7_TA (2011) 0094. Retrieved from http://www.europarl.europa.eu/sides/getDoc.do?pubRef=-//EP//TEXT+TA+P7-TA-2011-0094+0+DOC+XML+V0//EN.
European Parliament. (2013a, 13 June). *Freedom of Press and Media in the World*. P7_TA-PROV(2013)0274. Retrieved from http://www.europarl.europa.eu/document/activities/cont/201306/20130620ATT68106/20130620ATT68106EN.pdf.
European Parliament. (2013b, 3 July). *The situation of fundamental rights: standards and practices in Hungary*. P7_TA-PROV(2013)0315. Retrieved from http://www.europarl.europa.eu/sides/getDoc.do?type=TA&language=EN&reference=P7-TA-2013-315.
European Parliament. (2013c, 21 May). *The EU Charter: standard setting for media freedom across the EU*. P7_TA(2013)0203. Retrieved from http://www.europarl.europa.eu/sides/getDoc.do?pubRef=-//EP//TEXT+TA+P7-TA-2013-0203+0+DOC+XML+V0//EN.
European Parliament and the Council of the European Union. (2002). Directive 2002/22/EC *EU of the European Parliament and the Council on universal service and users' rights relating to electronic communications networks and services*. OJ L 108 of 24.04.2002.
European Parliament and the Council. (2010, 15 April). *Directive 2010/13/EU of the European Parliament and the Council of 10 March 2010 on the coordination of certain provisions laid down by law, regulation or administrative action in Member States concerning the provision of audiovisual media services (Audiovisual Media Services Directive)*. O.J. 15.04.2010 L 95/1-24. Retrieved from http://eur-lex.europa.eu/legal-content/EN/TXT/PDF/?uri=CELEX:32010L0013&from=EN.
Fossum, J. E., & Schlesinger, P. (Eds.). (2007). *The European Union and the public sphere. A Communicative space in the making?* London and New York: Routledge.

Freedom House: Freedom of the Press (2005–2014.) Retrieved from http://www.freedomhouse.org/report-types/freedom-press

Freedom House. (2011). Freedom of the Press 2011: Slovakia. Retrieved from http://www.freedomhouse.org/report/freedom-press/2011/slovakia.

Graham, David (Attentional) et al. (2011, 13 December). *Study on the implementation of the provisions of the Audiovisual Media Services Directive concerning the promotion of European works in audiovisual media services: Final Study Report.* Retrieved from http://ec.europa.eu/archives/information_society/avpolicy/docs/library/studies/art_13/final_report_20111214.pdf.

Hans Bredow Institute for Media Research et al. (2011). *INDIREG final report: Indicators for independence and efficient functioning of audiovisual media services regulatory bodies for the purpose of enforcing the rules in the AVMS Directive.* Retrieved from http://ec.europa.eu/avpolicy/docs/library/studies/regulators/final_report.pdf.

Harcourt, A. (2005). *The European Union and the regulation of media markets.* Manchester and New York: Manchester University Press.

Harcourt, A. (2012). Transnational media regulation in Central and Eastern Europe. In. J. Downey, & S. Mihelj (Eds.), *Central and Eastern European media in comparative perspective: Politics, economy and culture* (pp. 137–155). London: Ashgate.

Hume, E. (2011). *Caught in the middle: Central and Eastern European journalism at the crossroads: A Report to the Center for International Media Assistance.* Retrieved from http://www.nieman.harvard.edu/wp-content/uploads/pod-assets/Image/microsites/post-comm/CIMA-Central_and_Eastern_Europe-Report_3.pdf.

Humphreys, P.J. (2008). The principal axes of the European Union's audiovisual policy. In I. Fernández Alonso & M. de Moragas i Spà (Eds.), *Communication and cultural policies in Europe.* Collecció Lexikon 4 (pp. 151–182). Barcelona, Spain: Universitat Autònoma de Barcelona.

Iosifidis, P. (Ed.). (2010) *Reinventing public service communication: European broadcasters and beyond.* Basingstoke, UK: Palgrave Macmillan.

Jakubowicz, K. (2007). *Rude awakening: Social and media change in Central and Eastern Europe.* Creskill, NJ: Hampton Press.

Jakubowicz, K. (2010). From PSB to PSM: A new promise for public service provision in the information society. In B. Klimkiewicz (Ed.), *Media freedom and pluralism: Media policy challenges in the enlarged Europe* (pp. 13–128). Budapest, Hungary: CEU Press.

Jakubowicz, K. (2011). European melting pot? European integration and EU audiovisual policy at a crossroads. In M. Sükösd, & K. Jakubowicz, K. (Eds.), *Media, nationalism and European identities* (pp. 272–320). Budapest-New York: CEU Press.

Jakubowicz, K. (2012). Post-communist political systems and media freedom and independence. In J. Downey & S. Mihelj (Eds.), *Central and Eastern European media in comparative perspective: Politics, economy and culture* (pp. 15–40). London: Ashgate.

Just, N. (2009). Measuring media concentration and diversity: New approaches and instruments in Europe and the U.S. *Media, Culture and Society, 31*(1), 97–117. doi: 10.1177/0163443708098248.

Kaitatzi-Whitlock, S. (2005). *Europe's political communication deficit.* Bury St Edmonds, UK: Abramis Academic Publishing.

Klimkiewicz, B. (2014). *A polyvalent media policy in the enlarged Europe*. Krakow, Poland: Jagiellonian University Press.

McGoonagle, T. (2008). The quota quandary: An assessment of Articles 4–6 of the Television Without Frontiers Directive. In D. Ward (Ed.), *The European Union and the culture industries: Regulation and the public interest* (pp. 187–212). Aldershot, UK: Ashgate.

McQuail, D. (1992). *Media performance. Mass communication and the public interest*. London: Sage Publications.

Nicholson, T. (2012). *Gorila*. Bratislava, Slovakia: Vydavateľstvo Dixit.

Norris, P. (2006). The role of the free press in promoting democratization, good governance, and human development. In M. Harvey (Ed.), *Perspectives on advancing governance and development from the global forum for media development* (pp. 66–76). Brussels, Belgium: Global Forum for Media Development. Retrieved from https://internews.org/sites/default/files/resources/mediamatters.pdf.

Norris, P., & Odugbemi, S. (2009). Evaluating media performance. In P. Norris (Ed.), *Public sentinel: New media and the governance agenda* (pp. 3–29). Washington, DC: World Bank Publications.

Ó Fathaigh, R. (2015). Reply to Parliamentary Assembly's call to revise the European Convention on Transfrontier Television. *IRIS, 2015*(1), 1–2. Retrieved from http://merlin.obs.coe.int/iris/2015/1/article2.en.html.

Open Society Institute. (2005). *Television across Europe: regulation, policy and independence*. Retrieved from http://www.opensocietyfoundations.org/sites/default/files/volone_20051011_0.pdf.

Organization for Security and Co-operation in Europe. (2010). *Analysis and assessment of a package of Hungarian legislation and draft legislation on media and telecommunications*. Retrieved from http://www.osce.org/fom/71218.

Psychogiopoulou, E. (Ed.). (2012). *Understanding media policies: A European perspective*. Basingstoke: Palgrave Macmillan.

Reporters Without Borders. (2013). Press Freedom Index. (2005–2014) Retrieved from http://en.rsf.org/press-freedom-index-2013,1054.html.

Reporters Without Borders: Press Freedom Index. (2005–2013). Retrieved from http://en.rsf.org/press-freedom-index-2013,1054.html

Reporters Without Borders. (2013). *2013 World Press Freedom Index: Dashed hopes after spring*. Retrieved from http://en.rsf.org/press-freedom-index-2013,1054.html.

Reporters Without Borders. (2014). World Press Freedom Index 2005–2014. Retrieved from https://rsf.org/index2014/en-index2014.php.

Sarikakis, K. (2004). *Powers in media policy: The challenge of the European Parliament*. Oxford: Peter Lang.

Sasse, G. (2004). EU conditionality and minority right: Translating the Copenhagen Criterion into policy [Working Paper]. *EUI Working Papers. RSCAS 2005*(16). Retrieved from http://cadmus.eui.eu/bitstream/handle/1814/3365/05_16.pdf?sequence=1.

Schulz, W. (2004). Reconstructing mediatization as an analytical concept. *European Journal of Communication, 19*(1), 87–101. doi: 10.1177/0267323104040696.

Schulz, W., Valcke, P., & Irion, K. (Eds.). (2013). *The independence of the media and its regulatory agencies: Shedding new light on formal and actual independence against national context*. Bristol, UK: Intellect.

Siedentop, L. (2001). *Democracy in Europe*. New York: Columbia University Press.

Školkay, A., & Ondruchová-Hong, M. (2012). Slovakia: Reinventing media policy without a practical perspective. In E. Psychogiopoulou (Ed.), *Understanding media policies: A European perspective* (pp. 182–197). Basingstoke, UK: Palgrave Macmillan.

Splichal, S. (2001). Imitative revolutions: Changes in the media and journalism in East-Central Europe. *Javnost – The Public: Journal of the European Institute for Communication and Culture, 8*(4), 31–58. doi: 10.1080/13183222.2001.11008785.

Sükösd, M., & Jakubowicz, K. (Eds.). (2011). *Media, nationalism and European identities.* Budapest-New York: CEU Press.

Varga, P.J. (2011). Pan-European media: Attempts and limitations. In M. Sükösd, & K. Jakubowicz (Eds.), *Media, nationalism and European identities* (pp. 119–151). Budapest-New York: CEU Press.

Venturelli, S. (1998). *Liberalising the European media: Politics, regulation and the public sphere.* Oxford: Clarendon Press.

Voltmer, K. (2013). *The media in transitional democracies.* Cambridge, MA: Polity Press.

Ward, D. (2002). *The EU democratic deficit and the public sphere: An evaluation of EU media policy.* Washington, D.C.: IOS Press.

Ward, D. (Ed.). (2008). *The European Union and the culture industries: Regulation and the public interest.* Aldershot: Ashgate.

2002, 2003, 2004, 2005 Report on the Situation of Fundamental Rights in the European Union and its Member States, available at: http://ec.europa.eu/justice/fundamental-rights/document/index_en.htm.

12 Convergent Media Policy
Reflections Based Upon
the Australian Case

Terry Flew

Introduction: The Policy Challenges of Convergence

We are at a historic media policy juncture in the twenty-first century, where changes in the media environment are raising new questions about how media are regulated, how they should be regulated and indeed whether they should be regulated at all. It is widely acknowledged that existing laws, policies and regulations lag behind the technological, economic and socio-cultural changes associated with the Internet and media convergence. In 2011, Konrad von Finckenstein, then-Chair of the Canadian Radio–Telecommunications Commission (CRTC), observed that:

> [T]he [media] industry is going through fundamental change in technology, in business models and in corporate structures. It has become a single industry, thoroughly converged and integrated. Yet it continues to be regulated under … [a]cts, which date from 20 years ago. Authority continues to be divided among different departments and agencies.
> (von Finckenstein, 2011, p. 1)

In its 2013 Green Paper, *Preparing for a Fully Converged Audiovisual World: Growth, Creation and Values*, the European Commission has observed that 'lines are blurring quickly between the familiar twentieth-century consumption patterns of linear broadcasting received by TV sets versus on-demand services delivered to computers', and that 'if, in a converging world, linear and non-linear provision of similar content were to be treated as being in competition, then the current differences in [regulatory] regimes could clearly distort that relationship' (European Commission, 2013, pp. 1, 11). In Australia, the Australian Communication and Media Authority (ACMA) has argued that 'regulation constructed on the premise that content could (and should) be controlled by how it is delivered is losing its force, both in logic and in practice' (Australian Communication and Media Authority [ACMA], 2011, p. 6), the subsequent Convergence Review, commissioned by the Australian Government, concluded:

> Australia's policy and regulatory framework for content services is still focused on the traditional structures of the 1990s – broadcasting

and telecommunications. The distinction between these categories is increasingly blurred and these regulatory frameworks have outlived their original purpose (Australian Government, 2012, p. vii).

Such findings are similar to the Media Convergence Review conducted in Singapore in 2012, which found 'policy and regulatory frameworks, which were designed for traditional media platforms and industry structures, are no longer able to cope with the characteristics of the converged media environment' (MDA, 2012, p. 5).

It can thus be seen that, in multiple national and regional contexts, the Internet and media convergence have been key drivers of the need to rethink media regulation. Moreover, the relationship of media convergence to policy convergence, and the greater harmonisation of media, telecommunications and information laws and policies, also arises from media globalisation and the challenges presented to national regulators of digital content platforms that lack a clear territorial basis. Other significant drivers of change in the media environment that necessitate new approaches to media policy include the blurring of boundaries between media forms and industries, the greater ability of media consumers to themselves become producers of media content and the capacity of media users to access the same content across multiple devices, including tablet PCs, smart phones, and Internet-enabled 'smart' televisions.

In this chapter, I consider the Australian case, with particular reference to a series of reports undertaken for the Australian government between 2011 and 2012, in order to identify possible insights of relevance to policy makers in Europe and elsewhere. The key reviews that took place in Australia over 2011–2012 were the Convergence Review (Australian Government, 2012), the Independent Media Inquiry (Finkelstein, 2012), and the Australian Law Reform Commission's [ALRC] Review of the National Classification Scheme (Australian Law Reform Commission [ALRC], 2012). The chapter is intended to contribute to wider debates about the role of media and communication academics in the policy process and whether digital convergence has generated new opportunities for engagement by practitioners (Aslama & Napoli, 2009), and for moving – as Natascha Just and Manuel Puppis (2012, p. 12) have observed – from 'communications scholars' liking for self-castigation with regard to their assumed failure to actively inform and contribute to policy processes', towards greater 'self-confidence about their work' and its practical significance in policy formation. This chapter offers a qualified defence of the ongoing significance of public interest principles as they apply to media regulation and media policy reform. I note that these observations are made in part on the basis of having been a participant-observer in such processes, through secondment from the university sector to chair the ALRC's National Classification Scheme Review (Flew, 2014a).

Does Media Convergence Lead to Policy Convergence?

An important issue raised in the public policy literature is whether policy convergence is occurring, with changes in the external environment experienced simultaneously by multiple nation states leading to the adoption of broadly similar policy responses. Drezner (2001, p. 53) has defined policy convergence as 'the tendency of policies to grow more alike, in the form of increasing similarity in structures, processes and performances', and there are arguments that policy convergence has occurred as a consequence of economic globalisation or the diffusion of neo-liberal ideologies (Iosifidis, 2016; Flew, 2016). Knill (2005) has argued that policy convergence needs to be considered in light of its relationship to *policy transfer*, or the adoption of ideas developed in one national context and their application in another (c.f. Pratt, 2009), and to policy diffusion, or 'the socially mediated spread of policies across and within political systems' (Knill, 2005, p. 766).

Knill argues that an important distinction needs to be made between the sharing of ideas among key institutional actors in response to common policy challenges – in the media policy sphere, the challenges of convergence of platforms and services would be a case in point – and whether they are leading to the adoption in practice of similar policies. There is a disjuncture between the question of whether broadly similar policy and regulatory instruments may be adopted, as a result of the need to harmonise policies through supranational law and international treaty obligations to take one example, and whether the underlying structure of belief and ideas, and its embedding in policy institutions and practices, has actually been transformed. The literature on comparative national capitalisms draws attention to 'the persistence of diversity in capitalism and the uneven and experimental nature of systemic change' (Lane & Wood, 2009, p. 532), and various comparative studies have indicated that even in those areas where one would expect pressures for regulatory harmonisation to be strongest, historically and institutionally grounded forms of national differentiation continue to be important (Marsh & Sharman, 2009; Meseguer & Gilardi, 2009; Morgan, 2009).

The rise of the mass media of film and broadcasting in the twentieth century generated common regulatory responses in many countries based around common concerns about the social impact of mass media and the relationship of the public good to commercialisation. The BBC model of public service broadcasting was adopted in many countries – particularly those of the British Commonwealth – while the incorporation of film into national cultural policies as pioneered in France proved to be highly influential elsewhere in Europe. Broadcast media were subject to extensive government regulation on the basis of 'public good' characteristics of the media product; the need to manage access to spectrum; concerns about concentration of ownership and the capacity of media owners to influence public debate; and regulations to deal with potential risks to children and others from exposure to harmful media content (Doyle, 2013; Picard, 2011). While many of these regulations have been 'negative', in the sense of setting controls over access to the broadcast spectrum or restrictions on what can be screened, there have also been 'positive' regulations that aimed to stimulate various forms of local content production, including local drama, provision for cultural and linguistic minorities, children's programming and documentary and factual programming.

While there were commonalities in the forms that media regulation took between nations, there were also important historical differences in the institutional forms these took. Most notably, there was the 'great divergence' (van Cuilenberg & McQuail, 2003, p. 190) between the European and United States models in the period after World War II, with the European model placing much greater stress upon public service broadcasting and media as an instrument of social reform than the commercially driven U.S. approach. The European Union continues to identify PSB as a distinctive element of the European model, defining the mission of public broadcasting as being 'directly related to the democratic, social and cultural needs of each society and to the need to preserve media pluralism' (Schejter, 2008, p. 1610). At the same time, macro-histories of media regulation (e.g., Freedman, 2008; Van Cuilenberg & McQuail, 2003;) have tended to see the period from the 1980s onwards as one of greater policy convergence towards the U.S. model, particularly as media policy has become more influenced by telecommunications policy. Such policy frameworks are seen as being more pragmatic and consumer-focused rather than normative and social policy-driven and strongly shaped by an economic and technological logic of promoting competition and the development of new markets.

Why Regulate? The Politics of Media Regulation

Changes to media regulations are only partly shaped by technological changes. No less important are questions of *why* media regulations take the form they do and what are their normative and political foundations. Media regulation has traditionally been explained in terms of *public interest* criteria, where 'regulation is established in response to the conflict between private corporations and the general public [and] the creation of regulatory agencies is viewed as the concrete expression of the spirit of democratic reform (Horwitz, 1989, p. 23). Van Cuilenburg and McQuail observed that:

> Policy formation in this, as in other fields, is generally guided by a notion of the 'public interest', which democratic states are expected to pursue on behalf of their citizens. In general, a matter of 'public interest' is one that affects the society as a whole (or sections of it) rather than just the individuals immediately involved or directly affected.
> (van Cuilenburg & McQuail, 2003, p. 182)

The normative proposition that underpins public interest theories of regulation is that 'regulatory administration neither adds to nor subtracts from the policy decided by law makers ... [and] civil servants are simply office carriers dedicated to carrying out the duties that constitute their particular role' (Christensen, 2011, pp. 97–98). However, critics have argued that the history and conduct of regulatory institutions has seen instances of regulatory failure, the protection of vested interests by regulators, and undue political influence over the regulatory process (Horwitz, 1989, pp. 27–29).

The critique of public interest theories of regulation has come from two very distinct directions. *Economic capture theories* have argued that regulatory failure arises out of two interrelated processes: regulated businesses use the process as a way of securing economic rents and controlling the entry of new competitors into the market and government regulators serving their own interests by working closely with regulated businesses, to the detriment of the public interest (Christensen, 2011, pp. 97–99). Drawing upon neo-classical economics and applying rational choice theory to the political and policy spheres, these theories identify the problem of regulatory reform as being one where the benefits of the *status quo* are concentrated among a small number of industry and policy 'insiders', and the costs of change are well understood by these interests, whereas the benefits of change are more uncertain and diffused among the population more broadly (Dunleavy & O'Leary, 1987, pp. 108–111). One of the best known early accounts of regulatory capture theory was that of the Chicago economist Ronald Coase. In his critique of the U.S. Federal Communications Commission (FCC) and its approach to regulating commercial broadcasters, Coase observed that:

> It is difficult to operate closely with an industry without coming to look at its problems in industry terms ... the Commission, although thinking of itself as apart from and with different aims from the industry, will nonetheless be incapable of conceiving of or bringing about any radical changes in industry practices or structure. In fact, the regulation of the broadcasting industry by the Federal Communications Commission resembles a professional wrestling match. The grunts and groans resound throughout the land, but no permanent injury seems to result.
>
> (Coase, 1966, p. 442)

What is known as the 'positive theory of regulation' (Hoskins, McFadyen & Finn, 2004: pp. 304–307) has typically been accompanied by championing of the role played by markets and competition in economic transformation. The recommendations arising from such theories thus typically support deregulation, or a reduced role of governments in controlling the activities of private corporations, combined with measures to increase the level of overall competition in those industries (Berg, 2008; c.f. Stedman-Jones, 2012, pp. 126–133). Alternatively, technological change and changing consumer tastes and preferences are seen as themselves being drivers of regulatory change. Cable and satellite television, and the growing use of the Internet to enable alternative modes of content delivery and new services, are seen as undermining the traditional foundations of media regulation. The resulting 'crisis of regulation' is identified as providing a 'window of opportunity' for deregulatory arguments.

The second major critique of public interest theories of regulation comes from *capitalist state theories*, which have critiqued liberal pluralism for being both politically naïve and intellectually complicit in regimes of power and domination. These neo-Marxist critics have argued that regulatory agencies, and particularly those who head them, come to hold common class interests with those who own and control the major private corporations, as part of what C. Wright Mills termed a *power elite*, or what may now (post-Occupy) be termed 'the one per cent' (Gitlin, 2012; Mills, 1956). Ralph Miliband proposed, in *The State in Capitalist Society* (1968), that the locus of state power in modern capitalist societies had 'shifted from the legislative to the executive branch of government and to independent administrative or regulatory agencies' (Barrow, 2007, p. 91). This meant that even though governments 'speak in the name of the state and are formally invested with state power, [that] does not mean that they effectively control that power' (Miliband, 1968, pp. 49–50). In the current context, such arguments have been associated with critiques of the political ideology of *neoliberalism*, where it is argued that 'human well-being can best be advanced by liberating individual entrepreneurial freedoms and skills, within an institutional framework characterized by strong private property rights, free markets and free trade', and that 'the role of the state is to create and preserve an institutional framework appropriate to such practices' (Harvey, 2005, p. 2).

Capitalist state theories tend to look for the dominant corporate interests in a field such as media policy to determine whether they are the real forces driving such changes. Hesmondhalgh summarises the neo-Marxist perspective on media policy as one where 'in general, policy bodies in modern capitalism work towards combining the accumulation of capital on the part of businesses with a certain degree of popular legitimation', even if such an analysis 'does not always account for how they operate in practice' (Hesmondhalgh, 2013, p. 125). This perspective has aligned with the wider claim that neoliberalism has been the ascendant ideology in media policy internationally since the 1980s. Hesmondhalgh proposed that the political influence of neoliberalism 'helped to de-legitimate public ownership and certain forms of regulation in nearly all forms of economic activity' (p. 131). Freedman has argued that a shift towards neoliberalism in U.S. and UK. media policy drove 'a much narrower and more consumer-oriented role for the media' and a much greater focus on 'the largely economic benefits that may accrue from the exploitation of the media industries' (Freedman, 2008, p. 219). For these authors, the claims that media policy-making is constructed through a pluralistic frame is largely illusory, although there is an ambiguity in these accounts as to whether the belief in media pluralism has always been an illusion (i.e., the mass media have always in practice been controlled by capitalists and their allies in state agencies), or whether it has become less pluralistic over time with the adoption of neo-liberal ideologies by governments and policy makers.

Mindful of the complex politics of media policy reform and the power of the vested interests involved, this chapter nonetheless offers a qualified defence of public interest principles as they apply to media regulation and media policy reform. With regard to economic capture theories, a clear lesson of over three decades of measures to promote greater competition, including the privatisation of public assets, is that such changes have frequently led to more regulation, as various policy trade-offs that may have once been internalised within large corporations now become the responsibility of government agencies required to adjudicate on competing claims. As Baldwin, Cave, and Lodge observe, 'an initial emphasis on economic regulation that was supposed to "wither away" over time has been replaced by a realisation that there is a continuing need for regulatory oversight', and for 'newer conversations about regulation [as] it has become accepted ... that regulation is necessary for the functioning of a market economy (Baldwin, Cave & Lodge, 2012, pp. 9, 10).

At the same time, regulation is not simply about government agencies implementing command-and-control regulations over private entities. Scott (2004, pp. 146–147) has observed that whereas conventional legal and economic thinking has tended to prioritise formal legal arrangements and sharp dichotomies between market and state, and public and private, regulation scholarship that has been more informed by sociological and socio-legal theories that have pointed towards 'a blunting of the sharp distinction between states and markets and between the public and the private'. From this perspective, practices of governance that 'invoke other bases of control than hierarchy and state law' (Scott, 2004, p. 147) are of interest, including co-regulation, industry self-regulation, incentives-based regulation, and forms of 'soft law', including the capacity of regulatory design to reshape behaviour (Freiberg, 2010). A number of theorists of regulation have referred to the rise of the *regulatory state*, whose tasks have become more multi-faceted over the period, and which seeks new forms of partnership with corporations, NGOs and the community in order to govern complex economic relations and manage 'wicked problems' (Baldwin et al., 2012, pp. 373–387; Braithwaite, 2008). The Australian Communications and Media Authority (ACMA), for example, interprets its mission as a media and communications regulator as having a *capacity-building* dimension, that not only entails providing an information base that supports industry co-regulatory arrangements, but provides resources to citizens to enable them to more effectively participate in shaping regulatory practice (Australian Communications and Media Authority[ACMA], 2015).

226 Terry Flew

Reliance upon simple binary oppositions between market and state, and public and private, can also obscure the actual forms that policy debates take, and how they are in practice shaped by competing interests among capitalists and branches of industry themselves, as well as between corporate and other interests. It points to the need for policy to be seen as more complex and multifaceted than simply being an application of either 'public interest' rationales by regulators themselves, or the imposition of a neo-liberal orthodoxy dictated by the corporate sector. To take one example, demands for copyright law reform are not simply a bottom-up phenomenon, where digitally empowered ICT users seek to be liberated from the shackles of copyright restrictions that serve established corporate interests. There are also strong corporate interests that support more extended fair use provisions, most notably the ICT/platform-based giants such as Google, whose business models differ significantly from those of the incumbent copyright-based creative industries (Lobato, 2012, pp. 72–85, Cunningham Flew and Swift, 2015, pp. 123–126).

The Policy Challenges of Convergence

While noting that media convergence is always a process rather than an end-state, it can be understood as having at least four dimensions. At a technological level, it refers to the combination of computing, communications and content around networked digital media platforms. Economically, it involves both the metamorphosis of established media institutions as digital content producers and distributors, and the rise of new, digitally based companies such as Google, Apple, Microsoft, Amazon and others as significant media-content providers. At a social level, it is related to the rise of social network media and Web 2.0 services such as Facebook, Twitter and YouTube, the proliferation of user-created content, and multi-screen accessing of media content (e.g., accessing TV programs from tablet computers). Finally, at a content or textual level, convergence is associated with the re-use and remixing of media into what has been termed a 'transmedia' model, where stories and media content (for example, sounds, images, written text) are dispersed across multiple media platforms. A further question, with which we opened this chapter, is whether these broader patterns of media convergence also point towards policy convergence, both at a national level with greater harmonisation of media, telecommunications and information laws and policies, and, globally, with pressures to respond to the challenge of digital content platforms that lack a clear territorial basis.

Media convergence occurs in parallel with a series of other changes in the global media and communications environment that include (1) increased access to, and use of, high-speed broadband Internet; (2) the globalisation of media platforms, content and services (digital media content can be sourced, distributed and accessed to/from any point in the world); (3) an acceleration of platform and service innovation that makes it increasingly difficult to define the 'industry' that major digital companies are operating in; (4) the proliferation of user-created content and the associated shift of media users from audiences to participants, resulting in the blurring of a once relatively clear distinction between media producers and consumers and (5) a blurring of public-private and age-based distinctions, as all media content is increasingly distributed and consumed online, in environments that are public in terms of their access platforms yet private in terms of their consumption, making it more difficult to restrict access to online content through age-based verification measures.

These radical changes in the media landscape require a rethink of both core media policy principles and appropriate policy instruments. There are big shifts occurring in how we identify the key *media industry actors*, as the relationship between devices, platforms, services and content are becoming increasingly blurred. New media giants such as Google, Apple, Amazon, Facebook etc. possess a different relationship to media regulation than the more traditional media giants such as Time-Warner, News Corporation, Disney, and other big media conglomerates. The differences are apparent with ownership and content rules, for instance, as these have traditionally been premised upon a relatively stable definition of a media industry.

Addressing the perennial question of whether the concentration of media ownership is increasing or decreasing, media economist Eli Noam (2009) has argued that the 'digital optimists' were right to identify the emergence of new forms of competition in the 1990s, and that the Internet had been an important part of that trend, but that the 'digital pessimists' have also been right to observe an increase in media concentration in the 2000s. Noam argues that the key to understanding media ownership questions today lies in recognizing that a *two-tier media system* has been evolving, with large *integrator* firms operating in oligopolistic market structures at its core, surrounded by a large number of specialist firms that undertake much of the actual content production (Noam, 2009, pp. 436–437). The rise of the platform-based digital media companies has shifted power relations for traditional media conglomerates such as Time-Warner, Disney, News Corporation, Viacom/CBS and Sony, as they are more reliant upon the platform providers to distribute their content, thus losing the monopoly rents that could accrue from direct sale to consumers (Steirer, 2015). Moreover, in many of the traditional media markets, their challengers are now big ICT and software companies, as newspapers compete for reader attention with online news portals; TV networks battle with YouTube for the attention of screen media consumers; TV programs, and music and movies, are increasingly downloaded from iTunes or Netflix (Winseck, 2011).

As with questions of industry structure, issues of regulatory parity increasingly arise between 'old media' and 'new media' platforms and services. This has both a historical dimension, as the broadcasting industry has traditionally been subject to extensive forms of regulation, but it also has a territorial dimension, in terms of parity between nationally based media and 'deterritorialised' media platforms such as YouTube and IPTV. These issues arise most strongly with regard to broadcasting, as it has been regulated by governments, not only because of perceived influence in a given community, but also because governments have possessed the power to allocate access to spectrum, and hence can attach conditions to the awarding of licences. The broadcast licensing regime has been challenged worldwide by cable and satellite television since the 1980s and criticised for being anti-competitive and thwarting innovation and the development of new services. Even where new services such as subscription television can be held accountable to national laws and regulations as part of their operating conditions, this is not the case with services such as YouTube or new Internet Protocol TV (IPTV) services, which effectively operate outside of national territorial jurisdictions.

In the Australian context, the issue of regulatory parity particularly arises around the issue of domestic content requirements. The Convergence Review argued that government intervention to support the production and distribution of Australian content, as well as content arising from particular local regions within Australia, continued to be in the public interest, as 'there are considerable social and cultural benefits from the availability of content that reflects Australian identity, character and diversity. If left to the market alone, some culturally significant forms of Australian content, such as drama, documentary and children's programs, would be under-produced' (Australian Government, 2012, p. viii). While it is difficult to quantify the impact of existing Australian content standards for commercial free-to-air broadcasters, the Review estimated that the cost difference between imported content and locally produced content in the same program genre would be in the range of 1:4 to 1:10. Even if there is an audience preference for locally produced content, it was concluded that 'while some Australian content may deliver higher ratings and therefore higher advertising revenues over time, in most cases this will not offset the substantially higher production costs' (p. 64). The removal of existing Australian content requirements for commercial free-to-air broadcasters would lead to an overall reduction in expenditure on local production of 43 per cent, with a 90 per cent decrease in local drama expenditure and the complete disappearance of locally produced children's programming, resulting in significant job losses in the Australian film and television industries, as well as having adverse social and cultural impacts (pp. 65–66).

The question of equivalent treatment of media content across platforms, as digital content now moves easily between print, broadcast and online and can be accessed across multiple devices, is an ongoing subject of policy debate. It arose in the ALRC's review of the national classification scheme, where it was acknowledged that 'traditional distinctions based on how content is accessed or delivered are becoming less relevant' (ALRC, 2012, p. 25). While one outcome of convergence has been that there is an increasing fragmentation of media audiences into a plethora of non-overlapping niches, the ALRC nonetheless took the view that the concept of community standards in relation to media was not simply an artefact of limited media outlets and that 'the development of the Internet does not in itself provide a rationale for abandoning restrictions on content or regulations based on community standards' (ALRC, 2012, p. 84).

What such developments point to is the concept of *platform neutrality* in media and communication policy and whether 'classification should be focused upon content rather than platform or means of delivery' (ALRC, 2012, p. 93). This restates earlier debates around regulatory responses to convergence seen in the formation of new agencies such as Ofcom in the UK and the ACMA in Australia (ACMA, 2015; Lunt & Livingstone, 2012), although the thinking then was shaped by the convergence of broadcasting and telecommunications. In a similar vein, the Convergence Review proposed that 'regulation of significant media entities, which are increasingly operating across a range of platforms, is specifically designed to be platform neutral' (Australian Government, 2012, p. 13), based on its concept of a Convergent Service Enterprise (CSE), discussed below. As the implications of such a change point towards fewer regulations of broadcasting or new attempts to regulate Internet content such as the Labor government's unsuccessful attempts to introduce mandatory Internet filtering of 'Refused Classification' content, indicates the political complexities of changes for which a principled case can be made in the context of media convergence.

It is important to note that being outside of national regulatory systems is not the same as being unregulated. What goes up onto YouTube or onto Facebook can be managed, although it is through *ex post* mechanisms such as user 'flagging' for potentially inappropriate forms of content (Crawford and Lumby, 2011). On an international scale, some of the dilemmas this presents were seen in Google's response to protests worldwide about the 'Innocence of Muslims' video posted on YouTube: while rejecting a U.S. State Department request to take down the video, and successfully defending its right to host the video in the U.S. Federal Court, it nonetheless geo-blocked access to the video in Libya, Egypt, India, Malaysia, Indonesia and Pakistan, for fear of further inflaming Muslim feelings about the offending video. Whatever the merits of the approach Google took to the video, it can be argued that 'the incident shows ... Google is acting like a court, deciding what content it keeps up and what it pulls – all without the sort of democratic accountability or transparency we have come to expect on questions of free expression and censorship' (Rosen, 2012). Such decisions are now being made by global Internet platform/service providers on a daily basis, e.g., with execution videos being posted by entities such as the Islamic State. The jurisdictional bases upon which such decisions are being made, and the level of public accountability for these decisions, remain unresolved questions.

Paradoxes of Media Influence

The question of the appropriate scope of convergent media policy raises questions of media influence. The contemporary media influence question can be seen as having two elements. The first is determining the threshold of influence for media content and its providers and when a media outlet or company can be deemed 'big enough' for regulation to be appropriate in light of the rapid growth of user-created content and small-scale online distribution platforms. The second issue is the continued validity of distinctions between 'media content' and personal communication and the related expectation that the latter should have 'free speech' protections from government oversight or censorship. As differences between modes of communications based on their 'mass' or 'public' qualities are blurred in the context of media convergence, and as the relationship between platform and content becomes more fluid, these are issues that need to be considered in new ways (Flew, 2014b).

The various Australian media policy reviews in 2011–2012 dealt in different ways with media influence, but continued to see an ongoing role for public interest regulations in addressing it. The Convergence Review identified government regulation of media ownership as continuing to be important as 'concentration of services in the hands of a small number of operators can hinder the free flow of news, commentary and debate in a democratic society. Media ownership and control rules are vital to ensure that a diversity of news and commentary is maintained' (Australian Government, 2012, viii). In the Australian media policy reviews, two attempts were made to define the point at which a media entity may be deemed sufficiently influential as to warrant regulation. The first approach was that of the Finkelstein Review into news media regulation, which proposed that news media and small press 'publishers' that would be subject to the jurisdiction of the News Media Council would include news internet sites that exceed 15,000 hits per annum, paralleling a readership for print-based media of 3,000 print copies per month (Finkelstein, 2012, p. 295). This proposal was widely criticised as necessarily intruding upon blogging and very small online media that made no claims to be 'journalism' in its traditional forms (Flew & Swift, 2013).

A new approach to measuring media power and influence was developed by the Convergence Review with its concept of a Content Service Enterprise (CSE). The rationale behind CSEs was that 'a regulatory framework [should be] built around the scale and type of service provided by an enterprise rather than the platform of delivery' (Ausstralian Government, 2012, p. 7). In such a context, it was proposed that the locus of regulation needed to shift from industries and platforms to companies themselves:

> The legislation currently declares that the degree of regulation should be in proportion to the level of 'influence' a category of service is 'able to exert in shaping community views in Australia' ... *Under the*

Review's approach, the focus of regulation is significant enterprises that provide professional content to Australians (Australian Government, 2012, pp. 7, 9).

The Convergence Review proposed three criteria whereby a media firm could be considered to be a CSE:

1 Professionally produced content over whose distribution it had effective control
2 Significant revenues derived from Australian-sourced content (the Review proposed a threshold figure of $50 million a year)
3 Significant Australian audience and/or number of Australian users(the threshold proposed was 500,000 per month)

Using these criteria, it was proposed that the major radio and television broadcasters were CSEs, as were the News Limited and Fairfax media groups. Significantly, just outside of the revenue/user thresholds were Google, Apple and the leading Australian telecommunications company, Telstra. So while the CSEs in practice were largely the already-regulated broadcasters, the Convergence Review clearly flagged that since 'the relative influence of significant media enterprises will change over time', the CSE framework would 'provide a flexible model under which community expectations of major media entities may be fulfilled into the future, regardless of the technology or delivery platform used' (Australian Government, 2012, p. 13). It rejected the proposition that there should be an 'in principle' rejection of measures to 'regulate the Internet', and held that overseas media enterprises operating in Australia should be subject to Australian regulations, since 'any enterprise with a significant presence in Australia should be accountable in Australia ... Just as online banking is regulated in the same way as banking in the branch, significant media enterprises should be expected to meet the expectations of the Australian public irrespective of the platform used' (p. 13).

The concept of CSEs had its critics, as did the more general call for new regulatory frameworks developed in the Convergence Review and other Australian media policy reviews. Leonard (2012) noted that the CSE concept was unusually radical, as it placed the threshold of regulation around questions of firm size, in contrast to the more traditional focus of what industry a firm is in. It was apparent that figures used to calculate the threshold would be disputed; it is difficult, for instance, to determine the Australian revenues of multinational companies such as Google or Apple. At the same time, such questions are by no means unique to media policy: there has in recent years been a growing campaign to ensure that such global companies pay a reasonable share of company tax in the countries they are located and not be able to shift funds to low-tax havens (Drucker, 2012). The key question raised here is whether it becomes appropriate at some threshold point to think of Internet companies as media companies, and hence appropriately the subjects of media policy and regulation and not simply conduits for personal communication, which is seen as appropriately free from censorship in open, democratic societies.

Leonard (2012, p. 3) also observed that 'the broad cross-platform agenda [made] the Report unusual, if not unique, in global terms'. He observed that the Convergence Review's commitment to basing regulations on the size and influence of a content provider, rather than on the platform upon which content was delivered, was ground-breaking in terms of aiming to 'future proof' media legislation in the face of unpredictable convergence dynamics. At the same time, such regulatory radicalism also ran the risk of upsetting both the established media players by not treating them as unique and special, and requiring industry protection as a *quid pro quo* for public interest obligations, while being seen as threatening the largely *laissez-faire* media landscape in which the new media players have been able to emerge and flourish. For instance, Google Australia commissioned a study by the Boston Consulting Group titled *Culture Boom: How Digital Media are Invigorating Australia* (Belza, Forth, Purnell & Zwillenberg, 2012), which argued that local content regulation in the new media environment was unnecessary, as Australian online content creators were already generating a consumer surplus for Australians, as well as generating new export opportunities.

Political Opportunity Lost: The Fate of Media Policy Reform in Australia

The government's response to the various media reviews was a long time coming, with the Minister for Broadband, Communications and the Digital Economy, Sen. Stephen Conroy, taking almost a year after receiving the reports to finally present a submission to the Cabinet. When the proposed legislation to be submitted to Parliament was finally presented by the Minister on March 12, 2013, it was decidedly low-key in relation to the ambitions of the various media inquiries, focusing almost exclusively on the current concerns of existing media players, rather than the future-facing issues raised by media convergence and high-speed broadband. There was no discussion, for instance, of CSEs, nor the new policy and regulatory framework that the Convergence Review advocated. At any rate, facing near-universal opposition from media proprietors and the opposition parties and lacking a majority in the Parliament, Labor abandoned its proposed legislation 10 days after it was presented to the public.

During the 2013 Australian Federal election campaign, neither the Liberal Party nor the Labor Party released a media policy, and subsequent to the election of a new Coalition government, the focus has shifted away from both legislative reform and the National Broadband Network (NBN), with the new government more concerned with reducing NBN funding and support for national public broadcasting than changing the rules for commercial media in Australia. While the Liberal-National Party government has an intention to deregulate media ownership rules, arguing that they no longer act as guarantors of media diversity and that the Internet is diversifying news and information sources regardless of platform-based ownership rules (DCA, 2014), there appears to be no intention to advance this agenda in its current term. At the same time, rejection of the recommendations of the ALRC to liberalise Australia's copyright laws suggests that it is more likely to act to protect the interests of incumbent media interests than to pursue a more thoroughgoing deregulatory policy agenda (Flew, 2015).

Conclusion

This chapter has identified a range of challenges to media policy arising out of changes in the global media environment associated with convergence. This includes the growing uncoupling of media content from particular devices and platforms, as well as related developments such as media globalisation, the rise of user-created content, accelerated innovation in media and related industries, and the blurring of age-based and public/private distinctions in terms of access to media content.

It considered three Australian media enquiries undertaken during 2011–2112: the Convergence Review, the ALRC National Classification Review, and the Finkelstein Review into News Media, to observe how they have sought to address five contemporary dilemmas of media policy: (1) determining who is a media company; (2) regulatory parity between 'old' and 'new' media; (3) treatment of similar media content across different platforms; (4) distinguishing 'big media' from user-created content; and (5) maintaining a distinction between media regulation and censorship of personal communication, given the very different history and architecture of the Internet as compared to broadcast media. At the heart of these are questions of what media influence now means in a convergent media environment, what are the threshold levels of potential influence to warrant media regulation and how could a shift occur from regulations based upon platforms to ones based upon content.

I have elsewhere described this in terms of a 'policy window', presented by the Labor government's commitment a National Broadband Network, and the implications this would have for existing media policies, as it would be a major driver of convergence of media and communications access devices and content delivery platforms (Flew, 2014a). The media inquiries considered here struggled to find the right balance in addressing these questions, and certainly did not adequately engage politicians sufficiently to make the transition to policies that could gain sufficient support to be implemented.

234 Terry Flew

At the same time, I would argue that the questions themselves remain at the core of twenty-first century media policy and that the criticisms by some economic capture theorists that they simply shore up an outdated broadcast-era settlement are misplaced, as are those which simply read off media policy changes as reflections of an ascendant global neo-liberalism. They point towards new ways of promoting the concept of a 'public interest' in convergent media environments, and seeing media policy as more than simply an ideological cloak for the nefarious activities of meddling bureaucrats or multinational media moguls. In doing so, we also need to recognise that the circumstances in which public interest regulation is being pursued have become considerably more complex and potentially contradictory in the context of convergent media.

References

Aslama, M., & Napoli, P.M. (2011). Bridging gaps, crossing boundaries. In M. Aslama & P. M. Napoli, (Eds.), *Communications research in action: Scholar-activist collaborations for a democratic public sphere* (pp. 333–336). New York, NY: Fordham University Press.

Australian Communications and Media Authority. (2011). *Broken concepts: The Australian communications legislative landscape*, Melbourne: ACMA.

Australian Communications and Media Authority. (2015). *Evidence informed regulatory practice – An adaptive response, 2005–2015*, Melbourne, AUS: ACMA.

Australian Government. (2012). *Convergence review: Final report*. Convergence Review Committee. Available from http://www.abc.net.au/mediawatch/transcripts/1339_convergence.pdf.

Australian Government. (2014, June). *Media Control and Ownership. Policy Background Paper No. 3*. Department of Communication. Retrieved from https://www.communications.gov.au/publications/media-control-and-ownership-policy-background-paper-no3.

Australian Law Reform Commission. (2012). *Classification – Content regulation and convergent media. ALRC Report 118*. Retrieved from http://www.alrc.gov.au/sites/default/files/pdfs/publications/final_report_118_for_web.pdf.

Australian Law Reform Commission. (2013). *Copyright and the digital economy. ALRC Report 122*. Retrieved from http://www.alrc.gov.au/sites/default/files/pdfs/publications/final_report_alrc_122_2nd_december_2013_.pdf.

Baldwin, R., Cave, M., & Lodge, M. (2012). *Understanding regulation: Theory, strategy, and practice* (2nd edition). Oxford: Oxford University Press.

Barrow, C.W. (2007). Ralph Miliband and the instrumentalist theory of the state: A (mis)conception of an analytic concept. In P. Weatherly C.W. Barrow & P. Burnham (Eds.), *Class, power and the state in capitalist society: Essays on Ralph Miliband* (pp. 84–108). Basingstoke, UK: Palgrave.

Belza, J., Forth, P., Purnell, J., & Zwillenberg, P. (2012). *Culture boom: How digital media are reinvigorating Australia*. Boston, MA: Boston Consulting Group. Retrieved from http://www.ipa.org.au/library/publication/1207807254_document_berg_regulation.pdf.

Berg, C. (2008). *The growth of Australia's regulatory state: Ideology, accountability, and the mega-regulators*. Melbourne: Institute of Public Affairs. Retrieved

from http://www.ipa.org.au/library/publication/1207807254_document_berg_regulation.pdf.
Braithwaite, J. (2008). *Regulatory capitalism*. Cheltenham: Edward Elgar.
Christensen, J. G. (2011). Competing theories of regulatory governance: Reconsidering public interest theory of regulation. In D. Levi-Faur (Ed.), *Handbook of the politics of regulation* (pp. 96–110). Cheltenham, UK: Edward Elgar.
Coase, R. (1966). The economics of broadcasting and government policy. *American Economic Review*, 56(1–2), 440–447.
Copeland, P., & James, S. (2014). Policy windows, ambiguity and commission entrepreneurship: Explaining the re-launch of the European Union's economic reform agenda. *Journal of European Public Policy*, 21(1), 1–19. doi: 10.1080/13501763.2013.800789.
Crawford. K., & Lumby, C. (2011). *The adaptive moment: A fresh approach to convergent media in Australia*. Sydney: University of New South Wales, Journalism and Media Research Centre.
Cunningham, S., Flew, T. & Swift, A. (2015). *Media Economics*. Basingstoke, UK: Palgrave.
Department of Communication (2014) *Media Control and Ownership: Policy Background Paper No. 3*, June. http://www.communications.gov.au/__data/assets/pdf_file/0017/233513/Control_Background_Paper.pdf.
Doyle, G. (2013). *Understanding media economics* (2nd edition). London: Sage.
Drezner, D. (2001). Globalization and Policy Convergence. *International Studies Review*, 3(1), 53–78. doi: 10.1111/1521-9488.00225.
Drucker, J. (2012, 10 December). Google revenues sheltered in no-tax Bermuda soar to $10 Billion. *Bloomberg*. Retrieved from http://www.bloomberg.com/news/2012-12-10/google-revenues-sheltered-in-no-tax-bermuda-soar-to-10-billion.html.
Dunleavy, P. & O'Leary, B. (1987). *Theories of the state: The politics of liberal democracy*. London: Macmillan.
European Commission. (2013). *Preparing for a fully converged audiovisual world: Growth, creation and values*. [Green Paper]. Retrieved from http://eur-lex.europa.eu/LexUriServ/LexUriServ.do?uri=COM:2013:0231:FIN:EN:PDF.
Finkelstein, R. (2012). *Report of the independent inquiry into the media and media regulation*. Retrieved from http://apo.org.au/files/Resource/1205_finkelstein.pdf.
Flew, T. (2014a). Academics in the policy process: Engagement with Australian media inquiries 2011–2113. *Journal of Information Policy*, 4, 105–127. doi: 10.5325/jinfopoli.4.2014.0105.
Flew, T. (2014b). Changing influences on the concept of 'media influence'. *International Journal of Digital Television*, 5(1), 7–18. doi: 10.1386/jdtv.5.1.7_1.
Flew, T. (2015). Copyright and creativity: An ongoing debate in the creative industries. *International Journal of Cultural and Creative Industries*, 2(3).
Flew, T. (2016). National media regulations in an age of converging media: Beyond globalisation, neoliberalism and Internet freedom theories. In T. Flew, P. Iosifidis & J. Steemers (Eds.), *Global media and national policies: The return of the state*. Basingstoke, UK: Palgrave.
Flew, T., & Swift, A. (2013). Regulating journalists? The Finkelstein Review, the Convergence Review, and news media regulation in Australia. *Journal of Applied Journalism and Media Studies*, 2(1), 107–127. doi: 10.1386/ajms.2.1.181_1.
Freedman, D. (2008). *The politics of media policy*. Cambridge, MA: Polity Press.
Freiberg, A. (2010). *The tools of regulation*. Sydney, Australia: Federation Press.

Garnham, N. (2011). The political economy of communication revisited. In J. Wasko, G. Murdock, & H. Sousa (Eds.), *The handbook of political economy of communication* (pp. 41–61). Malden, MA: Wiley-Blackwell.

Gitlin, T. (2012). *Occupy nation: The roots, the spirit and the promise of Occupy Wall Street.* New York: HarperCollins.

Harvey, D. (2005). *A brief history of neoliberalism.* Oxford: Oxford University Press.

Hesmondhalgh, D. (2013). *The cultural industries* (3rd ed.). London: Sage.

Horwitz, R. (1989). *The irony of regulatory reform: The deregulation of American telecommunications.* Oxford: Oxford University Press.

Hoskins, C., McFadyen, S., & Finn, A. (2004). *Media economics: Applying economics to new and traditional media.* Thousand Oaks: Sage.

Iosifidis, P. (2016). Globalisation and the re-emergence of the regulatory state. In T. Flew, P. Iosifidis, & J. Steemers (Eds.), *Global media and national policies: The return of the state.* Basingstoke: Palgrave.

Just, N., & Puppis, M. (2012). Communication policy research: Looking back, moving forward. In N. Just & M. Puppis (Eds.), *Trends in communication policy research* (pp. 9–29). Bristol, UK: Intellect.

Jenkins, H. (2006). *Convergence culture: When new and old media collide.* New York: NYU Press.

Knill, C. (2005). Introduction: Cross-National policy convergence: Concepts, approaches and explanatory factors. *Journal of European Public Policy, 12*(5), 764–774. doi: 10.1080/13501760500161332.

Lane, C., & Wood, G. (2009). Capitalist diversity and diversity within capitalism. *Economy and Society, 38*(4), 531–351.

Leonard, P. (2012). Making converged regulation possible. *Communications Law Bulletin, 31*(2), 15–31.

Lobato, R. (2012). *Shadow economies of cinema: Mapping informal film distribution.* London: BFI/Palgrave Macmillan.

Lunt, P. & Livingstone, S. (2010) *Media Regulation: Governance and the Interests of Citizens and Consumers,* London: Sage.

Marsh, D., & Sharman, J. C. (2009). Policy diffusion and policy transfer. *Policy Studies, 30*(3), 269–288.

Meseguer, C., & Gilardi, F. (2009). What is new in the study of policy diffusion? *Review of International Political Economy, 16*(3), 527–543. doi: 10.1080/09692290802409236.

Miliband, R. (1968). *The state in capitalist society,* London: Merlin.

Mills, C.W. (1956). *The power elite.* New York: Oxford University Press.

Morgan, G. (2009). Globalization, multinationals and institutional diversity. *Economy and Society, 38*(4), 580–605. doi: 10.1080/03085140903190342.

Noam, E.M. (2009). *Media ownership and concentration in America.* Oxford: Oxford University Press.

Picard, R. (2011). Economic approaches to media policy. In R. Mansell & M. Raboy (Eds.), *The handbook of global media and communication policy* (pp. 355–365). Malden, MA: Wiley-Blackwell.

Pratt, A.C. (2009). Policy transfer and the field of cultural and creative industries: What can be learned from Europe? In L. Kong & J. O'Connor (Eds.), *Creative economies, creative cities: Asian-European perspectives* (pp. 9–23). Heidelberg, Germany: Springer.

Rosen, R. (2012, 14 September). What to make of Google's decision to block the 'Innocence of Muslims' movie? *The Atlantic*. Retrieved from http://www.theatlantic.com/technology/archive/2012/09/what-to-make-of-googles-decision-to-block-the-innocence-of-muslims-movie/262395/.

Schejter, A. (2008). European Union: Communication law. In W. Donsbach (Ed.), *The international encyclopedia of communication* (pp. 1609–1615). Oxford: Blackwell.

Scott, C. (2004). Regulation in the age of governance: The rise of the post-regulatory state. In J. Jordana & D. Levi-Faur (Eds.), *The politics of regulation: Institutions and regulatory reform for the age of governance* (pp. 145–174). Cheltenham, UK: Edward Elgar Publishing.

Singapore. Media Development Authority. (2012). *Media convergence review – Final report*. Retrieved from http://www.mda.gov.sg/RegulationsAndLicensing/Consultation/Documents/Media%20Convergence%20Review/Media%20Convergence%20Review%20Final%20Report.pdf.

Stedman-Jones, D. (2012). *Masters of the universe: Hayek, Freidman, and the birth of neoliberal politics*. Princeton, NJ: Princeton University Press.

Steirer, G. (2015). Clouded visions: UltraViolet and the future of digital distribution. *Television and New Media*, 16(2), 180–195. doi: 10.1177/1527476414524842.

Van Cuilenburg, J., & McQuail, D. (2003). Media policy paradigm shifts: Towards a new communications policy paradigm. *European Journal of Communication*, 18(2), 181–207. doi: 10.1177/0267323103018002002.

Von Finckenstein, K. (2011, 13 June). Speech by Konrad von Finckenstein, QC, chairman, Canadian Radio–Television and Telecommunications Commission. Retrieved from http://www.crtc.gc.ca/eng/com200/2011/s110613.htm.

Winseck, D. (2011). The political economies of media and the transformation of the global media industries. In D. Winseck & D.Y. Jin (Eds.), *The political economies of media: The transformation of the global media industries* (pp. 3–48). London: Bloomsbury.

13 Communications and Social Inclusion
Universal Service Policies in Europe and Latin America

Maria Stella Righettini and Michele Tonellotto

Introduction: When the Regulatory State Meets the Welfare State

The concept of the Regulatory State was developed to contrast a distinctive form of governance emerging from practices and from institutions of the Welfare State. The Welfare State uses distributive policies and deploys the tools of public expenditure, public ownership and direct State provision of benefits and services (Scott, 2000). By contrast, the Regulatory State emphasizes the problems of dismantling public monopolies, of self-restraint of political power, of control on public expenditure and of monitoring the efficiency and quality of public services through Independent Regulatory Agencies (IRAs). IRAs embody a cultural preference for competition and free market and, in theory, should be committed to facilitating private economic activity and initiative (Moran, 2003; Power, 1997; Scott, 2000). In practice, however, the challenge of addressing social issues in the context of vast privatizations of public utilities has always been a public concern, in order to guarantee citizens equal access to services.

As a consequence of the expansion of the Regulatory State in (former) public utilities, the boundaries between economic regulation and welfare programs are becoming more blurred. Nowadays, especially in light of technological evolution, securing quality standards for communication services, the increasing digital divide have a great deal to do with both citizen welfare and economic and social development. Universal Service programs are special welfare policies providing social inclusion through the provision of baseline levels of services to every resident of a country. Today, those programmes are mostly regulated and implemented by independent or semi-National Regulatory Agencies (NRAs) (World Bank, 2001), a hallmark of the Regulatory State (Majone, 1994). The large privatizations of public monopolies have produced a modification in the way States adopt and implement economic regulation as well as welfare policies. Over the last twenty years, relevant institutional change has occurred worldwide in the communication sector (Jordana, Levi-Faur & Fernandez i Marín, 2011) through the creation of IRAs as a new mode of regulation. According to the theory of expansion of the Regulatory State, the provision of communications infrastructures and services that emerged during the 1990s is based on an institutional separation between the functions of policy makers, technical regulators and service providers. This assumption has often also been extended to Universal Service programs in the telecommunications sector. IRAs in the telecommunications sector play a significant role in the framework of the Universal Service or Universal Access for telecommunications, which is seen as an instrument for shaping welfare programs in existing regulatory regimes (Gilardi, 2007; Estache, Laffont & Zhang, 2006). In order to analyse the interplay between Regulatory State and Welfare State, in this chapter, we adopt the notion of the 'regulatory regime' as the 'principles, norms, rules and decision-making procedures around which actors' expectations converge in a given issue' (Krasner, 1982, p. 185).

This chapter aims at analysing whether and, if so, how regulatory regimes in the telecommunications sector develop innovative welfare USO programs that include access to the Internet. How do national regulators react to common ICT challenges? How did they deal with the modernization of national Universal Service – or Access – programs? The chapter provides new insight into present and future developments of regulatory regimes and policies in the telecommunications sector and contributes to the discussion of Universal Service programs by taking into consideration a number of Latin American (*Mercosur*)[1] and EU countries, all of them dealing with a different idea of universality, different policy tools and procedures (Mueller, 2013).

Since the end of the nineteenth century, the concept of Universal Service has flourished, and it is now generally related to governments' ideas and choices for delivering a certain specified minimum level of service to everyone, reaching individuals in disadvantaged social and territorial conditions, and at affordable prices. Linking welfare programs to economic regulation is challenging since the latter was designed to correct market failures rather than to provide access and affordability to poor and disadvantaged users. In those contexts in which competitive markets do not lead to an equal-optimal allocation of resources,[2] regulatory agencies through specific programs should, at least according to the theory, act as 'benevolent agents for the public interest' (Baldwin, Cave & Lodge, 2012, p. 41). However, there is evidence that the growing inadequacy in coping with new technological challenges and the quasi-monopolistic powers achieved by providers in the communication market, especially in the Internet era, make the development of U.S. welfare policies increasingly important for social welfare into the future.

Universal Service: Between the Invisible Hand of the Market and the Paternalist State

Since the late 1980's, there has been considerable research on Universal Service content, settings, rules and economic consequences. Since the beginning of liberalisation the issue has been of great interest, in diverse economic sectors, among which is the telecommunications market. To date, most research has taken an economic approach, concentrating on the benefits and trade-offs resulting from the implementation of Universal Service Obligations in order to highlight positive and negative externalities caused by the co-existence of financial subsidies and competitive markets. Economists do not have a unanimous opinion on Universal Service (or Access) policies. Some (Kaserman, Mayo & Flynn, 1990) demonstrate how subsidies to specific operators made in order to promote Universal Service Obligations represent a distortion in competitive markets, which, on the contrary, would be able to satisfy all the necessities of the population with no need for specific policies for certain groups of people. Other scholars (Blackman, 1995) seek first to understand the significance of Universal Service agreements in free markets and the real needs of such policies in order to include certain groups of people, and then attempt to determine who will bear the economic burden of Universal Service agreements.

Petrazzini (1996) underlines the importance of liberalization in the communication sector, in order to allow the competitive market to reach the entire population and to adjust prices based on local necessities. The prevalent idea is that market regulation through Universal Service policies not only constitutes a distortion of the market, but also has little effect on telephone penetration rates, thus missing under-addressing the Universal Service agreement itself (Crandall & Wavermann, 2000). On the other hand, however, there are a number of studies that highlight the benefits gained by the efficient regulation of Universal Service in the communications sector (Graham, Cornford & Marvin, 1996; Mueller, 2013). These studies represent a shift from a focus on the financial sustainability of Universal Service policies to their real social and economic benefits, thus using a 'demand-side perspective' to formulate possible policy agendas for politicians. The scope of this work is to demonstrate how subsidies to Universal Service may well benefit a large number of people and thus promote social inclusion. Eriksson, Kaserman and Mayo (1998) analyse some examples of financial subsidies on Universal Service in several states, drawing empirical evidence on how this sort of intervention may influence the market. The authors show how *targeted* subsidies on specific policies are much more effective than general (*untargeted*) subsidies on economic subjects or groups of people, which could distort free markets in a more consistent fashion. The existing literature also includes a number of clear demonstrations of how policies promoting the distribution of Universal Service Obligations among a number of operators increase the capability to provide communication services more quickly, even in remote areas of a certain country (Choné, Flochel & Perrot, 2000, 2002). By contrast, when shifting attention to the social inclusion of different types of individuals (disabled people, Internet users), there is evidence that the identification of a single or a very small number of Universal Service providers is preferable (Bjorn, 2000). Somewhat differently, Garbacz and Thompson (2005) advocate implementing U.S. policies to promote the diffusion of mobile telephone services rather than fixed link services. They argue that complementary grants to mobile phone services and mainline phone services would be better able to ensure social inclusion for disadvantaged people, with less State intervention.

The rationales underlying the provision of USO are not only economic, but also social and political. The economic argument relates to the fact that USO provides incentives for investments in infrastructure, and USO subsidies to certain targeted groups of people can, when successful, help to boost productivity and economic growth, to promote regional and rural development, and to improve working conditions and public administration efficiency (Calvo, 2012; OECD, 2003). The social rationale for Universal Service Obligations refers to the need for all users to have access – and to be connected – to telecommunication networks in order to avoid exclusion and to fully participate in society, for instance by communicating with others and by accessing public and/or emergency services. For this reason, the USO is usually targeted at low income groups, people living in remote rural areas and disabled and other vulnerable groups (Crandall & Wavermann, 2000). Advocates of USO are now pressing for policies to provide not only consumers and vulnerable groups, but also public institutions, such as libraries and schools, with advanced technology and speed, at low cost. The symbolic value of USO is very important in its political rationale: public intervention must be socially responsive and able to guarantee a coherent method of 'governing' (Rubinstein Reiss, 2009). This implies that the degree of politicization of universality and access issues can vary according to the social relevance given to specific USO content. In some countries, it is generally perceived that the definition of the scope and the extent of USO for telecommunications should fall rest with the political domain and should be decided by elected and/or delegated institutions credibly committed to public interest. In the EU, the consolidation of telecommunication markets, the growth of the Regulatory State and the delegation of important tasks to national independent regulatory agencies have all significantly reduced the politicization of USO programs, and have tended to result in the delegation of most policy choices and changes on this issue to technical regulatory arenas. Historically in Europe, USO was established by state-owned monopolies, and often these services included uniform rating and entry restrictions (OECD, 2006). With the international spread of liberalization in telecommunications in the 1990s, in most countries the already- existing USO regime was simply modified and adjusted to fit the new economic and technological environment. The global spread of the Regulatory State has gradually achieved a prominent role in the handling of telecommunications services with rules, targets and with the re-definition of universal service itself (Jordana & Levi-Faur, 2006).

A Cross-Country Analysis of the Universal Service Regulatory Regimes

The main features of all USO regimes emerge from two major components: the *regime orientation* – i.e., the objectives and targets of the programs making up the regimes – and the *regime organization* – the delegation to IRAs, procedures and relationships between regulators and regulatees in any case

(Vogel, 1996, pp. 20–21). The theory of delegation (Braun & Gilardi, 2006) indicates that – in Europe, at least – the regulatory commitment of political governments in the field of public utilities has increasingly shifted to IRAs in order to create uniform rules and to improve policy-making and problem-solving capacities. IRAs are facing the increasing complexity of regulatory policy-making in the field of communication resulting from technological convergence and their involvement in a number of often conflicting communication public policy goals, such as the case of free market regulation and provision of economic grants to USO providers. Delegation in economic regulatory regimes increasingly occurs in the context of distributive programs where traditionally 'the relationships between policy makers and target groups play a major role in understanding regulation' (Braun, 2006, p. 147). In achieving distributive and redistributive policy goals, a stronger political commitment tends to modify the regulatory chain with a restriction of delegation to technical independent agencies. In normative terms, this could also mean that in pursuing their aim of integrating economic and welfare provisions, national governments reduce their distance from target groups (Braun, 2006, p. 148) and the agencies' technical independence becomes less important than the achievement of political distributive goals. A number of scholars have explored specific structural aspects of regulatory institutions, outlining the causal relationships between structural variables – notably the independence of RAs – and policy outcomes and effectiveness (Gilardi, 2007). These normative approaches stress the idea that the more IRAs are independent, the more policy goals are successfully fulfilled (Eisner, Worsham & Ringquist, 2000; Gilardi, 2009). Empirical work conducted for this chapter goes beyond this normative approach and explores how a set of institutional variables, including independence, can combine differently and can shape USO programs in order to innovate traditional programs and include the internet in USO policies or, by contrast, can shape programs in such a way that real change is resisted (Levi-Faur, 2010; Radaelli, Dente, Dossi, 2012).

The empirical work aimed to understand the regime orientation and organization of Universal Service or Access programs involving central institutions such as NRAs, and the circumstances under which such programs are put in place and policy innovation is achieved. Regarding the orientation of Universal Service programs, the research analysed a series of legislative reforms in order to understand:

1 The fine-tuning of USO *content* to the Internet era;
2 The USO *target* itself.
    The research then analysed a number of *organizational dimensions* and *working rules* of USO programs (Ostrom, 2005) raising the following questions:
3 What is the degree of delegation to NRAs in the communications sector to decide and deliver Universal Service programs with regard to the

majoritarian institutions? That is to say, who is the core actor regarding the Universal Service or Access? To what extent is Universal Service considered to be a depoliticized, technical issue, completely delegated to professional arenas or, conversely, something relevant for politics and political consent?

4 To whom is USO obligation applied? What type and number of providers participate in the program? In Universal Service or Universal Access programs, the provision of Obligations determines a delegation from regulators to providers and a public-private shared responsibility for the delivery of service and for the implementation of special welfare programs. This chain of delegation will make the jurisdiction more or less open, and makes providers more or less accountable.

5 What procedures are in place to select providers and regulate their activities? USO providers can be selected through public auction or by nomination, while price-caps, subsidies, cross subsidies, and quality standards affect the ways USO are implemented on the ground. The research examined whether economic accountability tools (public auction) were preferred to merely distributive (nomination) or redistributive tools (Special USO Fund) (Peters, 2000).

Table 13.1 Empirical dimensions of Universal Service Obligations regulatory regimes: orientation and organization

	Indicator	What is revealed
1. Type of target of USO programs	private and economic targets (groups of disadvantaged consumers) or public and social targets (territories, public services)	If USO is more consumer oriented or citizen oriented
2. Content of USO programs	Inclusion of internet	The degree of innovation in USO
Organization	*Indicator*	*What is revealed*
3. Degree of delegation to IRA, by central government	The level – high or low – of discretion of the IRA in the USO policy	The level of politicization of the issue
4. Type of Procedure of selecting USO providers	Public auction or nomination	*Openness* of procedures
5. Number and type of providers involved	Public or private or both	Type of Public-Private-Partnership in USO

The dimensions of Universal Service or Access programs illustrated above constitute empirical variables of what we called *orientation and organization* of welfare programs (Ostrom, 2005), and allow the comparison of which variables are most frequently associated with innovation in USO programs in the eight countries considered.

Comparison between EU member States and Latin American countries is particularly interesting because, despite significant differences in their social and political contexts, since the beginning of the 1980s both areas have developed wide-reaching liberalization programs accompanied by extensive reforms of the Regulatory State in the telecommunications sector. Until the 1980s, Latin America (LA) was similar to Europe (Jordana, Levi-Faure, 2006) in that both areas were characterized by utilities overseen by public monopolies, accompanied by fairly weak social regulation. Universal Service and Universal Access programs developed during the same period of time in both regions – from 1994 to 2002 – after extensive privatizations and liberalizations. The two areas have also vastly different technological contexts. Latin American countries, notwithstanding considerable economic growth in recent years, are still characterized by more limited fixed line phone services and network diffusion, when compared to Europe, due – at least in part – to the significant natural barriers that characterize the region. Despite all these differences, as evidenced by UNESCO in the Broadband Commission Annual Report (UNESCO, 2013), in recent years developments in new technologies and in mobile telephony have brought about changes worldwide, both in terms of markets and user dynamics, raising the number of consumers and overcoming diverse infrastructural barriers, increasing Internet penetration rates and internet users.

Table 13.2 Variation in growth of Internet users *between 2008 and 2012*

Latin America	
Argentina	26,9%
Brazil	16%
Chile	24,1%
Venezuela	18,1%
European Union	
France	12,3%
Italy	13,5%
Spain	12,4%
UK	8,6%

Source: Elaboration from data.worldbank.org

The four specific countries in LA and the EU have been chosen in order to assess the relative importance of an overlying governance 'superstructure' for USO, in particular whether it is purely economic or more broad-ranging in shaping regulatory USO programs.

Orientation of USO Programs: Innovation or Conservatism?

Since the end of the 19th century, the concept of Universal Service has been related to different types of communication services, in relation to which we can distinguish three generations of public Universal Service programs. The first generation – beginning at the end of nineteenth century – was related to the diffusion of postal services; the second generation saw the diffusion of fixed telephony, and finally, the third has heralded the advent of mobile phones and the Internet. After the postal and the telephone/telegraph eras, the idea of providing a baseline of communication services has now reached the Internet era as well. In a globalised world, access and quality of communication services are part of everyday economic and social life, and guarantee fundamental individual rights. An indicator of the on-going evolution of regulatory framework is, for example, the institutional convergence of postal, broadcasting and telecommunications regulation in order to better adapt to newly-available technological advances. The Internet age raises new questions concerning the role of public institutions and private enterprises in guaranteeing universal access to the Internet as a new condition for future social development. A communication service with adequate facilities and reasonable charges has always been the chief purpose of public regulation in this field, in an effort to facilitate social development and to correct competitive market failures.[3]

Historically, the first EU Directives introducing the concept of Universal Service with regard to communications go back to the early 1990s, when the European Commission began to regulate the provision of an Open Network for communications within its member states.[4] These documents were followed by a Council Resolution and Directives The latter aimed to harmonize the provision of fixed line phone services within and among Member States in an efficient and open fashion, and to define Universal Service as the possibility for every citizen to connect to the public phone network both from a fixed location and from a public telephone. In 1999, the European Commission launched a reform that led to the adoption of a series of Directives in 2002. Among them, the 'Framework Directive' 2002/21/EEC, provides a precise definition of Universal Service in its Article 2: [Universal Service is] *a minimum set of services of specified quality which is available to all users regardless of their geographical location, and in the light of specific national conditions, at an affordable price.* Another Directive issued in 2002, and amended in 2009, gives further details with regard to the content of Universal Service Obligations in every Member State.

The LA countries have not developed a common legal framework from Universal Service, due to the exclusively economic nature of Mercosur. Nevertheless, in comparing the legal frameworks in the EU and in Latin America, it emerges that there is a certain synchronism in the diffusion of the ideas of Universality, Obligation and Integration in telecommunication services in these two regional areas. Despite this synchronism, however, Latin American states tend to include Internet access in the Universal Service or Universal Access programs more quickly than do European countries (currently only Spain and Finland include Internet access in their Universal Service).

Table 13.3 The Evolution of the legal framework on USO in Telecommunication (UE–UK–FR–ES–IT)

Country	Definition of Universal Service and Contents of Obligations in electronic communications
EU	**1992:** ONP lease-lines Directive. provision of an Open Network for Communication within and among all EU Members (Directive 92/44/EEC).
	1994: Council Resolution 'On Universal Service principles in the telecommunications sector'. It states the necessity of providing some basic elements such as price and quality of services, access to disabled people, the provision of information effective instruments of settlement of disputes, public telephone facilities (Council Resolution 94/C48/01).
	1995: Directive 'on the application of open network provision (ONP) to voice telephony'. A first definition of Universal Service is given, along with legal dispositions about the harmonisation of the provision of fixed line phone services within and among Member States in an efficient and open way (Directive 95/62/EC).
	1998: Directive 'on the application of open network provision (ONP) to voice telephony and on universal service for telecommunications in a competitive environment'. Amendment to previous Directive (Directive 98/10/EC).
	1999: Launch of a project of reform of the Universal Service in Europe.
	2002: Telecom Package. Series of directives which include a Framework Directive and a Universal Service Directive, amended in 2009 (Directive 2002/21/EC and Directive 2002/22/EC) providing a series of Obligations on Universal Service for Member States: a) the connection to public phone networks from a fixed location and at an affordable price, in every case of local, national and international telephone calls, facsimile communications and data services; b) the access to at least one comprehensive directory and at least one comprehensive telephone directory inquiry service; c) the provision of public pay telephones or other public voice telephony access points; d) the access to the European emergency call number '112' and to other national emergency numbers free of charge from any telephone, including public devices; e) suitable measures to guarantee access to all telephone services at a fixed location for disabled users or with special social needs.
	2009: *Citizens' Right Directive*. Amendment to Directive 2002/22/EC. The new document introduces the possibility for Member State to include the access to the Internet for the entire population in the Universal Service Obligations (*Directive 2009/136/EC*); removes the reference to narrowband data rates and introduces the more flexible 'functional internet access'.
	Directive 2009/140 EC amends partially the Framework Directive of 2002 and others Directives on communications of the same year.

Communications and Social Inclusion 247

Country	Definition of Universal Service and Contents of Obligations in electronic communications
	2010: Public Consultation launched by the European Commission to re-define the Digital Agenda for Member States.
France	**2003**: Transposition of EU Directive into French legislation by the new *Code des Postes et des Communications électroniques*. The Code sets a definition of Universal Service and its Obligations, together with the individuation of US providers by Ministerial Decree (*Code des Postes et des Communications électroniques, articles L-35 to L-35–6*).
	2005: Individuation of *France Telecom* as the US provider (*Arrêté du 3 Mai 2005*).
	2009: Individuation of *Pages Jaunes* as provider of a phone book to all users of fixed line phone services.
Italy	**2003**: Transposition of European Legislation by the new *Codice delle Comunicazioni Elettroniche* (Code on Electronic Communications). This National Statement provides a general definition of Universal Service, lists a series of related Obligations and indicates the first US provider, that the Authority for Communications (Agcom) could theoretically change (*Codice delle Comunicazioni Elettroniche; articles 50, 54–59, 61*).
Spain	**2003**: Definition of Universal Service and its contents by National Statement. The same document gives the Ministry for Communications the power of nominating USO providers (*Ley 32/2003 de 3 noviembre 2003, General de Telecomunicaciones, articles 22–24*).
	2005: Another National Statement defines US Obligations in detail (*Real Decreto n. 424/2005*). Definition of some criteria to calculate the Net Cost deriving from the provision of US by market operators.
	2006: Definition of minimum quality standards by Ministerial Decree (*Orden ITC/912/2006*).
United Kingdom	**2003**: First definition of Universal Service and its contents and Obligations in TLC, along with a general reform of the telecommunications sector in UK. The Act creates Ofcom from the merging of Oftel with other regulatory bodies. The same Act defines for the first time the two USO providers (*Communication Act 2003, articles 65–72*). In the same year, the Secretary of State for Communications adopted an Order to define USO Obligations in details (*Electronic Communications (Universal Service) Order 2003*).
	2006: Statement of Ofcom partially revising some USO Obligations (like the necessity of public phones).
	2011: Amendment to the Order of 2003 (*Electronic Communications (Universal Service) (Amendment) Order 2011*). Statement of Ofcom of partial revision of Universal Service Obligations.

Sources: Official websites of Arcep, Agcom, Cmt and Ofcom

Changes in USO policies have already taken place in the past decades. European Union legislation gives member states the possibility to modify their USO programs and to substitute traditional USO elements, such as public pay telephony or telephone directory enquiry service, or printed telephone directories, in favour of new elements, such as Internet access. Table 13.3 shows that despite the fact the EU legal framework gives member states the possibility to innovate their domestic legislation, only Spain has already done this. The European Commission has raised the question of whether Universal Service is an appropriate way to foster economic development and, at the same time, to reduce the digital-divide . Currently, in European countries the national Functional Internet Access (FIA)speed is defined by NRA guidelines with a great variety in terms of both standards and capacity to defend user rights. Thus among the four European countries considered, Italy and the United Kingdom do not mention Internet access as part of Universal Service. The national governments of these two countries prefer to focus on the provision of basic phone services at an affordable price, phone books for subscribers, public telephones and special services for the disabled. Conversely, in France, the importance of access to the Internet for all is specifically mentioned in Article L-35-1 of the *Code des Postes et des Communications électroniques*. However, when determining the minimum quality standards to be followed in the provision of phone services, the decrees (*Arrêts*) issued by the French Ministry for Communications do not include access to the Internet among the basic services to be provided. By contrast, Spanish law specifically mentions access to the Internet for the population as as part of Universal Service provision, in the *Real Decreto n. 424/2005*. The same document sets a series of minimum quality standards for telephone and Internet connection services.

If European integration is one of the main factors contributing to isomorphism in institutional design and regulatory settings within its Member States, due to the implementation of a supranational legislative framework, there is no truly similar catalyst for Latin American countries in the field of telecommunications regimes. The intergovernmental economic union *Mercosur* has provided only a small number of Resolutions regarding certain aspects of the regulation of telecommunications. Only one of these documents deals with public services of basic telephony in border areas (*Servicios Públicos de Telefonía Básica en zonas fronterizas*), stating that phone operators and the governments of *Mercosur* member states must ensure connection for people in different countries through fixed line phone networks and the creation of adequate infrastructure in border areas.[5] Another Resolution, passed in 1999, assigns a common Emergency Number to all *Mercosur* members (*128*),[6] and a third document establishes a series of common rules with regard to the regulation of 'roaming' services for mobile telephony across countries.[7] Thus, in assessing Latin American countries, it is necessary to concentrate on national legislation in order to understand how each state copes differently with Universal Service.

In Europe, IRAs are now considered to be the main policy instrument of Universal Service implementation, whereas in Latin America the national governments still directly control this policy domain, adopting vastly different programs and strategies compared to their European counterparts. This divergence reflects an emerging distinction between the notions of Universal Service and Universal Access. If the first term, largely adopted among the four European countries analysed, refers to the provision of basic communication services to every household in the telecommunications market, the latter, adopted by all four Latin American countries examined, defines the right of every individual to have access and to be connected to a communication point, by means of public phones and public Internet points.[8] The difference may seem slight, but the implications are significant. The concept of Universal Service is more 'market-oriented', facilitating telecom operators in providing communication services to every home and expanding their own markets. In contrast, Universal Access programmes focus on the right of citizens to be connected to a communication point, private or public, even without becoming private customers of a particular service provider. The Latin American concept can thus be deemed to be more 'citizen-oriented'. European States exclusively use the words *Universal Service*. Other countries, while adopting measures which can be classified as 'Universal Access' programmes, still use the term 'Universal Service' in their legislation, thus using the two terms as synonyms. This is the case of Argentina, Brazil and Venezuela, while Chilean Law does not provide a clear definition of Universal Service or Access, defining only the obligations to be respected by service providers.[9] If the notions of Universal Service and Universal Access differ – the former being more market-oriented and the second being more citizen-oriented – in practice, the expression 'Universal Service' has been adopted in the legislation of several Latin American states. Among the four *Mercosur* countries analyzed- Argentina, Brazil, Chile and Venezuela – three specifically employ the words 'Universal Service' in their legislative documents, although the policies are characteristically 'Universal Access' measures, as shown in Table 13.3.

Table 13.4 The Evolution of the legal framework of US in Argentina, Brazil, Chile and Venezuela

Country	Definition of USO and Content of Obligations
Argentina	2000: National legislation foresees the access to the Internet as one of the possible contents of US but not as an obligation. Universal Service Obligations (USO) include the access to the following services: 1) fixed telephony network from every device, including remote areas of the Country; 2) public phones 3) services for disabled or disadvantaged people, including lower prices; 4) he access to the phone network for public venues such as schools, public libraries, hospitals. (*Decreto764/2000; articles 6, 26*).

(*Continued*)

Country	Definition of USO and Content of Obligations
	2008: Confirmation of previous indication without Internet access as an Obligation for the US provider. (*Decreto 558/2008*) The *Reglamento General de Servicio Universal* (General Guidelines on Universal Service) is adopted. **2009:** A Resolution launches the National Programme *Telefonía e Internet para Localidades sin Cobertura de Servicio Básico Telefónico*, for the development of infrastructures in areas with no access to the phone network. The programme is financed by the Fund for Universal Service (See below), but it has not yet been completed (*Resolución 88/2009*).
Brazil	**2001:** Resolution of Anatel listing the obligations that phone operators in charge of providing the US have to respect, including the provision of the Internet for households but also rural areas, schools, libraries, hospitals and other public venues. Such Obligations are implemented through the so-called 'General Plans of Objectives for Universal Service' (*PGMU* in Portuguese): project of technological development implemented by phone operators after public competition. The costs for the implementation of such activities are born by the operators. (*Resolução 269, de 9 de julho de 2001; article 6*). **1998:** PGMU-I (1999–2005) Development of infrastructures for fixed and mobile telephony and installation of public phones for the whole population, regardless social differences or geographical position (*Decree 2592/1998*) **2003:** PGMU-II (2006–2012) Development of phone services for fixed and mobile lines and installation of Internet access points (*backhaul* points) (*Decree 4769/2003*). **2011:** PGMU-III (2013–2019) Development of communication services in rural areas, remote zones of the Country, schools and public venues, hospitals, police stations, military stations, indigenous villages (*Decree 7512/2011*).
Chile	**2000:** The legislation of this Country does not provide a precise definition of Universal Service and its Obligations for phone operators. The contents of Universal Service for Telecommunications coincide with the objectives of the annual plans. Also Chile foresees a special State Fund in order to finance the costs that the operators meet when providing such services. The *Ley General de Telecomunicaciones n. 18168* of 02/10/1982 (Art. 28D, as modified in 2012) sets a list of general Obligations to be ensured. Annual plans foresee the provision of Internet access to households, schools, libraries, rural areas and other public venues.
Venezuela	**2000:** National legislation defines the Universal Service and its contents, among which the provision of the Internet for all, irrespective of social and geographical conditions. (*Ley Orgánica de Telecomunicaciones 28/03/2000; article 50*). Those goals are then concretely implemented through the formulation of specific Projects, like the cases of Brazil and Chile, which are assigned to one or more operators after a public competition. Every Project is published and assigned through specific decrees of *Conatel*.

Sources: Internet websites of Secom, Anatel, Subtel and Conatel.

Comparison between the various legal frameworks shows significant differences in the orientation of the Universal Service in telecommunications in the two areas. Innovation seems better associated with the presence of the 'universal access' idea in legislation, rather than that of 'universal service'. In three of the four Latin American countries (Brazil, Chile and Venezuela), all lacking supra-national coordination or legal constraints, the national USO programs have been developing and addressing the issue of Internet access, and all of them adopt a citizen-oriented notion of universal access rather than the market notion adopted by all four of the European states considered in this study.

Table 13.5 Orientation in USO programs

Innovation of USO Target	Including Internet in USO	Excluding Internet in USO
Citizen and consumer oriented	Brazil Venezuela Chile	Argentina
Only consumer oriented	Spain	Italy France United Kingdom

Apart from Argentina, all the Latin American legislative agendas give more importance to the inclusion of Internet access in their USO programs, as compared to the majority of European countries, and commitment to Universal access is seen as a stimulus for both social and economic development.

The inclusion of Internet access in telecommunications universal service raises other important questions, most importantly, that of what sort of technology for Internet access is to be guaranteed (broadband, satellite, or cable). The choice of technology has much to do with the politics of infrastructure and with the relationships between public and private actors in the USO programs. In European countries, a conservative approach to universal access might be justified by a high Internet penetration reached through appropriate infrastructural policies (Righettini & Nesti, 2014), or by certain characteristics of the telecommunication system structure, which will be addressed in the following section.

Understanding Diversity in USO Organization

According to Dahl and Lindblom (Dahl and Lindblom, 1953) when approaching the organizational differences between USO programs, it is important to focus on the details regarding the delegation of competencies from central governments to IRAs and the procedures shaping relationships between public and private actors involved in the USO programs.

Delegation to IRAs: Table 13.6, shows that NRA independence is in fact not a factor in influencing the fine-tuning innovations of USO content to the Internet era. Rather, it would appear evident that the inclusion of the Internet in the USO programs offered is addressed when the political commitment to this issue is higher. This consideration is supported by the case of Spain, where the independence of the IRA in the communication sector is lower (CMT) (Righettini & Nesti, 2014), compared to IRAs of other European countries. In the last two decades, the demands for changes resulting from the diffusion of the Internet, the increasing costs of public telephony and the spread of mobile telephony have caused Universal Service to return to the Spanish political arena to facilitate change in the traditional Universal Service programs and Obligations.

Table 13.6 Core USO actors in EU and Latin American regulatory regimes

Content of USO Type of Commitment	Including Internet in USO	Excluding Internet in USO
Independent – Technical – IRA	Brazil	France United Kingdom Italy
Semi-independent IRA and Political – Central Government or Parliament	Venezuela Chile Spain	Argentina

The Broadband Commission Annual Report (Broadband Commission, 2013) underlines the need to adopt a holistic approach to the new challenges in the telecommunication sector that also considers the diffusion of mobile telephony, where 'The holistic approach should take into account the feasibility of acquiring devices such as *tablets* and *smartphones*, and ensure that those accessing the networks have the right skills to access contents and add value' (Broadband Commission, 2013, p. 32). The Broadband Commission demonstrates how different regions adopt different approaches to extending US and Internet access. However, all these different strategies are implemented through national plans that must provide access to the entire population. This section considers the way the Universal Service program is shaped and organized and intended to function at the national level (Table 13.7).

As has recently been pointed out (Mueller, 2013) the procedures for selecting providers, to fix the number and nature of providers in USO programs have been gradually changing in many countries, due to the increasing degree of liberalization achieved by national telecommunication markets, by the spread of the new principle of net neutrality[10] and by the diffusion of mobile telephony. These changes seem not to have affected European national plans, however. In twenty countries, representing 60% of the membership of the Body of European Regulators in Electronic Communications (BEREC), the incumbent is still designated as universal service provider (USP) (BEREC, 2010) with only seven countries having designated multiple USPs for the different services. This indicates that the power given to incumbents in US programs and the connected risk of 'obligation traps' (OECD, 2004) – the dependence of regulators on information, standards and inputs coming from industry – is very high. Universal Service Obligation (USO) is frequently narrowly defined in ways that disfavour new technologies, favour incumbents and cause extensive waste and financing for non-commercial obligations that could often be raised in more efficient ways by multiple service providers rather than one preferred provider (OECD, 2004).

Table 13.7 The organization and orientation of the USO regimes in EU and Latin American States

Countries	Degree of Delegation To IRA	USO Providers — Number of operators	USO Providers — Characteristic of the USO operators	Market sectors	Contents and target of USO — USO Targets	Procedure for selecting USO providers
Argentina	Low Semi-independent authority (SECOM)	2	Private companies (dominant position)	Telephony	- Basic phone services - Public phones - Disabled people - Phone services to schools and libraries	- Nomination of US providers *without public procedures* - Public Fund - Quality standards - Price regulation
Brazil	Highly Independent Authority (ANATEL)	6	Private companies (with significant market power)	Telephony and Internet	- Basic phone services - Public phones - Disabled people - Internet to the entire population - Internet to schools and libraries	- Public consultations to assign US obligations - Public Fund - Price regulation
Chile	Low Central Government (Ministry in charge for Telecoms) (SUBTEL)	Several operators (variable number)	Private companies and public subjects (municipalities, cooperatives)	Telephony and Internet	- Basic phone services - Public phones - Disabled people - Internet to the entire population - Internet to schools and libraries	- *Public tender* to assign US obligation - Public Fund - Price regulation
Venezuela	Low Semi-independent authority (CONATEL)	Several operators (variable number)	Private companies and public subjects (municipalities, cooperatives)	Telephony and Internet	- Basic phone services - Public phones - Disabled people - Internet to the entire population - Internet to schools and libraries	- Public tender to assign US obligation - Public Fund - Price regulation
France	High Independent Authority (ARCEP)	2	France telecom: Majority share under public control	Telephony	- Basic phone services - Public phones	- Public tender to assign US obligation - Public Fund

(*Continued*)

Countries	Degree of Delegation To IRA	Number of USO operators	Characteristic of the USO operators	Market sectors	USO Targets	Procedure for selecting USO providers
Italy	High Independent Authority (AGCOM)	1	Pages Jaunes: private company	Telephony	- Disabled people - Phone Book - Basic phone services - Public phones - Disabled people - Phone Book	- Calculation of net costs - Quality standards - Price regulation - Nomination of US providers *without public procedures* - Public Fund (suspended from 2007) - Calculation of net costs - Quality standards - Price regulation
Spain	Low Central Government and Independent Authority (CMT)	2	Private company (with significant market power) Private company (dominant position)	Telephony and Internet	- Basic phone services - Public phones - Disabled people - Phone Book	- Public tender to assign US obligation - Public Fund - Calculation of net costs - Quality standards - Price regulation
United Kingdom	OFCOM High	2	Private companies	Telephony and Internet	- Basic phone services - Disabled people - Free emergency calls - Social prices or affordable prices for disadvantaged people - Public phones - Minimum quality standards for existing Internet lines	- Nomination of US providers *without public procedures* - Price regulation

Source: official websites of Secom, CNC, Anatel, Subtel, Conatel, Arcep, Agcom, CMT and Ofcom (2013), Berec Report on Universal Service 2010.

As illustrated by Table 13.8 below, in the eight countries considered the number of Universal Service Providers vary greatly: from the sole provider in Italy (Telecom Italy), to the six USO providers of Brazil. USPs in Latin American countries are generally multiple and overall tend to be much more numerous than in Europe. This may be due, at least in part, to the prevailing idea of universal access and to the policy tools used by regulators: the tendency is to attribute the Universal Service to operators not for the entire national territory, but for more restricted regions of the country, quite often recurring to the use of public auctions. In addition, Latin American countries also admit 'cooperatives' and 'municipalities' as USPs, thus extending the variety of public and private actors involved and granted in these programs. The different procedures utilised for the designation of USPs may be divided into 3 broad categories: nomination without consultation; nomination with public consultation and public tender.

Table 13.8 Procedures for selecting of USO providers

Number of Providers Type of procedure	Incumbent	Multiple (variable)
Public tender	France	Chile Venezuela Brazil Spain
Designation	UK Italy Argentina	

The procedures adopted. With regard to telecommunications, the main challenge for regulation seems to be that of guaranteeing conditions of transparency and impartiality in access to the network and its services in scenarios of convergent technologies (International Communication Union, 2013). As evidenced in Table 13.8, the use of public tenders generally increases the number of USO providers made available. By contrast, as in the case of Italy, the use of national law (the Italian Code of Communications) to assign the provision of USO to the incumbent Telecom Italia, limited *de facto* the Italian regulator's (AGCOM's) discretion to one USO provider (Table 13.7) (Righettini & Nesti, 2014). Transparent and competitive procedures would have positive consequences on the competitiveness and the quality standards of USO programs increasing the overall benefits deriving to disadvantaged users (Righettini & Nesti, 2014).

Interestingly, provider differentiation is higher in the states of the *Mercosur* area than in the four European countries examined in this chapter. The *Mercosur* countries include both public (non profit, and local governments) and private providers (enterprises). Universal access to the Internet is intended not only for the entire population of communications consumers, but also for citizens' right to connect from diverse locales, including public schools, libraries, police stations, hospitals and other public venues. Currently, in the EU, Belgium is the only country to include hospitals and public libraries as USO targets.

Conclusion: Determinants of Policy Change in USO

The comparison of Latin American and EU cases in this chapter leads to a number of conclusions. First, innovation seems to be more quickly addressed by regulatory regimes in which *political commitment* is stronger than *technical commitment*. Second, a factor facilitating USO innovation and Internet inclusion is the notion of USO itself. Comparison between Latin America and the EU shows that USO regimes can evolve along two different pathways: a *consumer-welfare regime (universal service)* or a *citizen-welfare regime (universal access)*. The first is 'market oriented', whereas the latter is more 'public oriented'. The idea of 'Universal Access' enhances the granularity of USO programs more than that of 'Universal Service', focusing more on citizens' rights and public institutions rather than on consumers and private interests.

Third, we see a different role played by national regulatory agencies in procedures for selecting USO providers. The European States perpetuate the traditional strong cooperation with the monopolistic incumbent, often using less transparent procedures and limiting the number of providers involved in public programs. Latin American states, on the contrary, have developed cooperation with multiple providers through more competitive procedures. Regulatory agencies choose USO providers and targets through specific procedures that can be more or less flexible and transparent, and allow new providers to access the sector or permit the replacement of the existing ones. Less transparent procedures are often crucial in shaping cooperation with incumbents or USO providers, and can also generate an incremental approach to change.

The chapter's comparison of four specific countries in Latin America and in EU indicates that there is a different ability to spread innovation in USO programs respectively in the Mercosur and EU territories. In particular the diffusion of innovation in USO distributive or redistributive programs seems faster when state governments 'espouse the cause' by supporting new ideas that shape the regime's formal rules and organization rather than the other way around through delegation to independent regulators. Innovation in USO is thus associated with: (1) strong political commitment and reduction of the role of neutral-technical regulation; (2) a notion of USO that is more citizen oriented; (3) more open and competitive procedures, assigning to a greater variety of providers the obligation to reach the largest number of people in a given territory. This USO configuration might be considered by European governments as a sort of check-list for future reforms. By far the most relevant policy implication of the above analysis is that changes to the idea of universality and new inclusion strategies require *political commitment to be carried out*, and this might be in conflict with a strong level of IRA independence. Legislative and governmental institutions often advocate relevant policy changes in the field of USO, especially when deciding relevant distributive or redistributive policies. In the absence of political advocacy, USO change may very well be slowed as a result of the lack of political legitimacy inherent to highly independent non-majoritarian IRAs. Previous evidence suggests that IRAs would rather avoid making these kind of decisions because their technical conclusions cannot overcome economic vetoes (Righettini & Nesti, 2014).

Notes

1. The *Mercado Común del Sur* in Portuguese *Mercado Comum do Sul,* in English *Southern Common Market* was created in 1991 with the Treaty of Asunción and the following Treaty of Ouro Preto (1994), which amended the first document and established a Secretary and an administrative structure. It is a free trade organisation between certain South American states, featuring common external tariffs and internal freedom of the movement of goods, individuals and currency. Current MERCOSUR members are Argentina, Brazil, Paraguay (whose membership was suspended in 2012), Uruguay, Venezuela and Bolivia. Other *Associated States* are Chile, Colombia, Peru, Ecuador, Guyana and Surinam. The scope of the organisation is to promote economic development by means of the free circulation of goods and individuals and of a common economic policy. In order to achieve this, member States are expected to progressively harmonize their national legislations, similarly to that which transpires in the EU. However, the decisions adopted by MERCOSUR still do not touch upon all market sectors, diversely from the European reality, and member States still have considerable freedom to determine legislative solutions to the regulation of important sectors of their economies, including Telecommunications. Recent negotiations to invest supranational bodies with new and more extensive competences, thus resulting in the transfer of some degree of sovereignty, have failed, and MERCOSUR States continue to retain significant independence in determining their respective economic policies. The following paragraphs will analyse the differences between the USO programs of the two regions.
2. That is to say, in those situations in which no single position can be improved without worsening that of another party at the same time.
3. From the Abstract of Bjorn W. (2000), Extending Telecommunications beyond the Market Toward Universal Service in Competitive Environments, World Bank, Washington DC.
4. Directive 92/44/EEC of on the application of open network provision to leased lines.
5. Resolución MERCOSUR/GMC/RES n. 66/97 de 1997.
6. Resolución MERCOSUR/GMC/RES n. 44/99 de 1999.
7. Resolución MERCOSUR/GMC/RES n. 19/01 de 2001.
8. The two definitions are reported in the website of the International Telecommunication Union: http://www.itu.int/itunews/manager/display.asp?lang=en&year=2007&issue=07&ipage=universal-access&ext=html (2013). *Universal Access: This usually means that everyone in a population has access to publicly available communication network facilities and services. Typically, it is provided*

through such means as pay telephones, community telecentres and community Internet access terminals. *Universal Service*: Policies in this area generally focus on promoting or maintaining universal connectivity of all households to public network facilities and services, and at affordable prices. *Either or both*: While universal service and universal access policies may differ, the concepts are closely related and the two terms are sometimes used interchangeably.

9. See for instance the Argentinian Reglamento General de Servicio Universal (Decreto n. 558/2008), the Brazilian Resolução n° 269, de 9 de julho de 2001, the Venezuelan Decreto n. 3227 of 8th of November 2004.

10. According to its inventor, net neutrality is a precondition for universal access: a principle that internet service providers and government should treat all data without discriminating or charging differentially by user, content, site, platform, application or mode of communication (Wu, 2003).

References

Armstrong, M. (2001). Access pricing, bypass and universal service. *The American Economic Review*, 91(2), 297–301.

Bjorn, W. (2000). *Extending telecommunications beyond the market: Toward universal service in competitive environments*. Retrieved from http://hdl.handle.net/10986/11439.

Blackman, R. (1995). Universal service: obligation or opportunity?. *Telecommunications Policy*, 19(3), 171–176.

Body of European Regulators for Electronic Communications (BEREC). (2010). *Report on universal service – Reflection for the future*. Retrieved from http://berec.europa.eu/eng/document_register/subject_matter/berec/reports/187-berec-report-on-universal-service-reflections-for-the-future.

Braun, D. (2006). Consequences of legitimizing independent regulatory agencies in contemporary democracies: theoretical scenarios, in *Delegation in Contemporary Democracies* (pp. 146–170). London and New York: Routledge.

Braun D., & Gilardi F. (2006). *Delegation in Contemporary Democracies*. London and New York: Routledge.

Broadband Commission. (2013). *The state of broadband 2013: Universalizing broadband*. Retrieved from http://www.broadbandcommission.org/documents/bb-annualreport2013.pdf.

Calvo, A. G. (2012). Universal Service Policies in the Context of National Broadband Plans. OECD Digital economy Papers, No. 203. OECD Publisher.

Choné, P., Flochel, L., & Perrot, A. (2000). Universal service obligations and competition. *Information Economics and Policy*, 12(3), 249–259. doi: 10.1016/S0167-6245(00)00014-7.

Choné, P., Flochel, L. & Perrot, A. (2002). Allocating and funding universal service obligations in a competitive market. *International Journal of Industrial Organisation*, 20(9), 1247–1276. doi: 10.1016/S0167-7187(01)00077-7.

Crandall, R., & Wavermann, L. (2000). *Who pays for universal service? When telephone subsidies become transparent*. Washington, DC: Brookings Institution Press.

Cremer, H., Gasmi, F., Grimaud, A., & Laffont, J.J. (2002). Universal Service: An economic perspective. *Annals of Public and Cooperative Economics*, 72(1) 5–43. doi: 10.1111/1467-8292.00158.

Crémer, J. (2000). Network externalities and universal service obligation in the Internet. *European Economic Review, 44*(4/6), 1021–1031. doi: 10.1016/S0014-2921(00)00041-6.

DiMaggio, P., & Hargittai, E. (2001). *From the 'digital divide' to 'digital inequality': Studying Internet use as penetration increases.* [Working paper]. Retrieved from https://www.princeton.edu/~artspol/workpap/WP15%20-%20DiMaggio%2B Hargittai.pdf.

DiMaggio, P., Hargittai, E., Neuman, R.W., & Roninson, J.P. (2001). Social Implications of the Internet. *Annual Review of Sociology, 27*, 307–336. doi: 10.1146/annurev.soc.27.1.307.

Eisner, M.A., Worsham, J., & Ringquist, E. (2000). *Contemporary regulatory policy.* Boulder, CO: Lynne Rinner Publishers.

Eriksson, R.C., Kaserman, D.L., & Mayo, J.W. (1998). Targeted and untargeted subsidy schemes: Evidence from postdivestiture efforts to promote universal telephone service. *Journal of Law and Economics, 41*(2), 477–502. doi: 10.1086/467398.

Estache, A., Laffont, J., & Zhang, X. (2006). Universal service obligations in LDCs: The effect of uniform pricing on infrastructure access. *Journal of Public Economy, 90*(6–7), 1155–1179. doi: 10.1016/j.jpubeco.2005.07.002.

Garbacz, C., & Thompson, H.J. (2005). Universal telecommunication service: A world perspective. *Information Economics and Policy, 17*(4), 495–512. doi: 1.0.1016/j.infoecopol.2005.03.001

Garnham, N. (1997). Universal service. In W.H. Melody (Ed.), *Telecom reform: principles, policies and regulatory practices* (pp. 199–204). Lyngby, Denmark: Technical University of Denmark. 2001.

Gasmi, F., Laffont, J.-J., & Sharkey, W. (2000). Competition, universal service and telecommunications policy in developing countries. *Information Economics and Policy, 12*(3), 221–248. doi: 10.1016/S0167-6245(00)00016-0.

Gilardi, F. (2007). The same, but different: Central banks, regulatory agencies, and the politics of delegation to independent authorities, Comparative European Politics, pp. 303–227.

Gilardi, F. (2009). *Delegation in the regulatory state: independent regulatory agencies in Western Europe.* Edward Elgar Publishing.

Gillett, S.E. (2000). Universal service: Defining the policy goal in the age of the Internet. *The Information Society: An International Journal, 16*(2), 147–179. doi: 10.1080/01972240050032906.

Goggin, G., & Newell, C. (2000). An end to disabling policies? Toward enlightened universal service. *The Information Society: An International Journal, 16*(2), 127–133. doi: 10.1080/01972240050032889.

Graham, S., Cornford, J., & Marvin, S. (1996). The socio-economic benefits of a universal telephone network: A demand-side view of universal service. *Telecommunications Policy, 20*(1), 3–10. doi: 10.1016/0308-5961(95)00049-6.

Hudson, H. (1994). Universal service in the information age. *Telecommunications Policy, 18*(8), 658–667. doi: 10.1016/0308-5961(94)90037-X.

International Telecommunication Union. (2013). *Trends in telecommunication reform 2013: Transnational aspects of regulation in a networked society.* Geneva: International Telecommunication Union.

Jordana, J., & Levi-Faur, D. (2005). The diffusion of regulatory capitalism in Latin America sectoral and national channels in the making of new order. *The Annals of the American Academy of Political and Social Science, 598*(1), 102–124. doi: 10.1177/0002716204272587.

Jordana, J. & Levi-Faur, D. (2006). Towards a Latin American regulatory state? The diffusion of autonomous regulatory agencies across countries and sectors. *International Journal of Public Administration, 29*(4/6), 335–366.

Jordana, J., Levi-Faur, D., & Fernández i Marin, X. (2011). The global diffusion of regulatory agencies: Channels of transfer and stages of diffusion. *Comparative Political Studies, 44*(10), 1343–1369. doi: 10.1177/0010414011407466.

Jordana, J., Levi-Faur, D. & Puig, I. (2005). The limits of Europeanization: Regulatory reforms in the Spanish and Portuguese telecommunications and electricity sectors. European *Integration Online Papers, 9*(10). Retrieved from http://eiop.or.at/eiop/pdf/2005-010.pdf.

Jordana, J., & Ramió, C. (2010). Delegation, presidential regimes and Latin American regulatory agencies. *Journal of Politics in Latin America, 2*(1), 3–30.

Jordana, J., & Sancho, D. (2002). The transformation of the Spanish telecommunications policy network during market liberalization. *Revista de Administração Pública, 36*(2), 319–350.

Kaserman, D.L., Mayo, J.W., & Flynn, J. E. (1990). Cross-Subsidization in telecommunications: Beyond the universal service fairy tale. *Journal of Regulatory Economics, 2*(3), 231–249. doi: 10.1007/BF00134062.

Krasner, S.D. (1982). *Structural Causes and Regime Consequences: Regimes as Intevening Variables, in International Organisation, 36*(2), 185–205.

Levi-Faur. (2010). Regulation and Regulatory Governance, in *Jerusalem Papers in Regulatin and Governance*, working paper.

Levin, S.L. (2010). Universal service and targeted support in a competitive telecommunications environment. *Telecommunications Policy, 34*(1–2), 92–91. doi: 10.1016/j.telpol.2009.11.010.

Majone, G. (1994). The rise of the regulatory state in Europe. *West European Politics, 17*(3), 77–101.

Malik, P., & de Silva, H. (2005). Diversifying network participation: Study of India's universal service instruments. [Working paper]. Retrieved from http://www.lirneasia.net/wp-content/uploads/2006/02/Malik%20de%20Silva%20Sept%202005%20final.pdf.

Milne, C. (1998). Stages of universal service policy. *Telecommunications Policy, 22*(9), 775–780. doi: 10.1016/S0308-5961(98)00045-7.

Moran, M. (2002). *The British regulatory state*. Oxford: Oxford University Press.

Mueller, M.L. (1996). Universal service from the bottom up: A study of telephone penetration in Camden, New Jersey. *The Information Society: an International Journal, 12*(3), 273–292. doi: 10.1080/019722496129468.

Mueller, M.L. (1997). Universal service in telephone history: A reconstruction. *Telecommunications Policy,17*(5),352–369.doi:10.1016/0308-5961(93)90050-D.

Mueller, M. (2013). *Universal service: Competition, interconnection and monopoly in the making of the American telephone system*. Washington, DC: AEI Press.

OECD. (2003). *Universal Service Obligations*. Paris: OECD Publications.

OECD. (2004). *OECD Reviewers of Regulatory Reform: Germany*. Paris: OECD Publications.

OECD. (2006). *Rethinking Universal Service for a Next Generation Network Environment*. Paris: OECD Publications.

Ostrom, E. (2005). *Understanding institutional diversity*. Princeton, NJ: Princeton University Press.
Peters, G.B. (2000). *Governance, Politics and the State*. Palgrave: Mc Millan.
Petrazzini, B.A. (1996). Competition in telecoms – Implications for universal service and employment. Retrieved from http://documents.worldbank.org/curated/en/1996/10/441228/competition-telecoms-implications-universal-service-employment.
Power, M. (1997). *The audit society*. Oxford: Oxford University Press.
Radaelli C.M., Dente B., Dossi S. (2012). *Recasting Institutionalism: Institutional Analysis and Public Policy*. Published on Line, Centre for European Governance, University of Exeter.
Righettini, M.S., & Nesti, G. (2013, June). *Independent regulatory agencies, implementation strategies and credible commitment. A comparative research on universal service policies in Italy and the UK*. Paper presented at the First International Conference on Public Policy, Grenoble, France. Retrieved from http://www.icpublicpolicy.org/IMG/pdf/panel_7_s2_righettini_nesti.pdf.
Righettini, M.S., & Nesti, G. (2014). *Indipendenza e credibilità. Istituzioni, imprese consumatori nella regolazione*. Rome: Carocci.
Rosston, G.L., & Bradley, S.W. (2000). The 'state' of universal service. *Information Economics and Policy, 12*(3), 261–283. doi: 10.1016/S0167-6245(00)00011-1.
Rubinstein Reiss, D. (2009). Agency accountability strategy after liberalization: Universal service in the United Kingdom, France and Sweden. *Law & Policy, 31*(1), 111–124. doi: 10.1111/j.1467-9930.2008.00277.x.
Scott, C. (2000). Accountability in the regulatory state. *Journal of Law and Society, 27*(1), 38–60.
Shi, J. (2008). Telecommunications universal service in China: Making the grade on a harmonious information society. *Journal of Technology Law & Policy, 13*(1), 115–148.
Valletti, T.M., Hoernig, S., & Barros, P.P. (2002). Universal service and entry: The role of uniform pricing and coverage constraints. *Journal of Regulatory Economics, 21*(2), 169–190. doi: 10.1023/A:1014387707275.
Vogel. (1996). *Kindred Strangers: the Uneasy Relationship Between politics and Business in America*. Princeton: Princeton University Press.
World Bank. (2002). Telecommunications and Information Services for the Poor: Toward a Strategy for Universal Service. World Bank Discussion paper n. 432.
Wu, T. (2003). Network neutrality, broadband discrimination. *Journal of Telecommunication and High Technology Law, 2*(1), 141–176.
Xia, J., & T.-J. Lu (2005). *Universal service policy in China: Building digital bridge for rural community*. [Working paper]. Beijing: Beijing University of Posts and Telecommunications, School of Economics and Management.

List of Contributors

Olga Batura is a Researcher at the Leuphana University of Lüneburg, Germany, and an Associate Professor at the European Humanities University in Vilnius, Lithuania. She defended a PhD thesis on regulation of universal service in telecommunications markets by the EU and WTO and worked on various topics of trade related to telecommunications, regulation of markets for electronic communications services and competition law at the Collaborative Research Center, 'Transformations of the State', of the University of Bremen and at the University of Hamburg.

Terry Flew is Professor of Media and Communications at the Queensland University of Technology, Brisbane, Australia. He is author of *The Creative Industries, Culture and Policy* (Sage, 2012), *Global Creative Industries* (Polity, 2013), *New Media: An Introduction* (Oxford, 2014) and *Media Economics* (Palgrave, 2015) and the founding editor of *Communication Research and Practice*. He was a member of the Australian Research Council College of Experts from 2013 to 2015, and in 2011–2012 chaired a review of Australia's National Classification Scheme. He is an International Communications Association (ICA) Executive Board member, and chairs the Global Communication and Social Change Division.

Stefan Gadringer is a University Assistant and PhD fellow in the Department of Communication Studies at the University of Salzburg, Austria, where he also obtained a Master's degree. His research areas include national and international communications policy, media and democracy, characteristics of new information and communication technologies and their implications for society and Internet governance.

Irini Katsirea has studied at the Free University of Berlin, the University of Leicester (LLM), UK, and Magdalene College, Cambridge (PhD), UK. She is Reader in International Media Law at the University of Sheffield. Her research interests are in the areas of EU and Comparative Media Law. She is the author of *Public Broadcasting and European Law. A Comparative Examination of Public Service Obligations in Six Member States* (Kluwer, 2008) and of *Cultural Diversity and European Integration in Conflict and in Harmony* (Ant. N. Sakkoulas (Athens), 2001). She has also published extensively in leading law journals, including the *Yearbook of*

European Law, the *European Law Review*, the *Cambridge Yearbook of European Legal Studies* and the *Journal of Media Law*. The research undertaken for the chapter in this volume was funded by the British Academy/Leverhulme Trust.

Jennifer Kavanagh is Lecturer in Law at Waterford Institute of Technology, Ireland, and has completed her PhD at the School of Law. Trinity College, Ireland. Her PhD thesis was entitled 'The "Education of Public Opinion" and the "Criticism of Government Policy": A Social Utility Examination of Irish Democracy under Articles 6.1 and 40.6.1'. Her teaching and research interests are in the areas of Constitutional Law, Administrative Law, Media Law and Politics and the Law. Her new book, *Electoral Law in Ireland,* is forthcoming from Bloomsbury Professional. She is a member of the Executive Committee of the Irish Political Studies Association. She is also a member of Academic Council of the Waterford Institute of Technology and a member of the Research, Innovation and Entrepreneurship sub-committee of Academic Council. She is a regular contributor to Irish national media on the areas of Constitutional Law and Media Law.

Beata Klimkiewicz is Associate Professor at the Institute of Journalism, Media and Social Communication, Jagiellonian University, Kraków, Poland. Her research interests include media pluralism and diversity, media policy in Europe, media reform in Central Europe and minority media. Her most recent publications in English include: *Media Freedom and Pluralism: Media Policy Challenges in the Enlarged Europe* (ed.; CEU Press, Budapest, 2010) and *A Polyvalent Media Policy in the Enlarged European Union* (Jagiellonian University Press (Krakow), 2014). She has been acting as an expert for the European Commission in developing indicators for measuring media pluralism and independence of media regulatory authorities. She contributed to the UNESCO report *World Trends in Freedom of Expression and Media Development*. She has also provided policy expertise in the Polish National Broadcasting Council and Ministry of Culture.

Eva Lievens is Professor of Law and Technology at the Law Faculty of Ghent University, and Guest Professor at KU Leuven, Belgium. She was previously a member of the Interdisciplinary Centre for Law & ICT (ICRI) at Katholieke Universiteit (KU) Leuven, Belgium, from 2003 to 2015. Her research focuses on legal challenges posed by new media and ICT phenomena with a specific focus on the protection of minors, fundamental rights and alternative regulatory instruments. She holds a law degree from the University of Ghent, a Masters degree in Transnational Communications and Global Media from Goldsmiths College, London, and a PhD in Law from KU Leuven.

Maria Löblich is Professor of Communication History and media cultures at Freie Universität Berlin, Germany. She holds a PhD in Communication

Science from Ludwig-Maximilians-Universität, Munich. Her research centres on the political processes of media and communication policy, the history of communication studies and qualitative methodology.

Maria Michalis is Reader in Communication Policy at the University of Westminster, London. Her research interests are in the field of communication policy and regulation with a view to advance understanding of how technological, market, social, political and ideological changes impact upon and are negotiated through power relations and structures as manifested in policy and regulation. She is author of *Governing European Communications* (Lexington, 2007) and sits on the editorial board of the Journal of Information Policy, the International Journal of Digital Television and the bi-lingual journal, *Comunicação e Sociedade*. She has represented the Voice of the Listeners and Viewers on the European Alliance of Listeners' and Viewers' Associations and was an invited expert at the European Social and Economic Committee's hearing on the European Commission's consultation on Connected TV. She is General Secretary of the International Association for Media and Communication Research.

Hallvard Moe is Professor of Media Studies at the University of Bergen, Norway. His media policy research has focused mostly on public service broadcasting. His latest book (co-authored) is *The Media Welfare State: Nordic Media in the Digital Era* (University Michigan Press, 2014). Together with Hilde Van den Bulck, he is currently working on an edited collection on teletext, to be published by Nordicom.

Francesca Musiani is a Researcher at the Institute for Communication Sciences (ISCC) of the French National Centre for Scientific Research (CNRS), Paris-Sorbonne and Université Pierre et Marie Curie, and an associate researcher at the Centre for the Sociology of Innovation at the École des Mines de Paris (MINES ParisTech-PSL). Her research focuses on Internet governance, from an interdisciplinary perspective, blending information and communication sciences with Science and Technology Studies (STS). She is the recipient of the Prix Informatique et Libertés 2013, awarded by the French Privacy and Data Protection Commission, and is currently a member of the Commission established by the French National Assembly in June 2014 to study rights and liberties in the digital age. She is a former author and current academic editor (Internet governance area) for the *Internet Policy Review*.

Manuel Puppis is Associate Professor in Media Systems and Media Structures in the Department of Communication and Media Research (DCM), University of Fribourg, Switzerland. He currently serves as chair of Communication Law and Policy Section of the European Communication Research and Education Association (ECREA) and board member of the Swiss Association of Communication and Media Research (SACM).

His research interests include media policy, media regulation and media governance, media systems in a comparative perspective, political communication and organization theory.

Maria Stella Righettini is Associate Professor in Public Policy and Policy Evaluation at the University of Padova, Italy. Her publications and research interests are in comparative research on independent regulatory agencies, regulatory policies, public accountability and administrative reforms. Her recent publications include 'Social Accountability in the Regulatory Policy Process: The Governance of Telecommunications in Italy and Spain' (in Bianculli, Fernandez i_Marin and Jordana, *Accountability and Regulatory* Governance) and the book, *Indipendenza Credibilità. Istituzioni, imprese e consumatori nella regolazione* (Editione Carocci, 2014), co-authored with Giorgia Nesti.

Seamus Simpson is Professor of Media Policy at the University of Salford, Manchester, UK. His research interests are in European and global communications policy, areas in which he has published widely. His research has been funded by the Economic and Social Research Council (ESRC) and the European Commission. He was part of the PricewaterhouseCoopers team which undertook the first EU-funded evaluation of the pan-European communications regulator, BEREC, in 2012. He is Chair of the Communication Law and Policy Division of the International Communication Association and an ICA Board of Directors member. In 2015, he joined the 'Oxford Research Encyclopedia: Communication' as a Senior Editor (Oxford University Press).

Michele Tonellotto graduated in Law, Institutions and European Integration at the University of Padova, Italy, in 2011. He is a Junior Researcher at the University of Padova and was a PhD student at the University of Potsdam, Germany, until 2014.

Josef Trappel is Professor of Media Policy and Media Economics at the Department for Communication Studies at the University of Salzburg, Austria. His scientific and research work concentrates on media and democracy, changes in mass media structures and their implications on mass communication, national and international media policy and media economics. He is the convenor of the Euromedia Research Group. His recent publications include *European Media in Crisis. Values, Risks and Policies* (Routledge 2015), *The Media for Democracy Monitor* (Nordicom, 2011) and *Media in Europe Today* (Intellect, 2011).

Hilde Van den Bulck (PhD) is Professor of Communication Studies and head of the *Media, Policy and Culture* research group at the University of Antwerp, Belgium. She combines expertise in media culture and identity with expertise in media policies and structures, looking at the impact of technological, economic, political and cultural developments on media structures and policies, with a focus on public service broadcasting. In both areas she has researched and published in books and ISI journals.

Corinna Wenzel is a Researcher in media policy and political communication. She was Research Assistant and PhD fellow in the Department of Communication Studies at the University of Salzburg, Austria, and the Academy of Sciences in Vienna. Her doctoral thesis *Media Policy in Times of Crisis* was completed in 2014. Her research focuses on national and international media policy, media and democracy and media law and public service broadcasting.

Mark Wheeler is Professor of Political Communications at London Metropolitan University. He is the author four books, including *Politics and the Mass Media* (Blackwell, 1997), *European Television Industries* (British Film Institute, 2005) (with Petros Iosifidis and Jeanette Steemers), *Hollywood: Politics and Society* (British Film Institute, 2006) and *Celebrity Politics* (Polity, 2013). He has contributed numerous peer reviewed articles to academic journals and has written many chapters in collected editions. He is currently co-authoring a monograph concerning the public sphere and the democratic role of the social media in global northern and southern states.

Index

2005 State Aid Action Plan 120, 121
2008 Press Act 203, 205
2010 Mass Media Act 206
2010 Press and Media Act 206

Abertis SA 127
academic researchers informing policy makers 11
acquis communautaire 199–200, 208, 211
Almunia, Joaquín 129
Ansip, Andrus 151
Apple (company) 168–9
application discrimination to Internet access 168–9
Argentina and Universal Service Obligations (USOs) 249–50, 253
Arpanet 34
Attorney General v. Paperlink 63
ATVOD. *See* Authority for Television on Demand (ATVOD)
audiovisual media services: access method 52; duration of material 48, 51; free circulation of 208–11; functional independence from written text 46, 48, 49; intertwined with written text 49; prominence compared to written text 50; protecting 208–11; regulating 41–54
Audiovisual Media Services Directive (AVMSD) 41–54; in Austria 45–47; in CEE Member States 208–12; in United Kingdom 43–45
Australia: media convergence in 219–34; media policy reform in 232–3; National Broadband Network 154; regulating domestic content requirements 228
Australian Communications and Media Authority (ACMA) 219, 225, 229
Australian Law Reform Commission (ALRC) 220, 228–9
Austria: regulating audiovisual media services 45–50; state-initiated self-regulation 107–8
Austrian Communications Authority 45
Austrian Regulatory Authority for Broadcasting and Telecommunications 45
Authority for Television on Demand (ATVOD) 43–45, 53
AVMSD. *See* Audiovisual Media Services Directive (AVMSD)

balkanisation 168
BBC 23; as model of public service broadcasting 221
BBC Food YouTube case 48
BBC Top Gear YouTube case 48
Bell Canada 167
Berlusconi, Silvio 125–6, 132
bias in media coverage 8–10, 71, 164, 200
BitTorrent 168
BKS 45–47
Body of European Regulators in Electronic Communications (BEREC) 153, 252
bottleneck regulation in broadcasting 170
Bowen, Howard 84
Bowman v. The United Kingdom 60
Brazil and Universal Service Obligations (USOs) 250, 253
British Broadcasting Corporation (BBC). *See* BBC
British National Audit Office (NAO) 154
Broadband Commission Annual Report 252
broadcasters 26–27, 120–9, 210, 228. *See also* public service broadcasters;

270   Index

duties of in Ireland 64; self-regulation in Germany 106
broadcasting: bottleneck regulation in 170; converging with online newspapers 40–41; influence from national level 14; liberalisation and marketisation of 4; policy framework in Ireland 60–62; regulating with social media 59–73; regulatory changes to 228
Broadcasting Act 2009 (Ireland) 64, 71
Broadcasting Authority of Ireland (BAI) 67–70, 73
Broadcasting Code on Referenda and Election Coverage 64
broadcast licensing 108, 228
Bundesrat (Swiss Federal Council) 108

cable broadcasting 9, 31, 101, 124, 128, 165, 170
Cameron, David 104
Canada and government-initiated self-regulation 100–2
Canadian Radio-television and Telecommunications Commission (CRTC) 100–2
capitalist state theory of regulation 224–5
Carson, Steve 69
Ceefax 23, 31
censorship: of the Internet 166–8; of personal communication 229, 230, 233
Central and Eastern Europe (CEE): 2004 EU enlargement and 197–201; implementing Audiovisual Media Services (AVMS) directive 208–11
CEO Coalition 78, 81
Charlie case 6
Charter of Fundamental Rights 82
children: minimizing risks on Internet 77–88, 106; rights in social networking environment 81–87; right to be protected 81–82
Children's rights and business principles (Unicef) 83, 86
Chile and Universal Service Obligations (USOs) 250, 253
citizen-welfare regime of Universal Service Obligations (USOs) 249, 256
civil defamation suits 204, 205
Coalition to make the Internet a better place for kids 79–80
Coase, Ronald 223

Collins, Richard 24
Comcast controversy of 2007 167–8
commercial media companies and publicly funded services 26, 32–34, 95–100, 119–32
Communications Act of 2003 (UK Parliament) 102
Community TV Policy (CRTC) 102
competition: digital switchover and 118–33; in EU telecommunications policy 141–56; liberalization and 240; net neutrality and 166; regulation and 13, 103, 223
Competition Directorate (EU) 118, 121, 122, 124, 126, 128–31
competition state 144
competitiveness 144–7
Concentra 28
Connected Continent initiative 148
Conroy, Stephen 232
consumers becoming producers of media 5
consumer welfare: policies of EU telecommunications policy 145; regime of Universal Service Obligations (USOs) 249, 256
content discrimination 168–9
controlled liberalisation of media policy 6
Convergence Review (Australian) 41, 219–20, 228, 233; establishing Convergent Service Enterprise (CSE) 230–3
Convergent Service Enterprise (CSE) 229, 230–3
Copenhagen criteria for EU membership 199, 207
copyright: distribution of audiovisual content and 7; law reform 226
co-regulation 98–99. *See also* governance; regulation; self-regulation; in Canada 101–2; during a crisis 95–112; in Germany 106–7; in United Kingdom 102–6
Corporate Social Responsibility (CSR) and Internet safety for children 84–88
Coughlan v. Broadcasting Complaints Commission 60, 62
Council of Europe (CoE) 12, 82; adopting European model of media policy 198–9
Council of Europe Guide to human rights for Internet users 85–86

Index 271

Croatia and digital switchover subsidies 130
culture: blocking content based on culture 167–70; digital switchover and 131; and EU enlargement 196, 198–9, 208, 210; media convergence and 221–2, 228
Culture Boom: How Digital Media are Invigorating Australia (Boston Consulting Group) 232
Czech Republic: freedom of the press in 202–4; implementing Audiovisual Media Services (AVMS) directive 208–11

Dahlgren, Peter 161, 163–4
Deep Packet Inspection (DPI) 164, 166–7
delegation in regulatory regimes 242–3
deregulation 151–5, 223–4
Deutsche Telekom 152
Digital Agenda for Europe, A (European Union) 2, 148, 176
Digital Cable Television (DCT) 119
digital divide 175–83, 238
digital inclusion 170–1
digital piracy 168
Digital Replacement Licences (DRLs) 122
Digital Satellite Television (DST) 119, 127–8
Digital Single Market policy 148, 155
digital switchover 6; controversy in Spain over obligations 127–8; in the European Union 118–33; subsidies for Eastern European member states 128–31
digital television (DTV) 118–19, 121
digital terrestrial decoders 126, 129
Digital Terrestrial Television (DTT) 119, 121, 122, 125–6
Diversity of Voices (CRTC) 101
DPI. See Deep Packet Inspection (DPI)

Eastern European member states and digital switchover subsidies 128–32
economic capture theory of regulation 223–4
economic growth and information and communication technology (ICT) 139–45
elections: equal broadcasting time to candidates 60–66; settings and regulating social media 59
Electronic News System 29

ethnic broadcasting in Canada 101
Ethnic Broadcasting Policy (CRTC) 100–1
EU 1; 2004 enlargement in Central and Eastern Europe (CEE) 197–201; advocating children's rights 82; Digital Agenda 2, 148, 176; engagement with media policy 12–15; evolution of legal framework on universal service obligations in 245–6; impact of enlarging its media policy 195–212; providing state aid for digital switchover 118–33; pushing medial convergence 6; universal service concept of 175–88; Universal Service Obligations (USOs) in 253–4
EU-28 176
EU Charter of Fundamental Rights 201
EU Member States: harmonizing national media policies with EU's policy 196–7; implementing universal service concept of the EU 177–8
EU Network of Independent Experts Reports 201
Europe: adopting Digital Agenda 148; media policy divergence between United States and 222
Europe 2020 strategy 130
European Agency for Fundamental Rights 201
European Commission (EC) 1, 13, 129; adopting Digital Agenda 148; involvement in universal access 245; making Internet safer for children 77–78, 85–88; media convergence and 219; net neutrality and 150, 163; providing public subsidies for digital switchover 118–33; revising the universal service concept 182–4; roaming mobile phone charges 148–9
European Convention on Transfrontier Television (ECTT) 199
European Council 149; network neutrality 150
European Council of Ministers 13
European Court of Justice 84
Europeanisation of national media policies 208–11
European Parliament 13, 149, 163; media policy in Hungary and 207; network neutrality 150
European Policy impacting digital switchover 131

European Strategy for a Better Internet for Children (European Commission) 77, 83, 86–88
European Telecommunications Network Operators' (ETNO) Association 151–2
European Union. *See* EU
European Union Treaty 12
European works protection 208–11
EU State Aid 118–23; in Spain for digital terrestrial television (DTT) 127–8
EU state aid for digital switchover 118–33
EU telecommunications policy 145–56; network access regulation and competition 151–4; network neutrality 149–51; roaming mobile phone charges 148–9
Everton TV case 47

Fabrimetal 31
Facebook 171, 226–7; making the Internet safer for children 79, 80; right to privacy 7
Federal Administrative Court 45
Federal Communications Commission (FCC) 153, 223
Federal Communications Senate. *See* BKS
Fehr, Hans-Jürg 108
Financieel Economische Tijd 33
Finkelstein Review into News Media 230, 233
Flanders and teletext 27–29, 35
Framework Directive 245
France and Universal Service Obligations (USOs) 247–8, 253
Freedman, Des 25
Freedom House 201–3
freedom of expression 6–7, 60; in EU enlargement in CEE countries 200; in Ireland 62–65; in the Irish Constitution 62–64
freedom of political debate 60–62, 65–66
Freedom of press and media in the world Resolution 207
freedom of speech 205
freedom of the media in 2004 post-accession period 201–5
freedom of the press 4, 65; corruption in Slovakia 205–6
Freedom of the Press reports 201–3
Freiwillige Selbstkontrolle Fernsehen (FSF) 106
Frontline debate (Ireland) 66–71
Functional Internet Access (FIA) speed 248

Gallagher, Séan 59, 66–68, 72
García Leiva, María Trinidad 120
Gebührenrefundierung 108
General comment on State obligations regarding the impact of the business sector on children's rights (United Nations) 83–84
geographic availability and EU's universal service concept 177–9, 245
German Telecommunications Act amendment 152
Germany: controversy over digital switchover subsidies 123–5, 132; government-initiated self-regulation in 106–7; regulation of press distribution in 170
gilded cages 168
Godin, B. 142–3
Google 226; making the Internet safer for children 80; preventing network overload 165; right to privacy 7; self-regulating content 229
Google Australia 232
Google Spain case 84
Gorilla Affair 205–6
governance 97–99. *See also* co-regulation; regulation; self-regulation; concept 7–8; external 98; internal 98
government-initiated self-regulation 99–112; in Canada 100–2; in Germany 106–7
Green Paper on Convergence (European Commission) 1
Guiding principles on business and human rights (United Nations) 83

Habermas, J. 163
Hayekian thought 141–2, 151, 154–5
Hesmondhalgh, D. 224
Higgins, Michael D. 59, 68
House of Lords Select Committee on Communications 41
human rights law in Ireland 65
Hungary: controversy over new media laws 206–8; freedom of the press in 202–4; implementing Audiovisual Media Services (AVMS) directive 208–11

ICT 5, 185; child safety online 85–86; economic growth and 139, 143–5, 147–8; in Europe 148; network access and 175–6
ICT Coalition for a Safer Internet for Children and Young People 80

Index 273

ICT Coalition for Children Online 78, 80, 81
ICT Coalition for the Safer Use of Connected Devices and Online Services by Children and Young People 78
ICT Principles Coalition 78
ICT Sector Guide on implementing the UN Guiding principles on business and human rights 88
Impress Project, The (Impress) 105
Increased involvement of the European Commission in ensuring respect towards media freedom and pluralism initiative 207
independent function test of audiovisual media services 46–47
Independent Press Standards Organisation (IPSO) 105
Independent Regulatory Agencies (IRAs) 238–9, 242, 249; degree of independency 251–2, 257
indirect press subsidies in Switzerland 109
industrial policy strand of EU telecommunications policy 145
information and communication technologies (ICT). *See* ICT
information sector, interest in 139–40
information society 140, 175–7
'Innocence of Muslims' video 229
innovation: in EU telecommunications policy 145–7, 154–6; forces driving 142–5; next generation networks (NGNs) and 151; triggering economic growth 142–3; Universal Service Obligations (USOs) and 256
integrator firms 227
Intellectual Property Rights (IPRs) 142
interactional dimension to net neutrality 168–9
Interactive Television (ITV) 35
inter-governmentalism impacting digital switchover 131
Internet: access 239, 248; by content providers 165–6; at European Union level 175–88; in Latin America 251; as avenue for users to protest content 10; contributing to economic growth 147–8; digital inclusion 170–1; diversity and control of content 166–8; epitomizing media convergence 1; growth of users 244; impacting media ownership 227; minimizing risks for children 77; neutrality 3, 7, 149–51, 161–72;

policy of the European Union 14; self-regulation of 78–88; teletext and 34–35
Internet Governance Forum 10
Internet Protocol TV (IPTV) services 228
Internet service providers (ISPs): controlling Internet access 167, 169, 171; and network neutrality 150–1
Ireland: broadcasting in 60–62; constitutional protection of freedom of expression 62–64; impact of European human rights law in 65; legislative protection of freedom of expression 64–65; media's impact of *The Frontline* presidential debate 66–73; public service broadcasting 59–73
Irish Constitution and right to freedom of expression 62–64
Irish Times v. Ireland 63
Italy: controversy over digital switchover subsidies 125–7, 132; Universal Service Obligations (USOs) in 247–8, 254

journalism 32, 70–71; neutrality of 162, 204–5; regulation of 3
Jugendmedienschutz-Staatsvertrag (JMStV) 106
Jugendschutzgesetz (JuSchG) 106
Juncker, Jean-Claude 88
Juncker European Commission 151
Just, Natascha 220

KommAustria 45–47, 108
Kroes, Neelie 163
Kuratorium 106

Landesmedienanstalten 106
Latin America: universal service in 245–51; Universal Service Obligations (USOs) in 253–4
Leech v. Independent Newspapers 62
Lehaen, Stijn 27
Leveson Inquiry 41, 104–5
liberalisation of media policy 4, 6, 9, 14, 97, 141, 146, 240
licence fees in Austria 108
Lingnes v. Austria 65

Macedonia and digital switchover subsidies 130
Maclaurin, Rupert W. 142
Madigan v. RTÉ 61–62
majority use test 182–3

market consolidation 151–5
market failure test 182
market fragmentation 151
market liberalisation 40, 141, 146
Martens, Jo 27
McGuinness, Martin 69, 70
media: boundary maintenance of sectors 33–34; changes in ownership 227; current structural changes in 96–97; democratic consolidation in Central and Eastern Europe (CEE) 197–201; ecosystems 25–27; equivalent treatment across platforms 228–9; influence of 230–2; pluralism in 224–5; public sector intervention in 4–6; regulating ownership 230; role in media policy making 8–10; traditional occurring 2; users influencing media policy 10
media convergence 1; blurring between the public and private 4–5, 7; broadcasting and social media 59; challenges of 9–10, 219–34; encouraged by European Union 6; globalizing and commericalising culture 5–6; governance of 3; leading to media policy convergence 221–2; media ecosystems and 25–27; of online newspapers and broadcasting 40–41; as technological nationalism/ democracy 5
Media Convergence Review (Singapore) 220
Media Council of the Media Authority for Berlin-Brandenburg (MABB) 123–5
media policy: challenges of media convergence 1–2, 226–9; consequences of 10–12; contentualising 1–15; convergence due to media convergence 221–2; declining relative importance of 111; harmonizing CEE's national policy with EU's policy 197–201; historical relevancy of 2; impact of EU enlarging on 195–212; liberalisation 4, 6, 9, 14, 97, 141, 146, 240; makers' preoccupation with new technology 23–27; making new forms of 6–8; neglect and technological determinism 25; politics of controlling public perception 8–10; polyvalent traits of 195–212; reform in Australia 232–3; regulation during crisis 95–112; researcher preoccupation with innovation 24–25; role of media organizations 8–10; transfer of 221–2
media regulation. *See* co-regulation; governance; regulation; self-regulation
Media Regulatory Authorities (MRA) 212
Mediaset 125–7, 132
Mercosur 245, 248, 255
Merton, R. K. 10–11
Micova, Sally Broughton 130
Miliband, Ralph 224
Mills, C. Wright 224
Milosavljevic, Marko 130
mobile operators 152–3
mobile phone services 240
Montenegro and digital switchover subsidies 130
Morrison, Rob 69
Murdoch, Rupert 125–6, 132
Murphy v. Independent Television and Radio Commission 63
must-carry rules on the Internet 165–6, 170

National Broadband Network (NBN) 154, 232–3
National Media and Communications Authority 206
National Regulatory Agencies (NRAs) 238; degree of delegation 242–3
neo-classical economics 141, 154–5
neo-liberalisation of media policy 4, 6, 9, 14, 97, 224
neo-Marxist perspective on media policy 224
Netflix 7
Netlog and self regulation of the Internet 79
net neutrality 3, 7, 149–51; communication research and 169–71; competition and 166; from public sphere perspective 161–72; and walled gardens 168–9
network access 2; as part of EU's universal service concept 184–8; regulation and competition 151–4
network neutrality. *See* net neutrality
new growth theories 141–3
New Media Broadcasting Undertakings (NMBUs) 102
news as a perishable commodity 62
News Corporation 125

News Media Council 230
newspapers: incorporating teletext 33; regulating online 40–41
new trade theory 143–4
next generation networks (NGNs) 3, 139, 143–5, 151–4; universal service concept and 181
Nicholson, Tom 205–6
Noam, Eli 227
non-linear audiovisual media services (AVMS) 42
Norsk rikskringkasting (NRK) 24, 27–29, 34–35
Norway and teletext 27–29, 34
NRK. *See* Norsk rikskringkasting (NRK)
NRK Atrivum 34

Observer and Guardian v. The United Kingdom 62, 65
Oettinger, Günther 151, 154
Ofcom. *See* Office of Communications (Ofcom)
Office of Communications (Ofcom) 43–45, 47–54, 102–3, 122, 229
on-demand audiovisual media services (AVMS) 42
on-demand programme services (ODPS) 43–45
Ondruchová-Hong, Mária 205
one per cent, the 224
online advertising in Austria 107–8
online newspapers: converging with broadcasting 40–41; regulating audiovisual material on their websites 41–54
Österreichischer Rundfunk (ORF) 107–8
Over The Top (OTI) services 7

P2P applications being blocked 168
parallel analogue and digital broadcasting 121, 128, 129
PBS. *See* public broadcasting services (PBS)
Penta group 205–6
Petit Press 206
Philips 31
phone-hacking scandal of *News of the World* 41, 104
platform neutrality in media policy 229
Poland: freedom of the press in 202–4; implementing Audiovisual Media Services (AVMS) directive 208–11
Policy determinations to the local programming improvement fund 2009 (CRTC) 102

Policy Framework for Broadcasting Distribution Undertakings (CRTC) 101
politics: of media regulation 222–6; of setting media policy 8–10
polyvalent media 195–212
Pool, Ithiel de Sola 26
positive theory of regulation 223
power elite in media regulation 224
Preparing for a Fully Converged Audiovisual World: Growth, Creation and Values (European Commission) 219
press: distribution regulation of 170; diversity in Switzerland 108–9; freedom of 4, 65, 205–6; regulation of 104–5
Press Complaints Commission (PCC) 104
Press Freedom Index 201, 203–4
Principles for the Safer Use of Connected Devices and Online Services by Children and Young People in the EU 80
privacy, right to 6–7
private enterprise and universal access to the Internet 245–51
ProSiebenSat.1 123, 124
prosumers 5
public: interest impacting media regulation 220, 222–4; intervention in media environment 4–6; perspective on net neutrality 161–72
public broadcasting services (PBS) 4; BBC model adoption of 221; differences in European and United States models 222; must-carry rules on Internet and 166; regulating in Ireland 59–73
public institutions and universal access to the Internet 245–51
public service broadcasters. *See also* broadcasters: *versus* the commercial press 32–34; online news provision 7; regulating 40–41; self-regulation in Austria 107; self-regulation in United Kingdom 103
Public Service Broadcasting Charter (Ireland) 64
Public Service Media (PSM) 200
public subsidies for digital switchover 118–33
Puppis, Manuel 220

276   Index

quality of access 187
quality of service 165, 186; EU's universal service concept and 179

radio broadcasting 2; regulation by the state 4
Radio Television Luxemburg (RTL) 123, 124
Radiotelevisone Italiana (RAI) 125
Raidió Teilifís Éireann (RTÉ) 59, 69–73; Public Service Statement of 64–65
Reagan, Ronald 97
Recognition Panel (UK) 105
Recommendation on the protection of human rights with regard to social networking services (Council of Europe) 82
regime organization of Universal Service Obligations (USOs) 241–4
regime orientation of Universal Service Obligations (USOs) 241–4
regulation. *See also* co-regulation; governance; self-regulation: of broadcasting and social media 59–73; of broadcasting merging with online newspapers 40–54; impact of media convergence on 220; increased parity between old and new media 227–8; new forms of 7–8; outside of national regulatory systems 229; politics of 222–6; resistance to reform 223; social networking services (SNS) 77–88; types of during a crisis 95–112
regulatory holidays 152
regulatory impact analysis 11
Regulatory State 225, 238–9
Renewed EU strategy 2011–14 for Corporate Social Responsibility, A (European Commission) 85, 87
Reporters Without Borders (RWB) 203–4
Reporting Requirements (CRTC) 102
representational dimension to net neutrality 164, 166–8
Resolution of 10 March 2011 on media law in Hungary 206
Review of the National Classification Scheme (Australia) 220, 228, 233
right of reply 203, 205
right to political expression 72
roaming mobile phone charges 148–9, 248
Rottey, Emmanuel 27

Royal Charter on Self-regulation of the Press (UK government) 104–5
Rundfunkänderungsstaatsvertrag (RFÄndStV) 106

Safer Social Networking Principles (SSNPS) 78–79
Schumpeter, J. 142
Schumpeterian thought 141–3, 145–7, 151, 155
Scope Guidance (ATVOD) 44–45
search engine operators protecting human rights 84
self-regulation 98–99. *See also* co-regulation; governance; regulation; in Austria 107–8; in Canada 100–2; during a crisis 95–112; definition 98; in Germany 106–7; possible failure of 80–81; of social networking services (SNS) 77–88; in Switzerland 108–9; in United Kingdom 102–6
Serbia and digital switchover subsidies 130
SES Astra 127
signal integrity case 7, 10, 26
Singapore on media convergence 220
Skolkay, Andrej 205
Sky Italia 125–7, 132
Sky Italia v. Mediaset 126–7
Slovakia: digital switchover subsidies and 129; freedom of the press in 202–4; implementing Audiovisual Media Services (AVMS) directive 208–11; journalistic corruption scandal in 205–6
Slovak Intelligence Service 205
Slovenia and digital switchover subsidies 130
SME newspaper 205–6
SNS. *See* social networking services (SNS)
social cohesion: *versus* competition in Germany 123–5; and digital switchover 123–5
social inclusion and communications 238–57
social liberalism 40
social media: impact on Ireland's presidential election of 2011, 66–73; regulating use in Ireland 70; regulating with broadcasting 59–73
social networking services (SNS): responsibility to protect children from the Internet 82–87; self regulation of 77–88

social network media 226
South Eastern European member states 130-2
Spain: controversy over digital switchover subsidies 127-8, 132; independency of Independent Regulatory Agencies (IRAs) 251-2; Universal Service Obligations (USOs) in 247-8, 254
Starks, Michael 120
state: invention in the market 141-2; monopolies 141; regulated self-regulation 98-99; regulation during a crisis 95-112
State in Capitalist Society, The (Miliband) 224
state-initiated self-regulation: in Austria 107-8; rising significance of 109-10; in Switzerland 108-9
Stiftungsrat 108
structural dimension to net neutrality 164-6
subsidies: for digital switchover 118-33; indirect press subsidies in Switzerland 109; targeted *versus* untargeted 240
Sun Video case 43-44, 47-48, 53
supra-nationalism impacting digital switchover 131
Switzerland's state-initiated self-regulation 108-9
Sympatico 167

take-up rates 119-21, 131-2, 180
technological determinism and policy neglect 25
technological neutrality 42, 119, 122-4, 126-8
Telecom Italia 255
telecommunications: blurring of mass and interpersonal 4-5, 7; influence from national level 14; universal access to 239-57
Telecommunications Single Market Policy 145-56
Telegraph's audiovisual services on website 50-51
Telemedien 106
Teletekst 27-29, 31
teletext: as add-on service 31; as commercial income stream 34-35; as forerunner to online newspapers 33; history in Norway and Flanders 27-29; the Internet and 34-35; lack of policy and policy research 30-32; neglect of by policy makers 23-25
television: broadcasting 2; similarity to audiovisual materials 47-48, 50-52; with teletext decoders 31
Television without Frontiers (TWF) Directive 4, 41, 199
Thatcher, Margaret 97
TirolerTageszeitung 45-46, 48, 51
trade agreements 101-2
traffic shaping processes on the Internet 166-8
transmedia model 226
transmission time devoted to national and European works 208-11
T-Systems 124
TT-junior 29
tweet: impacting presidential debate 66-73; verifying content of 69-70
#tweetgate 59-73
Twitter 7; regulating feeds in Ireland 59-73
two-tier media system 227

UN *Guiding principles on business and human rights* (United Nations) 85
United Kingdom: government-initiated self-regulation in 102-6; regulating audiovisual media services 43-45, 47-54; Universal Service Obligations (USOs) in 247-8, 254
United Nations 83, 85
United Nations Convention on the Rights of the Child 81, 83
United States: media policy divergence between European and 222; television investment in CEE Member States 210
Universal Access 239-57; contrasted with Universal Service 249-51
Universal Service: contrasted with Universal Access 249-51, 256; programs 238-57
universal service concept of the EU 175-88; access as minimum requirement 184-8; deficits of 177-80; electronic communications reality and 180-1; revising scope of 182-4
Universal Service Directive 177-80
Universal Service Obligations (USOs) 120, 127-8, 239-41; cross-country analysis of 241-4; determinants of policy change in 256-7; diversity in organization of 251-6; in EU and

Latin American states 253–4; market oriented 249, 256; orientation of 244–51
universal service providers (USPs) 252–6; selecting 255–6

Van Crombruggen, Linda 27
Venezuela and Universal Service Obligations (USOs) 250, 253
Verband Österreichischer Zeitungen (VÖZ) 107–8
video content on newspaper websites 40–41
videotex 30
Vlaams Radio and Television 24
von Finckenstein, Konrad 219
VRT 30
VTM text 28, 33

walled gardens 164, 168–9, 171
Web 2.0 social media 5
Welfare State 238–9
wireless infrastructure 2, 130, 154
written text intertwined with audiovisual material 49
Wu, Tim 162

YouTube 228

zero rating of the Internet 150